Developed fifty years ago by the National Bureau of Economic Research, the analytic methods of business cycles and economic indicators enable economists to forecast economic trends by examining the repetitive sequences that occur in business cycles. The methodology has proved to be an inexpensive and useful tool that is now used extensively throughout the world.

In recent years significant new developments have emerged in the field of business cycles and economic indicators. This volume comprises twenty-two articles by international experts who are working with new and innovative approaches to indicator research. Advancement has occurred in three broad areas. Researchers have developed new concepts and methods using recent advances in economic theory and time-series analysis that can rationalize the existing system of leading and coincident indicators. Also, they have found more appropriate methods for evaluating the forecasting records of leading indicators, especially with regard to the measurement of turning point probability. Finally, they have developed altogether new indicators; some of these represent imaginative new applications of existing technology, and others will contribute to the development of composite indices. The articles in this volume provide a cross-section of this research, examining the most important recent work in each area.

This will be an important book for forecasters in business, academe, and government as well as for scholars and graduate students in economics, business management, forecasting, and statistics.

Leading economic indicators

Leading economic indicators
New approaches and forecasting records

Edited by
KAJAL LAHIRI
State University of New York, Albany

and

GEOFFREY H. MOORE
Center for International Business Cycle Research
Columbia Business School

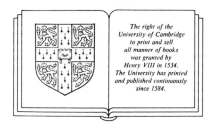

The right of the
University of Cambridge
to print and sell
all manner of books
was granted by
Henry VIII in 1534.
The University has printed
and published continuously
since 1584.

CAMBRIDGE UNIVERSITY PRESS

Cambridge
New York   Port Chester   Melbourne   Sydney

Dedicated to the memory of
WESLEY C. MITCHELL, 1874–1948
and
ARTHUR F. BURNS, 1904–1987

Published by the Press Syndicate of the University of Cambridge
The Pitt Building, Trumpington Street, Cambridge CB2 1RP
40 West 20th Street, New York, NY 10011, USA
10 Stamford Road, Oakleigh, Melbourne 3166, Australia

© Cambridge University Press 1991

First published 1991

Printed in the United States of America

Library of Congress Cataloging-in-Publication Data

Leading economic indicators : new approaches and forecasting records /
  edited by Kajal Lahiri and Geoffrey H. Moore.
    p.   cm.
  ISBN 0-521-37155-4
  1. Business cycles.   2. Economic forecasting.   3. Economic
indicators.   I. Lahiri, Kajal.   II. Moore, Geoffrey Hoyt.
HB3711.L43   1991
330′.01′12 – dc20   90-1757
                                                              CIP

British Library Cataloguing in Publication Data

Leading economic indicators : new approaches and forecasting
  records.
  1. Economic forecasting
  I. Lahiri, Kajal   II. Moore, Geoffrey H. (Geoffrey
  Hoyt) *1914–*
  330.0112

ISBN 0-521-37155-4 hardback

Contents

Contents

Preface

The immediate origin of this book was a conference held at the State University of New York at Albany in May 1987 at which a number of well-known exponents of leading indicators research were invited to offer their views on this subject. During the conference the need was felt for a volume that would systematically explain and evaluate the old and the new emerging techniques dealing with leading economic indicators. Thus, the volume is not the proceedings of the conference, but rather a collection of mostly previously unpublished articles broadly representing current research in this field. A number of authors were commissioned to write chapters on specific topics, and the two editors undertook to provide an appropriate framework. Many of the economists whose work has been central to the development of leading indicators report new research, review progress in specific areas, and discuss directions for further work. We hope that the book will prove useful to university economists and students interested in business cycles and forecasting, as well as to those in business firms, government agencies, and international organizations who wish to keep abreast of new developments in this field and adapt them for practical use.

The editors are grateful to the authors for their contributions, their involvement in revising their own chapters, and their patience during the course of the production of the book. We are also grateful to Rick Ashley, Mel Bers, Frank Diebold, G. S. Maddala, Steve McNees, Mike Niemira, Adrian Pagan, Ed Renshaw, Glenn Rudebusch, Feliks Tamm, Mark Watson, and Victor Zarnowitz for their encouragement, comments, and suggestions, which helped us to find an appropriate framework for the book. Finally, we are thankful to the University Foundation of the State University of New York at Albany, which sponsored the conference.

Kajal Lahiri
Geoffrey H. Moore

List of contributors

Dr. Ernst A. Boehm
Institute of Applied Economic and
  Social Research
University of Melbourne
Parkville, Victoria 3052
Australia

Dr. James M. Boughton
Research Department
International Monetary Fund 9-302
Washington, DC 20431

Professor William H. Branson
Department of Economics
Princeton University
Princeton, NJ 08540

Ms. Susmita Dasgupta
Department of Economics
State University of New York
Albany, NY 12222

Dr. Frank de Leeuw
Bureau of Economic Analysis
U.S. Department of Commerce
1401 K Street, N.W.
Washington, DC 20230

Dr. Francis X. Diebold
Department of Economics
University of Pennsylvania
Philadelphia, PA 19104

Mr. Chansik Hong
Department of Economics
University of Windsor
Windsor, ON N9B 3P4, Canada

Professor Philip A. Klein
Department of Economics
Pennsylvania State University
University Park, PA 16802

Professor Kajal Lahiri
Department of Economics
State University of New York
Albany, NY 12222

Dr. Allan P. Layton
Department of Economics
University of Queensland
St. Lucia, Brisbane
Queensland, Australia 4067

Dr. Stephen K. McNees
Federal Reserve Bank of Boston
600 Atlantic Avenue
Boston, MA 02106

Professor Geoffrey H. Moore
Center for International Business
  Cycle Research
Graduate School of Business
Columbia University
New York, NY 10027

xiv   **List of contributors**

Professor Salih Neftci
Department of Economics
CUNY – Graduate Center
33 West 42 Street
New York, NY 10036-8099

Mr. Michael P. Niemira
Mitsubishi Bank
Economics Research
225 Liberty Street
Two World Financial Center
New York, NY 10281

Professor Edward F. Renshaw
Department of Economics
State University of New York
Albany, NY 12222

Dr. Howard Roth
Security Pacific National Bank
P.O. Box 2097 Terminal Annex
Los Angeles, CA 90051

Dr. Glenn D. Rudebusch
Division of Research and Statistics
Board of Governors
Federal Reserve System
20th and Constitution Avenue, N.W.
Washington, DC 20551

Dr. Stephen J. Silver
Department of Business
  Administration
The Citadel
Charleston, SC 29409

Dr. Hermon O. Stekler
Department of Resource Policy and
  Analysis
National Defense University
Industrial College of Armed Forces
Washington, DC 20319-6000

Professor James H. Stock
John F. Kennedy School of
  Government
Harvard University
Cambridge, MA 02138

Dr. Feliks Tamm
Economic Consultant
910 Park Terrace
Fort Washington, MD 20744

Professor Mark W. Watson
Department of Economics
Northwestern University
Evanston, IL 60201

Dr. Roy H. Webb
Federal Reserve Bank of Richmond
P.O. Box 27622
Richmond, VA 32261

Professor Victor Zarnowitz
Graduate School of Business
University of Chicago
Chicago, IL 60637

Professor Arnold Zellner
Graduate School of Business
University of Chicago
Chicago, IL 60637

CHAPTER 1

Introduction

Kajal Lahiri and Geoffrey H. Moore

1.1   The leading indicator approach

The leading indicator approach to economic and business forecasting is based on the view that market-oriented economies experience business cycles within which repetitive sequences occur and that these sequences underlie the generation of the business cycle itself. Wesley Mitchell (1927), one of the founders of the National Bureau of Economic Research (NBER), first established a workable definition of business cycles, and Burns and Mitchell (1946) rephrased it as follows:

> Business cycles are a type of fluctuation found in the aggregate economic activity of nations that organize their work mainly in business enterprises: a cycle consists of expansions occurring at about the same time in many economic activities, followed by similarly general recessions, contractions and revivals that merge into the expansion phase of the next cycle; this sequence of changes is recurrent but not periodic. In duration business cycles vary from more than a year to ten or twelve years; they are not divisible into shorter cycles of similar character with amplitudes approximating their own.

The leading economic indicator (LEI) approach then is to find the repetitive sequences, to explain them, and to use them to identify and to forecast emerging stages of the current business cycle.

The approach differs from the usual econometric model, which does not differentiate business cycles from other economic fluctuations, except perhaps seasonal variation. It is particularly noteworthy that the NBER definition places no fixed requirement on the duration of expansions or contractions, their amplitude, or their scope because the observed sequences–leads and lags–are quite variable over time and are often systematically different at peaks and troughs, and because cycle phases vary widely in duration. As a result, the LEI approach emphasizes forecasts for somewhat indefinite periods of time rather than, say, individual quarters. This distinction is, however, a matter of emphasis. Leading indicators can be and are being used to forecast over uniform calendar time units, and not just around turning points. However, it is the LEI's emphasis on cycles that has contributed to its longevity and helped it to spread around the world. Early signals of recession or of recovery are of great interest to businessmen, policy makers, job seekers, and investors. In the 1930s and 1940s a system of leading, coincident, and lagging economic indicators was developed through a collective effort by a group of distinguished economists of the NBER including Moses Abramovitz, Arthur Burns, Milton Friedman, Gottfried Haberler, Wesley Mitchell, and Geoffrey Moore. For the United States, the system is presently maintained by the U.S. Department of Commerce (DOC). The Organization for Economic Cooperation and Development (OECD) in Paris publishes leading indexes monthly for twenty-two counties. In addition, the Center for International Business Cycle Research (CIBCR) at Columbia University Business School in New York reports indicators for eleven countries in North America, Europe, and the Pacific.

One of the crucial tests of an economic forecasting system such as LEI is its ability to survive repeated tests over time or in other countries. For example, consider Table 1.1, which contains the lead–lag record of eight leading indicators that were selected in 1950. When they were selected, the record extended back to the 1870s but ended in 1938. The table shows how the same series have performed at the sixteen business cycle peaks and troughs since 1948. We find that every one of the eight leaders continued to lead, on average, after 1948. Indeed, the leads have become longer rather than shorter. Only two of the indicators show some deterioration in their performance as leaders. It is interesting, too, that the indicators with long leads before 1938 also had longer leads after 1948, as the correlation between columns 5 and 6 shows. Nevertheless, despite this evidence that the essential characteristics of leading indicators persist, the need to change a list of indicators arises every few years because new series become available, because research has produced some new results, or because the economy has changed. Many examples of this process will be found in this book, as well as in Moore (1989) and Klein (1990).[1]

---

[1] It was once said that Andrew Carnegie, the steel tycoon, had his own private leading indicator of business activity, which was simply the number of factory chimneys blowing smoke. Mr. Carnegie reasoned that if the number was high, business was good. However, in today's economy, the Environmental Protection Agency probably would have rendered the indicator obsolete. This story highlights two important aspects of LEI: (a) They are easy to understand and (b) every indicator needs periodic review!

Table 1.1. *The historical record of U.S. leading indicators selected in 1950*

Indicator (1)	First year covered (2)	Number of timing comparisons		Average lead (+) or lag (−), in months		Percent leads	
		Before 1938 (3)	1948–82 (4)	Before 1938 (5)	1948–82 (6)	Before 1938 (7)	1948–82 (8)
Business failures, total liabilities	1879	29	11	−9	−12	90	91
Housing starts, number	1918	12	16	−6	−10	83	94
Stock price index	1873	32	14	−6	−7	78	100
New orders, durable goods	1921	7	16	−4	−6	86	88
New incorporations, number	1870	34	14	−3	−7	76	100
Average hours worked per week, manufacturing	1921	9	16	−3	−6	67	81
Building contracts, commercial and industrial	1929	11	14	−3	−4	73	43
Wholesale price index, basic commodities	1897	23	14	−2	−4	70	81
Total or average		157	115	−4	−7	78	81
Correlation coefficients (r)			+.91			+.51	

Source: The record before 1938 is from Geoffrey H. Moore, "Statistical Indicators of Cyclical Revivals and Recessions," Occasional Paper 31, National Bureau of Economic Research, New York, 1950. The record since 1948 for the same or nearly equivalent series was compiled by the Center for International Business Cycle Research, November 1986.

As an example of the ability of the leading indicator approach to be applicable to other countries, consider Table 1.2. It represents one of the results of a research program that began in 1973 at the National Bureau of Economic Research and is continuing today at the Columbia Business School's Center for International Business Cycle Research. The initial objective was to duplicate for each of the major industrial countries the leading indicators that had proved their worth in the United States. No country has exactly the same data set, but it is possible to obtain many of the same series or close relatives, and then to see whether the leading indicators led the business cycles in each country. Since business cycle chronologies did not exist for all countries, new chronologies were constructed for each country, using the concept of a growth cycle, or trend-adjusted business cycle. Table 1.2 give the lead–lag record, and we see that nearly all of the entries are leads. The entries for the eleven countries taken together (last column) also show that leads are typical for nearly every single one of the indicators. In short, economic indicators selected on the basis of U.S. experience perform in a similar way in many other countries. The leading indicator approach holds up in space (see Klein and Moore, 1985).

1.2   Overview

In recent years significant new developments have emerged in the field of business cycles and economic indicators (see Auerbach, 1982; Gorton, 1982; Gordon, 1986; Kling, 1987; Koch and Rasche, 1988; Diebold and Rudebusch, 1989; Kling and Bessler, 1989; Braun and Zarnowitz, 1989; Hamilton, 1989; Klein, 1990). After all, the methods used to construct these indexes have remained largely unchanged over the past thirty years. Clearly, the interest in this subject among economists is broadening. We can classify the current research on leading indicators into three broad categories. (a) New concepts and methods using recent developments in economic theory and time-series analysis are being developed that can help to rationalize or test the existing system of leading and coincident indicators. (b) More appropriate methods to evaluate the forecasting records of leading indicators are being developed. A closely related area of research deals with probabilistic definition of turning points. (c) Concurrently, we are seeing developments of new indicators around the world. Some of these are imaginative applications of the existing LEI technology; others are exploring new techniques.

The chapters that follow reflect the general outline sketched above, emphasizing the blend of emerging theories and careful data analysis in order to construct useful leading economic indicators. In Chapter 2

Table 1.2. *Lead/lag record of individual indicators at growth cycle peaks and troughs, eleven countries*

Leading indicators: U.S. titles and U.S. classification[a]	Median lead (−) or lag (+), in months											
	U.S.	Canada	U.K.	West Germany	France	Italy	Japan	Australia	Taiwan[d]	South Korea[e]	New Zealand	Eleven countries
Average workweek, manufacturing	−2	−4	−1	−4	−4	+2	−4	−3	−10	−8	+2	−3
New unemployment claims[b]	−3	−2	NA	0	−41	NA	NA	NA	NA	−3	NA	−2
New orders, consumer goods[c]	−2	−1	NA	NA	−12	NA	NA	NA	−4	−2	−2	−4
Formation of business enterprises	−6	NA	−9	−6	NA	−6	−12	−8	NA	NA	NA	−8
Contracts and orders, plant and equipment[c]	−2	+2	−2	−3	NA	NA	−2	−1	NA	−5	−2	−1
Building permits, housing	−8	−6	−10	−4	−8	−2	−9	−6	−5	NA	0	−6
Change in business inventories[c]	−1	0	−5	−2	+2	NA	−2	NA	NA	−1	−4	−2
Industrial materials price change	−6	−3	+3	−2	−2	0	−6	−2	NA	NA	0	−2
Stock price index	−4	−4	−6	−7	−7	−7	−6	−6	0	−4	−8	−6
Profits[c]	−3	−4	−4	−10	NA	NA	−10	−2	NA	NA	NA	−3
Ratio, price to labor cost	−8	0	−12	−8	−4	+2	−2	−12	NA	NA	+2	−4

Table 1.2. *Lead/lag record of individual indicators at growth cycle peaks and troughs, eleven countries (cont.)*

Leading indicators: U.S. titles and U.S. classification[a]	Median lead (−) or lag (+), in months											
	U.S.	Canada	U.K.	West Germany	France	Italy	Japan	Australia	Taiwan[d]	South Korea[e]	New Zealand	Eleven countries
Change in consumer debt[c]	−5	−6	−16	−20	NA	NA	−8	−8	NA	NA	−4	−8
Median, leading group	−4	−4	−6	−4	−5	−2	−6	−6	−4	−3	−2	−4

Note: NA = no indicator available.

[a]The indicators for each country are sometimes only roughly equivalent in content to the U.S. series. In some cases two series are used to match the U.S. series and the median includes all observations for both series. The periods covered vary for each indicator and each country, but all are within the years 1948–87.

[b]Inverted.

[c]In constant prices.

[d]Additional leading indicators for Taiwan, R.O.C., and medians at peaks and troughs are: exports[c], −6; money supply[c], −4.

[e]Additional leading indicators for South Korea are: accession rate, −3; letters of credit arrivals[c], −5; ratio of inventories to shipments[b], −2.

Frank de Leeuw supplies a convincing theoretical basis for leading indicators.[2] Using the dynamic production theory framework of Holt, Modigliani, Muth, and Simon (1960), he illustrates the response of orders, average hours and other indicators to shocks in demand, in production, and in expectations. In Chapter 3 Salih Neftci justifies the leading indicator approach as a filter in terms of a stochastically nonlinear time-series model. He argues that the methodology of leading indicators captures an aspect of real life (viz., a two-stage Markov process representing a business cycle) that econometric or time-series models miss. Recent research on macroeconomic dynamic factor models due to Sargent and Sims (1977), King, Plosser, and Rebello (1988a, 1988b), and others has suggested a theoretical foundation for coincident and leading index construction. In their NBER-sponsored research reported in Chapter 4, James Stock and Mark Watson implement the idea that comovements in many macroeconomic variables have a common element that can be captured by a single underlying unobserved variable. Their "single-index dynamic factor" model produces a coincident index that is strikingly similar to the index of coincident indicators currently compiled by DOC. They also investigated how their model can forecast the growth of the coincident indicator (or the reference cycle) using a variety of leading macroeconomic variables. They find that approximately two-thirds of the variance of the six-month ahead growth in the coincident index can be forecasted. This result is noteworthy in view of the fact that LEI is sometimes taken to be solely a predictor of turning points. In addition, Chapter 4 develops a method of estimating the probability that six months hence the economy will be in a recession or recovery.

Early detection of business cycle turning points has always been a major concern to policy makers, businessmen, and investors. Zarnowitz and Moore (1982) developed a "growth rate rule" to signal recessions and screen out false signals. Note that this type of signal detection from leading indicators does not give an explicit probability statement expressing the forecaster's degree of certainty regarding an upcoming turning point. Salih Neftci (1982) suggested a method using time-series analysis and the theory of optimum stopping to calculate the probability of a cyclical turning point. In Chapter 5 Michael Niemira goes through a step-by-step guide to the Neftci methodology, and demonstrates the usefulness of the probability method for forecasting turning points in international economic cycles. In Chapter 6, Roy Webb compares the

[2] For earlier discussions of why leading indicators lead, see Moore (1983) and Boschan and Zarnowitz (1975). Chow and Moore (1972) built a dynamic simultaneous equations model that incorporates leading indicators in an effort to present an explicit theoretical structure behind the DOC approach.

relative predictive power of Neftci's sequential probability rule, the vector-autoregressive (VAR) model, and a naive rule in detecting cyclical expansion and contraction. He finds that it is difficult to forecast the stage of the business cycle more accurately than by using an uninformative naive indicator. However, those results are tentative because of the short time interval considered.

Note that the Neftci methodology, while providing a significant extension of the Zarnowitz-Moore approach, does not predict the date on which the turning point is likely to occur. Wecker (1979) suggested an approach that permitted statements as to the probability of a turning point on any one date or any group of dates under consideration. By using Monte-Carlo simulation, future paths of the time-series are repeatedly generated for the event "time until the next turning point." This approach, however, needs a workable definition of a turning point, which is by no means a trivial problem. Kling (1987) has extended this framework to "debias" the probability assessments following the prequential principle of Dawid (1984). Given the small sample of postwar turning points, the Wecker-Kling methodology of debiasing probability assessments over turning point dates based on stochastic simulation seems to be particularly promising, and can potentially save researchers from unhealthy data-mining.

By using a similar procedure Arnold Zellner and Chansik Hong, in Chapter 7, have generated forecasts for turning points in annual growth rates for eighteen countries during 1974–85. Using Bayesian principles, they demonstrate that optimal turning point forecasts can be very sensitive to asymmetry in the loss structure. In the final chapter in Part I, Geoffrey Moore discusses his long-leading index and other new indicators and the benefits expected from them.

Part II deals with methods of evaluation and forecasting records of LEI. Both Stephen McNees (Chapter 9) and Hermon Stekler (Chapter 10) demonstrate how difficult it is to evaluate quantitative forecasts on their ability to predict turning points. The problem of defining what constitutes a turning point becomes an important issue. Using the rule for defining a recession as a two-quarter decline in real GNP, Stephen McNees shows that cyclical forecasts for the 1973–82 period had serious flaws. The existence of overoptimism during a recession is one of his interesting findings. Hermon Stekler emphasizes the need to pay more attention to leading indicators and to develop procedures that would locate the date of the expected turn in the economy given that a signal has occurred.

In Chapter 11 Stephen Silver tests the forecasting ability of each of the twelve economic series that comprise the LEI and creates two different leading indexes, one for the peaks and the other for troughs. He finds that this innovation significantly improves the ability of the leading indexes to predict historical turning points. Edward Renshaw, in Chapter 12, illustrates the superiority of a consensus approach by using a diffusion index and the downness properties of other leading indicators to differentiate between poor, medium, and super growth years for real GNP.

In Chapter 13 Allan Layton presents a coherent survey of research work that has been carried out in Australia using the LEI approach. The role of the LEI in predicting fluctuations in the telecommunication industry is statistically evaluated. He also finds evidence to suggest that Australia's economy is systematically led by cyclical fluctuations in the U.S. economy. In the next chapter, Francis Diebold and Glenn Rudebusch use a Bayesian sequential algorithm to produce ex ante probability forecasts for peaks and troughs from the composite LEI. They find substantial deterioration in forecasting performance using the real time composite indicator data relative to the final revised data. Another interesting finding is that turning point probabilities remained more or less constant over expansions and contractions. In Chapter 15 a practical implication of the problem of defining recession or recovery is illustrated by Geoffrey Moore and Victor Zarnowitz. They show how the particular definition of recession adopted by the Gramm-Rudman-Hollings law regarding the Federal deficit would lead to unwarranted results. Recessions would largely be over before they could be identified. In Chapter 16, which is the final chapter in Part II, Howard Roth evaluates a number of leading economic indicators of inflation, and finds that the composite indexes pass their tests quite impressively.

Part III includes a number of specialized leading indicators. In Chapter 17 James Boughton and William Branson study the usefulness of commodity prices as leading indictors of inflation (see Hall, 1982). By extending a model due to Frankel (1986), they show that commodity prices will not lead future prices in the presence of unaccommodated money supply unless reliable information is available about the nature and effect of the shocks. Empirically, the results indicate that commodity prices do have a useful role to play in this context. In Chapter 18 Susmita Dasgupta and Kajal Lahiri argue that information about future inflation extracted from the bond market should be included as one of the components in a composite indicator of inflation. This is an extension of earlier research by Mishkin (1981), Fama and Gibbons (1984), Kinal and Lahiri (1988), and others on inflation leading indicators. In the next essay (Chapter 19) Michael Niemira develops barometers of future activity for auto and non-auto retail sales. The leading indicators are then shown to lead successive stock market cycles in the respective markets. In Chapter 20 Ernst Boehm finds that a leading index for the service sector in Australia foreshadows that sector's activity just as the overall leading index foreshadows the total economy. As a result of the increasing importance of the service sector in modern economies, this research is bound to be pursued more in the future, as Layton and Moore (1989) have done for the United States. These papers illustrate how the NBER leading indicator approach can be successfully implemented for specialized sectors.

In Chapter 21, Philip Klein and Geoffrey Moore analyze the leading indicator value of surveys of buying prices, new orders, inventory change, and vendor performance conducted by the National Association of Purchasing Managers (NAPM). When the four NAPM survey series are combined together into a composite leading index, they find that it leads most of the business cycle turns since 1948. Survey data in many countries are becoming increasingly useful in leading indicator research for three basic reasons: (a) Since survey values vary less than the underlying series, they act as natural filters, (b) they are not subject to revision, and (c) they are available more promptly and easily. In the last paper (Chapter 22), Feliks Tamm discusses various aspects of the DOC inventory data in connection with their use as an LEI. He finds several interesting reasons why NAPM survey data on inventory changes should not be chosen over the DOC data in the construction of a composite index.

In conclusion let us note that for successful experimentation with the newly developed series and techniques described in this book we will need an effective system of leading, coincident, and lagging economic indicators. Thus, the need for painstaking time-series data analysis – an approach initiated by the NBER staff more than fifty years ago – is more pressing today if we want the newer concepts and methods to succeed in practice. The field of leading indicators is wide open. The problems that we face are challenging, and they invite the continued attention of economists and statisticians.

REFERENCES

Auerbach, A. J. (1982), "The Index of Leading Indicators: Measurement Without Theory, Thirty Five Years Later," *Review of Economics and Statistics,* 64, 589–95.
Boschan, C., and V. Zarnowitz (1975), "Cyclical Indicators: An Evaluation and New Leading Indexes," *Business Conditions Digest,* May, pp. v–x.
Braun, P., and V. Zarnowitz (1989), "Major Macroeconomic Variables and

Leading Indexes: Some Estimates of their Interrelations, 1886–1982," NBER Working Paper No. 2812.

Burns, A. F., and W. C. Mitchell (1946), *Measuring Business Cycles,* NBER Studies in Business Cycles No. 2. New York: Columbia University Press.

Chow, G. C., and G. H. Moore (1972), "An Econometric Model of Business Cycles," in B. G. Hickman, ed., *Econometric Models of Cyclical Behavior.* New York: Columbia University Press, pp. 739–81.

Dawid, A. P. (1984), "Statistical Theory: The Prequential Approach," *Journal of the Royal Statistical Society, Series A, 147,* 278–92.

Diebold, F. X., and G. D. Rudebusch (1989), "Scoring Leading Indicators," *Journal of Business, 62* (3), 369–691.

Fama, E. F., and M. R. Gibbons (1984), "A Comparison of Inflation Forecasts," *Journal of Monetary Economics, 13,* 327–48.

Frankel, J. A. (1986), "Expectations and Commodity Price Dynamics: The Overshooting Model" *American Journal of Agricultural Economics, 68,* 344–8.

Gordon, R. J. (1986), *The American Business Cycle: Continuity and Change,* NBER Studies in Business Cycles No. 25. Chicago: University of Chicago Press.

Gorton, G. (1982), "Forecasting with the Index of Leading Indicators," Federal Reserve Bank of Philadelphia Business Review (Nov.-Dec.), pp. 15–27.

Hall, R. E. (1982), *Inflation: Causes and Effects.* Chicago: The University of Chicago Press.

Hamilton, J. D. (1989), "A New Approach to the Economic Analysis of Nonstationary Time Series and the Business Cycle," *Econometrica, 57* (March), 357–84.

Holt, C. C., F. Modigliani, J. F. Muth, and H. A. Simon (1960), *Planning Production, Inventories, and Work Force.* Englewood Cliffs, N.J.: Prentice-Hall.

Hymans, S. H. (1973), "On the Use of Leading Indicators to Predict Cyclical Turning Points," *Brookings Papers on Economic Activity, 2,* 339–84, Washington, D.C., The Brookings Institution.

Kinal, T., and K. Lahiri (1988), "A Model for Ex Ante Real Interest Rates and Derived Inflation Forecasts," *Journal of the American Statistical Association, 83* (No. 403, Sept.), 665–73.

King, R. G., C. I. Plosser, and S. T. Rebello (1988a), "Production, Growth and Business Cycles I: The Basic Neoclassical Model," *Journal of Monetary Economics, 21,* 195–232.

(1988b), "Production, Growth, and Business Cycles II: New Directions," *Journal of Monetary Economics, 21,* 309–41.

Klein, P. A., ed. (1990), *Analyzing Modern Business Cycles: Essays in Honor of Geoffrey H. Moore.* Armonk, N.Y.: M. E. Sharpe.

Klein, P. A. and G. H. Moore (1985), *Monitoring Growth Cycles in Market-Oriented Economies.* Cambridge, Mass.: Ballinger Publishing Co. for the NBER.

Kling, J. L. (1987), "Predicting the Turning Points of Business and Economic Time Series," *Journal of Business, 60* (April), 201–38.

Kling, J. L., and D. A. Bessler (1989), "Calibration-based Predictive Distributions: An Application of Prequential Analysis to Interest Rates, Money, Prices, and Output," *Journal of Business, 62* (4), 477–99.

Koch, P. D., and R. H. Rasche (1988), "An Examination of the Commerce Department Leading-Indicator Approach," *Journal of Business and Economic Statistics, 6* (2, April), 167–87.

Layton, A. P., and G. H. Moore (1989), "Leading Indicators for the Service Sector," *Journal of Business and Economic Statistics, 7* (3, July), 379–86.

Mishkin, F. S. (1981), "The Real Interest Rate: An Empirical Investigation," *Carnegie-Rochester Conference Series on Public Policy, 15,* 151–200.

Mitchell, W. (1927), Business Cycles: The Problem and Its Setting, National Bureau of Economic Research Studies in Business Cycles, No. 1 and General Series No. 10.

Moore, G. H. (1983), *Business Cycles, Inflation, and Forecasting,* 2nd ed. Cambridge, Mass: Ballinger.

(1989), *Leading Indicators for the 1990's.* Homewood, Ill.: Dow Jones-Irwin.

Neftci, S. N. (1982), "Optimal Prediction in Cyclical Downturns," *Journal of Economic Dynamics and Control, 4* (August), 225–41.

Sargent, T. J., and C. A. Sims (1977), "Business Cycle Modeling Without Pretending to Have too Much a Priori Economic Theory," in C. A. Sims et al., eds., *New Methods in Business Cycle Research.* Minneapolis: Federal Reserve Bank of Minneapolis.

Wecker, W. E. (1979), "Predicting Turning Points of a Time Series," *Journal of Business, 52* (January), 35–50.

Zarnowitz, V., and G. H. Moore (1982), "Sequential Signals of Recession and Recovery," *Journal of Business, 55* (January), 57–85.

PART I
NEW CONCEPTS AND METHODS

CHAPTER 2

Toward a theory of leading indicators

Frank de Leeuw

They system of leading indicators is perhaps the least theoretical of forecasting tools. It began as a purely statistical classification of the 487 economic time-series that the National Bureau of Economic Research had
in its data bank as of 1937, in response to the concern of the administration over recovery from the 1937–8 recession (Mitchell and Burns,
1938). That project produced a list of leading indicators, but not an
index; the index was based on later analysis of a much more extensive
bank of series (Moore, 1950, 1955; especially 1955, pp. 69–71). The
National Bureau pioneers were well aware of leading business cycle theories, but the theories did not influence their procedures for classifying
time-series as leading, coincident, or lagging.

This chapter is an attempt to supply a theoretical basis for leading
indicators.[1] Readers may well ask, why bother? After all, the index of
leading indicators maintains its standing as a forecasting tool very successfully, in spite of the enormous amounts of time and resources
invested in competitors – in sophisticated new methods of time-series
analysis and in large and small econometric models that claim to have
solid theoretical foundations. If the index works, why not just use it?

The answer that Koopmans (1947) gave in his celebrated critique
"Measurement Without Theory" was essentially that the atheoretical
National Bureau approach (including, but not restricted to, leading indicators) could never lead to inferences about the probable effects of stabilization policies. He did not claim that his preferred econometric
model approach would lead to better forecasts, but rather that it could

---

[1] Alma Missouri capably performed the model simulations and regressions reported in
this chapter. Allan Blinder, Geoffrey Moore, Victor Zarnowitz, and colleagues at the
Bureau of Economic Analysis made helpful comments on an earlier draft.

15

assist policy makers in a way that the National Bureau approach could not.

The Koopmans critique is a special case of a more general point; that an approach based solely on statistical regularities has no carryover to any phenomena other than the ones that have been examined statistically. Not only will the leading indicator approach not lead to inferences about the probable effects of stabilization policies; it will not lead to inferences about other forecasting approaches, about the potential value of new indicator series, or about how changes in the structure of the economy might affect indicators. Thus, a more general reason for looking for a theoretical foundation for leading indicators is that it may lead to inferences or suggestions about a variety of related topics – perhaps including suggestions about forecasting.

This paper provides some basis for expecting such a payoff. Section 2.1 takes a first step toward a theory by discussing five rationales that could underlie one or more of the time-series in BEA's index of leading indicators:

1. Production time – the fact that for many goods it takes months or even years between the decision to produce and actual production
2. Ease of adaptation – the fact that certain dimensions of economic activity have lower costs of short-run variation than others (for example, weekly hours compared with employment)
3. Market expectations – the fact that some time-series tend to reflect, or to be especially sensitive to, anticipations about future economic activity
4. Prime movers – the view that fluctuations in economic activity are driven basically by a few measurable forces, such as monetary and fiscal policies
5. Change-versus-level – the view that changes in economic time-series generally turn up or down before levels

Earlier discussions of why leading indicators lead have discussed some of these rationales – typically, the first three (see Moore, 1978, including the references at the end, and Zarnowitz and Boschan, 1975).

The first three of these rationales directly affect business decisions about production, orders, employment, and inventories. To explore these three more carefully, Section 2.2 describes a theoretical model of leading indicators that incorporates them. The model is based on the dynamic theory of production pioneered by Holt, Modigliani, Muth, and Simon (1960). The section presents simulations of the model that show the response of orders, average hours, and other indicators to "shocks" in demand, in productivity, and in expectations. The model does not incorporate the last two rationales for two reasons; they do not have clear connections to a microeconomic theory like the dynamic theory of production. The prime mover rationale has been the subject of a subsequent paper (de Leeuw, 1989).

Section 2.3 points out that the model that was simulated in the second section implies that another forecasting approach, labeled the theory-based indicators approach, rests on the same rationales as the first three used to explain leading indicators. Under some circumstances, theory-based indicators ought to be a more robust forecasting tool than leading indicators. The two approaches have some similarities but also some important differences. Preliminary tests of the theory-based indicators approach using U.S. quarterly data are quite promising.

The final section, accordingly, concludes that this inquiry into the theoretical basis for leading indicators appears to have implications for an interesting alternative approach to forecasting.

2.1   Rationales for leading indicators

Before its 1989 revision, the index of leading indicators contained the following eleven time-series (they are arranged in an order useful for the discussion, with reference numbers to BEA's Statistical Indicators data bank in parentheses).

1. New orders, consumer goods and materials, 1982 dollars (8)
2. Contracts and orders, plant and equipment, 1982 dollars (20)
3. Housing units authorized by building permits, index (29)
4. Average weekly hours of production workers, manufacturing (1)
5. Vendor performance; percentage of companies receiving slower deliveries (32)
6. Stock prices, index (19)
7. Change in sensitive materials prices, percent (99)
8. Money supply (M2) in 1982 dollars (106)
9. Initial claims for unemployment insurance (5)
10. Change in business and consumer credit outstanding (111)
11. Change in manufacturing inventories on hand and on order, 1982 dollars (36)

Each series can be justified by one of five rationales – some by more than one. This section discusses these five rationales: production time (series 1–3), ease of adaptation (series 4–5), anticipations of future activity (series 6–7), prime mover (series 8), and change-versus-level (series 9–11). For each rationale, there is first a brief statement of its central idea, and then some comments and questions about it.

2.1.1   Production time

The first three series – new orders for consumer goods and materials, contracts and orders for plant and equipment, and housing units authorized by building permits – are all indicators of an early stage in a production process. These series might be expected to lead economic activity simply because it takes time to translate the placing of an order, the signing of a contract, or the taking out of a permit into actual production and delivery.

That simple explanation, however, rests on an equally simple, perhaps naive, view of expectations. New orders will be a leading indicator of production *if* producers do not try to anticipate demand changes, but simply wait until orders come in before beginning to produce. If, instead, producers succeed to some extent in anticipating bulges or shortfalls in orders, it is not clear that a lead–lag relationship ought to hold. Production could begin to rise or fall at the same time that new orders are expected to rise or fall; whether they do is, at least in part, a matter of costs of failing to fill orders promptly versus costs of changing production rapidly. It is only in the case of *unexpected* bulges or shortfalls in demand that a lead–lag relationship ought clearly to hold.

Seasonal variations in orders and production probably fit the successful anticipations model more closely than the naive model. Toy manufacturers do not wait until Christmas orders come in to start production; they no doubt anticipate a bulge in orders and plan to increase their production at the time that orders are expected to rise. For a toy retailer, to be sure, there must be at least a short lag between placing orders with a manufacturer and actually receiving toys. But for manufacturers, it is possible to try to match the timing of production with the timing of orders.

On the other hand, complex and limited-volume products, such as large commercial aircraft or new manufacturing plants, probably fit the naive model more closely than the successful anticipations model. In these cases, attempting to produce in advance of demand could lead to huge losses if the orders or contracts do not arrive, and to expensive changes in specifications even if they do. Airlines, consequently, do not expect to buy a new fleet of carriers "off the shelf"; they expect long delays between their demand decisions and delivery of new aircraft.

Which of the two models, the anticipatory or the naive, best fits business fluctuations generally is an open question.

2.1.2 *Ease of adaptation*

The fourt and fifth leading indicators, average weekly hours and vendor performance, can be rationalized as measuring dimensions of economic activity that can change rapidly without large transitional costs. For some elements of production – employment, for example – there are sizable costs associated with *changes* in addition to the recurrent costs associated with levels. Elements without such costs – easily adaptable variables – might be expected to be used heavily to absorb fluctuations in production, and might therefore reflect these fluctuations more than elements with high costs of change.

Businesses often vary average weekly hours in this way because they have lower costs of change than employment. Delivery times (measured by the vendor performance series) are also used in this way because they have low costs of change compared with other ways of responding to a surge or a drop in demand, at least in the short run (in the long run, chronic delays or even unpredictable delivery times have the cost of driving customers away).

Questions about expectations are at least as pertinent to this rationale as to the production time rationale. Under the naive view of no antici- pated change in demand, a rise in sales or orders would first cause a change in average hours or in delivery delays and later a change in employment or shipments. For demand changes that are expected, how- ever, the case for a lead–lag relationship is less clear. A normal seasonal bulge in orders, for example, could plausibly cause employment, aver- age hours, and production all to rise at approximately the same time. Even in the case of complex, customer-designed products (construction of a new factory, for example) if production plans are known in advance it is hard to see why hours should start rising before employment. Indeed, it is conceivable that a business anxious to assure itself of a capa- ble work crew will increase employment in advance of production and keep average hours to a minimum until full-scale production is under way.

Another problem with this rationale is that it rests entirely on demand-initiated changes – on business's response to changes in orders or sales. Supply-initiated changes (for example, a productivity improve- ment leading to higher output but lower employment) might have quite different implications for the timing of easily adaptable variables.

A third problem with the view of adaptable variables as leading indicators is that, even in the simple case of an unanticipated change in demand, the case for lead–lag relationship is unclear. What might be expected is an initial change in the adaptable variable at the same time that production increases, followed by a return to a normal level. An unexpected step-up in orders, for example, may lead to an increase in overtime hours at the time that production responds, in order to avoid abrupt increases in employment; but then, as employment increases, hours should return back to their normal level. The first, overtime-increasing, phase is an early (but contemporaneous rather than leading) indicator of production. The second, return-to-normal, phase is not an indicator of production at all.

2.1.3   *Market expectations*

Probably all of the leading indicators are sensitive in some degrees to changes in expectations about economic activity, but the sixth and seventh, stock prices and changes in sensitive materials prices, may be especially sensitive. It certainly is true that changes in expectations about economic activity are frequently cited as explanations of changes in these series. For stock prices, sensitivity to expected earnings may be at the root of the relationship. For materials prices, the anticipated degree of excess demand/excess supply may be most relevant (and might explain the use of price *changes,* if it is price changes rather than levels that respond to excess demand/excess supply).

   Other forces besides anticipations about economic activity are doubtless important for both series. To mention obvious examples: tax changes and interest rates influence stock prices; supply developments influence commodity prices; and speculative forces affect both series, adding to their volatility. These other forces, to be sure, affect future economic activity as well, but not in the same way as anticipations. For example, an increase in commodity prices is associated with rising economic activity if it is brought about by anticipations of strong demand, but not if it is brought about by the restrictive activities of a cartel or by some other supply restriction. The role of factors other than anticipations about economic activity is therefore a drawback of these two indicators.

   Direct measures of economic expectations, based on surveys of households or of businesses, have become available in recent years. They cannot match stock prices or commodity prices in frequency of measurement or length of historical record, but they raise fewer questions than these long-standing series about the role of non-expectational factors. Comparisons of the direct measures with the long-standing series might shed light on what the latter series are actually measuring.

2.1.4   Prime movers

Quite different from the first three rationales is the idea that leading indicators may represent the forces fundamentally responsible for short-run economic fluctuations. Only one indicator in the index, the money supply in 1982 dollars, fits this rationale.

The spirited debate in the 1960s and early 1970s about the "reduced-form" relationship of measures of economic activity to monetary and fiscal policies was essentially about this rationale. The approach lost popularity after receiving a good deal of criticism, although it has recently been defended in a paper by Brunner (1986) that reviews much of the past work (see also the discussion by Blinder, 1986).

It seems wise, in developing a theory of leading indicators, to treat this rationale separately from the first three. One reason is that changes in prime movers are generally not the variables that businesses use to signal a change in conditions; the leads of prime movers might be longer and more variable than leads and lags among orders, average hours, and other elements of short-term business behavior. An analogy may be helpful; predicting when a commuter will arrive at his bus stop based on when he leaves his house resembles the short-term business behavior approach, while predicting when he will arrive at his bus stop based on changes in the rewards/penalties of arriving at work early or late resembles the prime mover approach. The second approach, although it may produce more fundamental insights, seems more uncertain than the first and is hard to combine with it.

A second reason for treating the prime mover rationale separately is that the literature on the reduced-form approach has produced its special technical complexities related to the separation of exogenous and endogenous changes, the measurement of distributed lags, and other matters. It would be quite difficult to combine these with an investigation of the first three rationales.

2.1.5   Changes versus levels

For the remaining three leading indicators, the principal rationale that suggests itself is that changes in a time-series seem to be a leading indicator of levels. This generalization does not apply to all time-series contours; it does not apply to a saw-tooth contour, for example. But it does apply to the smoother contours that are typical of aggregate production and employment.

Changes in business and consumer credit clearly fit this rationale. Initial claims for unemployment insurance also fit, for it is when employment is falling that initial claims are highest and when employment is rising that initial claims are lowest. The change in inventories can also be rationalized in this way, since the level of inventories is broadly related to the level of business activity. (Inventory change is also a key element in short-run business behavior, however, suggesting that this indicator may be rationalized in a different way as well. The second and third sections of this paper will explore further this other possible rationale for inventory investment.)

The hypothesis that changes in time-series are leading indicators of levels underlies other forecasting tools besides the selection of some leading indicators. Diffusion indexes can be rationalized by the same hypothesis, as Broida (1955) pointed out many years ago. The ratio of the index of coincident indicators to the index of lagging indicators, sometimes used as a forecasting device, has the same rationale. To see this point, suppose that the lagging index were simply equal to the coincident index six months earlier. Then the ratio of the coincident index to the lagging index would be equal to one plus the six-month percent change in the coincident index – clearly, a measure of the change in economic activity.

The relationship of changes to levels is also an integral part of mathematical techniques of time-series forecasting – for example, ARIMA techniques (see Granger and Newbold, 1986). These techniques, like the leading indicator approach, are based on statistical rather than economic theory. They are in a sense a more recent and mathematically more complex implementation of the same combination of statistical care and theoretical agnosticism that gave birth to the leading indicator approach.

It seems wise to treat this rationale, like the prime mover rationale, separately from the others. In both cases, a voluminous literature full of its own technical complexities is one reason for the separation. In the case of the changes-versus-levels rationale, the basis in statistical analysis rather than economic theory is another reason for separate treatment from rationales that are based on how business firms might be expected to behave.

The next section of this chapter, therefore, will explore a theory that covers the first three rationales for leading indicators but not the other two. The other two will appear again toward the end of the chapter, but the task of integrating them with the first three is beyond the scope of the work this chapter describes.

2.2 A theoretical model

This section describes and simulates a model of a cost-minimizing firm, in order to gain a deeper understanding of the first three rationales for leading indicators discussed in section 2.1, namely, production time, ease of adaptation, and market expectations. That section concluded that the remaining two rationales, prime movers and change-versus-levels, are best treated separately from the first three, partly because they have quite different theoretical underpinnings and partly because they have their own complex statistical methodologies.

The simulations will show a good deal of variation in the timing and existence of lead–lag relationships.[2] Orders, average hours, changes in inventories, and changes in unfilled orders sometimes lead output and employment, but they cannot be depended on to do so. Simulation outcomes are sensitive to whether production is for stock or to order, to whether "shocks" occur in demand or in productivity, and to how expectations are formed.

2.2.1 Description of the model

The model is inspired by the pioneering work of Holt, Modigliani, Muth, and Simon (1960). It describes the short-run behavior of a business that forms expectations about demand and that attempts to minimize the costs of meeting those demands. Costs are associated with:

1. The level of employment
2. The change in employment
3. Departures of average hours from some normal level
4. Departures of the stock of inventories from some normal multiple of sales
5. Departures of unfilled orders from some normal multiple of output

---

[2] A definition of a lead–lag relationship is appropriate at this point: a variable X will be said to be a leading indicator of a variable Y if the correlation of $Y(t)$ with past values of X, $X(t - i)$, is much higher than the correlation of $X(t)$ with past values of Y, $Y(t - i)$.

It is convenient to deal separately with a firm that produces solely to order (and hence has no finished goods inventories) and a firm that produces solely for stock (and hence has no new or unfilled orders). The costs facing the first type of firm, for each time-period, are represented by the following equation:

$$C(t) = b_0 + b_1[E(t)\overline{H}] + b_2[E(t)(H(t) - \overline{H})]^2$$
$$+ b_3[\overline{H}(E(t) - E(t - 1))]^2 + b_4[U(t) - c_1 Q(t)]^2 \quad (1)$$

where

$C(t)$ = cost of production in period t
$E(t)$ = employment in period t
$H(t)$ = average hours per period in period t
$\overline{H}$ = normal or minimum-cost level of $H(t)$
$U(t)$ = unfilled orders at the end or period t
$Q(t)$ = quantity of output in period t
$N(t)$ = quantity of new orders in period t [this variable appears in equation (3)]
b_0–b_4 = cost parameters dependent on technology, on market conditions such as wage rates and recruitment costs, and on laws affecting such production elements as overtime hours and unemployment insurance (these also affect $\overline{H}$)

Note that the three "imbalance" terms in the equation are squared, implying (a) that imbalances in both directions – for example, net firing as well as net hiring – are costly, and (b) that the costs rise more than in proportion to the amount of imbalance. Justification for a cost function of this form appears in Holt et al. (1960, Chapter 3).

The firm's problem is to minimize the discounted sum of present and future costs, subject to two constraints; a short-run production function

$$Q(t) = c_2[E(t)H(t)] \quad (2)$$

and an unfilled order identity

$$U(t) = U(t - 1) + N(t) - Q(t) \quad (3)$$

A firm that produces to stock and has no unfilled orders faces an analogous cost function, the identical production function, and an inventory identity:

$$C(t) = a_0 + a_1[E(t)\overline{H}] + a_2[E(t)(H(t) - \overline{H})]^2$$
$$+ a_3[\overline{H}(E(t) - E(t - 1))]^2 + a_4[J(t) - c_3 S(t)]^2 \quad (4)$$

$$Q(t) = c_4[E(t)H(t)] \tag{5}$$

$$J(t) = J(t - 1) + Q(t) - S(t) \tag{6}$$

where the new variables are

$S(t)$ = quantity of shipments in period t
$J(t)$ = stock of finished goods inventories at the end of period t

Again, the firm's problem is to minimize the discounted sum of present and future costs, subject to the two constraints.

The solutions for the two versions of the model appear in the appendix to this chapter. For understanding this section, it is not necessary to follow the details of the solution, though it is worth noting that the details include two additional assumptions that simplify the problem of handling discounted costs far in the future.

The points about the solution that are important for understanding this section are the following:

1. In order to minimize costs, the firm must form expectations about future orders or future sales.
2. How these expectations are formed – whether by simple no-change assumptions, by sophisticated forecasts, or in other ways – can affect the simulation results (the simulations that follow show results for two ways of forming expectations).
3. Given these expectations and all the cost parameters, the firm makes its current decisions about output, employment, and average hours by balancing the costs of employment change and of disequilibrium in hours, inventories, and unfilled orders.
4. At the same time, the firm makes plans for future values of these variables, but these future plans are subject to revision each period as conditions facing the firm change.

The firm's period-by-period decisions are presented in this section graphically, in the form of responses to "shocks." The presentation first deals with shocks to demand, then with a shock to expectations about demand, then with a shock to productivity, and finally with the sensitivity of results to changes in two key parameters.

The results can also be presented algebraically as reduced-form equations that express the current decision variables – output, employment, and average hours in period t – as a function of (a) observed and expected demand (orders or shipments), (b) the initial level of inventories or unfilled orders, and (c) past values of decision variables. The next section of the paper exploits this reduced-form approach.

2.2.2   Simulations (1): Step changes in demand

The first, and most familiar, simulations to be presented are step changes in demand. New orders or shipments are set at a level of 100 from periods 1 through 5, then raised to a level of 120 from periods 6 through 15, and then returned to a level of 100. Figure 2.1 (for the orders model) and Figure 2.2 (for the shipments/inventory model) show these demand changes in the top panels and some of the responses to them in the remaining panels.

The figures show *differences* between the simulation results for step changes in demand and simulation results for a baseline run of the model in which orders or shipments are kept at 100 for every period. Parameters are set so that in the baseline run, output and employment are 100 every period, average hours are 1.0 each period, and inventories or unfilled orders are 200 at the end of each period. These baseline values are subtracted from the step change simulation values; thus, the top panels show values of 0 and 20 rather than 100 and 120.

Except where otherwise noted, simulations are based on values of 1.0 for the parameters a_0 through a_4, b_0 through b_4, c_2 and c_4, and on values of 2.0 for c_1 and c_3. In general, the qualitative results are surprisingly insensitive to parameter changes. Two examples of the sensitivity of the model to changes in parameters are presented at the end of this section.

Orders model: Figure 2.1 shows, just below the line depicting new orders, the time-path of output under two sets of assumptions about how expectations are formed. The first assumption is perfect foresight; the firm is assumed to know in advance about the step increase, and later the step decrease, in orders. The second assumption is a variant of adaptive expectations in which the firm (a) initially forecasts new orders of 100 each period (correct until period 6), and then (b) continually updates its forecast by adding to its previous forecast half of its latest forecast error.

For output, the alternative assumptions about expectations make very little difference. Under both assumptions, output responds to a step increase by a gradual rise, and to a step decrease by a gradual fall. Orders thus lead output – even in the perfect foresight case, where the discussion in the first part of this chapter indicated doubt about what the output response would be.

The path of employment, shown in the next panel, broadly resembles that of output, but expectations make more difference here. In the perfect foresight case, but not in the adaptive expectations case, employment starts rising before the step increase in orders whereas output is essentially flat until the increase takes place. Evidently, advance knowl-

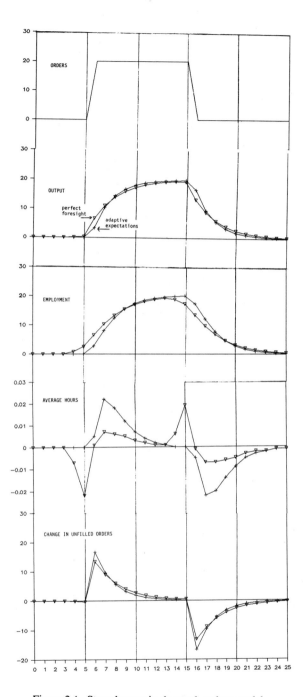

Figure 2.1. Step changes in demand, orders model.

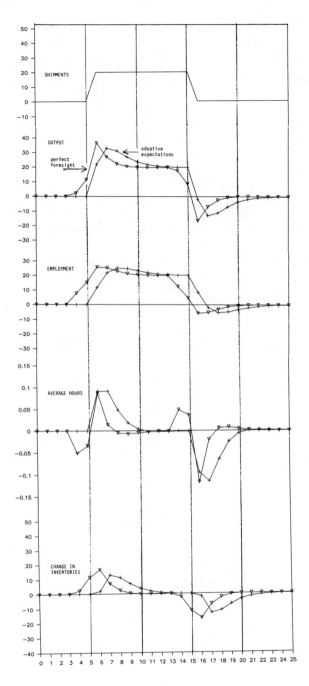

Figure 2.2. Step changes in demand, shipments model.

edge of the coming increase in demand enables the firm to reduce the costs associated with changing employment by doing some hiring in advance. The same behavior, in reverse, takes place before the step decrease in orders.

Differences between output and employment behavior are reflected in the next panel, depicting average weekly hours. In the adaptive expectations case, the step increase in demand is followed by increases in both employment and average hours, thereby spreading the increased costs between change-in-employment costs and overtime-hours costs. After two periods, hours begin to return to their normal level. The initial rise in hours can be described as a leading indicator of rising output but the subsequent return to normal cannot, for output approaches the new level of orders rather than returning to its old levels. An accurate characterization of hours in this case is as a coincident indicator of the *change* in output.

Under perfect foresight, the behavior of hours is quite different. As noted earlier, employment begins to rise in advance of the (known) step increase in orders, in order to limit costs of changing employment. The newly hired workers are not yet needed, however, so the firm reduces its average hours until orders actually increase. The reverse behavior occurs in advance of the step decrease in orders. The upshot is that average hours have, if anything, an inverse leading relationship to output.

The change in unfilled orders, shown in the final panel of Figure 2.1, is not a component of the index of leading indicators, but it is classified as a leading indicator and it is of special interest in the next section of this chapter. It rises at the time orders increase and then falls back to its old level. Its behavior is better described as a leading indicator of the change in output than as a leading indicator of the level of output. Both assumptions about expectations lead to this characterization.

Shipments/inventory model: Figure 2.2 goes over the same ground for the shipments/inventory model. In this model it is shipments rather than new orders that undergo two step changes, an increase in period 6 and a decrease in period 16. As before, the panels of the chart show the results under two assumptions about expected shipments, perfect foresight and a variant of adaptive expectations (described earlier for the orders mdoel).

The response of output is more complex in this model than in the orders model because output is needed to build up inventories to their new target level as well as to meet a changed level of final demand. Output therefore overshoots the new shipments level at first and then gradually approaches that level. Furthermore, the way in which expectations are formed makes a difference in this model, even for output. The overshooting is earlier and sharper in the perfect foresight variant, when the need for new inventories is known further in advance, than in the adaptive expectations variant.

The behavior of employment generally resembles the behavior of output. As in the orders model, however, in the perfect foresight case employment rises more than output in the period just preceding the increase in demand, while in the adaptive expectations case neither output or employment changes until the step increase in demand takes place.

The behavior of average hours once again is very sensitive to the assumption about expectations. In the case of adaptive expectations, average hours and a leading indicator of output at the upper turning point and a coincident indicator at the lower one. In the case of perfect foresight, hours behavior is too irregular to characterize in any simple way. An initial drop in hours reflects hiring in advance of demand and then a sharp increase reflects the desire to build up inventories as well as meeting the new level of demand; a subsequent return to normal continues until the step decrease in demand is in sight.

The change in inventories, like the change in unfilled orders, is generally classified as a leading indicator, and will be of special interest in the next section of this chapter. In these simulations, it is best described as an imperfect coincident indicator of output. The difference between inventory behavior under the two assumptions about expectations parallels the difference between output behavior under those two assumptions.

To sum up: the one result of the simulations so far that clearly resembles the usual pattern observed in statistical classification of time-series is that new orders are a good leading indicator of output. Other simulation results do not conform so well to the usual statistical patterns; a simple lead–lag relationship to output or employment is not generally the best description of the behavior of hours, of changes in unfilled orders, or of changes in inventories.

In part, the failure to conform to the usual patterns is due to the use of step changes in orders or shipments rather than smoother swings. Simulations of smooth swings (not shown) conform to the usual patterns more closely than Figures 2.1 and 2.2. Even for smooth swings, however, many of the differences from the usual patterns remain.

2.2.3   Simulations (2): Change in expectations

From changes in actual demand, we turn now to simulations of changes in *expectations* about demand, holding actual demand constant. Both actual and expected demand (orders in the orders model, shipments in the shipments/inventory model) are set at 100 through period 5, as in the baseline simulation. From period 6 through period 15 actual demand continues at 100, but expected demand – for the period just ahead *and* for the subsequent periods – is raised to 120. After period 15, expected demand reverts to 100, again equal to actual demand. These are not plausible simulations, but they have the value of isolating the leads and lags the model generates solely in response to a change in expectations.

There is no distinction between adaptive expectations and perfect foresight in these simulations because it is expectations themselves that are being set exogenously to determine their relation to the behavior of the rest of the model. There remains, however, a distinction between the shipments/inventory model and the orders model.

In the shipments/inventory simulation, Figure 2.3 shows that output responds to the changes in expectations by sharp, short changes in the same direction. The change in expectations is a coincident indicator of the level of output.

The employment response is not quite so sharp or so short as the output response. Average hours, reflecting the difference between these two responses, is a coincident indicator of output. The change in inventories is also a coincident indicator of ouput; inventory change and output are, in fact, identical because shipments do not change.

In the orders model, output, employment, and average hours are much less responsive to step changes in expectations than in the shipments/inventory model. The change in unfilled orders, in contrast to the change in inventories, moves inversely to output – in fact, one is exactly equal to the other with the sign reversed because new orders are unchanged.

Step changes in expectations, to sum up, do not give rise to lead–lag relationships in either model. In the shipments/inventory model, they cause temporary bulges in output, hours, and the change in inventories and a somewhat longer bulge in employment. In the orders model, they cause much smaller changes. Neither model will generate standard leading indicator results when changes in expectations about demand are an important source of shock.

2.2.4   *Simulations (3): Change in productivity*

To simulate a change in productivity, the parameters that set the relation of output to total hours (c_2 in the orders model, c_4 in the shipments/inventory model) are increased from their baseline values of 1.0 to new values of 1.2 in period 6. They are then kept at 1.2.

By itself, this change would tend to reduce employment but keep out-

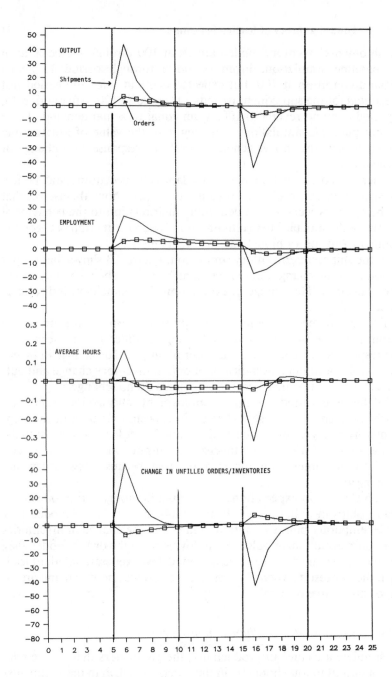

Figure 2.3. Step changes in expected demand, both models.

put unchanged. The reason output would not change is that demand, represented by orders or shipments, is set outside the model. Buyers are in effect assumed not to respond to the change in productivity (or to the relative price reduction that would presumably accompany it), unless the path of demand is deliberately modified to allow for such a response.

The simulations allow for such a response, by letting demand increase from 100 in periods 1–5 to 120 in period 6 and subsequent periods. The demand response is arbitrary, but at least the simulations show a *possible* set of model outcomes for a productivity improvement accompanied by an increase in demand. Furthermore, because the demand response is the same as the upward demand shock underlying Figures 2.1 and 2.2, it is possible to compare these simulation results with those earlier ones to isolate the effect of the productivity change alone.

The results for the orders model are depicted in Figure 2.4. Output responds to the increase in orders with a lag, so that orders are a leading indicator of output. Employment declines at first, responding more to the productivity improvement than to the demand increase, but eventually the effects of the two forces balance and employment is unchanged. The dip in employment is smaller and later under adaptive expectations than under perfect foresight ("perfect foresight" here refers to foresight about both the level of demand and the improvement in productivity).

Under adaptive expectations, average hours follow the same pattern as employment. They are a coincident indicator of employment but not of output. Under perfect foresight, average hours first rise, then fall, and then stabilize. They are not an indicator of either employment or output. Under both assumptions about expectations, unfilled orders give an advance signal of the rise in output, but then return to their old level while output stabilizes at a new higher level.

Result for the shipments/inventory model, shown in Figure 2.5, conform less to standard lead–lag patterns than results for the orders model. Under adaptive expectations, output, employment, average hours, and the change in inventories all peak at the same time, while shipments reach their peak one period earlier. Under perfect foresight, even shipments peak at the same time as the other variables, and average hours initially move inversely to output and employment.

A productivity shock, to sum up, yields only a few results that resemble standard time-series findings with respect to leading indicators. These few favorable results occur in the orders model rather than in the shipments/inventory model.

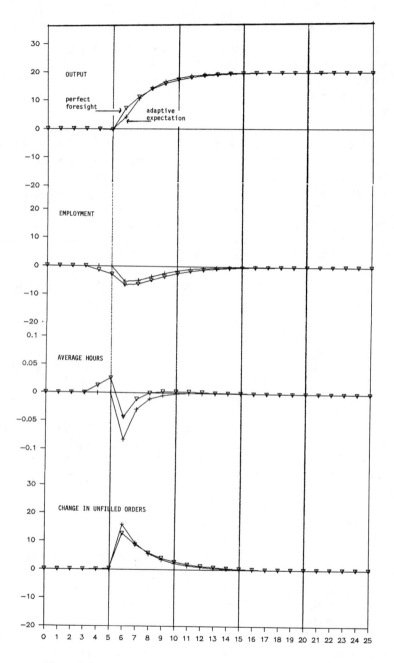

Figure 2.4. Productivity improvement accompanied by demand increase, orders model.

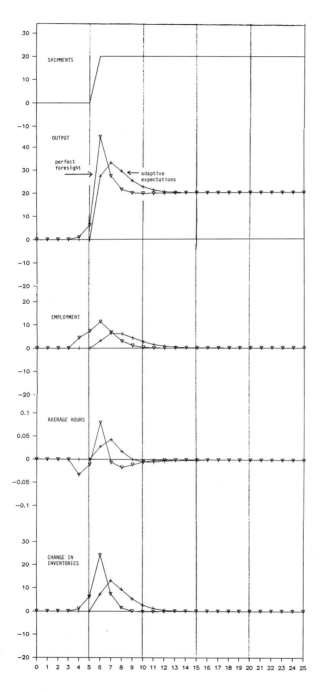

Figure 2.5. Productivity improvement accompanied by demand increase, shipments/inventory model.

2.2.5   *Simulations (4): Sensitivity to parameter changes*

A few additional simulations will illustrate the sensitivity of the model to changes in key cost parameters. The simulations employ the same step changes in demand as Figures 2.1 and 2.2 – an increase of 20 starting in period 6 and ending in period 16. The cost parameters that differ from baseline values are the one that measures the cost of employment changes and the ones that measure the cost of imbalance in inventories and in unfilled orders.

Figures 2.6 and 2.7 show the results of step changes in demand when the parameter expressing the cost of employment changes (b_3 in the orders model, c_3 in the shipments/inventory model) is quintupled, from a value of 1.0 to a value of 5.0. Figures 2.8 and 2.9 show the results of step changes in demand when the parameter expressing the cost of imbalance in inventories or unfilled orders (b_4 in the orders model, c_4 in the shipments/inventory model) is quintupled.

In all four figures, results from Figure 2.1 or 2.2 appear directly below the results using the new parameters. In Figure 2.6, for example, the "output" panel contains four lines. The top two show output under adaptive expectations and under perfect foresight with an employment change parameter of 5.0. The bottom two, taken from Figure 2.1 and plotted on a displaced vertical scale, show output under adaptive expectations and under perfect foresight with an employment change parameter of 1.0. Comparing the top two lines with the bottom two shows the impact of the new parameter.

Although the parameter changes are drastic ones, Figures 2.6 and 2.8 show very little impact of the new parameters. Figures 2.7 and 2.9 show slightly more impact; the behavior of output and employment is smoother in Figure 2.7 and more volatile in Figure 2.9 under the new parameters. Nevertheless, the generalizations about leads and lags made on the basis of Figures 2.1 and 2.2 seem to hold as well for the new parameters in Figures 2.6 through 2.9. Apparently in the theoretical model, even large changes in cost parameters do not have significant effects on the qualitative response of output, employment, average hours, unfilled orders, and inventories to changes in demand.

2.2.6   *Conclusions*

The phrase "mixed results" best describes the relation of the simulations based on the theoretical model of a cost-minimizing firm to the standard findings about leading indicators based on analysis of actual time-series. In the simulations, as in time-series analysis, new orders generally seem

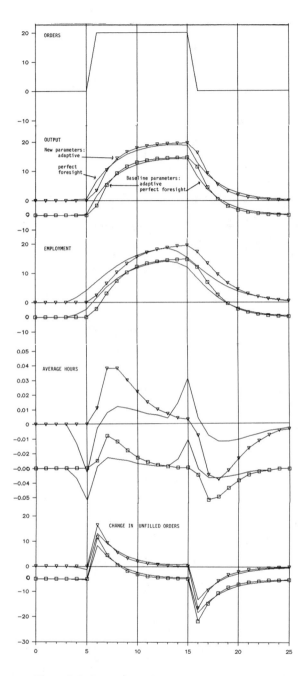

Figure 2.6. Step changes in demand, orders model. High cost-of-employment-change parameter.

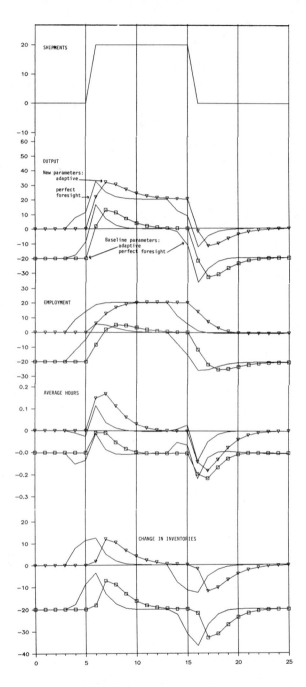

Figure 2.7. Step changes in demand, shipments/inventory model. High cost-of-employment-change parameter.

38

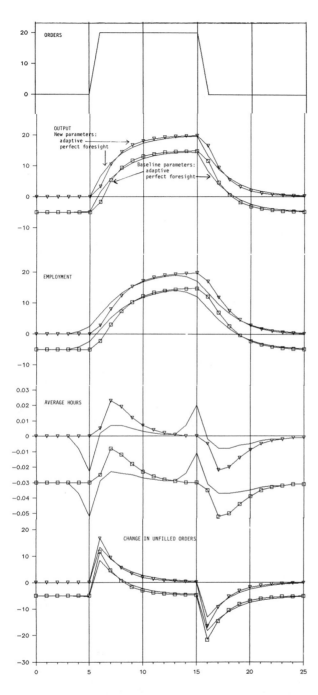

Figure 2.8. Step changes in demand, orders model. High cost-of-unfilled-orders-imbalance parameter.

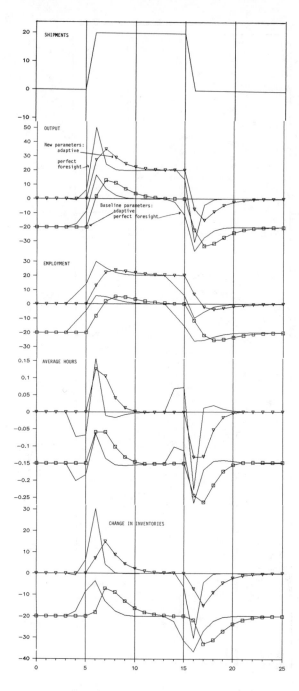

Figure 2.9. Step changes in demand, shipments/inventory model. High cost-of-inventory-imbalance parameter.

to be a leading indicator of output; but for average hours, the change in unfilled orders, and the change in inventories, simulation results vary depending on the kind of shock being simulated and the way in which expectations are assumed to be formed.

There are, basically, two possible explanations for these mixed results. One is that the model does a poor, or at least a mixed, job of representing key aspects of business decisions. The other is that the kind of shock and of expectations that produce relatively successful simulations – that is, those whose results tend to conform to the results of time-series analysis – are more frequent in the real economy than the kind of shock and of expectations that produce unsuccessful simulations. The first kind of shock (and of expectations), if this is the explanation, accounts for many of the correct signals emitted by leading indicators, while the second kind accounts for many of the false signals.

We do not know which of the two explanations is the correct one. As long as the second one *may* be correct, however, it is worth exploring the model further to see if there is some way of using its forecasting potential that is less sensitive than leading indicators to the nature of shocks and expectations. The next section is an attempt to explore the model in this way.

2.3   An alternative approach: Theory-based indicators

The previous section used a theory of the cost-minimizing firm as a basis for simulations of shocks in demand, in expectations, and in productivity. Some of the results resembled standard results for leading indicators, but many did not. This section uses the same theory in a different way, developing a set of "theory-based indicators" derived directly from the theory rather than from simulations of shocks. If the underlying theory has some validity, then the theory-based indicators ought to be useful for forecasting – possibly more useful than the standard leading indicators.

The section first presents reduced-form equations based on the theory. It then discusses the forecasting approach that they imply, and contrasts this approach with the leading indicator approach. Finally, it displays the results of some preliminary empirical explorations of the theory-based indicator approach, using U.S. quarterly data from 1953 to date.

2.3.1   *Reduced-form equations*

The model of the cost-minimizing firm introduced in the last section implies that the firm's decisions for this time period depend basically on four types of information: initial conditions, past history, expectations, and parameter values. Minimizing the discounted sum of the various types of cost the theoretical firm faces, in other words, reduces to a relationship between current output or current employment on the one hand and the four types of information on the other.

The term *initial conditions* refers to the stock of unfilled orders and the stock of inventories remaining at the end of the previous period. The former stock enters the orders model, the latter stock the shipments/inventory model.

Past history could in principle refer to past values of all the variables in the model; but, as the appendix shows, for the model of this paper it reduces to just one variable, last period's employment. It is clear that last period's employment should affect current decisions, because of the costs associated with changes in employment.

The term *expectations* refers to expected new orders and expected sales. Finally, the term *parameter values* refers to all of the parameters of the cost function and the production function, and also to "normal" hours H and to the discount rate r.

For the baseline parameters of the orders model, the reduced-form equations for current output and current employment are:

$$Q(t) = -.002 + .032E(t - 1) + .317U(t - 1) \\ + .317NE(t) + .011NE(t + 1) + .005NE(t + 2) \quad (7)$$

$$E(t) = -.253 + .391E(t - 1) + .167U(t - 1) \\ + .167NE(t) + .070NE(t + 1) + .042NE(t + 2) \quad (8)$$

where:

$Q(t)$ = quantity of output in period t
$E(t)$ = employment in period t
$U(t)$ = unfilled orders at the end of period t
$NE(t)$ = quantity of new orders expected in period t, as of period $t - 1$

The simulations shown in Figure 2.1 of the previous section were equivalent to calculated values based on these equations. In the simulations, new orders in period t were assumed to be known – that is, $NE(t)$ was equal to $N(t)$. $NE(t + 1)$ and $NE(t + 2)$ were generated according to two alternative assumptions about expectations. In this section, when the equations are to be used directly as a basis for forecasting, it is appropriate to let $NE(t)$ differ from $N(t)$.

The corresponding equations for the shipments/inventory model in the baseline case are:

$$Q(t) = .135 + .121E(t - 1) - .654J(t + 1)$$
$$+ 1.589SE(t) + .485SE(t + 1) + .113SE(t + 2) \quad (9)$$

$$E(t) = -.235 + .412E(t - 1) - .292J(t - 1)$$
$$+ .535SE(t) + .252SE(t + 1) + .387SE(t + 2) \quad (10)$$

where:

$J(t)$ = the stock of inventories at the end of period t

$SE(t)$ = quantity of shipments expected in period t, as of period $t - 1$

What these four equations state is that, in theory, this quarter's output and employment are related to lagged employment, lagged unfilled orders, lagged inventories, and expected new orders and shipments. These are the "theory-based indicators" that can be used in forecasting economic activity as an alternative to the leading indicator approach.

The theory-based indicators approach is more attractive the less sensitive the reduced-form equations are to changes in parameters – parameters that were arbitrarily chosen for the baseline run of the model. Table 2.1 suggests that they are not very sensitive. The table compares coefficients of the reduced-form equations for the baseline run with coefficients for two other runs: the high-cost-of-employment-change run (see Figures 2.6 and 2.7 in the previous section) and the high-cost-of-imbalance-in-unfilled-orders/inventories runs (see Figures 2.8 and 2.9 in the previous section). While changes in some of the coefficients are large, there is only one change in sign and the orders of magnitude show few changes. On the whole, Table 2.1 supports the case for exploring the theory-based alternative to the standard leading indicator approach.

A second question about the reduced-form equations is whether their forecasting implications are limited to forecasts one period ahead, as they seem to be in equations (7) through (10). The answer is no. The employment equation for last period, to begin with, can easily be substituted into the current output and employment equations to replace the $E(t - 1)$ term with variables two periods ago. Similarly, the unfilled orders identity and the inventory identity can be substituted into the current output and employment equations to replace $U(t - 1)$ and $J(t - 1)$ with lagged output and stocks two periods ago. Finally, the expected new orders and sales terms can reflect expectations as of two

Table 2.1. *Sensitivity of reduced-form equations for output to parameter changes*

	Coefficient of				
	$E(t-1)$	$U(t-1)$	$NE(t)$	$NE(t+1)$	$NE(t+2)$
Orders model:					
1. Baseline parameters	.032	.317	.317	.011	.005
2. Change-in-employment parameter from 1.0 to 5.0	.022	.314	.314	.018	.017
3. Unfilled-order-imbalance parameter from 1.0 to 5.0	.007	.330	.330	.003	.000
	$E(t-1)$	$J(t-1)$	$SE(t)$	$SE(t+1)$	$SE(t+2)$
Shipments/inventory model:					
1. Baseline parameters	.121	−.654	1.589	.485	.113
2. Change-in-employment parameter from 1.0 to 5.0	.035	−.614	1.401	.402	.391
3. Inventory-imbalance parameter from 1.0 to 5.0	.041	−.883	2.465	.307	−.046

or more periods ago rather than current expectations. With these substitutions, forecasts of $Q(t)$ and $E(t)$ would be based on variables two periods ago rather than one period ago. Forecast errors would no doubt grow with the forecast horizon, but the theory-based approach itself does not limit the forecasting horizon.

2.3.2   Forecasting with theory-based indicators

Before forecasting on the basis of the reduced form of the theoretical model, it is important to face two issues. The first is how to handle the statistical fact that time-series corresponding to many of the indicators are dominated by trends. For discovering relationships useful for forecasting between output and employment and the theory-based indicators, trend-dominated variables are suspect. It is preferable to convert the variables to rates of change or to divide them by some measure of the trend of output.

The second issue is how to represent expectations about demand. At least two approaches are feasible. The first is to assume that expected changes are related to recent actual changes, and hence to introduce these changes as indicators. The second is to use a time-series that purports to measure expectations – either a series like stock market prices that is widely viewed as highly sensitive to expectations, or a series based on an explicit survey of business or household expectations.

These two issues suggest modification of equations (7) through (10). A plausible output equation, which combines both the orders model and the shipments/inventory model, is the following:

$$\dot{Q}(t) = a_0 + a_1\dot{E}(t-1) - s_2 dJ/Y(t-1) + $$
$$a_3 dU/Y(t-1) + a_4\dot{D}(t-1) + a_5 E\dot{X}P(t-1) \quad (11)$$

where dots refer to rates of change from the previous period and:

$Q(t)$ = a measure of output
$E(t)$ = employment
$dJ/Y(t)$ = change in inventories divided by the level of output
$dU/Y(t)$ = change in unfilled orders divided by the level of output
$D(t)$ = a measure of recent final demand
$EXP(t)$ = a measure sensitive to expectations about demand

Empirical counterparts to these theoretical variables will be introduced and tested later in this section. The analogous employment equation is

$$\dot{E}(t) = b_0 + b_1\dot{E}(t-1) - b_2 dJ/Y(t-1) + $$
$$b_3 dU/Y(t-1) + b_4\dot{D}(t-1) + b_5 E\dot{X}P(t-1) \quad (12)$$

Before presenting any empirical work, however, it is useful to compare the theory-based equations (11) and (12) with some of the standard leading indicators. Note, first of all, that the dependent variables in equations (11) and (12) are rates of change in output and employment, not the level of these variables or of business activity more broadly.

On the right-hand side of the equations, the first term – the change in employment – is not on any list of leading indicators. Like other variables in the equations, it is not necessarily *in itself* a leading indicator; rather, the theory implies that in combination with the other variables in the equation it will be of use in forecasting output and employment.

The next two variables in the equations, changes in inventories and in unfilled orders, are both standard leading indicators. However, in the equations, inventory change is expected to have a negative coefficient, whereas as a leading indicator it has been found to have a positive relationship to economic activity. Its role as a theory-based indicator is in a sense opposite to its role as a leading indicator. The change in unfilled orders, in contrast, is a variable that both approaches treat in the same way.

The final two variables, representing expected changes in demand, are not specified precisely enough in the equations to identify them with specific time-series whose lead–lag status has been classified. Of the two time-series chosen below to represent these variables, one is a leading indicator and the other is not.

Clearly, there are major differences between the theory-based indicators in equations (11) and (12) and the standard leading indicators. The theory-based indicators, for reasons explained in section 2.1, omit any measures whose rationale is that they are prime movers or that they measure changes that are expected to precede levels. Quite apart from these omissions, however, the theory-based indicators differ in coverage and, in one case, in expected sign from the standard leading indicators.

2.3.3   Empirical explorations

To make a preliminary judgment about whether the theory-based indicators approach is worth pursuing, it is useful to perform some regression tests using the simplest variables easily at hand to represent the variables in equations (11) and (12). If the approach has promise, the signs of coefficients in these tests ought generally to accord with those in the equations, and predictions of output and employment based on the test results ought to lead actual output and employment. Results from such tests can be thought of as a lower bound to the potential of the theory-based indicators approach, on the grounds that a more careful selection of variables would probably improve, or at least not worsen, the results.

The regression tests reported here make use of the following variables:

1. *Output growth*
   (a) The quarterly growth rate of the index of coincident indicators (quarterly rate)
   (b) The quarterly growth rate of GNP in 1982 dollars (quarterly rate)
2. *Employment growth*
   The quarterly growth rate of employment on nonagricultural payrolls (quarterly rate)

3. *Inventory change*
   Nonfarm inventory investment (GNP component) as a percent
   of GNP (both in 1982 dollars)
4. *Unfilled orders change*
   Change in constant-dollar (1982 dollars) unfilled orders in manufacturing during a quarter, as a percent of GNP in 1982 dollars
   (latter at annual rate, former at quarterly rate)
5. *Expected change in demand*
   (a) Percent change from previous quarter in selected GNP
       components (see text; quarterly rate)
   (b) Index of consumer sentiment compiled by Survey Research
       Center, University of Michigan (1967 = 100)

All of the variables are measured quarterly, although it would be
quite feasible and interesting to experiment with monthly data. The first
variable representing expected demand is simply the most recent quarterly percent change in the sum of four components of constant-dollar
GNP: producers' durable equipment, nonresidential structures, residential structures, and state and local purchases. These are the four components for which the current percent change is significantly and positively related to the previous quarter's percent change. The second
variable representing expectations is the index of consumer sentiment
compiled by the Survey Research Center (University of Michigan). The
level of the index rather than its percent change enters the regressions
because the level reflects expected increases minus expected decreases
(plus 100).

Regression results appear in Table 2.2. There are three dependent
variables: the quarterly percent change in real GNP (the first measure of
the change in output), the quarterly percent change in nonagricultural
employment, and the quarterly percent change in the index of coincident indicators (the second measure of the change in output).

The results are encouraging. Signs of coefficients – negative for the
inventory investment variable, positive for the others – are in accord
with the theoretical expectation in every case. T-ratios are generally
greater than 2.0. Durbin-Watson ratios are between 1.7 and 2.1.

Since the independent variables are each lagged one quarter, it is possible to calculate one-quarter ahead forecasts based on these equations.
The percent changes that the equations predict can be cumulated to
yield predicted levels of the dependent variables. Figure 2.10 shows predicted levels of the index of coincident indicators, based on the equation
in the final column of Table 2.2. Also shown in Figure 2.10 are the
indexes of leading and coincident indicators.

Table 2.2. *Regression results, quarterly percent changes in GNP, nonagricultural employment, and the index of coincident indicators, 1953.2–1987.4*

	GṄP	Ė	IĊI
Ė(−1)	.276 (1.4)	.431 (4.3)	.457 (1.3)
DU/GNP(−1)	.092 (4.6)	.070 (7.1)	.214 (6.4)
DJ/GNP(−1)	−.856 (−5.6)	−.239 (−3.1)	−1.060 (−4.1)
SAĿES(−1)	.141 (2.3)	.082 (2.7)	.313 (3.0)
CONS(−1)	.021 (2.8)	.007 (1.8)	.034 (2.7)
Constant	−.818 (−1.4)	−.204 (−0.7)	−2.079 (−2.0)
R̄²	.41	.68	.51
SEE	.79	.39	1.34
DW	2.1	1.7	1.7

GṄP = percent change in GNP, 1982 dollars (not at annual rate); Ė = percent change in nonagricultural employment; ICI = percent change in index of coincident indicators; DU/GNP = change in manufacturers' unfilled orders (1982 dolalrs) divided by GNP (1982 dollars, annual rate); DJ/GNP = nonfarm inventory investment divided by GNP in current dollars (annual rate); SAĿES = percent change in sum of producers' durable equipment, nonresidential structures, residential structures, state and local government expenditures, all in 1982 dollars; CONS = index of consumer sentiment, 1967 = 100 (source: University of Michigan); SEE = standard error of estimate; DW = Durbin-Watson ratio. Numbers in parentheses are *t*-ratios.

The predicted percent changes are *not* based on the preliminary estimates of the variables as of the date of each prediction; they are based on the latest revised estimate for each variable as of July 1987. In this respect, the predicted values for each quarter differ from forecasts that could have been made at the time. The procedure adopted, however, can be defended on the basis that the other two series in the chart are on the same, latest-revised-estimate, basis.

Figure 2.10 indicates that the theory-based index leads the coincident index by an average of one quarter at turning points, as it was designed to do (as noted earlier, the approach could be used to forecast more than one quarter ahead, presumably with some loss of accuracy). The index occasionally fails to lead – for example, in the downturn at the beginning of 1980. The index of leading indicators always leads, by an average of two quarters. But the problem of false leads, notably in 1967 and 1984, is more pronounced for the index of leading indicators than for the theory-based index.

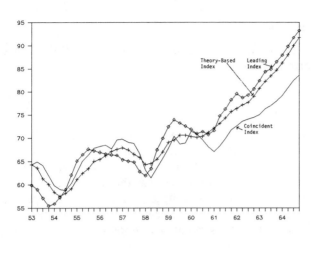

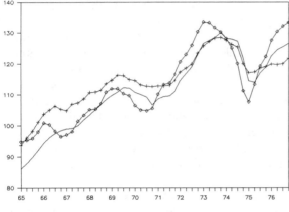

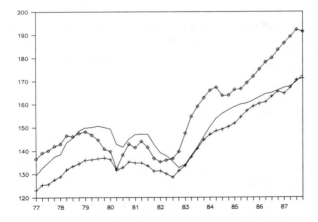

Figure 2.10. Indexes of business activity: coincident index, leading index, and theory-based index.

All in all, these preliminary results suggest that the theory-based approach is worth pursuing.

2.4   Conclusions

The premise of this chapter was that the search for a theoretical basis for leading indicators could yield useful insights about the behavior of the economy. The particular insight that has been emphasized is that the very same theory of a cost-minimizing firm that can be used to rationalize most of the leading indicators suggests an alternative approach to forecasting, labeled "theory-based indicators." Under some circumstances, theory-based indicators might be a more robust forecasting tool than the traditional leading indicators.

Preliminary empirical tests suggest that the theory-based indicator approach is worth pursuing. Even the fairly crude representation of the approach in section 2.3 seems to have some forecasting potential. The value of the approach could well be enhanced by (a) more careful construction of variables, (b) development of forecasts more than one quarter ahead (discussed in section 2.3.2), and (c) integration of the approach with the two rationales for leading indicators that it leaves out, the "prime mover" and the "change-versus-level" rationales.

The theory-based indicators approach is only one possible payoff from the search for a theoretical basis for leading indicators. The informal approach of section 2.1 could perhaps lead to suggestions for developing new indicators that fit into the traditional approach, or to ways of adapting the approach to economies with a different structure than the U.S. economy. At the other extreme, a more rigorous specification of the theory of the cost-minimzing firm than is attempted in section 2.2 (and the appendix) might lead to insights about the implications of lead–lag relationships for the way in which businesses form expectations. Possible payoffs from the search for a theory of leading indicators, in short, extend well beyond the scope of this chapter.

Appendix: Model solution

Orders model

In the orders model, the firm faces the following cost function, production function, and orders identity:

$$C(t) = b_0 + b_1[E(t)\overline{H}] + b_2[E(t)(H(t) - \overline{H})]^2$$
$$+ b_3[H(E(t) - E(t - 1))]^2 + b_4[U(t) - c1Q(t)]^2 \quad \text{(A.1)}$$

$$Q(t) = c_2[E(t)H(t)] \tag{A.2}$$

$$U(t) = U(t - 1) + N(t) - Q(t) \tag{A.3}$$

where:

$C(t)$ = cost of production in period t
$E(t)$ = employment in period t
$H(t)$ = average hours per period in period t
$\overline{H}$ = normal or minimum-cost level of $H(t)$
$U(t)$ = unfilled orders at the end or period t
$Q(t)$ = quantity of output in period t
$N(t)$ = quantity of output in period t
$b_0–b_4, c_1, c_2$ = parameters dependent on technology, on market conditions such as wage rates and recruitment costs, and on laws affecting such production elements as overtime hours and unemployment insurance (these also affect H).

The firm's problem is to minimize the discounted sum of present and future costs, or:

$$DSC(t) = \sum_i [C(t + i)/(1 + r)^i] \tag{A.4}$$

where r is a discount rate (we ignore expected future changes in r).
The general procedure for solution is as follows:

1. Substitute equation (A.3) into equation (A.1) to eliminate $U(t)$ [but not $U(t - 1)$].
2. Solve equation (A.2) for $H(t)$ and substitute into equation (A.1) to eliminate $H(t)$.
3. Write out equation (A.1) with these substitutions, and write corresponding equations for periods $t + 1, t + 2$, and so on.
4. Substitute equation (A.3) for periods $t + 1, t + 2, \ldots$ into these equations to eliminate $U(t), U(t + 1)$, and so on.
5. Substitute these equations into the discounted-sum equation (A.4).
6. Differentiate equation (A.4) after these substitutions with respect to $E(t), Q(t), E(t + 1), Q(t + 1)$, and set the derivatives equal to zero.
7. Solve the resulting set of simultaneous equations for E and Q (all periods).
8. Use equations (A.2) and (A.3) to go from these solutions to solutions for H and U.

This procedure encounters two problems. The first is that the solution involves new orders in future periods – orders not yet received at the time output and employment decisions must be made. We deal with this problem by substituting expected new orders, $NOE(t + i)$, for actual new orders, $NO(t + i)$. The conditions under which this so-called "certainty-equivalent" assumption is justified were discussed by Holt et al. (1960, chapter 6). In the simulations of section 2.2 and the regressions of section 2.3, we make alternative assumptions about the formation of expectations.

The second problem is that in, principle, this procedure will produce an infinite number of equations that have to be solved even to obtain current-period output and employment. To deal with this problem without sacrificing anything essential, we add two assumptions that amount to imposing the expectation that the firm will reach equilibrium conditions at the end of two periods. First, the firm assumes unfilled orders to equal c_1 times output by the end of period $t + 2$; and second, the firm assumes average hours to equal normal hours by period $t + 2$. Mathematically, the assumptions are:

$$U(t + 2) = c_1 Q(t + 2) \tag{A.5}$$

$$H(t + 2) = \overline{H} \tag{A.6}$$

These assumptions may shorten or lengthen some of the adjustment paths in the model, compared with the far more complex case of adjustment taking three or more periods. They do not, however, force the adjustment to an exogenous change to take only two periods; as the simulations in section 2.2 demonstrated, they permit quite complex and lengthy responses to exogenous changes. They are merely a way of simplifying the calculations that the firm makes each period by basing them on known data and on expectations up to two periods ahead. The generalizations about leads and lags suggested by solutions under these simplifying assumptions would probably be almost identical for more general solutions of the model.

Under these assumptions, at the end of step 6 there are four simultaneous equations in the four unknowns $E(t)$, $E(t + 1)$, $Q(t)$ and $Q(t + 1)$. In matrix form, the equations are

$$
\begin{bmatrix}
B11 & B12 & B13 & B14 \\
B21 & B22 & B23 & B24 \\
B31 & B32 & B33 & B34 \\
B41 & B42 & B43 & B44
\end{bmatrix}
\begin{bmatrix}
E(t) \\
E(t + 1) \\
Q(t) \\
Q(t + 1)
\end{bmatrix}
=
\begin{bmatrix}
Z1 \\
Z2 \\
Z3 \\
Z4
\end{bmatrix}
$$

$$\text{(A.7–A.10)}$$

where

$$B11 = [b_2 + b_3 + b_3/(1 + r))]\overline{H}$$
$$B12 = -(b_3\overline{H})/(1 + r)$$
$$B13 = -b_2/c_2$$
$$B14 = 0$$
$$B21 = -(b_3\overline{H})$$
$$B22 = [b_2 + b_3 + (b_3/(1 + r))]\overline{H}$$
$$B23 = b_3/[(1 + r)(1 + c_1)c_2]$$
$$B24 = b_3/((1 + r)(1 + c_1)c_2)] - (b_2/c_2)$$
$$B31 = -(b_2\overline{H})/c_2$$
$$B32 = (b_3\overline{H}/[(1 + r)^2(1 + c_1)c_2]$$
$$B33 = (b_2/c_2^2) + [b_4(1 + c_1)^2] + [b_4/(1 + r)] + b_3/[(1 + r)(1 + c_1)c_2]^2$$
$$B34 = [b_4(1 + c_1)/(1 + r)] + b_3/[(1 + r)(1 + c_1)c_2]^2$$
$$B41 = 0$$
$$B42 = -[(b_2\overline{H})/c_2] + (b_3\overline{H})/[1 + r)(1 - c_1)c_2]$$
$$B43 = [b_4(1 + c_1)] + b_3/[(1 + r)(1 + c_1)^2c_2^2]$$
$$B44 = (b_2/c_2^2) + [b_4(1 + c_1)^2] + [b_3/((1 + r)(1 + c_1)^2c_2^2)]$$
$$Z1 = -(b_1/2) + (b_3\overline{H})E(t - 1)$$
$$Z2 = -(b_1/2) + [b_3/((1 + r)(1 + c_1)c_2)][U(t - 1) + N(t) + NE(t + 1) + NE(t + 2)]$$
$$Z3 = [b_4(1 + c_1)][U(t - 1) + N(t)] + [b_4/(1 + r)][U(t - 1) + N(t) + NE(t + 1)] + [b_3/((1 + r)(1 + c_1)c_2)^2][U(t - 1) + N(t) + NE(t + 1) + NE(t + 2)] + [b_1/(2(1 + r)^2(1 + c_1)c_2)]$$
$$Z4 = [b_1/(2(1 + r)(1 + c_1)c_2)] + [b_4(1 + c_1)][U(t - 1) + N(t) + NE(t + 1)] + [b_3/((1 + r)(1 + c_1)^2c_2^2)][U(t - 1) + N(t) + NE(t + 1) + NE(t + 2)]$$

The solutions for $E(t)$ and $Q(t)$ represent the firm's final decisions for these variables. The solutions for $E(t + 1)$ and $Q(t + 1)$ represent plans, still subject to alteration in the next period when this period's $E(t + 1)$ and $Q(t + 1)$ become $E(t)$ and $Q(t)$, and when there is new information on orders and on any parameter changes.

Given the solutions for $E(t)$ and $Q(t)$, equation (A.2) can be used to solve for $H(t)$. From the solution for $Q(t)$ and the predetermined $U(t - 1)$ and $N(t)$, equation (A.3) can be used to solve for $U(t)$.

Numerical examples of the solution equation for $Q(t)$ under several sets of parameters are shown in Table 2.1 (section 2.3).

The shipments/inventory model

In the shipments/inventory model, the firm faces the following cost function, production function, and inventory identity:

$$C(t) = a_0 + a_1[E(t)\overline{H}] + a_2[E(t)(H(t) - \overline{H})]^2$$
$$+ a_3[H(E(t) - E(t - 1))]^2 + a_4[J(t) - c_3 S(t)]^2 \quad (A.11)$$

$$Q(t) = c_4[E(t)H(t)] \quad (A.12)$$

$$J(t) = J(t - 1) + Q(t) - S(t) \quad (A.13)$$

where the variables are as defined for equations (A.1)–(A.3) and:

$S(t)$ = quantity of shipments in period t
$J(t)$ = stock of inventories of finished goods at the end of period t

Parameters a_0 through a_4 take the place of b_0 through b_4 in the orders model, and c_3 and c_4 take the place of c_1 and c_2. As in the orders model, the firm wishes to minimize the discounted sum of future costs, given by:

$$DSC(t) = \sum_i [C(t + i)/(1 + r)^i] \quad (A.14)$$

The solution procedure is exactly analogous to that for the orders model. The stock of inventories enters the shipments/inventory model at the same places that the stock of unfilled orders enters the orders model. The simplifying assumptions to avoid dealing with expectations about the far future, in the case of the shipments/inventory model, are

$$J(t + 2) = c_3 S(t + 2) \quad (A.15)$$

$$H(t + 2) = \overline{H} \quad (A.16)$$

In matrix form, the solution to the shipments/inventory model can be expressed as

$$
\begin{bmatrix}
A11 & A12 & A13 & A14 \\
A21 & A22 & A23 & A24 \\
A31 & A32 & A33 & A34 \\
A41 & A42 & A43 & A44
\end{bmatrix}
\begin{bmatrix}
E(t) \\
E(t + 1) \\
Q(t) \\
Q(t + 1)
\end{bmatrix}
=
\begin{bmatrix}
Z5 \\
Z6 \\
Z7 \\
Z8
\end{bmatrix}
$$

$$(A.17–A.20)$$

where:

$$A11 = [a_2 + a_3 + (a_3/(1 + r))]\overline{H}$$
$$A12 = -(a_2\overline{H})/(1 + r)$$

$A13 = -a_2/c_4$

$A14 = 0$

$A21 = -a_3\overline{H}$

$A22 = [a_2 + a_3 + (a_3/(1 + r))]\overline{H}$

$A23 = a_3/[c_4(1 + r)]$

$A24 = a_3/[c_4(1 + r))] - (a_2/c_4)$

$A31 = -(a_2\overline{H})/c_4$

$A32 = (a_3\overline{H})/[1 + r)^2c_4]$

$A33 = (a_2/c_4^2) + a_4 + [a_4/(1 + r)] + [a_3/((1 + r)c_4)^2]$

$A34 = [a_4/(1 + r)] + [a_3/((1 + r)c_4)^2]$

$A41 = 0$

$A42 = -[(a\overline{H})/c_4] + (a_3\overline{H})/[(1 + r)c_4]$

$A43 = a_4 + [a_3/((1 + r)c_4^2)]$

$A44 = (a_2/c_4^2) + a_4 + [a_3/((1 + r)c_4^2)]$

$Z5 = -(a_1/2) + (a_3\overline{H})E(t - 1)$

$Z6 = -(a_1/2) - [a_3/((1 + r)c_4)][J(t - 1) - S(t) - SE(t + 1) - (1 + c_3)SE(t + 2)]$

$Z7 = -a_4[J(t - 1) - (1 + c_3)S(t)] - [a_4/(1 + r)][J(t - 1) - S(t) - (1 + c_3)SE(t + 1)] - [a_3/((1 + r)c_4)^2][J(t - 1) - S(t) - SE(t + 1) - (1 + c_3)SE(t + 2)] + [a_1/(2(1 + r)^2c_4)]$

$Z8 = [a_1/(2(1 + r)c_4)] - a_4[J(t - 1) - S(t) - (1 + c_3)SE(t + 1)] - [a_3/((1 + r)c_4^2)][J(t - 1) - S(t) - SE(t + 1) - (1 + c_3)SE(t + 2)]$

As in the orders model, solutions for $H(t)$ and $J(t)$ can be derived from the solutions for $Q(t)$ and $E(t)$ by using equations (A.12) and (A.13). Numerical examples of the solution equation for $Q(t)$ are shown in Table 2.1 (section 2.3).

REFERENCES

Blinder, A. S. (1986), "Ruminations on Karl Brunner's Reflections," in R. W. Hafer, ed., *The Monetary versus Fiscal Policy Debate.* Rowman and Allanheld, pp. 117–26.

Broida, A. (1955), "Diffusion Indexes," *American Statistician,* June, pp. 7–16.

Brunner, K. (1986), "Fiscal Policy in Macro Theory: A Survey and Evaluation," in R. W. Hafer, ed., *The Monetary versus Fiscal Policy. Debate.* Rowman and Allanheld, pp. 33–116.

De Leeuw, F. (1989), "Leading Indicators and the 'Prime Mover' View," *Survey of Current Business 69* (August), 23–9.

Granger, C. W. J., and P. Newbold (1986), *Forecasting Economic Time Series* (second edition). Academic Press.

56   **Frank de Leeuw**

Holt, C. C., F. Modigliani, J. F. Muth, and H. A. Simon (1960), *Planning Production. Inventories, and Work Force.* Prentice-Hall.

Koopmans, T. C. (1947), "Measurement Without Theory," *The Review of Economics and Statistics 29* (August), 161–72.

Mitchell, C., and A. F. Burns (1938), "Statistical Indicators of Cyclical Revivals," reprinted in G. H. Moore, ed., *Business Cycle Indicators.* Princeton University Press, 1961, vol. 1, pp. 162–83.

Moore, G. H. (1950) "Statistical Indicators of Cyclical revivals and Recessions," reprinted in G. H. Moore, ed., *Business Cycle Indicators.* Princeton University Press, 1961, vol. 1, pp. 184–260.

(1955), "Leading and Confirming Indicators of General Business Changes," reprinted in G. H. Moore, ed., *Business Cycle Indicators.* Princeton University Press, 1961, vol. 1, pp. 45–109.

(1978), "Why the Leading Indicators Really Do Lead," reprinted in G. H. Moore, ed., *Business Cycles, Inflation, and Forecasting.* Ballinger, 1983, pp. 339–51.

Zarnowitz, V., and C. Boschan (1975), "Cyclical Indicators: An Evaluation and New Leading Indexes," reprinted in Bureau of Economic Analysis, *Handbook of Cyclical Indicators: A Supplement to Business Conditions Digest.* U.S. Government Printing Office, 1977, pp. 170–83.

CHAPTER 3

A time-series framework for the study of leading indicators

Salih N. Neftci

From the point of view of a time-series analyst there are two questions of interest that concern the methodology dealing with the use of leading and coincident indicators. The first is the "surprising" longevity of the approach while competing methodologies such as large-scale econometric models or time-series representations have been subject to a fair amount of criticism over the years. This issue, we shall see, can be disposed of easily. It is the second question that is more substantial. Is the main contribution of the leading indicators approach to forecasting business cycle turning points one of convenience, or is it that the leading indicators capture an aspect of turning point prediction that econometric models or time-series representations miss?

Why is it not surprising that the methodology of leading indicators seems to have been subject to less controversy than the econometric models or time-series representations? Mainly because the latter two approaches impose explicit restrictions on observed phenomena and hence subject themselves to productive criticism and improvement. The approach of leading indicators, on the other hand, imposes few, if any, restrictions on the reality and is more robust. But it also generates less controversy and leads to fewer advances in understanding economic phenomena.

These comments notwithstanding, it *is* possible that the methodology of leading indicators captures an aspect of real phenomena that econometric models or time-series representations miss. This chapter deals with this question and shows under what conditions the approach has some special raison d'être. I argue that if economic time-series indeed go through explicit phases of a "business cycle," then the index of leading indicators may provide a crude filtering of the state of the cycle.

In order to do this, I introduce an abstract model. The model is driven by a finite-state Markov process, and I characterize leading and

57

coincident indicators as two time-series each having potentially three *unobservable* components: a trend, a noise, and a Markov process. This last is assumed to switch between two states, say, upswing and downswing. The Markov process is not observed individually and thus the switch times are not directly observed either. Using the model, I then show that under some conditions, an index of leading indicators may provide a consistent estimate of the present state of the Markov process.

3.1   The model

Let X_{1t} and X_{2t} denote the leading and coincident indicators, respectively. Also, assume that time is continuous and that X_{1t} and X_{2t} are influenced by three main components.

The first component is a two-state Markov process denoted by O_t, which measures the state of the business cycle. O_t is assumed to fluctuate between two states, s_1 and s_2, where s_1 characterizes upswings and s_2 characterizes downswings. O_t is not directly observed but is known to influence X_{it} ($i = 1, 2$).

The second component is a (possibly) serially correlated random variable that acts as a noise and disguises the true state of the Markov process O_t. Thus the individual components are unobserved but their sum is observed. This suggests the following pair of equations:

$$dX_{1t} = O_t dt + A_1(X_{1t})dt + B_1 dW_{1t} \tag{1}$$

$$dX_{2t} = O_{t-u}dt + A_2(X_{2t})dt + B_2 dW_{2t} \tag{2}$$

where the W_{1t}, W_{2t} are two standard Wiener processes, and B_1, B_2 are constants that we need to take into account because of the non-unit variances of the observed leading and coincident indicators. The $A_i(X_{it})$ represent the serially correlated components of the X_{it}, and u is a positive number that stands for the *lead time* of the leading indicators. Note that because we are dealing with changes on the left-hand side of equation (1) we assume that the trend terms have been dropped.

Let O_t be a first-order Markov process that switches between two regimes of the business cycle. These states are denoted by s_1 and s_2. The following important probabilities are associated with this Markov process. The unconditional probability of occupying a state is denoted by

$$P(O_t = s_1) = p \qquad P(O_t = s_2) = 1 - p \tag{3}$$

and the transition probabilities by

$$P(O_t = s_1 \,|\, O_{t-s} = s_1) = p_{11}(s) \tag{4}$$

$$P(O_{t-s} = s_2 \,|\, O_t = s_2) = p_{22}(s) \tag{5}$$

with

$$P(O_t = s_2 | O_{t-s} = s_1) = 1 - p_{11}(s) \tag{6}$$

$$P(O_t = s_2 | O_{t-s} = s_1) = 1 - p_{22}(s) \tag{7}$$

Hence the statistical problem faced by the econometrician is to extract the state of the Markov processes O_t given the information set at time t. Let I_t denote this information set. It is well known that the optimal MSE estimate of the O_t will be given by

$$\text{Min } E\{(O_t - \hat{O}_t)^2 | I_t\} \qquad \hat{O}_t \epsilon I_t \tag{8}$$

where I_t is the information set, which in this case consists of the past and contemporaneous values of the X_{it}.

It is easy to see that this minimization will yield the estimator

$$\begin{aligned}
\hat{O}_t &= E[O_t | I_t] \\
&= s_1 P(O_t = s_1 | I_t) + s_2 P(O_t = s_2 | I_t) \\
&= (s_1 - s_2) P(O_{it} = s_1 | I_t) + s_1
\end{aligned} \tag{9}$$

Thus the estimate of $\hat{O}_t$ is proportional to the a posteriori probability $P(O_t = s_1 | I_t)$ that the O_t will be in state s_1 given the information at time t.

It should be pointed out here that the Markov process O_t will capture the serially correlated component of the leading and coincident indicators created by the "business cycle." The $A_i(\dots)$ are then used to capture any serial correlation in the noise.

As shown in the next section, under some fairly plausible assumptions a carefully calculated index of leading indicators may provide an alternative estimate of the O_t. This estimate will be consistent and may in fact have a small variance as well.

3.2   The index of leading indicators as a filter

Suppose, now, we have several "leading indicators" all relating to the coincident series with a pair of equations such as in equations (1) and (2). We thus have K leading indicators with

$$dX_{1t} = O_t dt + A_1(X_{1t})dt + B_1 dW_{1t}$$

$$\begin{matrix} \cdot & \cdot & \cdot & \cdot \\ \cdot & \cdot & \cdot & \cdot \\ \cdot & \cdot & \cdot & \cdot \end{matrix} \tag{10}$$

$$dX_{Kt} = O_t dt + A_K(X_{Kt})dt + B_K dW_{Kt}$$

where the Wiener processes W_i are assumed to be independent across the i. Also note that we assumed that the state of the O_t affects all leading indicators with a coefficient of one and with the same lead time u. These latter assumptions can be changed easily without affecting the main thrust of the argument.

Now let L_t denote the index of leading indicators defined by

$$L_t = \alpha_1 X_{1t} + \cdots + \alpha_K X_{Kt} \tag{11}$$

where the α_i ($i = 1, K$) are appropriately chosen weights with the property $\Sigma \alpha_i = 1$.

We then have

$$dL_t = \Sigma \alpha_i O_t + \Sigma \alpha_i A_i(X_i) + \Sigma \alpha_i B_i dW_{it} \tag{12}$$

$$dL_t = O_t + \delta_t + \epsilon_t \tag{13}$$

where ϵ_t denoted the weighted sum of the Wiener processes shown in equation (12) and δ_t represents the weighted sum of the serially correlated components of X_{it}. We use equation (13) to discuss the conditions under which leading indicators may have a special contribution to turning point prediction.

If, as assumed in equation (8), the Wiener processes affecting the X_t are independent, then the ϵ_t shown in expression (13) will be a weighted sum of K independent Wiener processes with mean zero. If K is "large," then we expect ϵ_t be very close to zero. This makes dL_t approach O_t, but the two can still be very different if δ_t is "large" in some statistical sense. It turns out that the ability of the leading indicators in capturing the behavior of O_t depends exactly on this point. To the extent that the leading indicators have serially correlated components other than the business cycle that are correlated across series, an index of leading indicators would fail to capture the state of the business cycle. On the other hand, if the correlations across X_{it} are mainly due to the business cycle, then O_t will be able to capture most of the serial correlations in the leading indicators.

Under these conditions dL_t, which represents the "change" in the index of leading indicators, will be a very good estimate of the present state of the system. In short dL_t will be a crude filtering equation.

As new data become available, L_t will provide a good and convenient estimate of the state of the business cycle, O_t, or whether a switch from an upturn regime to a downturn regime has occurred. It should be noted that econometric models or vector autoregressions will not explicitly provide an estimate of the state of business cycle – if this latter is well defined, that is.

The leading indicators approach thus becomes a quick and reasonably accurate way to assess the state of the business cycle if economic time-series are affected by variables that we represented by O_t. These variables are basically jump processes that make observed data go through some explicit "regimes." If such regimes do not exist and economic time-series are basically of the sum of the remaining two components that we denoted by $A(\ldots)$ and $B(\ldots)$ in equation (1), then the leading indicators approach loses this property of acting as a nonlinear filter. Under these conditions the only advantage of the approach would be in the ease of calculating a new index, which consists of an average of twelve numbers, in contrast to large-scale econometric models or VARs, which require more involved calculations.

Also note that this framework suggests restrictions on the economic time-series that qualify as leading indicators. We basically want the following properties to be present in such time-series:

1. We want these time series to be smooth – in order for ϵ_t to be small.
2. We want these series to represent different aspects of the economy so that any serially correlated noise factors become independent of each other – in order for δ_t to be small.
3. We naturally want the lead time to be as large as possible so that the filter issues an early signal.

It is interesting that a comparison of these properties with the methodology outlined in Moore (1983), for example, yields several similarities as to how leading indicators should be selected.

3.3 Conclusions

This chapter outlined a stochastically nonlinear time-series model that can be used for selecting and combining leading indicators. It also showed that under the conditions (a) that economic time-series are affected by various "regimes" of a business cycle and (b) that these series do not contain much serially correlated noise, an index of leading indicators may provide a reasonable estimate of the "state" of the business cycle.

REFERENCES

Diebold, F. X., and G. D. Rudebusch (1989), "Scoring the Leading Indicators," *Journal of Business, 62* (3), 369–91.

Klein, P. A., and G. H. Moore (1983), "The Leading Indicator Approach to Economic Forecasting," *Journal of Forecasting.*

(1985), *Monitoring Growth Cycles in Market Oriented Economies.* NBER.

Mitchell, W. C., and A. Burns (1938), *Statistical Indicators of Cyclical Revivals.* NBER.

Moore, G. H. (1983), *Business Cycles, Inflation and Forecasting.* Ballenger.

Neftci, S. N. (1982), "Optimal Prediction of Cyclical Downturns," *Journal Economic Dynamics and Control.*

CHAPTER 4

A probability model of the coincident economic indicators

James H. Stock and Mark W. Watson

Since their initial development in 1938 by Wesley Mitchell, Arthur Burns, and their colleagues at the National Bureau of Economic Research, the Composite Indexes of Coincident and Leading Economic Indicators have played an important role in summarizing the state of macroeconomic activity. This chapter reconsiders the problem of constructing an index of coincident indicators. We will use the techniques of modern time-series analysis to develop an explicit probability model of the four coincident variables that make up the Index of Coincident Economic Indicators (CEI) currently compiled by the Department of Commerce (DOC). This probability model provides a framework for computing an alternative coincident index. As it turns out, this alternative index is quantitatively similar to the DOC index. Thus this probability model provides a formal statistical rationalization for, and interpretation of, the construction of the DOC CEI. This alternative interpretation complements that provided by the methodology developed by Mitchell and Burns (1938) and applied by, for example, Zarnowitz and Boschan (1975).

The model adopted in this chapter is based on the notion that the comovements in many macroeconomic variables have a common element that can be captured by a single underlying, unobserved variable.

This chapter reports background research under the NBER Project on Cyclical Indicators. At the time this went to press (August 1990), the most recent indexes produced under this project are the experimental coincident, leading, and recession indexes described in Stock and Watson (1989). The authors thank Robert Hall, Geoffrey Moore, Lawrence Summers, John Taylor, and numerous colleagues for helpful advice. Myungsoo Park provided skillful research assistance. An earlier version of this paper was circulated under the title, "What Do the Leading Indicators Lead? A New Approach to Forecasting Swings in Economic Activity." Financial support for this project was provided by the Sloan Foundation, the National Science Foundation, and the National Bureau of Economic Research.

In the abstract, this variable represents the general "state of the economy." The problem is to estimate the current state of the economy, that is, this common element in the fluctuations of key aggregate time-series variables. This unobserved variable – the state of the economy – must be defined before any attempt can be made to estimate it. In technical terms, this requires formulating a probability model that provides a mathematical definition of the unobserved state of the economy. In nontechnical terms, this problem can be phrased as a question: What do the leading indicators lead?

Our proposed answer to this question is given in section 4.1. This section presents a parametric "single-index" model in which the state of the economy, referred to as C_t, is an unobserved variable common to multiple aggregate time-series. Because this model is linear in the unobserved variables, the Kalman filter can be used to construct the Gaussian likelihood function and thereby to estimate the unknown parameters of the model by maximum likelihood. As a side benefit, the Kalman filter automatically computes the minimum mean square error estimate of C_t using data through period t. This estimate, $C_{t|t}$, is the alternative index of coincident indicators computed using the single-index model.

The single-index model is estimated using data on industrial production, real personal income, real manufacturing and trade sales, and employment in nonagricultural establishments from 1959 to 1987. The results are reported in section 4.2. Also in this section, the estimated alternative index $C_{t|t}$ is compared with the DOC series. The similarity between the two is striking, particularly over business-cycle horizons.

Section 4.3 presents an initial investigation into forecasting the growth of $C_{t|t}$ using a variety of leading or predictive macroeconomic variables. The main conclusion is that a parsimoniously parameterized time-series model with $C_{t|t}$ and six leading variables can forecast approximately two-thirds of the variance of the growth in $C_{t|t}$ over the next six months.

A conceptually distinct forecasting problem is explored in section 4.4. A traditional focus of business cycle analysis has of course been identifying expansions and contractions. Several recent forecasting exercises have focused on forecasting turning points; see, for example, Hymans (1973), Wecker (1979), Zarnowitz and Moore (1982), Neftci (1982), Kling (1987), and Zellner, Hong, and Gulati (1987). Rather than focusing on turning points, the approach taken in section 4.4 is to forecast directly the binary variable representing whether the economy is in a recession or expansion six months hence. The main conclusion is that, among the binary-response models considered, expansions can be forecasted fairly reliably, recessions less so.

4.1 The coincident indicator model: Specification and estimation

One approach to studying aggregate fluctuations is to pick an important economic time-series, say employment or GNP, as the object of interest for subsequent analysis and forecasting. This decided, life becomes relatively easy, since economists have decades of experience constructing models to analyze and to forecast observable time-series variables. From the perspective of business cycle analysis, however, this approach is rather limited. Individual series measure more or less well-defined concepts, such as the value of all goods and services produced in a quarter or the total number of individuals working for pay. But these series measure only various facets of the overall state of economic activity; none measure the state of the economy [in Burns and Mitchell's (1946) terminology, the "reference cycle"] directly. Moreover, even the concepts that the series purport to measure are measured with error.[1]

The formulation developed here is based instead on the assumption that there is a single unobserved variable common to many macroeconomic time-series. This places Burns and Mitchell's (1946) reference cycle in a fully specified probability model. The proposed model is a parametric version of the "single-index" models discussed by Sargent and Sims (1977), in which the single unobserved index is common to multiple macroeconomic variables. Estimates of this unobserved index, constructed using variables that move contemporaneously with this index, provide an alternative index of coincident indicators. This index can then be forecasted using leading variables.

4.1.1 The single-index model

Let X_t denote an $n \times 1$ vector of macroeconomic time-series variables that are hypothesized to move contemporaneously with overall economic conditions. In the single-index model, X_t consists of two stochastic components: the common unobserved scalar time-series variable, or "index," C_t, and an n-dimensional component that represents idiosyncratic movements in the series and measurement error, v_t. Both the

---

[1] Most modern research on the forecasting potential of the index of leading indicators has focused on its ability to forecast not the reference cycle, but some observable series such as industrial production or unemployment [e.g., Stekler and Schepsman (1973), Vaccara and Zarnowitz (1978), Sargent (1979), Auerbach (1982), and Koch and Raasche (1988)]. Our perspective is closer to that underlying the work of Diebold and Rudebusch (1989) and Hamilton (1987). For a historical review of the development of the leading indicators, see Moore (1979).

unobserved index and the idiosyncratic component are modeled as having linear stochastic structures. In addition, C_t is assumed to enter each of the variables contemporaneously. This suggests the formulation

$$X_t = \tilde{\beta} + \gamma C_t + v_t \tag{1}$$

$$\tilde{\phi}(L)C_t = \delta + \eta_t \tag{2}$$

$$\tilde{D}(L)v_t = \epsilon_t \tag{3}$$

where L denotes the lag operator, $\tilde{\phi}(L)$ is a scalar lag polynomial, and $\tilde{D}(L)$ is a lag polynomial matrix. According to equation (1), C_t enters each of the n equations in equation (1), although with different weights.

As an empirical matter, many macroeconomic time-series are well characterized as containing stochastic trends; see, for example, Nelson and Plosser (1982). A theoretical possibility is that these stochastic trends would enter through C_t; in this case, each element of X_t would contain a stochastic trend, but this trend would be common to each element. Thus X_t would be cointegrated of order (1,1) as defined by Engle and Granger (1987). Looking ahead to the empirical results, however, this turns out not to be the case: while we cannot reject the hypothesis that the coincident series we consider individually contain a stochastic trend, neither can we reject the hypothesis that there is no cointegration among these variables.[2] The system (1)–(3) is therefore reformulated in terms of the changes (or, more precisely, the growth rates) of the variables. Specifically, assume that $\tilde{\phi}(L)$ and $\tilde{D}(L)$ can be factored so that $\tilde{\phi}(L) = \phi(L)\Delta$ and $\tilde{D}(L) = D(L)\Delta$, where $\Delta = 1 - L$. Let $Y_t = \Delta X_t$ and $u_t = \Delta v_t$, so that equations (1)–(3) become

$$Y_t = \beta + \gamma \Delta C_t + u_t \tag{4}$$

$$\phi(L)\Delta C_t = \delta + \eta_t \tag{5}$$

$$D(L)u_t = \epsilon_t \tag{6}$$

In practice, X_t will be a vector of the logarithms of time-series variables, so that Y_t is a vector of their growth rates. The lag polynomials $\phi(L)$ and $D(L)$ are assumed to have finite orders p and k, respectively, and non-zero β permits different drifts in Y_t.

---

[2] A different way to make this point is that we are examining comovements among the first differences of the coincident variables at frequencies other than zero. Were the common factor ΔC_t the only source of power at frequency zero in the spectra of the first differences, the spectral density matrix of the first differences would be singular at frequency zero and the series would be cointegrated. Harvey, Fernandez-Macho, and Stock (1987) discuss modeling strategies for unobserved-component models with cointegrated variables.

The main identifying assumption in the model expresses the core notion of the single-index model that the comovements of the multiple time-series arise from the single source C_t. This is made precise by assuming that $(u_{1t}, \ldots, u_{nt}, \Delta C_t)$ are mutually uncorrelated at all leads and lags. (When there are four or more variables, this imposes testable overidentifying restrictions, which will be examined empirically below.) This is achieved by assuming that $D(L)$ is diagonal and that the $n + 1$ disturbances are mutually uncorrelated:

$$D(L) = \text{diag}(d_1(L), \ldots, d_n(L) \ldots, d_n(L)$$

and

$$E \begin{bmatrix} \eta_t \\ \epsilon_t \end{bmatrix} [\eta_t \; \epsilon_t'] = \Sigma = \text{diag}(\sigma_\eta^2, \sigma_{\epsilon_1}^2, \ldots, \sigma_{\epsilon_n}^2)$$

In addition, the scale of ΔC_t is identified by setting $\text{var}(\eta_t) = 1$. (This is a normalization with no substantive implications.)

A final identifying assumption is required to estimate the mean growth rate for $C_{t|t}$. This mean is calculated here as a weighted average of the growth rates of the constituent series. The weights are those implicitly used to construct $\Delta C_{t|t}$ from the original data series. That is, in this model $\Delta C_{t|t}$ can be written

$$\Delta C_{t|t} = W(L)Y_t \tag{7}$$

where $W(L)$ is a $1 \times n$ lag polynomial vector. The mean of $\Delta C_{t|t}$ equals $W(1)\mu_Y$, where $W(1) = \Sigma_{i=0}^{\infty} W_i$ and μ_Y denotes the mean of Y_t. This implies

$$\delta = \phi(1)W(1)\mu_Y$$

Taken together, these assumptions provide sufficient identifying restrictions to estimate the unknown parameters of the model and to extract estimates of C_t.

4.1.2 State space representation

The first step toward estimating the model (4)–(6) is to cast it into a state space form so that the Kalman filter can be used to evaluate the likelihood function. This formulation has two parts, the state equation and the measurement equation. The state equation describes the evolution of the unobserved state vector, which in this case consists of ΔC_t, u_t, and their lags. The measurement equation relates the observed variables to the elements of the state vector.

The state equation obtains by combining equations (5) and (6).

Because one objective is to estimate the level of C_t using information up to time t, it is convenient to augment these equations at this point by the identity $C_{t-1} = \Delta C_{t-1} + C_{t-2}$. The transition equation for the state is thus given by

$$
\begin{bmatrix} C_t^* \\ u_t^* \\ C_{t-1} \end{bmatrix} = \begin{bmatrix} \delta \\ 0_{(p+nk)\times 1} \end{bmatrix} + \begin{bmatrix} \phi^* & 0 & 0 \\ 0 & D^* & 0 \\ Z_c & 0 & 1 \end{bmatrix} \begin{bmatrix} C_{t-1}^* \\ u_{t-1}^* \\ C_{t-2} \end{bmatrix}
$$

$$
+ \begin{bmatrix} Z_c' & 0 \\ 0 & Z_u' \\ 0 & 0 \end{bmatrix} \begin{bmatrix} \eta_t \\ \epsilon_t \end{bmatrix} \quad (8)
$$

where:

$$C_t^* = [\Delta C_t \quad \Delta C_{t-1} \cdots \Delta C_{t-p+1}]'$$
$$u_t^* = [u_t' \quad u_{t-1}' \cdots u_{t-k+1}']'$$
$$\phi^* = \begin{bmatrix} \phi_1 \cdots \phi_{p-1} & \phi_p \\ I_{p-1} & 0_{(p-1)\times 1} \end{bmatrix}$$
$$D^* = \begin{bmatrix} D_1 \cdots D_{k-1} & D_k \\ I_{n(k-1)} & 0_{n(k-1)\times n} \end{bmatrix}$$
$$Z_c = [1 \quad 0_{1\times(p-1)}]$$
$$Z_u = [I_n \quad 0_{n\times n(k-1)}]$$

and where I_n denotes the $n \times n$ identity matrix, $0_{n\times k}$ denotes an $n \times k$ matrix of zeros, and $D_i = \text{diag}(d_{1i}, \ldots d_{ni})$, where $d_j(L) = 1 - \Sigma_{i=1}^k d_{ji} L^i$.

The measurement equation is obtained by writing equation (4) as a linear combination of the state vector:

$$
Y_t = \beta + [\gamma Z_c \quad Z_u \quad 0_{n+1}] \begin{bmatrix} C_t^* \\ u_t^* \\ C_{t-1} \end{bmatrix} \quad (9)
$$

The system (8) and (9) can be rewritten more compactly in the standard form,

$$\alpha_t = \mu_\alpha + T_t \alpha_{t-1} + R\zeta_t \quad (10)$$
$$Y_t = \beta + Z\alpha_t + \xi_t \quad (11)$$

where

$$\alpha_t = (C_t^{*\prime} \quad u_t^{*\prime} \quad C_{t-1})^\prime$$
$$\zeta_t = (\eta_t \quad \epsilon_t^\prime)^\prime$$

and where the matrices T_t, R, and Z respectively denote the transition matrix in equation (8), the selection matrix in equation (8), and the selection matrix in equation (9), and $\mu_\alpha = (\delta 0_{1 \times (p+nk)})^\prime$. The covariance matrix of ζ_t is $E\zeta_t\zeta_t^\prime = \Sigma$. For generality, a measurement error term ξ_t (assumed uncorrelated with ζ_t) has been added to the measurement equation (11), and the transition matrix T_t is allowed to vary over time. In the empirical work below, however, the measurement noise is set to zero and the time invariant transition matrix in equation (8) is used.[3]

4.1.3 Estimation

The Kalman filter is a well-known way to compute the Gaussian likelihood function for a trial set of parameters; for a discussion, see Harvey (1981). The filter recursively constructs minimum mean square error (MMSE) estimates of the unobserved state vector, given observations on y_t. The filter consists of two sets of equations, the prediction and updating equations. Let $\alpha_{t|\tau}$ denote the estimate of α_t based on $(y_1, \ldots, y_\tau)$, let $E[\xi_t\xi_t^\prime] = H$, and recall that $E[\zeta_t\zeta_t^\prime] = \Sigma$. Also, let $P_{t|\tau} = E[(\alpha_{t|\tau} - \alpha_t)(\alpha_{t|\tau} - \alpha_t)^\prime]$. With this notation, the prediction equations of the Kalman filter are

$$\alpha_{t|t-1} = \mu_\alpha + T_t\alpha_{t-1|t-1} \tag{12}$$

$$P_{t|t-1} = T_t P_{t-1|t-1} T_t^\prime + R\Sigma R^\prime \tag{13}$$

The forecast of Y_t at time $t - 1$ is $Y_{t|t-1} = \beta + Z\alpha_{t|t-1}$. The updating equations of the filter are

$$\alpha_{t|t} = \alpha_{t|t-1} + P_{t|t-1}Z^\prime F_t^{-1}\nu_t \tag{14}$$

$$P_{t|t} = P_{t|t-1} - P_{t|t-1}Z^\prime F_t^{-1}ZP_{t|t-1} \tag{15}$$

where $F_t = E[\nu_t\nu_t^\prime] = ZP_{t|t-1}Z^\prime + H$ and $\nu_t = Y_t - Y_{t|t-1}$.

The Kalman filter equations (12)–(15) permit recursive calculation of the predicted state vector, $\alpha_{t|t-1}$, and of the covariance matrix of this estimate, $P_{t|t-1}$, given the assumed parameters in T_t, R, Σ, H, and Z,

---

[3] The state space representation in equations (8) and (9) is not unique. In practice, it is computationally more efficient to work with a lower-dimensional state vector. This can be achieved by filtering Y_t, $\gamma\Delta C_t$, and u_t in equation (4) by $D(L)$ and treating ϵ_t as a measurement error. The resulting state vector has dimension $p + 1$.

and given initial values for $\alpha_{t|t}$ and $P_{t|t}$. For exact maximum likelihood estimation, these initial values are taken to be the unconditional expectation of α_t and its covariance matrix, $E[(\alpha_t - E\alpha_t)(\alpha_t - E\alpha_t)']$; that is, $P_{0|0} = \Sigma_{j=0}^{\infty} T_{t-j}^{j} \Sigma T_{t-j}^{j'}$. Alternatively, one could set $P_{0|0}$ to an arbitrary constant matrix. In this case, the estimates are asymptotically equivalent to maximum likelihood.

The Gaussian log likelihood is then computed (up to an additive constant) as

$$\mathcal{L} = -\frac{1}{2}\sum_{t=1}^{T} v_t' F_t^{-1} v_t - \frac{1}{2}\sum_{t=1}^{T} \ln(\det(F_t)) \tag{16}$$

The Gaussian maximum likelihood estimates of the parameters are found by maximizing $\mathcal{L}$ over the parameter space.

4.1.4   Construction of the leading index and weights (W_i)

The alternative index of coincident indicators from the single-index model is the MMSE estimator of C_t constructed using data on the coincident variables available through time t. This is denoted by $C_{t|t}$. The Kalman filter produces the MMSE estimator $\alpha_{t|t}$ of the state vector given $(Y_1, \ldots, Y_t)$. In the notation of equation (8), the alternative index of coincident indicators is $C_{t|t} = (Z_c \quad 0_{1\times(p-1)} \quad 0_{1\times nk} \quad 1)\alpha_{t|t}$. The weights implicitly used by the Kalman filter to construct $C_{t|t}$ from the coincident variables can be calculated by computing the response of $C_{t|t}$ to unit impulses in each of the observed coincident variables. The variance of $C_{t|t}$ is $Z_c \quad 0_{1\times(p-1)} \quad 0_{1\times nk} \quad 1)p_{t|t}(Z_c \quad 0_{1\times(p-1)} \quad 0_{1\times nk} \quad 1)'$.

It is worth noting that this framework also permits the calculation of retrospective estimates of the state of the economy, $C_{t|T}$, and more generally $\alpha_{t|T}$. Estimates of α_t based on the entire sample are computed using the Kalman smoother [see Harvey (1981)].

The weighting polynomial $W(L)$ in equation (7) can be obtained directly from the Kalman filter matrices. Because $\Delta C_{t|t} = e_1'\alpha_{t|t}$, where $e_1 = (1 \quad 0 \quad \cdots \quad 0)'$, the problem of finding the weights implicitly used to construct $\Delta C_{t|t}$, is a special case of the problem of finding the corresponding weights for $\alpha_{t|t}$. The estimate $\alpha_{t|t}$ computed by the Kalman filter is linear in current and past observations on Y_t. By substituting the relationship $v_t = Y_t - (\beta + Z\alpha_{t|t-1})$ into equation (14) and then using equation (12), one obtains:

$$\alpha_{t|t} = (I - G_t Z)(\mu_\alpha + T_t\alpha_{t-1|t-1}) + G_t Y_t - G_t\beta \tag{17}$$

where $G_t = P_{t|t-1}Z'F_t^{-1}$ is the Kalman gain. When the data are expressed as deviations from their means (as is done in the empirical estimation below), β is "concentrated out" of the likelihood. In addition, when T_t is time invariant (so that $T_t = T^*$), G_t converges nonstochastically to the steady-state Kalman gain, G^*. Under these conditions, equation (17) can be rewritten,

$$(I - KL)\alpha_{t|t} = G^*Y_t \tag{18}$$

where $K = (I - G^*Z)T^*$ and by construction $(I - G^*Z)\mu_\alpha = G^*\beta$. The weights $W(L)$ are obtained by inverting $(I - KL)$ in equation (18) and selecting the first row of the resulting infinite order moving average:

$$\Delta C_{t|t} = e_1' \sum_{j=0}^{\infty} K^j G^* Y_{t-j} \tag{19}$$

4.2   Empirical results for the coincident model

This section presents estimates of the single-index model using four monthly time-series for the United States from 1959:2 to 1987:12. The series are those used to construct the DOC coincident index: industrial production (IP), total personal income less transfer payments in 1982 dollars (GMYXP8), total manufacturing and trade sales in 1982 dollars (MT82), and employees on nonagricultural payrolls (LPNAG). The data were obtained from the August 1988 release of CITIBASE. Throughout, we adopt the CITIBASE mnemonics for the variables when applicable.

4.2.1   Preliminary data analysis

The first step in specifying the model is to test for whether the series are integrated and, if they are, whether they are cointegrated. For each of the coincident indicators, Dickey and Fuller's (1979) test for a unit root (against the alternative that the series are stationary, perhaps around a linear time trend) was unable to reject (at the 10 percent level) the hypothesis that the series are integrated. The subsequent application of the Stock-Watson (1988) test of the null hypothesis that the four series are not cointegrated against the alternative of cointegration failed to reject at the 66 percent significance level. Thus these tests provided no evidence against the hypothesis that each series is integrated but they are not cointegrated. We therefore estimated the model (3)–(6) using for Y_t the first difference of the logarithm of each of the coincident series, standardized to have zero mean and unit variance.

The single-index model imposes the restriction that all the comovements in the series arise from a single source. Tests of this restriction, against the hypothesis that the coincident indicators have a spectral density matrix that is finite and nonsingular but otherwise unrestricted, were implemented by Sargent and Sims (1977). Their test examines the implication that the spectral density matrix of Y_t, averaged over any frequency band, will have a factor structure in the sense of conventional factor analysis; thus the dynamic single-index restrictions may be tested by testing the "single-factor" restrictions for a set of these bands and then aggregating the results. Specifically, since ΔC_t and Δu_t are by assumption uncorrelated at all leads and lags, equation (4) implies that $S_Y(\omega) = \gamma S_{\Delta C}(\omega)\gamma' + S_u(\omega)$, where $S_Y(\omega)$ denotes the spectral density matrix of Y_t at frequency ω, and so on. Because $S_{\Delta C}(\omega)$ is a scalar and $S_u(\omega)$ is diagonal, this implies a testable restriction on $S_Y(\omega)$. Performing this test for the coincident indicator model over six equally spaced bands constructed using Y_t (where the averaged matrix periodogram provides the unconstrained estimate of the spectrum) provides little evidence against the dynamic single-index structure: the χ^2_{30} test statistic is 19.8, having a p-value of 92 percent.

4.2.2   Maximum likelihood estimates

The parameters of two single-index models were estimated using IP, GMYXP8, MT82, and LPNAG over the period 1959:2–1987:12. In both models, a second-order autoregressive specification was adopted for ΔC_t, so that $p = 2$. In the first, the errors u_t are modeled as an AR(1) ($k = 1$); in the second, they are modeled as an AR(2) ($k = 2$). The log likelihood for the AR(1) model is 327.77, and for the AR(2) model is 341.38. A likelihood ratio test easily rejects the hypothesis that the additional four autoregressive parameters are zero. We therefore adopt the AR(2) specification henceforth.

The maximum likelihood estimates of the parameters of the single-index model are presented in Table 4.1. The negative estimates of d_{li} for IP and MT82 indicate that the idiosyncratic component of these series exhibits negative serial correlation, although the idiosyncratic component of LPNAG exhibits substantial positive serial correlation. The estimated model for the unobserved component exhibits substantial first-order – but limited second-order – dependence, with roots of (.60, −.05).

Statistics that examine the fit of the single-index model are presented in Table 4.2. The tests assess whether the disturbances in the observed variables are predictable: if the estimated model is correctly specified, they should be serially uncorrelated. The results suggest satisfactory specifications for the IP, GMYXP8, and MT82 equations. However, the disturbance in LPNAG is forecastable by each lagged disturbance and

Table 4.1. *Estimated single-index model of coincident variables*

| Parameter | Coincident variable | | | |
	IP	GMYXP8	MT82	LPNAG
γ_i	0.717	0.521	0.470	0.602
	(0.037)	(0.044)	(0.030)	(0.041)
d_{1i}	−0.040	−0.087	−0.414	0.108
	(0.091)	(0.042)	(0.052)	(0.050)
d_{2i}	−0.137	0.154	−0.206	0.448
	(0.083)	(0.049)	(0.059)	(0.068)
$\sigma_i(\times\ 10^{-2})$	0.488	0.769	0.735	0.540
	(0.035)	(0.026)	(0.030)	(0.030)

$$\Delta C_t = 0.545\Delta C_{t-1} + 0.032\Delta C_{t-2} + \eta_t$$
$$\quad\ (0.062) \qquad\quad (0.065)$$
$$\mathcal{L} = 341.38$$

Notes: The estimation period is 1959:2–1987:12. The parameters were estimated by Gaussian maximum likelihood as described in the text. The parameters are $\gamma = (\gamma_1, \ldots, \gamma_4)$, $D(L) = \mathrm{diag}(d_1(L), \ldots, d_4(L))$ with $d_i(L) = 1 - d_{i1}L - d_{i2}L^2$, and $\Sigma = \mathrm{diag}(\sigma_1^2, \ldots, \sigma_4^2)$. Asymptotic standard errors (computed numerically) appear in parentheses.

variable in the model, indicating misspecification of the LPNAG equation. A possible source of this misspecification is that LPNAG is not an exactly coincident variable, but slightly lags the unobserved factor. This could be investigated by including lags of C_t in the equation for LPNAG in (4). Alternatively, one might change the dynamic specification for u_{4t}. We do not, however, pursue these options for two reasons. First, with the exception of the LPNAG equation, the overall fit of the model appears to be good. Second, and more important, our primary objective is to see whether a purely coincident single-index model can rationalize the DOC coincident index; adopting a mixed coincident/lagging single-index specification would defeat this purpose. We therefore proceed with the coincident single-index model of Table 4.1, but raise the apparent misspecification of the LPNAG equation as an issue for future research.

4.2.3   Comparison between $C_{t|t}$ and the DOC series

We now examine the relation between the contemporaneous estimate $C_{t|t}$ of C_t obtained using the coincident single-index model and the

Table 4.2. *Marginal significance levels of diagnostic tests for single-index model*

Regressor	Dependent variable			
	e_{IP}	e_{GMYXP8}	e_{MT82}	e_{LPNAG}
e_{IP}	.625	.445	.063	.014
e_{GMYXP8}	.320	.986	.786	.034
e_{MT82}	.198	.952	.810	.004
e_{LPNAG}	.359	.790	.163	.000
$\Delta\ln(\text{IP})$	.593	.464	.196	.002
$\Delta\ln(\text{GMYXP8})$	.366	.986	.905	.008
$\Delta\ln(\text{MT82})$	.219	.875	.628	.000
$\Delta\ln(\text{LPNAG})$	.241	.556	.189	.000

Notes: The entries in the table are p-values from the regression of e_y against a constant and six lags of the indicated regressor; the p-values correspond to the usual F-test of the hypothesis that the coefficients on these six lags are zero. No attempt was made to correct the test statistic or the distribution for degrees of freedom, other than the usual correction for the number of regressors. The series e_y denotes the one-step ahead forecast errors from the single-index model. That is, e_y is $y_t - y_{t|t-1}$, where $y_{t|t}$ is computed using the Kalman filter applied to the estimated model reported in Table 4.1.

Table 4.3. *Comparison of growth rates of $C_{t|t}$ and C_t^{DOC}: Summary statistics*

Growth rates (on an annual basis) of:	Sample mean (%)	Sample standard deviation (%)
Commerce series	3.53	8.98
$C_{t|t}$	2.96	4.80

Contemporaneous correlation between C_t^{DOC} and $C_{t|t}$: 0.936

Index of Coincident Indicators published by the Department of Commerce, henceforth referred to as C_t^{DOC}. The summary statistics reported in Table 4.3 indicate that these series are highly correlated, but that the standard deviation of the growth rate of C_t^{DOC} exceeds that of $C_{t|t}$ by 80 percent. This is a consequence of how C_t^{DOC} is constructed: the weights on the deviations of the constituent series from their means sum to 1.8, while the weights implicitly used to construct $\Delta C_{t|t}$ sum to 1. This dif-

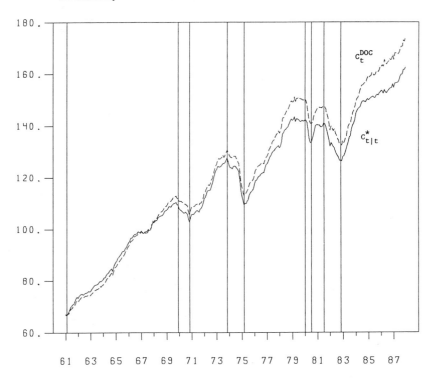

Figure 4.1. $C^*_{t|t}$ and C^{DOC}_t, 1961–87.

ference affects the graphical presentation of the series in levels, but of course not the correlation or other functions of centered moments estimated using their growth rates.

To facilitate a graphical comparison, we calculated a series $C^*_{t|t}$ by scaling $\Delta C_{t|t}$ to have the same variance as the growth in C^{DOC}_t and to have the same mean as $\Delta C_{t|t}$. This modified growth rates series was then used to construct the levels series $C^*_{t|t}$, indexed to equal 100 in January 1967. The series C^{DOC}_t and $C^*_{t|t}$ are plotted in Figure 4.1. Although the mean growth rates differ, the two series exhibit a striking similarity. One of the few noticeable differences between the two series is the somewhat slower average growth of $C^*_{t|t}$ from 1984 to 1987.

A comparison of the weights used in the construction of the growth rates of C^{DOC}_t and $C^*_{t|t}$ provides an additional indication of their similarity. These weights, normalized to add to one, are presented in Table 4.4. The two sets of weights are generally similar. For example, contemporaneous values receive most of the weight in $C_{t|t}$ (and 100 percent in

Table 4.4. *Weights on coincident variables used in constructing* C_t^{DOC} *and* $C_{t|t}$

	Lag	IP	GMYXP8	MT82	LPNAG
C_t^{DOC}	0	.156	.227	.138	.479
	1	.000	.000	.000	.000
	2	.000	.000	.000	.000
	3	.000	.000	.000	.000
	4	.000	.000	.000	.000
$C_{t|t}$	0	.271	.163	.072	.668
	1	.031	.026	.036	−.029
	2	.052	−.016	.021	−.271
	3	.005	.000	.003	−.019
	4	.003	−.001	.001	−.014
	>4	.000	.000	.000	−.002
	Total	.361	.173	.134	.332

Notes: The weights are normalized so that they add to one. The weights implicitly used to construct C_t^{DOC} were computed by regressing the growth rate of the Commerce series on contemporaneous values of the growth rates of the four series used in its construction: industrial production (IP), real person income (GMYXP8), real manufacturing and trade sales (MT82), and employment at nonagricultural establishments (LPNAG). Thus the weights for all lags other than the contemporaneous variables are zero by construction. The R^2 of this regression, estimated from 61:1 to 87:12, is .937. Reasons why the R^2 would be less than one include rounding error and minor differences between our data and those used by the DOC to construct the index. The weights implicitly used to construct $C_{t|t}$ were obtained by computing the responses of $C_{t|t}$ to unit impulses to each of the four series using the Kalman filter.

C_t^{DOC}). The major exception is that a second lag of LPNAG receives a substantial negative weight.

A final measure of the relation between $C_{t|t}$ and C_t^{DOC} is the coherence between their growth rates; this is plotted in Figure 4.2. The very high estimated coherence at low frequencies (in excess of 95 percent for periods over two years) indicates that the two series are very similar at horizons associated with the business cycle.

In summary, these measures all suggest that the coincident index $C_{t|t}$ estimated using the single-index model agrees closely with the current DOC CEI, especially at business cycle frequencies.

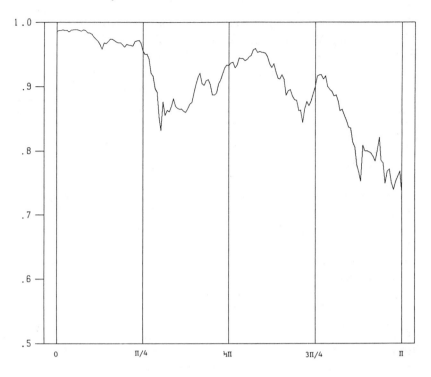

Figure 4.2. Coherence between $\Delta C_{t|t}$ and $\Delta \ln(C_t^{DOC})$.

4.3   Forecasts of the coincident index using leading variables

This section explores one approach to forecasting the coincident series $C_{t|t}$. Rather than considering $C_{t|t}$ directly, we focus on forecasting the growth of $C_{t|t}$ over six months, denoted by $f_t(6)$. The strategy is to construct a parsimoniously parameterized system of autoregressive equations, where the parameterization is suggested by the data. The resulting "base" model is then used to assess the marginal predictive content of additional candidate leading variables.

4.3.1   *Autoregressive systems to forecast $f_t(6)$*

Summary statistics for several autoregressive systems are presented in Table 4.5. In addition to $\Delta C_{t|t}$, each system includes five key leading variables: manufacturing and trade inventories (IVMT82), manufacturers' unfilled orders (MDU82), housing starts (HSBP), the yield on a con-

Table 4.5. *Performance of various systems for forecasting $f_t(6)$*
Variables: $C_{t|t}$, IVMT82, MDU82, HSBP, FYGT10, FYGT10-
FYGM3

	R^2 between $\hat{f}_t(6)$ and $f_t(6)$		
Model	61:1–87:6	61:1–79:9	79:10–87:6
A. Classival VARs			
1. VAR(6)	.578	.585	.565
2. VAR(12)	.654	.633	.673
B. Bayesian VARs			
3. BVAR(12), $\gamma = .2$	.620	.614	.626
4. BVAR(12), $\gamma = .1$	.577	.585	.567
C. VARs with $\Delta FYGT10$			
5. VAR(12)	.538	.534	.632
6. BVAR(12), $\gamma = .1$	.473	.475	.542
D. Mixed systems:			
$[p_{ii}, i > 1; p_{ij}, i \neq j > 1; p_{11}; (p_{12}, p_{13}, p_{14}); (p_{15}, p_{16})]$			
7. (1, 1, 12, 12, 12)	.633	.630	.636
8. (1, 1, 4, 12, 12,)	.615	.601	.634
9. (1, 1, 4, 12, 8)	.607	.590	.634
10. (1, 1, 4, 8, 8)	.587	.597	.573

Notes: $f_t(6) = C_{t+6|t+6} - C_{t|t}$, where $C_{t|t}$ is estimated from the single-index model reported in Table 4.1; $\hat{f}_t(6)$ denotes the six-month ahead forecast of $C_{t|t}$ computed using the relevant estimated system, i.e., $\hat{f}_t(6) = \hat{C}_{t+6|t+6} - C_{t|t}$. All systems were estimated in RATS using the six variables listed. The γ parameter in the Bayesian VARs represents different degrees of tightness in the Bayesian prior, with the lower value corresponding to a more tight prior. The estimation period was 1961:1–1987:12; the R^2 measures were computed for different subsamples using the $\hat{f}_t(6)$ generated by the autoregressive model estimated over the entire period. The mixed systems impose many zero restrictions; the p_{ij} notation in the specification of the mixed systems refers to the number of lags of the jth variable in the ith equation in the autoregressive system. $C_{t|t}$, IVMT82, and MDU82 appear in growth rates and HSBP and FYGT10–FYGM3 appear in levels. In parts A, B, and D, FYGT10 appears in levels; in part C it appears in first differences.

stant-maturity portfolio of ten-year treasury bonds, and the spread between the ten-year bond yield and the interest rate on ninety-day T-bills. Note that $\Delta C_{t|t}$, not $f_t(6)$, enters the autoregressions. The six-month forecast of $C_{t|t}$, $\hat{f}_t(6)$, is computed from the estimated systems.

The classical VAR(12), while delivering the highest R^2 between $\hat{f}_t(6)$ and $f_t(6)$, has many parameters and thus might be expected to be unstable. The Bayesian VARs reported in Table 4.5 impose "smoothness priors," in effect imposing restrictions that might mitigate this problem. Unfortunately, the predictive performance of the Bayesian VARs deteriorates substantially when the tightness of the prior is increased. As an alternative, part D reports results for a set of models that are relatively parsimoniously parameterized, but that do not result in a marked deterioration of six-step ahead forecasting performance. In these, the equations for IVMT82, MDU82, HSBP, FYGT10, and FYGT10-FYGM3 each include one lag of each of the six variables, while the $\Delta C_{t|t}$ equation includes the indicated number of lags (p_{ij}) of the six variables. Of these, model 9 was selected as the "base" model for subsequent analysis.

4.3.2   An examination of additional variables

This base model provides a framework for assessing the marginal predictive content of alternative leading variables. This is done by including trial variables, one at a time, as additional leading variables in the mixed autoregressive system. The results for selected variables are reported in Table 4.6. (The variable definitions are provided in the appendix.)

The strongest evidence of additional predictive content comes from yields on various financial instruments. Theory suggests that bond and stock prices will incorporate expectations of various aspects of future economic performance and so should be useful leading indicators. Yet it is perhaps surprising that these variables provide additional useful information because the base model already includes two interest rates (FYGT10 and FYGM3) and an interest-sensitive series, HSBP. These high R^2 values should be interpreted cautiously, however. For the interest rates, at least, the two largest R^2 values drop in the 1980s, indicating potential instability of these series as useful leading indicators. It is also interesting to note that stock prices help to forecast $f_t(6)$ not by predicting $\Delta C_{t|t}$ directly, but rather by helping to forecast the other variables in the system, which in turn are useful in forecasting $\Delta C_{t|t}$.

Among selected BCD leading indicators (part A of Table 4.6), only IVPAC makes a statistically strong contribution to the $\Delta C_{t|t}$ equation, but including IVPAC actually reduces the six-step ahead forecasting performance. Measures of productivity, prices, exchange rates, and services make only modest contributions. Two of the measures of money and credit – FMBASE and FCBCUC – made substantial improvements in the R^2. However, money and credit variables must be viewed with suspicion as stable leading indicators because of recent changes in financial

Table 4.6. *Tests of the marginal predictive value of alternative leading variables*

Series	Transfor-mation	*F*-tests: *p*-values lags 1–12	lags 7–12	R^2 between $\hat{f}_t(6)$ and $f_t(6)$ 61:1–87:12	61:1–79:9	79:10–87:12
Base model		—	—	.607	.590	.634
A. Selected leading Indicators						
bus	Δln(x)	.093	.699	.624	.622	.628
lhu5	Δln(x)	.091	.389	.624	.609	.643
condo9	Δln(x)	.642	.406	.618	.603	.641
hsfr	Δln(x)	.719	.502	.617	.612	.626
ipi	Δln(x)	.384	.569	.621	.604	.650
ipmfg	Δln(x)	.345	.279	.626	.623	.640
ipcd	Δln(x)	.204	.648	.642	.642	.636
gmcd82	Δln(x)	.612	.430	.615	.592	.655
ivm28	Δln(x)	.693	.945	.645	.648	.634
mocm82	Δln(x)	.868	.876	.615	.594	.649
mpcon8	Δln(x)	.831	.544	.603	.602	.606
ivpac	Δln(x)	.001	.212	.579	.568	.596
rcar6d	Δln(x)	.949	.667	.610	.594	.634
B. Productivity						
loutbm	Δln(x)	.192	.367	.599	.558	.633
lboutum	Δln(x)	.945	.722	.604	.591	.631
C. Prices						
pw	Δln(x)	.689	.904	.629	.628	.619
pwfc	Δln(x)	.712	.637	.611	.595	.636
ppsmc	none	.216	.057	.632	.632	.637
punew	Δln(x)	.104	.136	.605	.600	.624
pzunew	Δln(x)	.180	.344	.610	.607	.620
D. Exchange rates and trade						
exrwt1	Δln(x)	.746	.575	.613	.598	.636
exrwt2	Δln(x)	.639	.426	.616	.599	.642
exnwt1	Δln(x)	.694	.461	.616	.605	.640
exnwt2	Δln(x)	.656	.359	.618	.604	.643
tbl	none	.459	.207	.624	.599	.662
E. Services						
gmws	Δln(x)	.371	.192	.619	.607	.657
lpsp	Δln(x)	.398	.647	.611	.613	.621
lpgov	Δln(x)	.166	.119	.621	.615	.641
lpspng	Δln(x)	.884	.934	.612	.608	.627

Table 4.6. *(cont.)*

Series	Transfor-mation	F-tests: p-values lags 1–12	lags 7–12	R^2 between $\hat{f}_t(6)$ and $f_t(6)$ 61:1–87:12	61:1–79:9	79:10–87:12
F. Money and credit						
fmld82	$\Delta\ln(x)$	1.000	.997	.607	.593	.632
fm2d82	$\Delta\ln(x)$	.873	.977	.624	.613	.629
fmbase	$\Delta\ln(x)$	.110	.045	.641	.637	.687
fcln82	$\Delta\ln(x)$	.203	.815	.608	.575	.674
fcbcuc	$\Delta\ln(x)$	.701	.963	.648	.650	.622
fclbmc	$\Delta\ln(x)$	.125	.037	.633	.772	.238
cci30m	$\Delta\ln(x)$	.567	.537	.642	.640	.641
G. Stock prices and volume						
fspcom	$\Delta\ln(x)$	.317	.393	.673	.649	.696
fsdj	$\Delta\ln(x)$	.420	.384	.645	.630	.659
fspin	$\Delta\ln(x)$	.300	.308	.672	.647	.697
fsvol	$\Delta\ln(x)$	.171	.112	.639	.614	.671
H. Nominal and ex-post real interest rates						
fyff	none	.077	.986	.680	.703	.616
fygt1	none	.436	.668	.636	.594	.699
fycp	none	.007	.756	.739	.751	.691
fyffr	none	.037	.982	.614	.595	.644
fygm3r	none	.188	.923	.623	.618	.626
fygt1r	none	.086	.972	.615	.599	.639
fygt10r	none	.571	.641	.612	.585	.664

Notes: The base model in the first line of this table is the mixed VAR, model 9 in Table 4.5. For each of the variables, the base model was augmented by the trial variable, with twelve lags of the trial variable in the $C_{t|t}$ equation and one lag of the trial variable entering each of the remaining six equations. The p-values reported in the third and fourth columns refer to the F-tests of the hypothesis that the coefficients on the indicated lags of the trial variable in the $C_{t|t}$ equation are zero. The R^2 measures in the final two columns are described in the notes to Table 4.5.

markets [see Friedman (1988) for a discussion]. This is highlighted by the very poor performance of the six-month ahead forecasts based on FCLBMC in the 1980s.

In summary, the leading variables in the base model, along with some of the variables in Table 4.6, indicate that approximately two-thirds of the variance of the six-month ahead growth in $C_{t|t}$ can be forecasted using restricted autoregressive systems. The next step, left for further research, is to assess the stability of these systems.

4.4   Forecasts of recessions using leading variables

This section presents an initial exploration of the possibility of predicting whether six months hence the economy will be in an NBER-dated recession. The approach taken here is to estimate several binary logit models. The dependent variable is R_{t+6}, where $R_t = 1$ if the economy is in an NBER-dated recession in month t and $R_t = 0$ if it is not. The predictive variables are the forecasts $f_t(1), \ldots, f_t(6)$ calculated from an eight-variable mixed autoregressive system with $C_{t|t}$, IVMT82, MDU82, HSBP, FYGT10, FYGT10-FYGM3, FYCP, and IPCD. In addition, individual leading variables were included, both singly and as a group.

The logit models were estimated by maximum likelihood. It is important to recognize that this likelihood is misspecified: because the dependent variable refers to an event six months hence, the errors in the latent variable equation (and the six-step ahead prediction errors) will in general have a moving average structure. Thus this procedure should be viewed simply as providing a convenient functional form for exploring the predictability of R_{t+6}.

The results are reported in Table 4.7. The first noteworthy result is that the one- through six-step ahead forecasts of $C_{t|t}$, produced by the eight-variable mixed autoregression, by themselves produce a substantial reduction in the unexplained variance of R_{t+6}. In addition, these results suggest that expansions can be forecasted accurately, but that the probability of correctly forecasting a recession six months hence is approximately two-thirds. Considerable gains can be made by incorporating variables in addition to $\hat{f}_t(1), \ldots, \hat{f}_t(6)$; financial variables seem particularly useful in this regard.

The predictions $R_{t+6|t}$ of the six-month ahead NBER forecasts, computed using model 15 in Table 4.7, are plotted in Figure 4.3. The dating convention in this figure is that $R_{t|t-6}$ is plotted; for example, in the figure the July 1982 probability is the forecast of the binary July 1982 recession/expansion variable, made using data through January 1982. The actual NBER-dated recessions are indicated by vertical lines. This plot bears out the false positive and false negative rates presented in the final two columns of Table 4.7. On the one hand, false recession forecasts occur relatively rarely, with the largest false recession forecasts occurring during 1967 and throughout 1979. On the other hand, the six-

Table 4.7. *Logit models to predict NBER-dated recessions at a six-month horizon*
Variables in base model: constant, $\hat{f}_t(1)$, $\hat{f}_t(2)$, ..., $\hat{f}_t(6)$

Series	Additional predictive variables No. of lags	R^2	False positive rate	False negative rate
1. Base model	—	.448	.090	.452
2. MDU82	5	.456	.089	.447
3. IVMT82	5	.491	.084	.423
4. HSBP	5	.513	.080	.403
5. FYGT10	5	.486	.984	.423
6. FSPRD	5	.551	.074	.372
7. FYCP	5	.479	.084	.420
8. IPCD	5	.530	.076	.380
9. EXNWT2	5	.453	.089	.448
10. LHU5	5	.482	.084	.422
11. LBOUTU	5	.469	.087	.436
12. FSPCOM	5	.497	.083	.416
13. MDU82, IVMT82, HSBP, FYGT10, FSPRD, FYCP, IPCD	1	.597	.067	.334
14. FYGT10, FSPRD, FYCP, FSPCOM	1	.551	.073	.366
15. FYGT10, FSPRD, FYCP, FSPCOM	3	.613	.062	.309

Notes: The estimation period is 1961:1–1987:12. The dependent variable in the logit regressions has a value of one if there is an NBER-dated recession six months in the future, and has a value of zero if six months hence there is a NBER-dated expansion. The mean value of this variable over the estimation period is .167. The "base model" has only $[1, \hat{f}_t(1), \hat{f}_t(2), ..., \hat{f}_t(6)]$ as regressors. Contemporaneous values (and the number of lags indicated in the second column) of the additional predictive variables were included as well in the remaining models. The R^2 is computed using the actual (0/1) recession probabilities and their six-month ahead forecast computed by the logit model. The second-to-last column (false positive rate) presents the average fraction of times that a recession is forecast when in fact no recession occurs, and the final column (false negative rate) presents the average fraction of times that no recession is forecasted when in fact a recession occurs.

month ahead recession probabilities rarely approach one when in fact a recession does occur. For example, the six-month ahead probability of a recession incorrectly drops below 50 percent during the middle of the 1970 contraction.

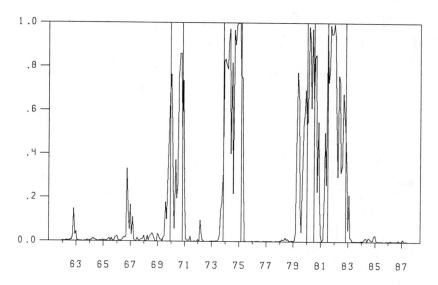

Figure 4.3 NBER-dated recessions and forecasts of their probability of occurring, made six months prior using model 15 of Table 4.7.

4.5   Conclusions

The single-index model provides an explicit probability model for the definition and estimation of an alternative index of coincident indicators. The empirical model produces a coincident index that is strikingly similar to the index currently computed by the Department of Commerce, particularly at the low frequencies associated with business cycles. The main evidence of misspecification in the empirical model appears in the equation for the employment series, LPNAG. One possible explanation, to be explored in future research, is that employment is a lagging rather than an exactly coincident series.

The forecasting exercises of sections 4.3 and 4.4 indicate that time-series models which incorporate leading variables can provide useful forecasts of the growth of the coincident index, and of a variable that indicates whether the economy is in a recession or expansion six months hence. This is unsurprising in the sense that these leading variables are so categorized because of their tendency to move in advance of the coincident index. The main contribution of these empirical investigations is rather to provide some specific models with which to make these forecasts, and some statistical measures of the within-sample forecast quality. A noteworthy finding from this investigation is that financial prices and yields appear to have greater predictive value than do measures of real output, real inputs, or prices of foreign or domestic goods.

Appendix: Variable definitions

Unless otherwise noted, the data were obtained from the August 1988 release of CITIBASE. The variable definitions are those in CITIBASE.

Coincident variables

IP	INDUSTRIAL PRODUCTION: TOTAL INDEX (1977 = 100,SA)
GMYXP8	PERSONAL INCOME: TOTAL LESS TRANSFER PAYMENTS, 82$(BIL$,SAAR)
MT82	MFG & TRADE SALES: TOTAL, 1982$(MIL$, SA)(BCD57)
LPNAG	EMPLOYEES ON NONAG. PAYROLLS: TOTAL (THOUS.,SA)

Additional variables

BUS	INDEX OF NET BUSINESS FORMATION (1967 = 100;SA)
CCI30M	CONSUMER INSTAL.LOANS: DELINQUENCY RATE,30 DAYS & OVER (%,SA)
CONDO9	CONSTRUCT.CONTRACTS: COMM'L & INDUS.BLDGS(MIL.SQ.FT.FLOOR SP.;SA)
EXNWT1	Trade-weighted nominal exchange rate, U.S. vs Canada, France, Italy, Japan, U.K., W. Germany (authors' calculation)
EXNWT2	Trade-weighted nominal exchange rate, U.S. vs France, Italy, Japan, U.K., W. Germany (authors' calculation)
EXRWT1	Trade-weighted real exchange rate, U.S. vs Canada, France, Italy, Japan, U.K., W. Germany; real rates based on CPI's (authors' calculation)
EXRWT2	Trade-weighted real exchange rate, U.S. vs France, Italy, Japan, U.K., W. Germany; real rates based on CPI's (authors' calculation)
FCBCUC	CHANGE IN BUS AND CONSUMER CREDIT OUTSTAND.(PERCENT,SAAR)(BCD111)

FCLBMC	WKLY RP LG COM'L BANKS:NET CHANGE COM'L & INDUS LOANS(BIL$,SAAR)
FCLN82	COMMERCIAL & INDUSTRIAL LOANS: OUTSTANDING,82$(MIL$,SA)
FM1D82	MONEY STOCK: M-1 IN 1982$ (BIL$,SA)(BCD 105)
FM2D82	MONEY STOCK: M-2 IN 1982$(BIL$,SA)(BCD 106)
FMBASE	MONETARY BASE, ADJ FOR RESERVE REQ CHGS(FRB OF ST.LOUIS)(BIL$,SA)
FSDJ	COMMON STOCK PRICES: DOW JONES INDUSTRIAL AVERAGE
FSPCOM	S&P'S COMMON STOCK PRICE INDEX: COMPOSITE (1941–43 = 10)
FSPIN	S&P'S COMMON STOCK PRICE INDEX: INDUSTRIALS (1941–43 = 10)
FSVOL	STOCK MRKT: NYSE REPORTED SHARE VOLUME (MIL.OF SHARES;NSA)
FYCP	INTEREST RATE: COMMERCIAL PAPER, 6-MONTH (% PER ANNUM,NSA)
FYFF	INTEREST RATE: FEDERAL FUNDS (EFFECTIVE) (% PER ANNUM,NSA)
FYFFR	FYFF less 12-month CPI inflation rate (authors' calculation)
FYGM3R	FYGM3 less 12-month CPI inflation rate (authors' calculation)
FYGT1	INTEREST RATE: U.S.TREASURY CONST MATURITIES,1-YR.(% PER ANN,NSA)
FYGT10R	FYGT10 (10-year U.S. Treasury int rate) less 12-month CPI inflation rate (authors' calculation)
FYGT1R	FYGT1 less 12-month CPI inflation rate (authors' calculation)
GMCD82	PERSONAL CONSUMPTION EXPENDITURES: DURABLE GOODS,82$
GMWS	PERSONAL INCOME: WAGE & SALARY, SERVICE INDUSTRIES (BIL$,SAAR)
HSFR	HOUSING STARTS: NONFARM (1947–58);TOTAL FARM&NONFARM (1959–) (THOUS.,SA)
IPCD	INDUSTRIAL PRODUCTION: DURABLE CONSUMER GDS (1977 = 100,SA)
IPI	INDUSTRIAL PRODUCTION: INTERMEDIATE PROD (1977 = 100,SA)

IPMFG	INDUSTRIAL PRODUCTION: MANUFACTUR-ING (1977 = 100,SA)
IVM28	MFG INVENTORIES: CHEMICALS & ALLIED PRODUCTS (MIL$,SA)
IVPAC	VENDOR PERFORMANCE: % OF CO'S REPORT-ING SLOWER DELIVERIES(%,NSA)
LBOUTUM	Quarterly output per hour of all persons, business sector, distributed evenly across months in quarter, lagged two months (authors' calculation, based on CITIBASE series LBOUTU).
LHU5	UNEMPLOY.BY DURATION: PERSONS UN-EMPL.LESS THAN 5 WKS (THOUS.,SA)
LOUTBM	Quarterly output per hour of all persons, nonfinancial corporate sector, distributed evenly across months in quarter, lagged two months (authors' calculation, based on CITIBASE series LOUTB).
LPGOV	EMPLOYEES ON NONAG. PAYROLLS: GOV-ERNMENT (THOUS.,SA)
LPSP	EMPLOYEES ON NONAG. PAYROLLS: SER-VICE-PRODUCING (THOUS.,SA)
LPSPNG	LPSP less LPGOV (authors' calculation)
MOCM82	2 MFG NEW ORDERS: CONSUMER GOODS & MATERIAL,82$(BIL$,SA)
MPCON8	CONTRACTS & ORDERS FOR PLANT & EQUIP-MENT IN 82$(BIL$,SA)
PPSMC	CHANGE IN SENSITIVE CRUDE and INTERM PRODUCERS' PRICES(%)BCD98
PUNEW	CPI-U: ALL ITEMS (SA)
PW	PRODUCER PRICE INDEX: ALL COMMODITIES (NSA)
PWFC	PRODUCER PRICE INDEX: FINISHED CON-SUMER GOODS (NSA)
PZUNEW	CPI-U: ALL ITEMS (NSA)
RCAR6D	RETAIL SALES: NEW PASSENGER CARS, DOMESTIC (NO.IN THOUS.;NSA)
TB1	Trade Balance as percent of personal income: total merchandise and trade exports less imports (current dollars), divided by current dollars personal income (authors' calculation, based on CITIBASE series FTM, FTE, F6TED, F6TMD, and GMPY)

REFERENCES

Auerbach, A. J. (1982), "The Index of Leading Indicators: 'Measurement Without Theory,' Thirty-five Years Later," *Review of Economics and Statistics, 64* (4), 589–95.

Burns, A. F., and W. C. Mitchell (1946), *Measuring Business Cycles.* New York: NBER.

Dickey, D. A., and W. A. Fuller (1979), "Distribution of the Estimators for Autoregressive Time Series with a Unit Root," *Journal of the American Statistical Society, 74* (366), 427–31.

Diebold, F. X., and G. D. Rudebusch (1989), "Scoring the Leading Indicators," *Journal of Business, 62,* 369–91.

Engle, R. F., and C. W. J. Granger (1987), "Co-Integration and Error Correction: Representation, Estimation and Testing," *Econometrica, 55,* 251–76.

Friedman, B. M. (1988), "Monetary Policy Without Quantity Variables," NBER Working Paper No. 2552.

Hamilton, J. D. (1987), "A New Approach to the Economic Analysis of Nonstationary Time Series and the Business Cycle," manuscript, University of Virginia.

Harvey, A. C. (1981), *Time Series Models.* Oxford: Philip Allan.

Harvey, A. C., F. J. Fernandez-Macho, and J. H. Stock (1987), "Forecasting and Interpolation Using Vector Autoregressions with Common Trends," *Annales d'Economie et de Statistique, No. 6–7,* 279–88.

Hymans, S. (1973), "On the Use of Leading Indicators to Predict Cyclical Turning Points," *Brookings Papers on Economic Activity, 2,* 339–84.

Kling, J. L. (1987), "Predicting the Turning Points of Business and Economic Time Series," *Journal of Business, 60* (2), 201–38.

Koch, P. D., and R. H. Raasche (1988), "An Examination of the Commerce Department Leading-Indicator Approach," *Journal of Business and Economic Statistics, 6* (2), 167–87.

Mitchell, W. C., and A. F. Burns (1938), *Statistical Indicators of Cyclical Revivals.* New York: NBER.

Moore, G. H. (1979) "The Forty-Second Anniversary of the Leading Indicators," in William Fellner, ed., *Contemporary Economic Problems, 1979.* Washington, D.C.: American Enterprise Institute, 1979; reprinted in G. H. Moore, *Business Cycles, Inflation, and Forecasting,* second edition. Cambridge, Mass.: NBER, 1983.

Neftci, S. N. (1982), "Optimal Prediction of Cyclical Downturns," *Journal of Economic Dynamics and Control, 4,* 225–41.

Nelson, C. R., and C. I. Plosser (1982), "Trends and Random Walks in Macroeconomic Time Series," *Journal of Monetary Economics,* 129–62.

Sargent, T. J. (1979), *Macroeconomic Theory.* New York: Academic Press.

Sargent, T. J., and C. A. Sims (1977), "Business Cycle Modeling without Pretending to Have Too Much a-priori Economic Theory," in C. Sims et al., *New Methods in Business Cycle Research.* Minneapolis: Federal Reserve Bank of Minneapolis.

Stekler, H. O., and M. Schepsman (1973), "Forecasting with an Index of Leading Series," *Journal of the American Statistical Association 68,* No. 342, 291–6.

Stock, J. H., and M. W. Watson (1988), "Testing for Common Trends," *Journal of the American Statistical Association, 83* (404), 1097–1107.

Stock, J. H., and M. W. Watson (1989), "New Indexes of Coincident and Leading Economic Indicators," NBER Macroeconomics Annual 1989, 351–94.

Vaccara, B. N., and V. Zarnowitz (1978), "Forecasting with the Index of Leading Indicators," NBER Working Paper No. 244.

Wecker, W. E. (1979), "Predicting the Turning Points of a Time Series," *Journal of Business, 52* (1), 35–50.

Zarnowitz, V., and C. Boschan (1975), "Cyclical Indicators: An Evaluation and New Leading Indexes," in U.S. Department of Commerce, Bureau of Economic Analysis, *Business Conditions Digest,* May 1975, reprinted in *Handbook of Cyclical Indicators.*

Zarnowitz, V., and G. H. Moore (1982), "Sequential Signals of Recession and Recovery," *Journal of Business, 55* (1), 57–85.

Zellner, A., C. Hong, and G. M. Gulati (1987), "Turning Points in Economic Time Series, Loss Structures and Bayesian Forecasting," manuscript, Graduate School of Business, University of Chicago.

CHAPTER 5

An international application of Neftci's probability approach for signaling growth recessions and recoveries using turning point indicators

Michael P. Niemira

Early detection or even timely recognition of business cycle turning points has always been a major concern of policy makers, businesses, and investors. Clearly, early recognition would allow the government policy maker to trigger countercyclical policy measures, businesses to change their own sales or investment strategy, and investors to reallocate assets among alternative investments to optimize their return. The typical way of monitoring and forecasting cyclical turning points is to use leading indicators. Unfortunately, no leading indicator is 100 percent perfect, which means it is sometimes difficult to tell whether or not the leading indicator signal is real. Over the years, numerous systems have been developed to screen out false signals. When these systems were put to the real-life test of forecasting turning points, some of these systems have worked well while others have not. Nearly all the methods for screening turning point signals have been ad hoc creations that may or may not have credibility with other users. However, there is one method, proposed by Salih Neftci of City University of New York (CUNY), that adds a new dimension to screening out false signals. This method is based on economic theory and statistical methods.

Neftci has proposed a method that uses sequential analysis to calculate the probability of a cyclical turning point. This method is based on a theoretical and empirical claim that the onset of a recession is marked by a pronounced decline in aggregate economic activity. Neftci (1982)

Thanks to Geoffrey H. Moore, Jean Maltz, Salih Neftci, Gerald Zukowski, and Margaret Reed for their assistance and comments.

and Palash and Radecki (1985) tested this claim using the U.S. Department of Commerce's composite index of leading indicators to signal a recession when the cumulative downturn probability rises above 90 percent (that is, allowing for a 10 percent chance of error). This approach has worked remarkably well as a decision rule system for recognizing significant changes in a composite index of leading indicators and signaling the onset of "classical" business cycle recessions for the United States. However, the Neftci methodology raises a number of interesting questions and possibilities for other applications. For example:

1. Does the sharp cyclical decline and rebound in leading indicators that is present in business cycle behavior also characterize "growth cycles"?
2. Can this method be successfully applied to spotting recessions and recoveries in the United States, Japan, England and West Germany?
3. What are the implications of the Neftci method for forming composite leading indicators of the business cycle?

5.1   A review of decision rule systems for spotting business cycle turning points

There are two basic types of decision rule systems for interpreting movement in composite indicators – the growth rate rules and the probability rules. Among the former are the Zarnowitz-Moore (1982) and Institute for Trend Research (ITR)[1] approaches. These methods use a sequence of "signals" or "check points" in growth rates to spot and confirm turning points. The probability methods include the Chaffin-Talley (1974, 1986) statistical hypothesis test, the Anderson (1966) discriminant analysis approach, and the Neftci sequential analysis method. These probability methods all share a common ground in that they attempt to classify observations as coming from either the "recession population" or the "expansion population." However, the Chaffin-Talley and Anderson methods are static in the sense that they look at each observation independently, whereas the Neftci method accumulates probabilities from the start of the previous turning point. This particular dynamic characteristic of the Neftci method is a major improvement over its predecessors.

---

[1] The Institute for Trend Research uses a technique called "pressure curves." The interaction of the "12/12" and "3/12" moving growth rates is used to determine the phase of the business cycle.

5.2   A step-by-step guide to the Neftci methodology
(based on Niemira and Kahan, in press)

The Neftci methodology allows for a statistically optimal evaluation of monthly movement in a leading indicator by drawing upon three pieces of information. The first is the likelihood that the latest observation in the leading indicator is from the recession sample or the recovery/expansion sample. The second piece of information used is the likelihood of a recession (recovery) given the current length of the expansion (recession) relative to its historical average. Finally, these two components are combined with last month's probability estimate in order to incorporate previous information.

The logic underlying this method is that business activity declines rapidly when a business cycle peak had been reached, that activity in sensitive (leading) indicators shows sharp declines prior to a recession or shortly thereafter, and that sharp increases in sensitive indicators occur prior to a recovery or shortly thereafter.

Neftci formulates the problem of forecasting turning points as recognizing when this abrupt switch in probability distributions has occurred. This method can be applied to both recessions and expansions as follows:

Step 1: Set up probability distributions: The historical series must be segmented into two distributions – a growth recession and a growth cycle expansion case. From these two segments the historical probability distributions are developed (using a three-period centered average to smooth the raw data). Alternatively, a theoretical distribution (such as the normal distribution, etc.) might be used.

Step 2: Develop a prior probability distribution: The user determines a subjective probability distribution that a recession (recovery) will develop so many months after the expansion (recession) begins. In doing so, the user should take note that McCulloch (1975) showed that once an expansion or recession has exceeded its historical minimum duration, the probability of a turning point is independent of its age. Therefore, a simple strategy would be to have probabilities build to the average duration and then hold constant.

Step 3: Apply the Neftci recursive formula: Neftci derived a probability formula using optimal stopping time theory. When this formula is used, what is predicted is the time of the occurrence and not the level of the economic variable. The formula is

$$\text{Prob}_t = \frac{[\text{Prob}_{t-1} + (\text{Prior}\,(1 - \text{Prob}_{t-1}\,\text{Prob1})]}{[\text{Prob}_{t-1} + (\text{Prior}\,(1 - \text{Prob}_{t-1})\,\text{Prob1}) + (1 - \text{Prob}_{t-1})\,\text{Prob2}\,(1 - \text{Prior})]}$$

where Prob is the probability of a recession (recovery) in the near term, Prior is the prior probability determined in step 2, Prob1 is the probability that a new observation is in the downturn (upturn) distribution, and Prob2 is the probability that the new observation comes from the upturn or expansion case (downturn).

Step 4: Interpret the results: When the cumulative probability exceeds the preset level of confidence, say 95 percent, then a signal of a turning point occurs.

Step 5: Look for the next turning point: An operational rule used to reset the probability back to zero and search for the next turning point is to reset it after the cumulative probability increases to 100 percent.

5.3   Application to international growth cycles

Previous studies using the Neftci method have applied the technique to classical business cycles. But two types of business cycles exist. The first type, the "classical" cycle, is more familiar, while the second type, the "growth" cycle, is more common. The growth cycle concept is the typical way the business cycle is measured by the Japanese, English, and other European governments. In short, a classical business cycle is an absolute decline and rebound in economic activity, whereas a growth cycle is a pronounced positive and negative deviation around the trend rate of growth in the economy. Clearly implicit in the measurement of growth cycles is some trend rate of growth. The selection of "the" proper trend is by no means universally agreed upon. Numerous methods exist for measuring growth cycles that may give differing turning point dates. [For a more complete discussion of the alternative techniques, see Niemira and Kahan (in press).] Some of these alternative chronologies, however, would suggest a very different picture of the usefulness of leading indicators for forecasting growth recessions. For the purpose of this study, the National Bureau of Economic Research (NBER)/Center for

International Business Cycle Research (CIBCR) growth cycle chronologies are used for the United States, Japan, England, and West Germany as the basis for comparison with the probability signals.

5.4 A monitoring device sans a turning point chronology

The main value of the Neftci criteria is in real-time monitoring of the growth cycle. On a current monitoring basis, a turning point chronology would not be available until at least six months after the turning point in the economy. However, since the severity of a recession is generally determined after six months, early recognition holds the possibility of a quicker countercyclical policy response that could lessen the severity of the downturn. Even if policy is not changed, the business planner could reevaluate sales or earnings forecasts to better cope with the changing phase of the cycle. The individual country discussions below are divided into two parts: (a) the historical track record and (b) the growth cycle monitor based on data available in early 1987 and not associated with a turning point chronology.

5.5 Growth cycles in the United States

On average, the Neftci probability signals are coincident with growth cycle turning points in the United States.[2] The time span between the signal and actual turning point varies from a lead of thirteen months at a 90 percent probability to a lag of four months (see Table 5.1). Although this application does not provide lead time, on balance it does function well as a system for timely recognition of growth cycle turning points. Furthermore, there is very little difference in turning point recognition time between a 90 percent and a 95 percent probability criterion. Consequently, it is better to use the 95 percent criterion as the threshold for a turning point signal.

It is characteristic of this application that these probabilities generally rise very rapidly. For example, the probability of a growth recession was 14.3 percent in April 1966 but rose to 97.8 percent one month later. This contrasts with the typical pattern of the classical cycle that tends to rise more gradually. Of course, what is interesting about this "abrupt" change is that it fits the Neftci methodology perfectly.

Although the segmenting of the sample between recession and expan-

---

[2] For the *classical* business cycle in the United States, the average lead time is ten months using a 90 percent rule or six months using a 95 percent criterion.

Table 5.1. *Turning point signals of the U.S. growth cycle using the CIBCR chronology and U.S. Department of Commerce composite index of leading indicators, 1951–86*

Turning point		Neftci signal			Lead (−)/lag (+), mo.		
Type	Date	90%	95%	100%	90%	95%	100%
High	Feb 1951	Oct 1950	Oct 1950	Nov 1950	−4	−4	−3
Low	Jul 1952	Jun 1952	Jun 1952	Sep 1952	−1	−1	+2
High	Mar 1953	Jun 1953	Jun 1953	Aug 1953	+3	+3	+5
Low	Aug 1954	Jun 1954	Jul 1954	Sep 1954	−2	−1	+1
High	Feb 1957	Jan 1956	Feb 1956	May 1956	−13	−12	−9
Low	Apr 1958	Jun 1958	Jun 1958	Jul 1958	+2	+2	+3
High	Feb 1960	Oct 1959	Oct 1959	Feb 1960	−4	−4	0
Low	Feb 1961	Apr 1961	May 1961	Jun 1961	+2	+3	+4
High	May 1962[a]	No signal	No signal	No signal	NA	NA	NA
Low	Oct 1964	No signal	No signal	No signal	NA	NA	NA
High	Jun 1966	May 1966	May 1966	Aug 1966	−1	−1	+2
Low	Oct 1967	Jun 1967	Jul 1967	Dec 1967	−4	−3	+2
High	Mar 1969	Jul 1969	Aug 1969	Dec 1969	+4	+5	+9
Low	Nov 1970	Dec 1979	Jan 1971	Feb 1971	+1	+2	+3
High	Mar 1973	Jul 1973	Aug 1973	Oct 1973	+4	+5	+7
Low	Mar 1975	May 1975	May 1975	Jun 1975	+2	+2	+3
High	Dec 1978[b]	Apr 1979	Apr 1979	Sep 1980	+4	+4	+21
Low	Dec 1982	Dec 1982	Dec 1982	Feb 1983	0	0	+2
High		Jul 1984	Jul 1984	Jul 1984	NA	NA	NA
Low		Dec 1985	Dec 1985	Dec 1986	NA	NA	NA
Overall Average					−0.4	0.0	+3.3
Average at highs					−0.9	−0.5	+4.0
Average at lows					0.0	+0.5	+3.3
Median at highs					+0.5	+1.0	+3.5
Median at lows					+0.5	+1.0	+2.5

[a]In June 1962, the probability of a growth recession rose to 86.2 percent only to edge lower thereafter.
[b]After signaling the growth recession, the probabilities receded sharply to 0 percent in May 1980 (reflecting the 1980 *business* cycle recovery) but then moved up briskly to 90 percent by July 1980, 95 percent by September 1980, and 100 percent by September 1981.
Source: Center for International Business Cycle Research (CIBCR); PaineWebber.

sion is done independently of any specific turning point chronology, it is interesting to compare the signals of turning points with other chronologies. Two of those "other" chronologies are the Higgins-Poole (Higgins, 1979; Poole, 1975) and Beveridge-Nelson (1981) methods. Both of these alternative chronologies shown in Tables 5.2 and 5.3 are based on

Table 5.2. *Turning point signals of the U.S. growth cycle using the Higgins-Poole chronology and U.S. Department of Commerce composite index of leading indicators, 1950–86*

Turning point		Neftci signal			Lead (−)/lag (+), mo.		
Type	Date	90%	95%	100%	90%	95%	100%
High	Aug 1950	Oct 1950	Oct 1950	Nov 1950	+2	+2	+3
Low	Jul 1952	Jun 1952	Jun 1952	Sep 1952	−1	−1	+2
High	Oct 1952	Jun 1953	Jun 1953	Aug 1953	+8	+8	+10
Low	Jan 1954	Jun 1954	Jul 1954	Sep 1954	+5	+6	+8
High	May 1955	Jan 1956	Feb 1956	May 1956	+8	+9	+12
Low	Apr 1958	Jun 1958	Jun 1958	Jul 1958	+2	+2	+3
High	May 1959	Oct 1959	Oct 1959	Feb 1960	+5	+5	+9
Low	Dec 1960	Apr 1961	May 1961	Jun 1961	+4	+5	+6
High	Apr 1962[a]	No signal	No signal	No signal	NA	NA	NA
Low	Jan 1963	No signal	No signal	No signal	NA	NA	NA
High	Dec 1965	May 1966	May 1966	Aug 1966	+5	+5	+8
Low	May 1967	Jun 1967	Jul 1967	Dec 1967	+1	+2	+7
High	Dec 1967	Jul 1969	Aug 1969	Dec 1969	+19	+20	+24
Low	Nov 1970	Dec 1970	Jan 1971	Feb 1971	+1	+2	+3
High	Feb 1973	Jul 1973	Aug 1973	Oct 1973	+5	+6	+8
Low	Mar 1975	May 1975	May 1975	Jun 1975	+2	+2	+3
High	Apr 1978[b]	Apr 1979	Apr 1979	Sep 1980	+12	+12	+29
Low	Jan 1982	Dec 1982	Dec 1982	Feb 1983	+11	+11	+13
High	Jan 1984	Jul 1984	Jul 1984	Jul 1984	+6	+6	+6
Low	Jun 1986	Dec 1985	Dec 1985	Dec 1986	−6	−6	+6
Overall average					+4.9	+5.3	+8.9
Average at highs					+7.8	+8.1	+12.1
Average at lows					+2.1	+2.6	+5.7

[a] In June 1962, the probability of a growth recession rose to 86.2 percent only to edge lower thereafter.
[b] After signaling the growth recession, the probabilities receded sharply to 0 percent in May 1980 (reflecting the 1980 *business* cycle recovery) but then moved up briskly to 90 percent by July 1980, 95 percent by September 1980, and 100 percent by September 1981.
Source: Niemira and Kahan (in press); PaineWebber.

methods that extrapolate the trend in the time-series by either a smoothing method (exponential smoothing or a moving average) or an ARIMA model. When the Higgins-Poole method was used for determining deviations from trend, the overall length of time necessary for signaling a turning point was five months, on average, after the turning point occurred, using a 90 percent probability rule (see Table 5.2). On the other hand, the Beveridge-Nelson method found far more growth cycles

Table 5.3. *Turning point signals of the U.S. growth cycle using the Beveridge-Nelson chronology and U.S. Department of Commerce composite index of leading indicators, 1950–86*

Turning point		Neftci signal			Lead (−)/lag (+), mo.		
Type	Date	90%	95%	100%	90%	95%	100%
High	Aug 1950	Oct 1950	Oct 1950	Nov 1950	+2	+2	+3
Low	Jul 1951	Jun 1952	Jun 1952	Sep 1952	+11	+11	+14
High	Nov 1952	Jun 1953	Jun 1953	Aug 1953	+7	+7	+9
Low	Dec 1953	Jun 1954	Jul 1954	Sep 1954	+6	+7	+9
High	Mar 1955	No signal	No signal	No signal	NA	NA	NA
Low	Jul 1956	No signal	No signal	No signal	NA	NA	NA
High	Dec 1956	Jan 1956	Feb 1956	May 1956	+6	+7	+5
Low	Feb 1958	Jun 1958	Jun 1958	Jul 1958	+4	+4	+5
High	Nov 1958	No signal	No signal	No signal	NA	NA	NA
Low	Aug 1959	No signal	No signal	No signal	NA	NA	NA
High	Jan 1960	Oct 1959	Oct 1959	Feb 1960	−3	−3	+1
Low	Feb 1961	Apr 1961	May 1961	Jun 1961	+2	+3	+4
High	Dec 1961[a]	No signal	No signal	No signal	NA	NA	NA
Low	Dec 1962	No signal	No signal	No signal	NA	NA	NA
High	Feb 1966	May 1966	May 1966	Aug 1966	+3	+3	+6
Low	Feb 1967	Jun 1967	Jul 1967	Dec 1967	+4	+5	+10
High	Dec 1967	Jul 1969	Aug 1969	Dec 1969	+19	+20	+24
Low	Nov 1970	Dec 1970	Jan 1971	Feb 1971	+1	+2	+3
High	Feb 1973	Jul 1973	Aug 1973	Oct 1973	+5	+6	+8
Low	Jan 1975	May 1975	May 1975	Jun 1975	+3	+3	+4
High	Aug 1975	No signal	No signal	No signal	NA	NA	NA
Low	Oct 1976	No signal	No signal	No signal	NA	NA	NA
High		Apr 1979	Apr 1979	Sep 1980	NA	NA	NA
Low		Dec 1982	Dec 1982	Feb 1983	NA	NA	NA
High		Jul 1984	Jul 1984	Jul 1984	NA	NA	NA
Low		Dec 1985	Feb 1986	Dec 1986	NA	NA	NA
Overall average					+5.0	+5.5	+7.5
Average at highs					+5.6	+6.0	+8.0
Average at lows					+4.4	+5.0	+7.0

[a] In June 1962, the probability of a growth recession rose to 86.2 percent, only to edge lower thereafter.
Source: Beveridge and Nelson (1981); PaineWebber.

that were totally missed by the probability signals (see Table 5.3). What should be noted, however, is that these late or missed signals may be a problem with the chronologies themselves or with the choice of the leading indicators in which the Neftci method is applied and not this technique for screening turning points.

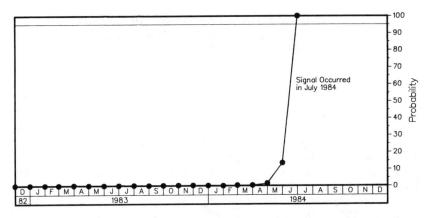

Figure 5.1. Probability of a growth recession in the United States (using Neftci method). A signal of a turning point occurs when the probability exceeds 95 percent.

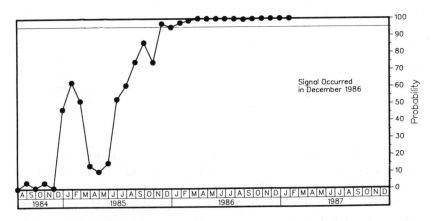

Figure 5.2. Probability of a growth recovery in the United States (using Neftci method). A signal of a turning point occurs when the probability exceeds 95 percent.

5.6 The U.S. economic slowdown: 1984–6

The U.S. economy entered a growth recession in July 1984 that continued until December 1986, based on this probability-based monitoring scheme (see Figures 5.1 and 5.2). The actual turning point is assumed to have occurred once the probability equaled 100 percent. In the case of the July 1984 turning point the probability equaled 100 percent and exceeded the 95 percent threshold level at the same time. With the

Table 5.4. *Growth Cycle Turning Point Signals for the United Kingdom Using the CIBCR Chronology and the CIBCR U.K. Composite Leading Indicator (1961-1986)*

Turning point		Neftci signal			Lead (−)/lag (+), mo.		
Type	Date	90%	95%	100%	90%	95%	100%
High	Mar 1961	Jan 1961	May 1961	Aug 1961	−2	+2	+5
Low	Feb 1963	Apr 1963	May 1963	Sep 1963	+2	+3	+7
High	Feb 1966	Jul 1965	Jul 1965	Aug 1966	−7	−7	+7
Low	Aug 1967	Nov 1967	Jan 1968	Mar 1968	+3	+5	+7
High	Jun 1969	Jan 1970	Feb 1970	Feb 1970	+7	+8	+8
Low	Feb 1972	Aug 1972	Aug 1972	Jan 1973	+6	+6	+11
High	Jun 1973	Jun 1974	Jun 1974	Sep 1974	+12	+12	+15
Low	Aug 1975	Jan 1976	Mar 1976	Jan 1977	+5	+7	+17
High	Jun 1979	Feb 1980	Feb 1980	Jul 1980	+8	+8	+13
Low	Jun 1983	Jul 1981	Jan 1983	Dec 1983	−23	−5	+5
High		Jul 1985	Jul 1985	Apr 1986	NA	NA	NA
Low							
Overall average					+1.1	+3.9	+9.5
Average at highs					+3.6	+4.6	+9.6
Average at lows					−1.4	+3.2	+9.4

Source: Center for International Business Cycle Research (CIBCR); Paine-Webber.

advantage of hindsight, the growth cycle high- and low-point calls were a correct assessment of business conditions. Subsequent to that 1986 signal of a low in the growth cycle, real GNP accelerated sharply at the beginning of 1987 and the momentum continued into that year. Indeed, the average real growth over the six quarters following the December 1986 low signal was 4.8 percent – substantially above the 1975–86 growth rate of 2.5 percent. This timely recognition of growth cycle turning points highlights the value of the Neftci methodology for on-going analysis of business conditions.

5.7   Growth cycles in the United Kingdom

Between 1961 and 1983, the British economy has undergone five slow-downs. The Neftci probability method has picked up each of these episodes with varying degrees of success (see Table 5.4). On average, a 90 percent probability rule signaled a turning point within one month of its occurrence. A 95 percent probability criterion increased the lag to

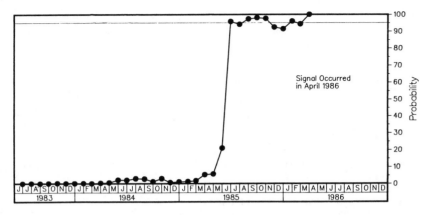

Figure 5.3. Probability of a growth recession in the United Kingdom (using Neftci method). A signal of a turning point occurs when the probability exceeds 95 percent.

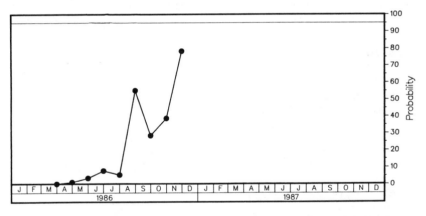

Figure 5.4. Probability of a growth recovery in the United Kingdom (using Neftci method). A signal of a turning point occurs when the probability exceeds 95 percent.

four months, on average. Though 80 percent of the signals lagged their turning point, the 1973 growth cycle signal was the slowest, coming one year after.

A renewed sense of optimism on the U.K. economy was evident in the financial press in early 1987, and this optimism was warranted according to the Neftci technique. Through December 1986, the U.K. economy continued in a growth recession that began in early 1986 (see Figure 5.3). However, the probability of an expansion increased to 78 percent by December 1986 (see Figure 5.4).

Table 5.5. *Growth cycle turning point signals for the Japanese economy using the CIBCR chronology and the CIBCR Japanese composite leading indicator, 1957–86*

Turning point		Neftci signal			Lead (−)/lag (+), mo.		
Type	Date	90%	95%	100%	90%	95%	100%
High	May 1957	Jul 1957	Jul 1957	Aug 1957	+2	+2	+3
Low	Jan 1959	Dec 1958	Jan 1959	Mar 1969	−1	0	+2
High	Jan 1962	Sep 1961	Sep 1961	Dec 1961	−4	−4	−1
Low	Jan 1963	Feb 1963	Mar 1963	Jul 1963	+1	+2	+6
High	Jul 1964	Oct 1964	Nov 1964	Mar 1965	+3	+4	+8
Low	Feb 1966	Jan 1966	Jan 1966	Mar 1966	−1	−1	+1
High	Jun 1970	May 1970	May 1970	Aug 1970	−1	−1	+2
Low	Jan 1972	Jul 1972	Jul 1972	Oct 1972	+6	+6	+9
High	Nov 1973	Apr 1974	Apr 1974	May 1974	+5	+5	+10
Low	Mar 1975	Aug 1975	Aug 1975	Jan 1976	+5	+5	+10
High	Jan 1980[a]	Jun 1980	Jun 1980	Sep 1980	+5	+5	+8
Low	Jun 1983	May 1983	May 1983	Oct 1983	−1	−1	+4
High		Feb 1986	Feb 1986	Feb 1986	NA	NA	NA
Low							
Overall average					+1.6	+1.8	+4.8
Average at highs					+1.7	+1.8	+4.3
Average at lows					+1.5	+1.8	+5.3

[a] An earlier signal of a growth recession was flashed in April 1977 when the probability rose to 93 percent and then exceeded 95% by May 1977, though the 100 percent mark was never reached. The probabilities then fell sharply to 0 percent by November 1978.
Source: Center for International Business Cycle Research (CIBCR); PaineWebber.

5.8   Growth cycles in Japan

Between 1957 and 1983, the average growth cycle probability signal occurred two months after the turning point in the Japanese economy. These signals, using either a 90 percent or 95 percent rule, were "roughly coincident" with the turning point (see Table 5.5). Using a 95 percent rule, the length of time associated with these six growth cycles ranged from a lead of four months in 1961 to a lag of six months after the turning point that occurred in 1972.

The Japan Economic Institute (JEI), in an analysis of the Japanese economy, suggested that the 1983 economic expansion ended in the first quarter of 1986 (Jones, 1987). The Neftci signal of this turning point was consistent with the JEI analysis; a turning point signal was flashed in February 1986 when the probability of a growth recession rose from 88 percent to 100 percent (see Figure 5.5). While this technique did not

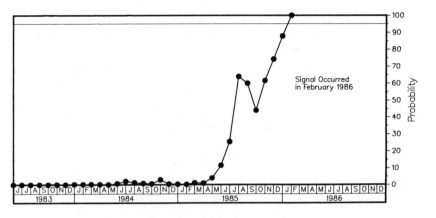

Figure 5.5. Probability of a growth recession in Japan (using Neftci method). A signal of a turning point occurs when the probability exceeds 95 percent.

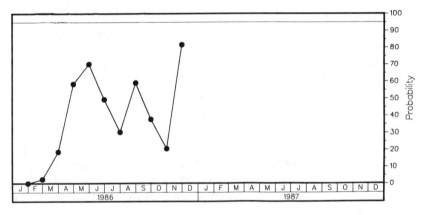

Figure 5.6. Probability of a growth recovery in Japan (using Neftci method). A signal of a turning point occurs when the probability exceeds 95 percent.

provide any advance notice of the growth recession, it clearly performed well as a timely detection of the turn.

Moreover, the Japan Economic Research Center concluded that the "Japanese economy bottomed out in the January–March 1987 quarter" (*The Japan Economic Journal*, April 4, 1987). Through December, the probability of a recovery increased to nearly 90 percent – suggesting that better times were indeed ahead, though not quite high enough to lend full support to this research finding (see Figure 5.6).

Table 5.6. *Growth cycle turning point signals for the West German economy using the CIBCR chronology and the CIBCR West German composite leading indicator, 1961–86*

Turning point		Neftci signal			Lead (−)/lag (+)		
Type	Date	90%	95%	100%	90%	95%	100%
High	Feb 1961	Oct 1960	Oct 1960	Dec 1960	−4	−4	−2
Low	Feb 1963	Oct 1963	Oct 1963	May 1964	+8	+8	+15
High	May 1965	Jun 1965	Jun 1965	Jul 1965	+1	+1	+2
Low	Aug 1967	Oct 1967	Oct 1967	Nov 1967	+2	+2	+3
High	May 1970	Jan 1970	Jan 1970	Apr 1970	−4	−4	−1
Low	Dec 1971	Oct 1972	Oct 1972	Dec 1972	+10	+10	+12
High	Aug 1973	Apr 1973	Jun 1973	Jul 1973	−4	−2	−1
Low	May 1975	Nov 1975	Dec 1975	Mar 1976	+6	+7	+12
High	Feb 1980	Mar 1980	Mar 1980	Apr 1980	+1	+1	+2
Low	Jul 1983	Apr 1983	Apr 1983	Sep 1983	−3	−3	+2
High		Dec 1985	Jan 1986	Feb 1986	NA	NA	NA
Low							
Overall average					+1.3	+1.6	+4.4
Average at highs					−2.0	−1.6	0.0
Average at lows					+4.6	+4.8	+8.8

Source: Center for International Business Cycle Research (CIBCR); PaineWebber.

5.9   Growth cycles in West Germany

Between 1961 and 1983, the West Germany economy experienced five growth recessions. The average lead time, using a 95 percent criterion with the sequential probability method, was two months at peaks, though at troughs the signal lagged by an average of five months (see Table 5.6).

The West Germany economy entered a growth recession in February 1986 when the probability rose to 100 percent (see Figure 5.7). Through December 1986, the German recovery was nowhere in sight, as suggested by a meager 2 percent probability of an expansion (see Figure 5.8). Again from the standpoint of hindsight this reading appeared correct.

5.10   New application of the method

This chapter has demonstrated the usefulness of the Neftci probability method for spotting turning points in international economic cycles. The evaluation undertaken in this paper was to determine whether or

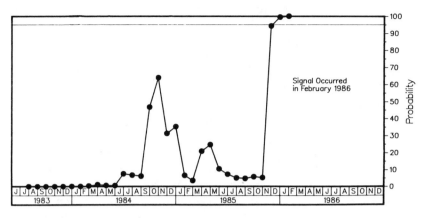

Figure 5.7. Probability of a growth recession in West Germany (using Neftci method). A signal of a turning point occurs when the probability exceeds 95 percent.

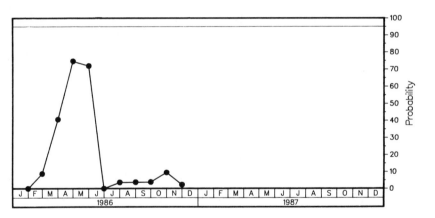

Figure 5.8. Probability of a growth recovery in West Germany (using Neftci method). A signal of a turning point occurs when the probability exceeds 95 percent.

not a signal was flashed and when it occurred relative to the "actual turn." Of course, the actual turning point is, in part, a judgment call based on the methodology used. Therefore, if a particular composite leading indicator does not seem to work well in calling turning points, it may be becasue of three factors: (a) the leading indicator was not constructed properly; (b) the chronology used to compare the turning point signals is not a proper representation of the aggregate trend-adjusted cycle; or (c) the growth recession/recovery environment is not sufficiently different. The results in this chapter seem to suggest that the third factor is least likely, since it was shown that aggregate indicators for four countries did undergo a "switch" even under growth cycle phases.

A further result of this study was that the leading indicators together with the Neftci probabilities worked best for the United States and worst for the United Kingdom at a 95 percent criterion. Why is this so? One possible explanation is that the NBER/CIBCR method, which constructed the international composites by using series similar to those in the U.S. composite, may not be the best approach for selecting foreign cyclical indicators to be included in their composites because of differences in data or economic structures. One way to assess the suitability of individual components for inclusion into composite indicators is to apply a "Neftci criterion" to the selection of economic indicators. Use of the Neftci criterion (that is, the ability to forecast a turning point in the probabilistic sense for selecting cyclical indicators) could provide a major step forward in the methodology used to form composite indicators.

Clearly, the Neftci technique has much merit as a decision rule system for forming and interpreting composite indicators. But even beyond this application, it is easy to envision more specialized uses of the Neftci method, such as the use of composite, diffusion, or individual indicators to signal a turning point in the stock market, commodity price cycles, or even company sales. This sequential classification of information provides a major tool for economic forecasting and monitoring of cyclical processes.

Appendix: Components of the composite leading indexes

Components for the United States (compiled by the U.S. Department of Commerce).

1. Average workweek, manufacturing
2. Initial claims for state unemployment insurance
3. Manufacturing new orders for consumer goods and materials (1982 dollars)
4. Vendor performance
5. Contracts and orders for plant and equipment (1982 dollars)
6. Building permits
7. Change in inventories on hand and on order (1982 dollars)
8. Change in sensitive materials prices
9. Stock prices

10. Money supply (M2, 1982 dollars)
11. Change in business and consumer credit

Components for the United Kingdom (compiled by the Center for International Business Cycle Research).

1. Average workweek, manufacturing
2. New companies registered
3. Business failure
4. New orders, engineering industries
5. Construction new orders
6. Housing starts
7. Change in stocks and work in progress
8. Stock price index
9. Companies profits less U.K. taxes
10. Ratio, price to unit labor costs
11. Increase in hire purchase debt

Components for Japan (compiled by CIBCR).

1. Index of overtime hours, manufacturing
2. Business failures
3. New orders for machinery and construction
4. Dwelling units started
5. Change in inventories
6. Change in raw material prices
7. Stock price index
8. Operating profits, all industry
9. Ratio, price to unit labor costs
10. Change in consumer and housing credit outstanding

Components for West Germany (compiled by CIBCR).

1. Number of persons working shortened hours
2. Applications for unemployment compensation
3. Insolvent enterprises
4. New orders by investment goods industry
5. Residential construction orders
6. Real inventory change
7. Change in basic materials prices
8. Stock price index
9. Net income from entrepreneurial activity (real)
10. Ratio, price to unit labor cost
11. Real change in consumer credit

REFERENCES

Anderson, L. C. (1966), "A Method of Using Diffusion Indexes to Indicate the Direction of National Economic Activity," *Proceedings of the American Statistical Association*, pp. 424–34.

Beveridge, S., and C. R. Nelson (1981), "A New Approach to Decomposition of Economic Time Series into Permanent and Transitory Components with Particular Attention to Measurement of the 'Business Cycle,'" *Journal of Monetary Economics, 7,* 151–74.

Chaffin, W. W., and W. K. Talley (1974), "Diffusion Indexes and Indifference Bands," *Proceedings of the American Statistical Association*, pp. 408–11.

Chaffin, W. W., and W. K. Talley (1986), "Diffusion Indexes and a Statistical Test for Predicting Turning Points in Business Cycles," mimeo.

Higgins, B. (1979), "Monetary Growth and Business Cycles: The Relationship Between Monetary Decelerations and Recessions," *Economic Review*, Federal Reserve Bank of Kansas City, April, pp. 12–23.

Jones, R. (1987), "FY 1987 Outlook for the Japanese Economy," *JEI Report*, Japan Economic Institute, No. 6A, February 13.

McCulloch, J. H. (1975), "The Monte-Carlo Cycle in Business Activity," *Economic Inquiry, 13* (3), 303–21.

Neftci, S. (1982), "Optimal Prediction of Cyclical Downturns," *Journal of Economic Dynamics and Control*, pp. 225–41.

Niemira, M. P., and S. Kahan (in press), *Measuring, Monitoring, and Forecasting Economic Cycles.* New York: John Wiley & Sons.

Palash, C. J., and L. J. Radecki (1985), "Using Monetary and Financial Variables to Predict Cyclical Downturns," *Federal Reserve Bank of New York Quarterly Review*, Summer, pp. 36–45.

Poole, W. (1975), "The Relationship of Monetary Decelerations to Business Cycle Peaks: Another Look at the Evidence," *The Journal of Finance, 30* (June), 697–712.

Zarnowitz, V., and G. H. Moore (1982), "Sequential Signals of Recession and Recovery," *The Journal of Business, 55,* (1), 57–85.

CHAPTER 6

On predicting the stage of the business cycle

Roy H. Webb

6.1   The business cycle and economic forecasting

Macroeconomic forecasts are traditionally stated as point estimates. Retrospective evaluations of forecasts usually assume that the cost of a forecast error increases with the arithmetic magnitude of the error. As a result, measures such as the root-mean-square error (RMSE) or the mean absolute error (MAE) are most often used to summarize forecast performance.

For many users, however, the traditional approach may not correspond with their own uses and evaluations of macro forecasts. The premise of this chapter is that it could be valuable for many users to accurately predict the stage of the business cycle several quarters ahead. For example, a government policymaker accountable to the electorate might well want the economy to be expanding in the quarter before an election; the actual levels of real GNP and other variables would be of secondary importance. Another example is that a producer of capital goods might expect two quite different sales levels to be associated with a particular level of real GNP, depending on whether the economy is expanding or contracting.

In short, when a variable such as real GNP is predicted, the relevant

An earlier version of this paper, "The Business Cycle and Economic Forecasting," was presented to the Western Economic Association in July 1986 and to the Federal Reserve System Research Committee on Business Analysis in November 1986. The author is indebted to Francis Diebold, Thomas Humphrey, Anatoli Kurpianov, and Stephen McNees for helpful comments, and to Eric Hill and William Whelpley for valuable research assistance. The analyses and conclusions are solely the author's and do not necessarily reflect the views of the Federal Reserve Bank of Richmond or the Federal Reserve System.

loss function may not be a simple linear or quadratic function of the forecast error. This chapter therefore proposes a measure to supplement the traditional summaries of forecast errors. The new measure attempts to capture the extent to which the stage of the business cycle is accurately predicted.

Using that measure, the record of major economic forecasters is reviewed. The results indicate that these forecasters have not predicted the stage of the business cycle very well. Do they represent the state of the art, or are there better ways to predict the timing of peaks and troughs? In an attempt to answer that question, this chapter details two alternatives to conventional forecasting methods, examines the evaluation of cyclical forecasts, and compares the results of different methods.

6.2   Forecast evaluation methodology

6.2.1   *Obstacles*

A major obstacle to evaluating forecasts of the economy's turning points is the small sample. If the data that are used to predict turning points are constant dollar values from the U.S. income and product accounts, quarterly data are available only from 1947. There are only eight cyclical peaks and eight troughs over that interval. If the sample is extended back before World War II, then there are two problems. One is the reliability of data. The other is the comparability of prewar and postwar business cycles. The expanded role of government, the declining share of agricultural and manufacturing employment, the provision of deposit insurance, and the growing importance of services have all affected the economy's cyclical behavior. The postwar business cycle is therefore substantially different from its prewar counterpart.

Given a very small sample of turning points, formal statistical tests and informal judgments have little power or meaning. To finesse that problem, it is possible to reorient the question slightly. Instead of focusing on the prediction of turning points, one can instead focus on the prediction of the stage of the business cycle. The comparative performance of different methods, however, will still be determined by a relatively small number of observations in the neighborhood of turning points.

6.2.2   *This chapter's approach*

The approach of this chapter is to focus on prediction of a cyclical indicator variable – a binary variable that indicates whether the economy is in a cyclical expansion or contraction. First, predictions from major forecasting services will be examined. Next, forecasts from a vector autoregressive (VAR) model and from a sequential probability technique will be examined. Data from 1952 to 1969 will be used to estimate those two alternative models; remaining data will be used to examine post-sample predictions.[1]

In order for some methods to generate a recession signal, a statistical definition of recession is necessary. For example, historical forecasts that are available from major forecasting services give real GNP estimates but usually do not give an explicit prediction of whether a recession will begin. A statistical definition can be used both to define the timing of recessions and to convert real GNP forecasts into forecasts of expansion or recession.

The most common statistical definition is that a recession is a period of at least two consecutive quarterly declines in real GNP. In symbols, quarter t is in a recession if $x_t < 0$ and either $x_{t-1} < 0$ or $x_{t+1} < 0$, where x_t is the growth rate of real GNP in quarter t (approximated by $400[\log(X_t) - \log(X_{t-1})]$, where X is the level of real GNP). That statistical definition, however, frequently departs from the timing of recessions made by the National Bureau of Economic Research (NBER), whose judgment is widely accepted as definitive. An alternative is that a quarter is part of a recession if it is part of a two-quarter real GNP decline; that is, quarter t is in a recession if either $x_t + x_{t-1} < 0$ or $x_t + x_{t+1} < 0$. Table 6.1 presents the timing of business cycles by the two statistical methods and the NBER's official judgment. The common method and the NBER differ in sixteen quarters; the alternative method and the NBER differ in thirteen quarters. The common method fails to define two recessions; the alternative does define each recession but also incorrectly defines an additional recession. Although neither statistical definition is perfect, the closer correspondence to the NBER's definition favors the alternative as the definition of recession that is used in this chapter.[2]

---

[1] The starting date, 1952 Q2, is a traditional starting date in empirical studies of money demand (i.e., Goldfeld, 1976). Macroeconomic consulting services have track records for quarterly forecasts dating back to the early 1970s; the cyclical peak 1969 Q4 is a convenient break-point that allows their forecasts to be compared with other methods.

[2] With a well-specified loss function it would not be necessary to guess at which definition of recession would be most useful. Instead, the events for which timing mattered could be directly derived. This paper does not attempt to specify individual loss functions. Instead, it assumes (a) that many users would value accurate predictions of whether the economy will be contracting or expanding, and (b) that a two-quarter real GNP decline is a valid measure of a contracting economy.

Table 6.1. *Alternative measures of cyclical turning points*

| | | Calendar quarters | | | | | |
| NBER | | Common statistical | | | Alternative statistical | | |
Peak	Trough	Peak	Trough	Dif	Peak	Trough	Dif
48-4	49-4	48-4	49-2	2	48-2	49-4	2
53-2	54-2	53-2	54-2	0	53-2	54-2	0
57-3	58-2	57-3	58-1	1	57-2	58-2	1
60-2	61-1	*	*	3	60-1	60-4	2
69-4	70-4	69-3	70-2	3	69-3	70-2	3
73-4	75-1	74-2	75-1	2	73-4	75-2	1
*	*	*	*	0	78-4	79-2	2
80-1	80-3	*	*	2	79-4	80-3	1
81-3	82-4	81-3	82-1	3	81-2	82-4	1
				16			13

Note: For both statistical methods, the Dif column is the number of calendar quarters that differ from the NBER's measure of recession. The common statistical method defines a quarter to be part of a recession if real GNP declines in it and an adjacent quarter ($x_t < 0$ and either $x_{t-1} < 0$ or $x_{t+1} < 0$, where x is the quarterly growth rate of real GNP). The alternative method defines a quarter to be part of a recession if real GNP declines over a two-quarter period including that particualr quarter (either $x_t + x_{t-1} < 0$ or $x_t + x_{t+1} < 0$). An asterisk represents the absence of recession according to the particular definition. The peak refers to the last quarter before the beginning of recession; the trough refers to the last quarter of recession.

Using the alternative definition, an indicator variable for the cyclical state of the economy can thus be constructed, with 0 indicating a quarter in recession and 1 indicating a quarter in expansion (more precisely, a non-recession). The performance of a forecaster can be measured by means of the following steps:

1. Convert a series of real GNP forecasts into a series of forecasts of the cyclical indicator.
2. Compute forecast errors by subtracting the predicted cyclical indicator values from the actual values.
3. Aggregate forecast errors, either by simply summing the number of quarters that the forecast differs from the cyclical indicator or calculating traditional measures such as mean absolute

Table 6.2. *Recessions predicted by major forecasting services*

Chase		DRI		WEFA		No change	
Peak	Trough	Peak	Trough	Peak	Trough	Peak	Trough
A. One-quarter ahead forecasts							
73-4	74-2	74-3	75-2	73-4	74-2	74-1	75-3
74-3	75-2			74-3	75-2		
78-4	81-1	79-2	80-3	79-2	80-3	79-1	79-3
81-2	81-3	80-4	81-1			80-1	80-4
81-4	82-2	81-4	82-2	81-4	82-2	81-3	83-1
		82-3	82-4	82-3	82-4		
B. Four-quarter ahead forecasts							
				74-2	74-3		
				75-2	75-3		
79-3	80-1	79-3	79-4				

Note: These forecasts of the cyclical indicator variable were derived from real GNP predictions of the major forecasting services. The peak refers to the last quarter before the beginning of recession; the trough refers to the last quarter of recession.

error or root mean square error.[3] The MAE is presented in Tables 6.2–6.5; it can also be interpreted as the fraction of incorrect forecasts.

4. Compare the measure of forecast error with a "naive" standard, based on information available to even a naive user. For a one-quarter ahead forecast the standard will be the prediction of no change in the cyclical state for the next quarter. It turns out that this simple forecast is not easy to beat. For horizons of several quarters ahead, another simple standard is hard to beat, namely, never predicting recession.

6.3 Conventional forecasts

This section reviews a sample of forecasts from the major consulting services: Chase Econometrics, Data Resources Inc. (DRI), and Wharton

---

[3] By examining statistics such as the MAE or RMSE one is implicitly restricting possible loss functions. In this case, if the loss from erroneously predicting expansion were not the same as erroneously predicting recession, then symmetric loss functions such as the MAE and RMSE would not be appropriate.

Table 6.3. *Accuracy of predictions of the stage of the business cycle by major forecasting services*

Forecaster-horizon	Recession quarters predicted	No. correct	Expansion quarters predicted	No. correct	MAE
Actual	17		34		
Chase-1	17	13	34	30	.16
Chase-4	2	1	49	33	.33
DRI-1	12	9	39	31	.22
DRI-4	1	0	50	33	.35
WEFA-1	13	11	38	32	.16
WEFA-4	2	1	49	33	.33
No change-1	17	13	34	30	.16
No recession-4	0	0	51	34	.33

Note: The forecast horizon is the number of quarters ahead for which forecasts are made. The first quarter forecasted in this table is 1971 Q3; the last is 1984 Q1. The no-change forecast is the lagged value of the cyclical indicator variable. The no-recession forecast is a constant prediction of expansion. MAE is the mean absolute error, that is, the average absolute value of the difference between the cyclical indicator variable and the estimated cyclical indicator variable constructed from real GNP forecasts from the major forecasting services.

Econometric Forecasting Associates (WEFA). Their forecasts were made near the end of each quarter[4] from 1971 to 1983 for the level of real GNP; for this study they were converted to forecasts of the cyclical indicator variable. Table 6.2 lists the recession quarters predicted and Table 6.3 contains accuracy measures for the forecasts and the naive comparisons. Several features of the tables are striking:

    1.   The forecasting services were usually correct when they predicted a recession one quarter ahead. WEFA had the highest

---

[4] The forecasts were most often made within two weeks of the end of each quarter. The WEFA forecasts before 1976 were made in mid-quarter, however. They would thus have had fewer data when making their forecasts than the other forecasters for a five-year period that includes a major recession. For forecasts made at the end of the quarter, the services had most of the weekly data and a large amount of monthly data for the quarter. They did not, however, have GNP figures and other data from the national income and product accounts, which would not be released until the third week of the next month.

    success rate at that horizon, 85 percent, with Chase lowest at 76 percent.

2.   Recessions were predicted less frequently than actually occurred. The bias toward underpredicting the frequency of recession worsened as the forecast horizon increased. There were seventeen quarters of recession over the sample period; DRI, for example, predicted recession in the next quarter only twelve times. At the four-quarter horizon, there were almost no forecasts of recession. Data not presented in the tables show that each service failed to forecast any recession quarters more than four quarters ahead.

3.   The high percentage of correct calls at the short horizon balanced the tendency to underpredict the frequency of recession. As a result, each major forecaster's one-quarter forecasts were no better than the no-change comparison, when compared by the mean absolute error.

4.   At the four-quarter horizon, each model did no better than a simple no-recession forecast. The very low number of long-range forecasts of recession may be an implicit acknowledgment by the forecasting services of the low accuracy of such forecasts. It is also possible that false predictions of recession were perceived to be more costly than false predictions of expansion.

6.4   Two other forecasting methods

Two other methods are used in this section to forecast the cyclical indicator variable. Both methods simulate forecasts that are based only on data up to the date on which the forecast would have been prepared. One-quarter ahead forecasts for 1975 Q1, for example, would be based only on data from 1974 Q4 and earlier. Results are summarized in Tables 6.4 and 6.5.

Both methods make minimal use of economic theory. It would naturally be preferable to have a well-specified theory that would allow prediction of cyclical turning points. At present, however, there is less than complete agrement as to the correct macro theory for steady states with certainty. More difficult, but also more relevant for business cycles, is the theory of dynamic adjustment between steady states. Although current models used by major forecasting services do contain many dynamic restrictions, they are typically not derived from dynamic optimizing behavior but are instead often chosen to raise the in-sample fit of particular equations. It is therefore conceivable that statistical methods that make minimal use of theory could predict the stage of the busi-

Table 6.4. *Recessions predicted by two statistical techniques*

One-quarter ahead						Four-quarter ahead	
VAR		Sequential probability		No change		VAR	
Peak	Trough	Peak	Trough	Peak	Trough	Peak	Trough
73-3	73-4	73-3	75-3	74-1	75-3	74-2	74-3
74-3	75-2					75-1	75-3
79-1	79-3	79-3	80-3	79-1	79-3	79-3	79-4
79-4	81-1			80-1	80-4	80-3	81-1
81-2	82-2	81-4	82-3	81-3	83-1	81-3	82-3
82-3	82-4					82-4	83-1

Note: The VAR forecasts were constructed from real GNP forecasts as in Table 6.2. Any sequential probabilty estimate of 0.9 or higher was defined to be a recession forecast; other values were defined as predicting expansion.

Table 6.5. *Accuracy of predictions of the stage of the business cycle by two statistical techniques*

Forecaster-horizon	Recession quarters predicted	No. correct	Expansion quarters predicted	No. correct	MAE
Actual	17		34		
VAR-1	17	13	34	30	.16
VAR-4	11	7	40	31	.25
Sequential probability	15	12	36	29	.16
No change-1	17	13	34	30	.16
No recession-4	0	0	51	34	.33

Note: The forecast horizon is the number of quarters ahead for which forecasts are made. The first quarter forecasted in this table is 1971 Q3; the last is 1984 Q1. The no-change forecast is simply the lagged value of the cyclical indicator variable. The no-recession forecast is a constant prediction of expansion. MAE is the mean absolute error, that is, the average absolute value of the difference between the cyclical indicator variable and the estimated cyclical indicator variable.

ness cycle more accurately than methods based on highly imperfect theory.

6.4.1 A sequential probability method

A statistical method for calculating cyclical peaks was proposed by Neftci (1982) and has also been used by Palash and Radecki (1985). It is based on the statistical properties of a time series believed to be a leading indicator of cyclical change, such as the U.S. Department of Commerce index of leading indicators, which was used by Neftci, or monetary aggregates, which were used by Palash and Radecki. The basic idea is that the leading indicator will behave differently in a downturn than in an upturn. Recent values can therefore be examined to determine the likelihood of their occurrence if a downturn were to be imminent. That probability is then combined with (a) data on the length of expansion and (b) the probability of recession that was last estimated; the result is a new estimate of the likelihood of recession.

Appendix A contains the details of this chapter's implementation of the sequential probability approach. It follows Neftci in using the index of leading indicators and in the information considered. It differs from Neftci in examining quarterly rather than monthly data, in its extension to predicting cyclical troughs, and by interpreting the method's signal as predicting a recession at a particular time. In this section, if the sequential probability method places a probability of 90 percent or higher on recession, the estimated cyclical indicator is set to recession for the next quarter.[5] This method is not used for forecasts more than one quarter ahead.

Although both Neftci and Palash-Radecki provided suggestive examples, neither compared their forecasts with forecasts produced by other methods. As a result, the relative power of that method is unknown. The comparison in this chapter with other forecasts is therefore of particular interest.

6.4.2 VAR model

Lupoletti and Webb (1986) have argued that VAR models produce forecasts of sufficient accuracy to compete with major forecasting services.

---

[5] The value 90 percent was used by Neftci. Neftci did not specify a particular time at which his method predicts a recession; that is, his signal would say that a recession was imminent but would not predict that the recession would begin in any particular quarter, say the current quarter plus k. Several possible values for k were therefore tested. Placing the prediction of recession one quarter ahead produced the most accurate forecast.

Also, they found that a VAR model's forecasts of real GNP lost less accuracy when made near a cyclical turning point (NBER definition) than did forecasts from major consulting services. For example, a five-variable VAR model used to predict real GNP four quarters ahead had an RMSE of 2.8 percent in post-sample forecasts from 1970 to 1983. Forecasts made within two quarters of cyclical turning points had the same RMSE. Chase Econometrics, on the other hand, had an RMSE of 2.5 percent for the entire period but had a 3.0 percent RMSE for forecasts made near turning points. The other major forecasting services also showed at least a 0.5 percent increase in errors of real GNP forecasts made near turning points.

Those results suggest that a VAR model might provide relatively accurate forecasts of the stage of the business cycle. Accordingly, Appendix B contains the details of a VAR model that is used in this chapter. It is a six-variable model (real GNP, GNP implicit price deflator, Treasury-bill rate, capacity utilization rate, monetary base, and federal spending) that was presented in Webb (1985). In this section, it is used to forecast real GNP; those values, in turn, are used to construct an estimated cyclical indicator variable as was done with predictions from the major forecasting services.

6.4.3   Caveats

Both methods examined in this section are used to produce simulated forecasts. That is, they were not made in real time and are therefore fundamentally different from the real-time forecasts summarized in Tables 6.2 and 6.3. The simulated forecasts have several advantages over their real-time counterparts, including the following:

1.   The simulated forecasts are made with the latest data, which have benefited from revisions that presumably improved their accuracy. Lupoletti and Webb, however, experimented with using preliminary data for four variables in a five-variable VAR model. Surprisingly, the accuracy of the forecasts was not dramatically worsened – in a few cases, the accuracy actually increased. The Neftci method uses the index of leading indicators, which is also subject to substantial revision. Hymans (1973) compared turning-point predictions from the revised index of leading indicators and predictions from originally released data. He found the "amazing result" that predictions based on originally released data were more accurate than predictions based on the latest revised data. For these models, it

therefore appears that using the most recent data does not grossly bias the accuracy comparisons with real-time forecasters.

2. The simulated forecasts had better data for the quarter on which each forecast was based. It is implicitly assumed that the simulated forecasts "knew" the exact values of the data for the base quarter. Real-time forecasters, however, would have had only incomplete data at the time they made their forecasts, the end of the quarter. The information differential ranges from fairly insignificant (such as for quarterly average Treasury-bill rates, for which data would have been known for eleven of thirteen weeks) to substantial (real GNP and the deflator were announced about three weeks after the end of the quarter for most of the period). While including current quarter GNP in the information set thus overstates the information available to forecasters, assuming no information for GNP would also be erroneous. In fact, by the end of the quarter enough data have usually been received to estimate GNP with reasonable accuracy.[6]

3. Also, excessive in-sample experimentation can result in models that fit the available data well but forecast poorly. To reduce that problem, the parameters for the sequential probability method were chosen from pre-1970 data. The VAR model was also constructed using data through 1969. For one-quarter ahead forecasts for a particular quarter, the model was estimated using data up to the previous quarter. The four-quarter forecasts were based on data up to the year-ago quarter. The results are therefore true post-sample forecasts. There still remains a subtle bias. If his forecasts for the 1970s had been poor, Neftci might well have not published his method. Similarly, if the VAR model had not forecasted well in earlier exer-

---

[6] For example, Robert Litterman has produced monthly forecasts of real GNP with a VAR model. Using forecasts that he made at the end of a quarter and the beginning of the next quarter (after data from the national income and product accounts were released), it is possible to determine whether there was solid information on real GNP at the end of the quarter. Forecasts from 1980 Q2 to 1985 Q1 were examined. In a regression of the post-release growth rate on the pre-release prediction, the constant was not significantly different from zero (at any conventional level), the slope coefficient was not significantly different from one (at the 99 percent level), and the R^2 was .73. The average difference between the two series was 0.065, and the average absolute difference was 1.89. It therefore appears that Litterman's mechanical method was able to extract considerable information about a quarter's GNP from available monthly series.

cises, its results would not have been published. The real-time forecasters had no similar luxury.

6.5   Results for the statistical methods

The one-quarter ahead forecasts from both techniques, shown in Tables 6.4 and 6.5, are similar to predictions from the major forecasting services. The VAR model predicted recession seventeen times, and was accurate thirteen – exactly the same as Chase Econometrics and the naive forecast. The sequential probability model, like DRI and WEFA, predicted fewer recession quarters than actually occurred. Its MAE was the same as for most of the other methods.

The only substantial difference in forecasting accuracy among the various methods is at the four-quarter horizon. The VAR model predicted eleven quarters of recession, in contrast to only one or two predicted by each of the forecasting services. The VAR model's accuracy rate for its recession predictions was 64 percent. That was accurate enough to lower its MAE below those of the other models and the naive comparison.

That the statistical methods were as accurate as forecasting services at the one-quarter horizon may at first glance seem rather surprising. The forecasting services study several hundred time-series, whereas the VAR model uses only six and the sequential probability technique two. The forecasting services also have the opportunity to incorporate economic theory into their models. And the services employ analysts who can use their judgment to adjust their forecasts for well-known data anomalies and for ad hoc events. For example, the Carter credit controls triggered the 1980 recession; their removal similarly triggered the following expansion. The ability to adjust for that one event would seemingly confer a sizable advantage to the forecasting services. Since none of the forecasting methods outperformed the naive forecast, however, perhaps it is just a straightforward matter to match the naive method and a difficult task to better it.

The VAR model's relatively accurate performance at the four-quarter horizon contradicts the conventional wisdom that atheoretical techniques do not provide accurate forecasts at longer intervals or at turning points. For example, as Fromm and Klein (1981) put it, "Not only do large [structural] models provide more detail over a wide spectrum of variables, but they also provide valuable information about the economy when it is really needed. They are better than other tools for forecasting at turning points." The results summarized in Tables 6.4 and 6.5 clearly contradict that view.

6.5.1 Probability forecasts

The statistical forecasts produce more information than just the binary estimates that were discussed above. The sequential probability method actually produces a direct estimate of the probability of recession, rather than simply a binary indicator. The VAR model not only forecasts real GNP, but also estimates the standard errors of the forecasts.[7] Is there any value to the additional information that each model produces? This section attempts to answer that question.

Probability forecasts can be evaluated in a similar manner to other forecasts. The actual series will be the same cyclical indicator variable that was used in previous sections; the predictor series will be the estimated probability of recession. It can be shown that forecasting any value except the estimated probability of recession will raise the expected squared forecast error.[8] In particular, reducing probability forecasts to a binary indicator would be expected to raise the average squared error. This type of forecast evaluation has been used in other areas, such as the evaluation of probabilistic weather forecasts by DeGroot and Fienberg (1983). Diebold and Rudebusch (1987) have used several statistics used by meteorologists, including the RMSE, to evaluate sequential probability forecasts of cyclical turning points. Kling (1987) has also generated forecasts of the probability of occurrence of statistical turning points.

Results are summarized in Table 6.6. The accuracy of the sequential probability technique changed very little when evaluated as a probabil-

---

[7] In the results presented here, the estimated standard error is based on the in-sample estimated covariance matrix. It therefore does not account for parameter uncertainty nor does it account for the effects of model misspecification. Doan, Litterman, and Sims (1984) compared in-sample estimates of a VAR model's forecast error with realized post-sample error distributions (which should reflect all sources of error). They found that in many cases the in-sample estimate was actually larger than the post-sample estimate.

[8] Let p be the "true" ex ante probability of expansion, f be the forecast, and e be the forecast error (the realized value of the cyclical indicator minus the forecast). The expected value of the squared error is

$$p(1 - f)^2 + (1 - p)f^2 \qquad (1)$$

where the first term is the probability of expansion times the squared error if the economy does expand, and the second term is the probability of recession times the squared error if the economy contracts. (For example, if the predicted probability of expansion f is .7, the error would be .3 if the economy expanded and .7 if it contracted.) Setting the derivative of expression (1) with respect to f equal to zero yields the first order condition $f = p$.

Table 6.6. *Accuracy of predictions of the stage of the business cycle: Probability forecasts made by two statistical techniques*

Forecaster-horizon	Binary forecasts		Probability forecasts	
	MAE	RMSE	MAE	RMSE
Sequential probability-1	.16	.40	.18	.40
VAR-1 OLS	.16	.40	.36	.46
VAR-4 OLS	.25	.50	.53	.57
VAR-1 SUR			.39	.47
VAR-4 SUR			.52	.55
VAR-1 OLS, debiased			.28	.38
VAR-4 SUR, debiased			.39	.44
No change-1	.16	.40	—	—
No recession-4	.33	.58	—	—

Note: The sequential probability forecast is the result of the formula in Appendix A. The VAR model and estimated forecast errors were estimated by ordinary least squares (OLS) and seemingly unrelated regression (SUR) methods.

ity forecast. The VAR forecast, however, was substantially less accurate at both the one-quarter and four-quarter horizons. It appears that simply assuming a normal error distribution for projected real GNP growth leads to an unrealistically low estimate of the probability of an expansion continuing. The four-quarter ahead forecast, for example, never showed a probability of 0.75 or higher for continued expansion. The result is that the VAR probability forecast is a biased predictor that overestimates the probability of cyclical change.

The robustness of this negative conclusion was checked by replacing ordinary least squares (OLS) estimates of the VAR model with seemingly unrelated regression (SUR) estimates. In principle, to the extent that (a) the errors across equations of the VAR model are contemporaneously correlated and (b) the independent variables in separate equations are uncorrelated, the SUR estimates of the covariance matrix would be more accurate. In an unrestricted VAR model the right-hand

sides of each equation are identical and there is consequently no gain to
SUR estimation. The VAR model in this chapter, however, has different
lag lengths for each variable in each equation, and SUR estimation is
therefore potentially attractive. Although the SUR-estimated covariance
matrix was changed substantially, the resulting cyclical probabilities
were not much different from OLS estimates.

Theil (1966) has suggested a procedure to remove the bias from forecasts. First, estimate

$$A_t = \alpha + \beta F_t + e_t \tag{1}$$

where A is the actual value, F is the forecast for A, α and β are estimated
coefficients, and e is a white noise error term. Then, if α is significantly
different from zero and β is significantly different from one, use those
coefficients to adjust the forecast and produce an unbiased forecast.

That procedure was used to remove the bias from the VAR (OLS)
probability forecasts. First, forecasts from 1970 Q1 to 1971 Q3 were
used to estimate the two parameters in equation (1).[9] Those values were
then used to estimate an unbiased forecast:

$$U_t = \hat{\alpha} + \hat{\beta} F_t \tag{2}$$

where F is the forecast from the VAR model and U is the estimated
unbiased forecast. The estimation was then repeated from 1970 Q1 to
1971 Q4 and another value for U calculated. The procedure was further
repeated, adding one quarter at a time, until a series for U_t was calculated for 1971 Q3 to 1984 Q1. The resulting series therefore approxi-
mates the extent to which a real-time forecaster could have reduced the
bias by studying past forecasts.

The results, shown in Table 6.6, were lower MAEs and RMSEs than
in the unadjusted VAR probability forecasts. Compared with the VAR
binary forecasts or the naive binary forecasts, the debiased forecasts had
higher MAEs but lower RMSEs. The differences do not reverse the conclusions of previous sections, and indicate that better methods of producing probability forecasts are needed.

6.6   Conclusion

It is difficult to forecast the stage of the business cycle more accurately
than by using an uninformative naive indicator. For one-quarter ahead

[9] Since the actual values were binary, and the forecasts were probabilities, OLS estimates
would be biased. Logit estimation was therefore used for all regressions discussed in this
paragraph.

forecasts, simply extrapolating the current stage would have been as accurate as using forecasts from the major consulting services during a thirteen-year interval. Four quarters ahead, the services rarely forecast recession; never forecasting recession would have been just as accurate.

Two statistical forecasting techniques were also examined. One, based on a proposal by Neftci, performed as well as the major forecasters but was no more accurate than the naive methods. The other technique, a VAR model, also had the same accuracy as major forecasters for one-quarter ahead forecasts. But at the four-quarter horizon, the VAR model predicted many of the recession quarters that did occur. Of the methods studied, only the VAR model's four-quarter predictions were more accurate than a naive comparison.

In principle, it might be preferable to work directly with the probability of expansion or recession, rather than confining attention to a binary indicator variable. In practice, however, it can be difficult to produce unambiguously useful estimates of probabilities. Both statistical techniques were used to make predictions of cyclical probabilities; the sequential probability technique's accuracy changed very little. Depending on the metric used for evaluation, the VAR probability forecasts were either more or less accurate than the VAR binary forecast and the naive methods.

These results are suggestive rather than definitive for several reasons. First, they are based on a thirteen-year period that may or may not closely correspond with the future. Second, that interval contained only three business cycles; a much larger sample would be desirable. Third, a specific loss function was not presented; instead it was assumed that predicting a two-quarter downturn would be useful. And finally, while the major forecasting services were judged on the basis of published forecasts, the two statistical techniques produced simulated forecasts. Although efforts were made to base the simulated forecasts on comparable data, definitive comparative results require real-time forecasts.

Appendix A: A sequential probability method for predicting the stage of the business cycle

The sequential probability method, as used by Neftci, Palash-Radecki, and Diebold-Rudebusch, employs a formula that takes time-series data and yields an estimate of the probability that a recession is imminent. The first step in applying that procedure is to choose an indicator variable. This paper uses the Department of Commerce index of leading indicators, as did Neftci and Diebold-Rudebusch.

The second step is to estimate a probability density that gives the probability (p) of downturn, based on the latest observation of the indicator. The approach taken by this chapter and by Neftci was to judgmentally estimate that probability distribution from smoothed historical data. For this chapter, the historical data were quarterly average values of the index of leading indicators from 1948 Q1 to 1970 Q2.

The third step is to estimate a probability distribution that gives the probability (q) of a recession, based on the length of expansion to date. This chapter uses the probabilities given by Neftci, converted from monthly to quarterly data. Differing from Neftci and Palash-Radecki, the method was extended to periods of recession, in which the probability of expansion was estimated.

The fourth step is to combine the probabilities estimated in steps two and three with the probability estimated during the last period (r_{-1}), yielding an updated probability of recession (r). In symbols,

$$r = a/(a + b)$$

where $a = [r_{-1} + q(1 - r_{-1})]p$ and $b = (1 - r_{-1})(1 - p)(1 - q)$.

Neftci interpreted the formula as predicting that a recession was imminent if r was at least 0.9. In this chapter the signal was interpreted as applying to a specific quarter. The formula was most accurate when interpreted as a one-quarter ahead forecast. In addition, the second and third steps were extended to periods of recession. The formula was then used to forecast troughs as well as peaks.

The sequential probability method is based on the assumption that the economy's behavior is substantially different in recession and expansion. That assumption is also necessary for the loss function for forecast errors that motivates this chapter.

Despite the intuitive appeal of that basic assumption, there are potential problems with the sequential probability approach. First, there is no guidance in choosing an indicator variable. One could easily choose an indicator that offered little predictive power.[10] Second, the length of an expansion may not be closely related to the probability of recession.

---

[10] The predictive value of the index of leading indicators has been extensively debated. Zarnowitz and Moore (1982) derived rules for using the index to predict cyclical turning points and found that the resulting forecasts were accurate enough to guide countercyclical policies. Since they used the same data for constructing their rules and for testing them, their results are analogous to in-sample forecasts. Their post-sample performance is unknown. Hymans (1973) was only able to construct fairly inaccurate methods for using the index to predict turning points. Commenting on that work, Alan Greenspan concluded, "Saul Hymans has done an impressive job in extracting about as much information as I think one can get from what I consider a very weak data base."

Table 6A.1. *Lag lengths in a VAR model*

Equation	Lag lengths					
	RTB	CU	FEX	GNP	IPD	MB
RTB	4	0	0	0	4	1
CU	2	5	5	0	0	4
FEX	2	0	4	0	0	0
GNP	1	1	7	9	0	4
IPD	0	5	0	1	4	2
MB	2	0	5	1	1	4

McCulloch (1975), for example, has argued that the age of an expansion is unrelated to the probability of expansion continuing. Consequently, the two sources of data in the sequential probability formula may not provide much useful information in predicting the stage of the business cycle.

Appendix B: Using a VAR model to predict the stage of the business cycle

The VAR model contains six variables: quarterly average values of the ninety-day T-bill rate (RTB) and capacity utilization rate in manufacturing (CU), the ratio of federal spending to GNP (FEX), and quarterly changes at annual rates for real GNP (GNP), the GNP implicit price deflator (IPD), and the monetary base estimated by St. Louis (MB). There is one equation for each of the six variables. Each equation contains a constant and a "counter" for the capacity utilization rate. [The counter is an integer that is zero in 1948 Q1 and that is incremented by one in a quarter when the capacity utilization rate rises and is decremented by one when the capacity utilization rate falls. The use of a counter was proposed by Neftci (1986).] Each equation has lag lengths set by the procedure described in Webb (1985), based only on data through 1969 Q4. The selection of individual lag lengths, as opposed to the usual practice of setting a common lag length for each variable in each equation, was performed in order to reduce the number of parameters estimated in each equation, while allowing long lags in the event that they were needed in a particular case. The resulting lag lengths are given in Table 6A.1. A zero entry indicates that the variable was excluded from that equation. Each lag begins with the first lagged value; no contemporaneous values are included in any equation.

Each equation was estimated by OLS through 1969 Q4. Forecasts were generated from one to six quarters ahead, and standard errors for two-quarter average GNP growth were projected from the estimated residuals. The model was then reestimated through 1970 Q1, and a new set of forecasts and estimated errors was produced. The procedure was repeated through 1984 Q1. GNP forecasts were then converted to forecasts of the cyclical indicator variable. The point estimates for two-quarter GNP growth and the estimated standard errors were used to construct the estimated probabilities of recession.

REFERENCES

DeGroot, M. H., and S. E. Fienberg (1983), "The Comparison and Evaluation of Forecasters," *The Statistician, 32,* 12–22.

Diebold, F. X., and G. D. Rudebusch (1987), "Scoring the Leading Indicators," Board of Governors of the Federal Reserve System Special Studies Paper No. 206.

Doan, T., R. Litterman, and C. Sims (1984), "Forecasting and Conditional Projection Using Realistic Prior Distributions," *Econometric Reviews, 3* (1), 1–100.

Fromm, G., and L. R. Klein (1981), "Scale of Macro-Econometric Models and Accuracy of Forecasting," in J. Kmenta and J. B. Ramsey, ed. *Large-Scale Macro-Econometric Models.* North-Holland, p. 377.

Goldfeld, S. M. (1976), "The Case of the Missing Money," *Brookings Papers on Economic Activity,* No. 3, 683–730.

Hymans, Saul H. (1973), "On the Use of Leading Indicators to Predict Cyclical Turning Points," *Brookings Papers on Economic Activity,* No. 2, 339–84.

Kling, J. L. (1987), "Predicting the Turning Points of Business and Economic Time Series," *Journal of Business, 60* (April), 201–37.

Lupoletti, W. M., and R. H. Webb (1986), "Defining and Improving the Accuracy of Macroeconomic Forecasts: Contributions from a VAR Model," *Journal of Business, 59* (April, part 1), 263–85.

McCulloch, J. H. (1975), "The Monte-Carlo Cycle in Business Activity," *Economic Inquiry, 13* (3), 303–21.

Neftci, S. N. (1982), "Optimal Prediction of Cyclical Downturns," *Journal of Economic Dynamics and Control, 4,* 225–41.

——— (1986), "Is There a Cyclical Time Unit?" *Carnegie-Rochester Series on Public Policy, 24,* 11–48.

Palash, C. J., and L. J. Radecki (1985), "Using Monetary and Financial Variables to Predict Cyclical Downturns," *Quarterly Review* (Federal Reserve Bank of New York), 10 (Summer), 36–45.

Theil, H. (1966), *Applied Economic Forecasting,* University of Chicago Press.

Webb, R. H. (1985), "Toward More Accurate Forecasts from Vector Autoregressions," *Economic Review* (Federal Reserve Bank of Richmond), 71 (July/August), 3–11.

Zarnowitz, V., and G. H. Moore (1982), "Sequential Signals of Recession and Recovery," *Journal of Business, 55* (January), 57–86.

CHAPTER 7

Bayesian methods for forecasting turning points in economic time-series: Sensitivity of forecasts to asymmetry of loss structures

Arnold Zellner and Chansik Hong

In our previous work (Zellner, Hong, and Gulati, 1987), we set forth and applied a Bayesian methodology for forecasting turning points in time-series building on previous work of Wecker (1979) and Kling (1987). We showed how optimal MELO (*m*inimum *e*xpected *l*oss) forecasts of turning points can be made. We also pointed out that such forecasts are very sensitive to the forms of loss structures as well as to values of probabilities of downturns and upturns. The sensitivity of optimal decisions to the forms of loss structures has also been emphasized in Zellner (1986). In this chapter, our approach to forecasting turning points is reviewed and then applied to forecast turning points in annual growth rates of real output for eighteen countries, 1973–84, using loss structures of varying degrees of asymmetry.

The plan of the chapter is as follows. In section 7.1, we describe procedures for making optimal forecasts of turning points. Section 7.2 incorporates a description of our data, forecasting model, and forecasting results. In section 7.3, a summary of results and some concluding remarks are presented.

7.1 Loss structures and turning point forecasting method

When forecasting turning points in time-series, it is important to consider loss structures very carefully in order to obtain good or optimal turning point forecasts. Such forecasts will reflect the relative costs of errors in forecasting turning points. If, for example, we consider the

Research financed in part by the National Science Foundation and by income from the H. G. B. Alexander Endowment Fund, Graduate School of Business, University of Chicago.

Table 7.1. *Loss structure for DT and NDT forecasts*

	Outcomes	
	DT	NDT
Forecasts		
DT	0	c_1
NDT	c_2	0
Probabilities	P_{DT}	$1 - P_{DT}$

mutually exclusive and exhaustive forecasts, downturn (DT) and no downturn (NDT), there are two errors that can be made, namely, (a) forecast DT and NDT occurs and (b) forecast NDT and DT occurs. If the second error is much more serious than the first error, it is clear that a forecaster will be very wary about deciding to forecast NDT. As will be seen, such behavior is incorporated in our optimal decision rules for forecasting turning points.

To formalize the considerations in the previous paragraph, we present a 2×2 loss structure in Table 7.1, in which losses have been scaled to equal zero when forecasts are correct. The loss associated with an incorrect DT forecast is denoted by c_1 and that with an incorrect NDT forecast by c_2. We shall see that optimal forecasts are determined in part by the ratio of c_2 to c_1. To derive optimal forecasts, there is a need to have probabilities associated with the mutually exclusive and exhaustive outcomes DT or NDT, a subject to which we now turn.

Probabilities associated with the outcomes DT and NDT, P_{DT} and $1 - P_{DT}$, respectively, can be computed given (a) past data, (b) a model for the observations and its predictive probability density function (pdf), and (c) definitions of DT and NDT. As explained below, with these three inputs, the probability of DT, P_{DT}, and the probability of NDT, $P_{NDT} = 1 - P_{DT}$, can be computed. With these probabilities available, we can compute expected losses associated with the choice of forecasting DT or of forecasting NDT, denoted by $E(L|DT_F)$ and $E(L|NDT_F)$, respectively. These expected losses are given by

$$EL|DT_F = 0 \cdot P_{DT} + c_1(1 - P_{DT}) = c_1(1 - P_{DT}) \quad (1)$$

and

$$EL|NDT_F = c_2 P_{DT} + 0(1 - P_{DT}) = c_2 P_{DT} \quad (2)$$

Table 7.2. *Loss structure for UT and NUT forecasts*

	Outcomes	
	UT	NUT
Forecasts		
UT	0	c_3
NUT	c_4	0
Probabilities	P_{UT}	$1 - P_{UT}$

If $EL|DT_F < EL|NDT_F$, that is, $c_1(1 - P_{DT}) < c_2 P_{DT}$, the optimal decision is to forecast DT. Thus a DT forecast will be chosen when

$$1 < (c_2/c_1)P_{DT}/(1 - P_{DT}) \tag{3}$$

It is seen that the decision to choose a DT forecast is critically dependent on two factors, the cost parameter ratio (CPR), c_2/c_1, and the odds relating to DT, $P_{DT}/(1 - P_{DT})$. For example, in the case of a symmetric loss structure ($c_1 = c_2$), a DT forecast will be chosen when $P_{DT}/(1 - P_{DT})$ > 1 or $P_{DT} > 1/2$. On the other hand, when $c_2/c_1 = 2$, a DT forecast will be selected when $P_{DT}/(1 - P_{DT}) > 1/2$ or $P_{DT} > 1/3$. Thus, as c_2/c_1 increases in value, a forecaster will be much more prone to choose the DT forecast. Similarly, as c_2/c_1 decreases in value, a forecaster will be less prone to choose the DT forecast. Empirical illustrations of these points will be presented in section 7.2.

The above analysis can be easily adapted to the problem of choosing between upturn (UT) and no-upturn (NUT) forecasts. In this case the loss structure is given in Table 7.2. In Table 7.2, P_{UT} is the probability associated with the outcome UT, which can be computed from a predictive pdf and a definition of UT. Then the expected losses associated with the choices of UT or NUT forecasts are

$$EL|UT_F = 0 \cdot P_{UT} + c_3(1 - P_{UT}) = c_3(1 - P_{UT}) \tag{4}$$

and

$$EL|NUT_F = c_4 P_{UT} + 0 \cdot (1 - P_{UT}) = c_4 P_{UT} \tag{5}$$

If $EL|UT_F < EL|NUT_F$, that is, $c_3(1 - P_{UT}) < c_4 P_{UT}$, or

$$1 < (c_4/c_3)P_{UT}/(1 - P_{UT}) \tag{6}$$

then UT is the optimal forecast. From relation (6), it is seen that this choice depends on the CPR, c_4/c_3, and the odds on UT, $P_{UT}/(1 - P_{UT})$.

If $c_4/c_3 = 1$, the case of a symmetric loss structure, relation (6) will be satisfied when $P_{UT} > 1/2$. Thus, if the computed value of P_{UT} is larger than 1/2, the optimal forecast is UT. If $c_4/c_3 = 2$, then UT will be an optimal forecast when $P_{UT} > 1/3$; or if $P_{UT} < 1/3$, the optimal forecast is NUT when $c_4/c_3 = 2$. The performance of these decision rules for forecasting UTs and NUTs is reported in section 7.2.

To implement the above decision rules for forecasting turning points, we require a definition of turning points and values for P_{DT} and P_{UT}, the probabilities of DT and UT, respectively. If we have observed y_1, y_2, ..., y_{n-1}, y_{n-2}, y_n and y_{n+1} is the first future, as yet unobserved observation, the definition of a downturn that we employ in our empirical work is $y_{n-2}, y_{n-1} < y_n > y_{n+1}$, that is, two previous observations less than y_n and y_n larger than y_{n+1}. Given this DT definition and with y_{n+1} as yet unobserved, the probability of a downturn, $P_{DT} = Pr(y_{n+1} < y_n | y_{n-2}, y_{n-1} < y_n, D)$, where D denotes past data and information about the model assumed to generate the data. This probability can easily be evaluated from the predictive pdf for y_{n+1}, given by

$$p(y_{n+1}|D) = \int_\Theta p(y_{n+1}|\theta)p(\theta|D)d\theta \quad -\infty < y_{n+1} < \infty \quad (7)$$

where $p(y_{n+1}|\theta)$ is the pdf for y_{n+1} given the parameter vector θ, $p(\theta|D)$ is the posterior pdf for θ given D, the past data, prior information, and model, and Θ is the parameter space containing θ. As is well known, by Bayes's theorem, the posterior pdf, $p(\theta|D) \propto \pi(\theta)\ell(\theta|\mathbf{y})$, where $\propto$ denotes "is proportional to," $\pi(\theta)$ is a prior pdf for θ, and $\ell(\theta|\mathbf{y})$ is the likelihood function for the observations, $\mathbf{y}' = (y_1, y_2, \ldots, y_n)$.

The predictive pdf in equation (7) can be employed to evaluate P_{DT} as follows:

$$P_{DT} = \int_{-\infty}^{y_n} p(y_{n+1}|y_{n-1}, y_{n-2} < y_n, D)dy_{n+1} \quad (8)$$

In our applications in section 7.2, $p(y_{n+1}|D)$ is in the form of a univariate Student-t pdf with $\nu = n - k$ degrees of freedom where n = number of past observations and k = number of coefficients in our forecasting equation [see equation (10)]. That is, t given by

$$t = (y_{n+1} - \hat{y}_{n+1})/s_f \quad (9)$$

has a univariate Student-t pdf with ν degrees of freedom [see, e.g., Zellner (1971, pp. 72ff)]. In equation (9), y_{n+1} is a random, as yet unobserved value and $\hat{y}_{n+1}$ and s_f are the mean and a measure of dispersion, respectively, of $p(y_{n+1}|D)$, which can be computed from the past n observations. From equation (9), $y_{n+1} = \hat{y}_{n+1} + s_f t$ and thus P_{DT} in equation (8) is equal to $Pr(\hat{y}_{n+1} + s_f t < y_n | D) = Pr\{t < (y_n - \hat{y}_{n+1})/s_f | D\}$. This last probability can be evaluated from the cumulative Student-t distribution since $(y_n - \hat{y}_{n+1})s_f$ has a given value. If $y_n = \hat{y}_{n+1}$, $P_{DT} = 1/2$; if $y_n > \hat{y}_{n+1}$, $P_{DT} > 1/2$; and if $y_n < \hat{y}_{n+1}$, $P_{DT} < 1/2$. Given the values of P_{DT} and the CPR, c_2/c_1, the decision rule in relation to (3) is operational.

To implement equation (6), the value of P_{UT} must be calculated. The definition of UT employed here is $y_{n-1}, y_{n-2} > y_n < y_{n+1}$. If $y_{n-1}, y_{n-2} > y_n$ is satisfied and y_{n+1} is as yet unobserved, $P_{UT} = Pr(y_{n+1} > y_n | D) = Pr(\hat{y}_{n+1} + s_f t > y_n | D) = Pr\{t > (y_n - \hat{y}_{n+1})/s_f | D\}$, which can be evaluated from the cumulative Student-t distribution function. Given a value for P_{UT} and the value of c_4/c_3, the decision rule in equation (6) is operational. That is, if $1 < (c_4/c_3)P_{UT}/(1 - P_{UT})$, forecast UT; otherwise forecast NUT.

With these decision rules for forecasting turning points described, we now turn to applications of these procedures in forecasting turning points in annual output growth rates for eighteen countries, 1973–84.

7.2   Model, data, and forecasting results

The statistical model we employ to generate turning point forecasts was used in our previous work [see Garcia-Ferrer et al. (1987), Zellner and Hong (1989), and Zellner, Hong, and Gulati (1987)]. It is the following third-order autoregressive-leading indicator model, denoted by AR(3)LI,

$$y_{it} = \alpha_{i0} + \alpha_{i1}y_{it-1} + \alpha_{2i}y_{it-2} + \alpha_{3i}y_{it-3} + \beta_{1i}SR_{it-1}$$
$$+ \beta_{2i}SR_{it-2} + \beta_{3i}GM_{it-1} + \beta_{4i}WR_{t-1} + \epsilon_{it} \quad (10)$$

where the subscripts i and t denote the ith country and tth year, respectively, and

y_{it} = growth rate of real output
SR_{it} = growth rate of real stock prices
GM_{it} = growth rate of real money
WR_t = "world return," the median of countries' SR_{it}s
ϵ_{it} = error term

The ϵ_{it}s are assumed independently drawn from a normal distribution with zero mean and variance σ_i^2 for all i and t. For each country, annual data from the early 1950s through 1972 were employed along with a diffuse prior distribution for the parameters to derive a posterior distribution for each country's parameters. This posterior distribution was employed to derive predictive pdfs for use in making turning point forecasts for 1973. For subsequent years' turning point forecasts, all previous data were employed to compute predictive pdfs for use in generating turning point forecasts [see, e.g., Zellner (1971, pp. 72ff) for derivation of the predictive pdf].

The data for the variables in equation (10) were obtained from the International Monetary Fund's International Financial Statistics data base at the University of Chicago. A diskette containing the data is available for a charge of $5.00 to cover mailing, handling, and other costs. The data relate to the following countries: Australia, Austria, Belgium, Canada, Denmark, Finland, France, Germany, Ireland, Italy, Japan, the Netherlands, Norway, Spain, Sweden, Switzerland, the United Kingdom, and the United States.

For the eighteen countries in the period 1973–84, there were fifty-three DTs and fifteen NDTs using the DT definition $y_{n-2}, y_{n-1} < y_n > y_{n+1}$ and the NDT definition $y_{n-2}, y_{n-1} < y_n \leq y_{n+1}$, and forty-five UTs and thirty-seven NUTs using the UT definition $y_{n-2}, y_{n-1} > y_n < y_{n+1}$ and the NUT definition $y_{n-2}, y_{n-1} > y_n \geq y_{n+1}$. In Table 7.3, the results of forecasting DTs and NDTs using various cost ratios, c_2/c_1 (see Table 7.1 for definitions of c_1 and c_2), are reported. It is seen that the percentages of correct DT forecasts vary from 84 to 94 percent. As explained in section 7.1, when $c_2/c_1 = 4$, it is optimal to forecast a DT when $P_{DT} > .2$. For these conditions, of sixty DT forecasts, fifty-one, or 85 percent, were correct. When $c_2/c_1 = 1/4$, it is optimal to forecast a DT when $P_{DT} > .8$ and in this case seventeen of eighteen, or 94 percent, of the DT forecasts are correct. With the condition $P_{DT} > .8$, a higher percentage of correct DT forecasts is found than in the case $P_{DT} > .2$. Also, in the former case, only eighteen DT forecasts were made since the cost of an erroneous DT forecast is relatively higher than in the case $c_2/c_1 = 4$. Indeed if c_2/c_1 were to assume a very large value, it would be optimal to forecast DT in almost every case in order to avoid the high cost, c_2, associated with an erroneous NDT forecast. Put otherwise, when c_2/c_1 is very large, an optimal forecaster becomes a pessimist in the sense of usually forecasting a DT.

With respect to the NDT forecasts reported in Table 7.3, they are not as good as the DT forecasts. The percentage of correct NDT forecasts ranges from 29 to 75 percent, with 75 percent correct when $c_2/c_1 = 4$, a situation in which an NDT forecast is made when $P_{NDT} > .8$. As the ratio c_2/c_1 falls in value, NDT forecasts are made more frequently since the cost of an incorrect NDT forecast decreases relative to that of an incorrect DT forecast. When $c_2/c_1 = 4$, only eight NDT forecasts were made whereas when $c_2/c_1 = 1/4$, fifty NDT forecasts were made. If $c_2/$

Table 7.3. *Forecasting downturns (DTs) and no-downturns (NDTs) in annual output growth rates, eighteen countries, 1973–84, using different loss structures*[a]

Cost ratio,[b] c_2/c_1	Forecast DT if:	Forecast	Correct	Incorrect	Total	Percent correct
4	P_{DT}[c] $> .2$	DT	51	9	60	85
		NDT	6	2	8	75
7/3	$P_{DT} > .3$	DT	47	9	56	84
		NDT	6	6	12	50
3/2	$P_{DT} > .4$	DT	38	7	45	84
		NDT	8	15	23	35
1	$P_{DT} > .5$	DT	35	5	40	88
		NDT	10	18	28	36
2/3	$P_{DT} > .6$	DT	29	4	33	88
		NDT	11	24	35	31
3/7	$P_{DT} > .7$	DT	24	3	27	89
		NDT	12	29	41	29
1/4	$P_{DT} > .8$	DT	17	1	18	94
		NDT	15	35	50	30

[a]A DT is defined to occur at $t = n$ if the growth rates satisfy $y_{n-2}, y_{n-1} < y_n > y_{n+1}$. NDT is defined to occur at $t = n$ if $y_{n-2}, y_{n-1} < y_n \le y_{n+1}$.
[b]See Table 7.1 for loss structure involving costs c_1 and c_2.
[c]P_{DT} is the calculated probability of a DT.

$c_1 = 0$, all forecasts would be NDT, the case of optimally optimistic forecasting.

In Table 7.4, the results for forecasting UTs and NUTs are reported. It is seen that from 61 to 74 percent of the UT forecasts are correct. Generally the percentage of correct UT forecasts rises as the ratio c_4/c_3 increases, or equivalently as the "cutoff" values for P_{UT} rise from .2 to .8. Also, when $c_4/c_3 = 4$, seventy-four UT forecasts were made whereas when $c_4/c_3 = 1/4$ there were only thirty-three UT forecasts, reflecting the fact that in the latter case, the cost of an incorrect UT forecast is relatively greater than in the former case. As regards NUT forecasts, from 55 to 100 percent of them are correct, with a greater percentage correct for higher values of c_4/c_3 (or when the cutoff value for $P_{NUT} = 1 - P_{UT}$ is high).

Table 7.4. *Forecasting upturns (UTs) and no-upturns (NUTs) in annual output growth rates, eighteen countries, 1973–84, using different loss structures*[a]

Cost ratio,[b] c_4/c_3	Forecast UT if:	Forecast	Correct	Incorrect	Total	Percent correct
4	$P_{UT}^c > .2$	UT	45	29	74	61
		NUT	8	0	8	100
7/3	$P_{UT} > .3$	UT	45	26	71	63
		NUT	11	0	11	100
3/2	$P_{UT} > .4$	UT	43	25	68	63
		NUT	12	2	14	86
1	$P_{UT} > .5$	UT	43	20	63	68
		NUT	17	2	19	89
2/3	$P_{UT} > .6$	UT	41	16	57	72
		NUT	21	4	25	84
3/7	$P_{UT} > .7$	UT	34	12	46	74
		NUT	25	11	36	69
1/4	$P_{UT} > .8$	UT	23	10	33	70
		NUT	27	22	49	55

[a] UT is defined to occur at $t = n$ if the growth rates satisfy $y_{n-2}, y_{n-1} > y_n < y_{n+1}$. NUT is defined to occur at $t = n$ if $y_{n-2}, y_{n-1} > y_n \geq y_{n+1}$.
[b] See Table 7.2 for loss structure involving costs c_3 and c_4.
[c] P_{UT} is the calculated probability of a UT.

Overall, the turning point forecasts reported in Tables 7.3 and 7.4 are reasonably good except for the NDT forecasts. The information in Table 7.5 sheds further light on the properties of the DT and NDT forecasts. When the calculated values of P_{DT} are in the intervals .60–.79 and .80–.99, the actual observed proportions of DTs (and NDTs) are close to these calculated values. However, when the calculated values of P_{DT} are in the intervals 0–.19, .20–.39 and .40–.59, the observed proportions of DTs are much higher than the P_{DT}s. Thus, for example, when $c_2/c_1 = 1$, an NDT forecast will be made when $P_{DT} < .5$ and as can be seen for such values the observed proportion of DTs is much higher than the calculated probabilities, a reflection of erroneous NDT forecasts. Perhaps unexpected shocks cause DTs and the calculated values of P_{DT} do not entirely reflect such shocks.

In Table 7.6, intervals for calculated values of P_{UT} and associated

Table 7.5. *Calculated probabilities of downturns (DTs) and observed outcomes, annual output growth rates, eighteen countries, 1973–84*[a]

Calculated P_{DT}	No. of cases	Outcomes DT	NDT	Observed proportion of DTs
0–.19	8	2	6	.25
.20–.39	14	12	2	.86
.40–.59	13	10	3	.77
.60–.79	15	12	3	.80
.80–1.00	18	17	1	.94
Totals	68	53	15	.78

[a] See footnote *a* in Table 7.3 for definitions of DT and NDT.

observed proportions of UTs are presented. Although the observed frequencies are not very great, the agreement between the calculated probabilities and observed proportions is better than in the case of Table 7.5.

In Table 7.7, realized losses have been computed for the DT and NDT forecasts and for the UT and NUT forecasts. If all turning point forecasts were correct, the realized loss would be zero. In the case of the DT and NDT forecasts, the realized losses range from 10.0 to 29.5 with a median of 20.0. Performance is better at the extreme values of the ratio c_2/c_1. Also, it is interesting to evaluate the performance of a forecaster who believes in a cycle of constant four-year period and who would always forecast DT given $y_{n-2}, y_{n-1} < y_n$. In the present case such a forecaster would forecast DT sixty-eight times with fifty-three, or 78 percent, correct and fifteen, or 22 percent, incorrect. The percentages of correct DT forecasts in Table 3 are somewhat higher than 78 percent. However, with $c_1 = 1$, this forecaster has realized loss equal to 15 which is better than the realized losses in Table 7.7 except for one case in which the optimal rule's realized loss is only 10.0.

The realized losses for UT and NUT forecasts in Table 7.7 range from 15.5 to 29.0 with a median loss of 22.0. In this case a believer in a cycle of constant four-year period would forecast UT in the eighty-two instances in which $y_{n-2}, y_{n-1} > y_n$ and would be correct in forty-five cases (or 54.9 percent) and incorrect in thirty-seven cases. With $c_3 = 1$ and thirty-seven incorrect UT forecasts, the realized loss of this forecaster is 37, much higher than all the realized losses associated with the optimal UT and NUT forecasts shown in Table 7.7.

Table 7.6. *Calculated probabilities of upturns (UTs) and observed outcomes, annual output growth rates, eighteen countries, 1974–85[a]*

| Calculated | | Outcomes | | Observed proportion |
P_{UT}	No. of cases	UT	NUT	of UTs
0–.19	8	0	8	.00
.20–.39	6	2	4	.33
.40–.59	11	2	9	.18
.60–.79	24	18	6	.75
.80–1.00	33	23	10	.70
Totals	82	45	37	.55

[a]See footnote *a* in Table 7.4 for definitions of UT and NUT.

With regard to the relative performance of DT/NDT and UT/NUT forecasts as measured by the realized losses in Table 7.7, the median losses 20.0 and 22.0, respectively, are very similar. For $c_2/c_1 = 1/4$ and $c_4/c_3 = 1/4$, the realized loss, 10.0, of the DT/NDT forecasts is lower than that of the UT/NUT forecasts, 15.5. Also when $c_2/c_1 = 4$ and $c_4/c_3 = 4$, the realized loss of the DT/NDT forecasts, 17.0, is quite a bit lower than that of the UT/NUT forecasts, 29.0. For intermediate values of the cost ratios, the realized losses are not far different.

7.3   Summary and concluding remarks

In this chapter we have utilized an AR(3)LI model given in equation (10) to forecast turning points in annual growth rates for eighteen countries, 1973–84, under various loss structures. It was found that optimal forecasts of turning points can be readily computed and are quite sensitive to asymmetry of loss structures. Since loss structures are often asymmetric, this finding is of great importance. With regard to the actual, applied forecasting results, it was found that DT, UT, and NUT forecasts were reasonably good, with the percentages of correct forecasts ranging from 84 to 94 percent for DT forecasts, 61 to 74 percent for UT forecasts, and 55 to 100 percent for the NUT forecasts as the loss structure cost parameters' ratios varied from 4 to 1/4. However, only 30 to 75 percent of the NDT forecasts were found to be correct as the ratio of loss structure cost parameters varied from 4 to 1/4. It may be that the

Table 7.7. *Realized losses in forecasting DTs and UTs in annual growth rates, eighteen countries, 1973–84*[a]

DT and NDT forecasts			UT and NUT forecasts		
c_1	c_2	Realized loss	c_3	c_4	Realized loss
1	4	17.0	1	4	29.0
1	7/3	23.0	1	7/3	26.0
1	3/2	29.5	1	3/2	28.0
1	1	23.0	1	1	22.0
1	2/3	20.0	1	2/3	18.7
1	3/7	15.4	1	3/7	16.7
1	1/4	10.0	1	1/4	15.5

[a]See Tables 7.1 and 7.2 for loss structures involving costs c_1, c_2, c_3, and c_4 and footnote a in Tables 7.3 and 7.4 for definitions of DT, NDT, UT, and NUT.

performance of NDT forecasts can be improved by the use of more informative prior distributions, quarterly or monthly data, and/or other variants of our AR(3)LI model. These possibilities will be investigated in future research.

In conclusion, a flexible procedure for generating optimal turning point forecasts was presented and applied to provide reasonably good turning point forecasts for annual growth rates of output for eighteen countries, 1973–84. The methods can be used in a variety of contexts to provide MELO (*m*inimum *e*xpected *lo*ss) forecasts of turning points of economic and other types of time-series data.

REFERENCES

Garcia-Ferrer, A., R. A. Highfield, F. Palm, and A. Zellner (1987), "Macroeconomic Forecasting Using Pooled International Data," *Journal of Business and Economic Statistics, 5*, 53–67.
Kling, J. L. (1987), "Predicting the Turning Points of Business and Economic Time Series," *Journal of Business, 60*, 201–38.
Wecker, W. E. (1979), "Predicting the Turning Points of a Time Series," *Journal of Business, 52*, 35–50.
Zellner, A. (1971), *An Introduction to Bayesian Inference in Econometrics.* New York: John Wiley & Sons (reprinted, 1987, Malabar, Fla.: Krieger Publishing Co.).
    (1986), "Bayesian Estimation and Prediction Using Asymmetric Loss Functions," *Journal of the American Statistical Association, 81*, 446–51.

Zellner, A., and C. Hong (1989), "Forecasting International Growth Rates Using Bayesian Shrinkage and Other Procedures," *Journal of Econometrics, 40*, 183–202.

Zellner, A., C. Hong, and G. M. Gulati (1987), "Turning Points in Economic Time Series, Loss Structures and Bayesian Forecasting," in S. Geisser, J. S. Hodges, S. J. Press, and A. Zellner (eds.), *Bayesian and Likelihood Methods in Statistics and Econometrics* (North Holland: The Netherlands), 1990, pp. 371–93.

CHAPTER 8

New developments in leading indicators

Geoffrey H. Moore

8.1 Long-leading versus short-leading indicators

Most of the leading indicators that have been in use for many years have relatively short leads, averaging about six or eight months at business cycle peaks, when recessions begin, and two to four months at troughs, when recoveries start. Since there are often delays of a month or so in reporting the figures, and even longer delays in judging whether a turn in an indicator is significant, a recession or recovery may be well under way before it can be recognized. One way to deal with this problem is to distinguish indicators with exceptionally long leads from others.

The new long-leading index currently published by the Center for International Business Cycle Research takes a step in this direction. Using the revised list of fifteen leading indicators (Moore, 1989), we classified as long-leading those that had average leads of at least twelve months at peaks and six months at troughs during 1948–82. The four indicators that qualified as long-leading were bond prices, real money supply (M2), new building permits for housing, and a profit margin indicator, the ratio of prices to unit labor costs in manufacturing. A long-leading index constructed from these series is shown in Figure 8.1, together with the short-leading index based on the other eleven series. Also shown is the Department of Commerce leading index as revised in March 1989, which contains two of the series in our long-leading group (money supply and housing permits), seven series in our short-leading group, and two other series.

One of the advantages of this grouping is that you may see a downturn in the long-leading index before you have seen anything like it in the short-leading index. Is a recession about to happen or not? If the downturn in the long-leading index continues, as it did in 1978 and

141

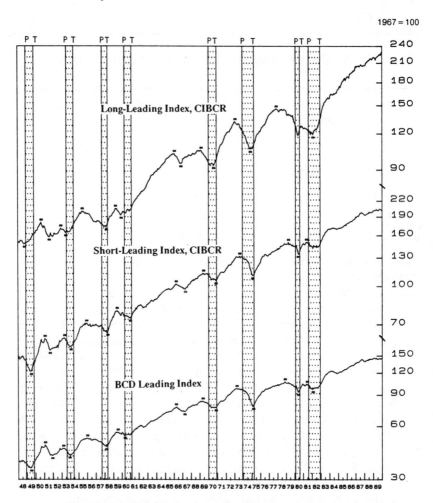

Figure 8.1. Long-leading and short-leading indexes. Shaded areas are business cycle recessions, from peak (P) to trough (T). Center for International Business Cycle Research, 1990.

1979, then you can be fairly sure that the short-leading index is going to follow suit, and if it does then a business cycle downturn is likely to follow within a few months. The same is true for the upturn side, though the sequences are apt to be shorter.

The lead in the long-leading index averages about fourteen months at downturns, and about eight months at upturns. The short-leading index has leads of about eight months at downturns and two months at

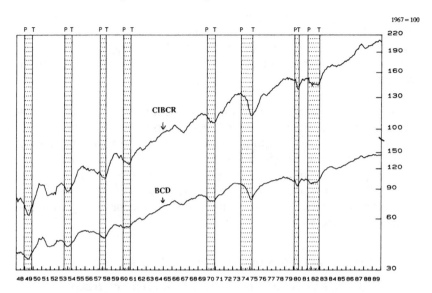

Figure 8.2. Promptly available leading index (CIBCR) and Department of Commerce leading index (BCD), 1948–88. Shaded areas are business cycle recessions, from peak (P) to trough (T). Center for International Business Cycle Research, 1990.

upturns. Hence there is about a six-month difference in the two indexes on the average, and that provides some time to appraise what is going on and make some projections as to what is likely to happen next.

8.2 Promptly available leading indicators

Another kind of leading index that we have been developing at the Columbia Center is a promptly available index. It is always useful to have information that is current and up-to-date and yet relevant to the future outlook. In 1980 we developed a weekly leading index, which is now published in *Business Week* magazine. It is the most promptly available leading index there is.

Another way to get at the same idea is to use monthly data that are promptly available, together with weekly or daily information, and construct a monthly index from those data. Figure 8.2 compares a promptly available monthly leading index, labeled CIBCR, with the BCD index shown in Figure 8.1. The two lines in Figure 8.2 are nearly parallel. The difference is that the one we call promptly available can be prepared within the first seven days of the month, with data for the preceding month, while the other one is available toward the end of that same month. Hence one index is available about three weeks ahead of the other, yet it tells virtually the same story. The average lead times are nearly identical in the two indexes. Hence one way to keep more up-to-date on the economic outlook is to look at these promptly available types of indicators.

The National Association of Purchasing Managers produces indicators that are very useful in this connection, and publishes them within the first seven days of the following month. Then we use measures of stock prices and bond prices and several weekly series that are available promptly. Several leading indicators of employment, such as the average workweek, become available in the first seven days of the month. Altogether, there are twelve leading indicators in the promptly available leading index shown in Figure 8.2.

8.3   Leading indicators for the service industries

The role of the service industries in the U.S. economy has become far more important than it was twenty, thirty, or fifty years ago. The number of people employed in the service industries is about 75 percent of the total number on nonfarm payrolls. Back in the 1920s and 1930s it was less than 60 percent. Clearly, the services deserve some attention in terms of the leading indicators. Figure 8.3 presents our new services leading index together with the Department of Commerce index. The latter purports to cover the entire economy, although it is largely dominated by figures for the goods-producing industries. Both indexes are shown in the form of growth rates. The level of activity in the services sector hardly ever declines, but the growth rate moves very strongly in relation to the business cycle. The growth rate in the entire economy, as reflected by the Department of Commerce index, has a much wider range of fluctuation and gets much farther down into negative territory in recessions. Since the services sector has acted as a stabilizing force in the economy, the services leading index gives an early clue as to how powerful that force is likely to be (see Layton and Moore, 1989).

8.4   Leading indicators of inflation

Another of the hitherto neglected areas in leading indicator studies is inflation. We have found that one can apply much the same approach to inflation that we have been applying for years to the physical dimensions of the economy. We use the rate of inflation, that is, the rate of growth in the price level, as the target. This is the bottom line in Figure 8.4, the rate of change in the consumer price index. It has fluctuated

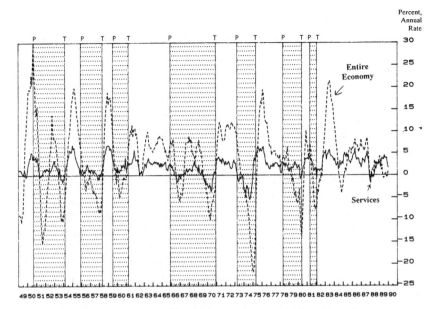

Figure 8.3. Growth rates in leading indexes for service industries and the entire economy. Growth rates are based on the ratio of the current month's index to the average index for the preceding twelve months, expressed as a compound annual rate. Shaded areas represent slowdowns from peak (P) to trough (T) in the service industries growth chronology. The leading index for the entire economy is published by the Department of Commerce.

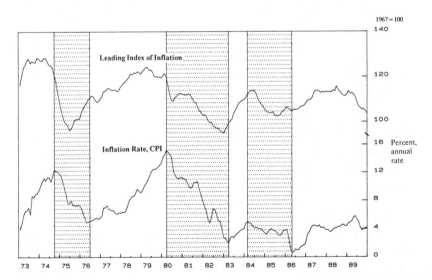

Figure 8.4. Leading index of inflation and CPI inflation rate, 1973–88. Shaded areas represent slowdowns in the inflation cycle, based upon the six-month smoothed growth rate in the consumer price index for all urban consumers.

widely, and can be used to develop an inflation cycle chronology, similar to the business cycle chronology.

Indicators that are believed to have a bearing upon future prospects for inflation can be tested against the inflation chronolgy. Among those that have qualified in this respect is the rate of change in industrial materials prices, which are very sensitive to market conditions and influence costs of production. Import prices have also become very important and sensitive indicators of future inflation in the United States. The growth rate in the volume of debt created in the economy is one of the more powerful leading indicators of inflation. A useful measure of labor market tightness is the percentage of the working-age population that is employed. Unlike the unemployment rate, which is another measure of labor tightness, the percentage of the working-age population employed takes into account people who are not presently in the labor force but might join if conditions change. Hence it has proved to be a more useful leading indicator of inflation. Other series that qualify as leading indicators of inflation include the Dun and Bradstreet survey of business expectations with regard to selling prices and the National Association of Purchasing Managers surveys of buying prices and vendor performance.

Hence the leading index of inflation shown as the top line in Figure 8.4 is composed of these seven components. It has led the CPI inflation rate peaks and troughs since 1949 by about six months, on average, with the usual wide variation in the length of leads. Judging from its record, it should prove helpful in judging when major swings in inflation are about to develop. Since these swings have a bearing on the movements in interest rates, the leading inflation index can also provide useful signals of emerging trends in rates of interest on bonds and other interest-bearing securities.

8.5   International leading indicators

Another new development in the leading indicators field is international. Many countries today are publishing leading, coincident, and lagging indexes, whereas twenty years ago only a few countries were so engaged. The trend seems likely to continue, in view of the growing interest in international trade and investment. Leading indexes that cover large groups of countries may also become popular in view of their relevance to the prosperity of individual countries both within and outside the group. Studies at the Columbia Center have shown, for example, that a leading index covering four European countries (the United Kingdom, West Germany, France, and Italy) provides useful forecasts

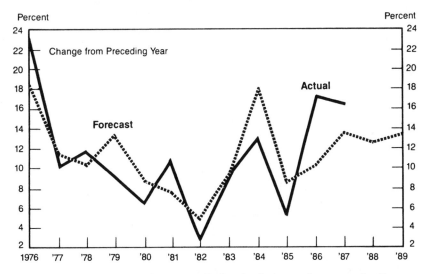

Figure 8.5. Growth in exports of Asian developing market economies. Forecast changes are based on the preceding December's six-month smoothed growth rate in the leading index for the G-7 countries as reported by the Center for International Business Cycle Research, Columbia Business School.

of U.S. exports to Europe as a whole. Similarly, the Center's leading index for the major developed (G-7) countries forecasts year-to-year changes in the exports of the Asian developing market economies, including Hong Kong, Korea, Singapore, Malaysia, India, the Philippines, and others (see Figure 8.5). Leading indicators provide measures of the potential demand for imports entering a country, and hence for the exports from other countries.

REFERENCES

Layton, A. P., and G. H. Moore (1989), "Leading Indicators for the Service Sector," *Journal of Business and Economic Statistics, 7* (3, July), 379–86.
Moore, G. H. (1989), *Leading Indicators for the 1990's.* Homewood, Ill.: Dow Jones-Irwin.

PART II

FORECASTING RECORDS AND METHODS
OF EVALUATION

CHAPTER 9

Forecasting cyclical turning points: The record in the past three recessions

Stephen K. McNees

Many economic decision-makers seem to attach special importance to the phase of the business cycle – whether the economy is in an expansion or a recession – above and beyond the exact magnitude of the change in economic activity. The Gramm-Rudman-Hollings legislation, for example, contains a special provision suspending the budget deficit targets in the event of a recession. This concern about the stage of the business cycle is both a cause and an effect of the pioneering work by the National Bureau of Economic Research in identifying and dating cyclical turning points, the times when the economy has shifted from one phase to another. The Bureau's cycle chronology reaches back to 1854 on a monthly basis and even further on an annual basis.

The origin of this empirical approach predates the development of the National Income and Product or GNP Accounts and thus predates the development of macroeconometric models of GNP. While the designation of cyclical turning points derives from analyses of monthly data, the quarterly GNP accounts are the language of most macroeconomic models and forecasts.[1] This presents a problem for those who ask,

The author wishes to thank Charles Ross for his useful research assistance. This chapter was previously published in the *New England Economic Review,* March/April 1987 [Eds.].

[1] A growing body of literature approaches the problem of forecasting turning points from a different perspective. See, for example, Neftci (1982), Palash and Radecki (1985), and Diebold and Rudebusch (1987). This literature deals with the statistical question of how best to extract a turning point signal (the probability that a turning point will occur at some future unspecified date) from actual values of a data series (typically monthly) such as the composite index of leading indicators. This chapter deals with how to extract turning point signals (that a turning point will occur on some specific future date) from quarterly forecasts of the magnitudes of macroeconomic variables. When forecasted data are considered, there is no need to classify data series as "leading" or "lagging" but only to determine how closely the series conforms to the business cycle chronology.

as many invariably do, how well cyclical turning points have been predicted. Most forecasts do not provide an explicit statement of when the economy will change from one phase to the next, and any attempt to assess their accuracy must first select the configuration of macroeconomic forecast data that can be taken as an indication that a cyclical turning point will occur. The assessment, in other words, is contingent on the procedure used to translate a forecast into a statement about turning points. This rather obvious point has seldom been sufficiently emphasized, which is unfortunate because, as the first section of this chapter shows, the most straightforward macroeconomic criteria for identifying and adding turning points do not conform closely to the official chronology of business cycle turning points. This follows from the fact that the procedures followed to identify and date turning points are based on a wide variety of monthly data rather than GNP and are essentially judgmental in the importance they attach to these diverse sources.[2]

Once a criterion for translating quarterly forecasts into turning points has been chosen, the task of evaluating forecast accuracy is still not totally straightforward. Other things equal, a long lead in anticipating (or a short lag in recognizing) the actual turning point is clearly desirable. But this consideration must be weighed against instances of false signals, anticipating turning points that did not materialize. Is a forecast made well before a turning point that falsely dates a cyclical turn shortly before the actual turn better or worse than one that correctly identifies the actual turn only well after it has occurred? Is a forecast that correctly anticipates a turn far in advance, but is subsequently revised, better or worse than one that consistently identifies the correct turn much later? Without a clear statement of the forecast users' interests, the accuracy of turning point forecasts cannot be reduced to a single, unambiguous quantitative index. For this reason, and because the number of turning points for which forecasts are available is quite small, the later sections of the chapter review the turning points of each of the last three recessions individually, without trying to reach broad conclusions applicable to all business cycles. Put differently, recent business cycles have exhibited many diverse and unprecedented characteristics. The following investigation is an attempt to describe history rather than an attempt to predict our ability to forecast the next turning point.

[2] For an excellent description of the National Bureau of Economic Research approach, see Moore (1983). See also Fels and Hinshaw (1968). This chapter does not attempt to evaluate the NBER turning point designations but rather considers how to infer turning points from quarterly forecasts.

9.1   What is a recession?

Broadly speaking, a recession (expansion) is a period in which the level of aggregate economic activity is declining (rising). It would be a mistake, however, simply to identify recessions (expansions) with quarters in which the level of real GNP declined (rose). Changes in real GNP have *not* been closely associated with the official National Bureau of Economic Research (NBER) business cycle chronology. For example, over the past forty years, real GNP has declined in eleven quarters classified as expansions and has risen in five quarters during recessions. Even this count excludes the quarters in which cyclical turns have occurred. In quarters classified as cyclical peaks, real GNP has increased six times and declined twice. In quarters classified as cyclical troughs, real GNP has increased four times and fallen four times. Clearly, the task of identifying cyclical turning points cannot be reduced to simply observing the direction of change of real GNP.

In recognition of this fact, a common rule of thumb has developed, classifying recessions as periods of two consecutive quarterly declines in real GNP.[3] This popular rule of thumb also bears little resemblance to the officially designated recession periods. Since 1947, real GNP has declined in two or more consecutive quarters only six times. Neither the 1960–1 recession nor the 1980 recession had that feature. Moreover, these six periods do not conform closely to the official recessions. The popular rule of thumb thus does not provide a very accurate criterion for establishing recession periods. The main moral of these examples is that magnitudes matter. One cannot reliably infer recessions and expansions by merely observing the direction of changes in real GNP.

A slightly different definition of recession is also implied in the special provision for suspending the Gramm-Rudman-Hollings law. Section 254 allows for suspension when "the [annual] rate of real economic growth for each of the most recent reported quarter and the immediately preceding quarter is less than one percent." This criterion for defining a recession improves upon the rule of thumb of two consecutive declines by identifying both the 1960–1 and 1980 recessions and by conforming much more closely to the official timing for the 1981–2 recession. However, it falsely identifies two recessions that never occurred in early 1973 and 1979. Moreover, by this criterion, the 1980 recession is in danger

---

[3] Zarnowitz and Moore (Chapter 15) point out the limitations of the two consecutive declines criterion but nevertheless apply it because that criterion appears in the Gramm-Rudman-Hollings law.

of extinction; a relatively small upward revision of real growth in 1980:III would eliminate it.

All three of these criteria based on real GNP fail to capture the *timing* of recessionary periods. The 1948–9, 1969–70, 1973–5, and 1981–2 recessions *all* were interrupted by one quarter of real growth in excess of 1 percent. A single quarter considered in isolation is too short a period from which to determine a cyclical turning point. Each of these criteria is concerned only with the change in real GNP in each quarter, without taking account of what occurs in adjacent quarters.

A simple modification of these criteria helps to correct this problem – defining a recession as a half-year (that is, two-quarter) period in which real GNP has declined. As illustrated in Table 9.1, this criterion conforms more closely to the officially designated recession and expansion periods. Specifically, this criterion identifies all postwar recessions but it also introduces two false signals, a false trough in 1949 and a false peak in 1979. Nonetheless, the timing of recessions implied by this definition is far closer to official recessions than the criteria previously considered. All but two cyclical peaks occurred in the first quarter of the first half-year decline in real GNP.[4] In the only two exceptions to this tendency, in 1953 and 1973 the cyclical peak occurred in the quarter preceding the half-year decline.

A half-year increase is somewhat less reliable a criterion for the timing of cyclical troughs. Five of eight cyclical troughs occurred in the first quarter of the first half-year increase in real GNP. However, the 1975:I trough occurred one quarter earlier, the 1961:I trough one quarter later, and the 1970:IV trough two quarters later than this general tendency suggests.

Thus, the criterion of defining half-year declines (increases) in real GNP as recessions (expansions) conforms to the official NBER designations somewhat better than the more commonly employed rules of thumb based on quarterly changes in real GNP. Even so, this criterion provides two false signals (from 1949:I to 1949:III and from 1978:IV to 1979:II) and can vary in timing from its normal relationship to cyclical turning points by as much as two quarters. It appears that no simple rule is sufficient to translate two quarterly real GNP changes into official cyclical turning points.

Changes in the quarterly average unemployment rate have conformed quite closely to official turning points, especially recession troughs. With minor exceptions, all postwar cyclical turning points have

---

[4] For example, after rising from 1981:I to 1981:III, real GNP declined from 1981:II to 1981:IV, and the cyclical peak occurred in 1981:III.

Table 9.1. *Alternative criteria for defining cyclical turning points*

Official NBER turning point	First half-year change in real GNP[a]	Consecutive "sizable" increases in the unemployment rate[b]
Peaks		
1948:IV	1948:IV	1948:IV
1953:II[c]	1953:III	1953:III
1957:III	1957:III	1957:III
1960:II	1960:II	1960:II
1969:IV	1969:IV	1969:IV
1973:IV	1974:I[d]	1974:II
1980:I	1980:I	1979:IV
1981:III	1981:III[e]	1981:III
False signal	1979:I	None
Troughs		
1949:IV	1949:IV	1949:IV
1954:II	1954:II	1954:II
1958:II	1958:II	1958:II
1961:I	1960:IV	1961:I
1970:IV	1970:II	1970:IV
1975:I	1975:II	1975:II
1980:III	1980:III	1980:III
1982:IV	1982:IV	1982:IV
False signal	1949:II	None

[a]Peak (trough) occurs in the first quarter of the first half-year decline (increase) in real GNP.
[b]Peak (trough) occurs in the quarter prior to two consecutive increases in the quarterly average unemployment rate of (less than) 0.3 or more percentage points.
[c]Trough month was in 1953:III (July).
[d]Based on preliminary data, peak was in 1973:IV.
[e]Based on preliminary data, peak was in 1981:II.

occurred in the quarter prior to changes in the behavior of the unemployment rate.[5] More precisely, cyclical peaks have tended to occur in the quarter *prior* to an increase of 0.3 percentage points or more in the

[5] Moore (1985) employs a one-half percentage point increase in the six-month average unemployment rate as a recession signal. Monthly criteria such as that one cannot be employed for the quarterly forecasts examined here.

unemployment rate, and cyclical troughs in the quarter *prior* to the first change of less than 0.3 percentage points in the unemployment rate. In the three exceptions to this tendency (the 1953 peak, the 1975 trough, and the 1980 peak), the turning point occurred within a month of the quarter implied. These exceptions are deemed to be minor given that it is not generally possible to establish timing on a monthly basis with quarterly data, the most common frequency for forecasted data. Alternatively, one need only qualify the observed tendency by modifying "prior quarter" with the phrase "plus or minus one month."

While "sizable" (henceforth taken to mean 0.3 percentage points or more) increases in the unemployment rate have been a necessary condition for peaks and the absence of "sizable" increases for troughs, this criterion has not been a sufficient one – the simple rule would produce false peaks in 1959:IV and 1963:I and a false trough in 1974:I. These instances further illustrate what was previously noted for real GNP – turning points cannot be identified from data for one quarter in isolation. The rule could be easily modified arbitrarily to omit all false signals. The simplest modification – requiring two consecutive "sizable" increases for peaks and their absence for troughs – suffices to eliminate all false signals but only by greatly displacing the dating of the 1973 peak, a matter that is discussed more fully below.

One could, of course, design more complex criteria for identifying turning points that would duplicate the official chronology. Such criteria would clearly be ad hoc in that they were devised solely to eliminate false signals and might well not hold for future turning points. More basically, such complex criteria would take us farther away from our primary concern – identifying the macroeconomic circumstances the forecast user would be likely to associate with a turn in the business cycle. The following analysis is, therefore, based on the following criteria: A cyclical peak is expected to occur in the first quarter of a half-year decline in real GNP and a cyclical trough in the quarter prior to two consecutive changes in the quarterly average unemployment rate of less than 0.3 percentage points. These criteria will be applied to available forecasts of three prominent forecasting organizations and one well-known survey-based consensus forecast (the ASA/NBER, here called Consensus A) to assess how well cyclical turning points have been predicted. An alternative consensus forecast (the Blue Chip, or Consensus B) and a fourth forecaster are also included when data are available.

9.2   Dating turning point signals

The traditional approach to evaluating turning point forecasts focuses on the difference between the time a signal of a turning point at some *unspecified* future date is issued and the time that a turning point actually occurs. Within this approach, the *variability* of this lead (lag) is probably even more important than the average lead (lag) time itself. For example, a forecaster could easily achieve very long lead times by calling the next peak as soon as a recession ends, so long as the date of the peak was unspecified. To account for such uninformative behavior, great attention must be placed on the variability of lead (lag) times of such turning point forecasts with unspecified dates. An alternative approach is followed here, one that stresses the importance of timing in forecasting turning points. Here a turning point signal is considered to have two components: a statement that a turning point will occur and a statement of *when* it will occur. A turning point signal is regarded as a false signal if it does not date the turning point correctly. This is a harsher standard than the traditional one in that it introduces more false signals. In the traditional approach, false signals are relatively rare: a false peak signal would only occur if a peak call were issued and later rescinded; a false trough signal would only occur if a recession were expected to persist indefinitely. This methodological difference has a major impact on the interpretation of the results: what are here called false signals of the 1980 peak would be regarded as long lead times in the traditional approach. The variability of the lead (lag) time of the correct peak signal is less critical here than it is in following the traditional approach.

To facilitate comparisons with other studies, the tables are organized as follows: the first three rows follow the traditional approach, showing the date the first peak call was issued along with the predicted peak and trough dates; the next two rows show the date the first correct peak call was made and the trough date of that forecast; the final two rows show the date of the first correct trough call and, because the date the trough was expected was frequently changed, the date that the correct trough was first consistently identified.

9.3   The 1973–5 recession

The poor performance in forecasting the severity of the 1973–5 recession has been described elsewhere (McNees, 1976). The focus here will be on forecasting the *timing* of the turning points rather than the *magnitudes* of the changes as such. As just discussed, the criterion used to identify the peak will be the first predicted half-year decline in real GNP. For all data prior to the December 1985 benchmark revision, this criterion conforms to the official designation of 1973:IV (November) as the cyclical peak. Specifically, before the latest revision, it appeared that the level of real GNP in 1974:I was lower than in 1973:III. On the basis of prior experience, this suggests that a peak occurred in 1973:IV. The criterion used to identify the trough will be the quarter *prior* to two consecutive quarters of expected increases in the unemployment rate of less than 0.3 percentage points. (Specifically, the quarterly average unemployment rate fell 0.4 and 0.2 percentage points in 1974:III and IV, respectively, after rising 0.6 percentage points in 1975:II.) Based on postwar experience, this would suggest that the trough occurred in 1975:II. To ensure that a perfect unemployment rate forecast would be regarded as having correctly identified the turning point, this date, rather than the March 1975 official date, is employed here. The criterion of the first half-year increase in real GNP would also place the trough in 1975:II.

Although muted murmurs of a 1974 recession could be heard as early as mid-1973, none of the forecasters examined here clearly signaled a recession. Even in their October forecasts, after the war in the Middle East had led to a 70 percent increase in the posted price of imported oil, the prevailing view continued to be one of sustained expansion. As shown in Table 9.2, it was not until November, the peak month, that two of these forecasters signaled a cyclical peak. One forecaster correctly signaled that the peak was at hand. (See rows 1 and 2.) The other forecaster expected only a one-quarter recession, starting in 1974:I, that is, that the first and only half-year decline in real GNP would occur 1973:IV to 1974:II. While this forecast is consistent with the most recent revised data, it is not consistent with any of the real GNP data prior to the 1985 rebenchmarking to 1982 dollars, or with the official designation of 1973:IV as the peak; thus, it can be regarded as a false signal in terms of timing. It was not until the January forecast that this forecaster recognized 1973:IV as the peak. (Compare rows 1 and 4.) In December, a third forecaster correctly recognized 1973:IV as the peak, but this forecaster was also expecting a very brief recession. Further evidence of the difficulty of calling the peak is the fact that the Consensus A forecast released in December did not show a recession. Thus, although none of these forecasters anticipated the 1973 peak, two correctly recognized it in the quarter in which it occurred; most forecasters did not recognize the peak until after it had occurred.

The trough of this recession proved even more elusive. In the spring of 1974, after the oil embargo had ended, most forecasters reached the view that the recession was over. The June Consensus A forecast, for example, showed no large increases in the unemployment rate after 1974:II. This overly optimistic view of the recession as a mere "energy spasm" seemed to be confirmed by the actual path of the unemployment rate, which held essentially flat through May. The 0.3 percent increase in June was dismissed by most as an aberration related to sea-

Table 9.2. *Forecasting cyclical turning points: 1973–5 recession*

	Consensus A[a]	Forecasters		
		1	2	3
1. First called a peak	Mar. 1974	Nov. 1973	Dec. 1973	Nov. 1973
2. Peak date called	1973:IV	1974:I	1973:IV	1973:IV
3. Corresponding trough	1974:III	1974:II[b]	1974:II	1975:I
4. First called correct peak	Mar. 1974	Jan. 1974	Dec. 1973	Nov. 1973
5. Corresponding trough	1974:III	1974:II	1974:II	1975:I
6. First called correct trough	Dec. 1974	Dec. 1974	Oct. 1974	Jan. 1975
7. Final call of correct trough	June 1975	Dec. 1974	July 1975	July 1975

[a]Consensus A is the ASA/NBER consensus forecast.
[b]Based on real GNP criterion because unemployment data unavailable from November 1973 forecast.
Note: Dates are approximate because monthly forecasts are not available from all forecasters.

sonal adjustment difficulties in the month when students enter the labor force.

In July, however, after GNP revisions revealed a massive inventory buildup, one forecaster predicted the recession would last into 1975. The September Consensus A forecast, however, showed 1974:IV as the last large increase in the unemployment rate and it was not until October that a different forecaster first correctly called the trough quarter. By the end of the year, all forecasters agreed that an upturn would occur in mid-1975. Only one forecaster, however, held consistently to the correct trough date. In early 1975, the others became more pessimistic, moving the onset of the expansion back to 1975:III. It was not until June that the Consensus A forecast consistently recognized that the large increases in unemployment would end in 1975:II.

Thus, in contrast to the peak, which was not anticipated but which was unequivocally recognized with a fairly short lag, prediction of the end of the recession was characterized by numerous false signals, predictions of troughs that never occurred. The early expectation was that the recession would be brief. This error was compounded in the spring of 1974 when all but one forecaster became even more optimistic. It was not until July that the first forecaster consistently indicated that the recession would last into 1975 and not until October that a forecaster first called the correct trough date. In December 1974, another forecaster correctly and consistently called the trough. All other forecasters became more pessimistic in early 1975 and did not finally settle consistently on the correct trough date until the expansion was already under way.

9.4   The 1980 recession

The 1975–80 expansion was the longest peacetime expansion in more than one hundred years. It is perhaps not surprising, therefore, that premature forecasts of the end of the expansion were issued as early as October 1978. As shown in Table 9.3, these early recession forecasts envisioned a brief recession in 1979. This view was not widely shared – neither of the two consensus forecasts at the end of 1978 showed a recession. This changed in early 1979 after the revolution in Iran had disrupted the world oil market. By March, both of the consensus forecasts concurred with the two individual forecasters who had, since late in 1978, been expecting a brief recession in 1979. The third individual forecaster saw no recession until the June forecast, which correctly anticipated that real GNP in 1979:II would be lower than it was in 1978:IV.

All previous half-year declines in real GNP had been associated with a cyclical peak. When actual data released in July confirmed the expected half-year decline in real GNP, it seemed to confirm that a cyclical peak had occurred in early 1979. With hindsight, we now realize that this was a false signal – the only half-year decline in real GNP not associated with a recession. It seems a bit odd, however, to criticize forecasts for accurately predicting the drop in real GNP. The problem in this instance is less in the forecasts than in the use of the criterion of a half-year decline in real GNP to infer a recession signal from the forecasts. Nevertheless, it seems fair to say that the false expectation of an imminent recession followed from the accurate real GNP forecast. In September, even before the sharp increase in interest rates in October 1979, all these forecasters were anticipating large increases in the unemployment rate for three or four consecutive quarters. In fact, despite the decline in real GNP in early 1979, the unemployment rate inched up slowly in late 1979. The failure of these forecasts, in other words, was the failure to anticipate that the unemployment rate would hold stable in the wake of declines in output, reflecting a collapse in labor productivity.

Table 9.3. *Forecasting cyclical turning points: 1980 recession*

	Consensus A	Consensus B[a]	Forecasters 1	2	3
1. First called a peak	Mar. 1979	Mar. 1979	Nov. 1978	Oct. 1978	June 1979
2. Peak date called	1979:III	1979:II	1979:I	1979:II	1979:I
3. Corresponding trough	1979:IV	1979:IV[b]	1979:IV	1979:III[c]	1980:II
4. First called correct peak	Mar. 1980	Feb. 1980	Feb. 1980	Jan. 1980	Mar. 1980
5. Corresponding trough	1980:III	1980:III	1980:IV	1980:IV	1980:IV
6. First called correct trough	Mar. 1980	Nov. 1979[b]	Oct. 1979	Sept. 1979	Nov. 1979
7. Final call of correct trough	Dec. 1980	Nov. 1980	Feb. 1981	Oct. 1980	Oct. 1980

[a]Consensus B is the Blue Chip consensus forecast.
[b]Based on real GNP criterion because unemployment data unavailable before February 1980.
[c]Based on real GNP criterion as the peak was not confirmed by the unemployment criterion.
Note: Dates are approximate because monthly forecasts are not available from all forecasters.

Although their peak predictions proved premature, none of these forecasters abandoned their recession forecasts. In December 1979, all were still expecting that a recession was already under way: all the individual forecasters had correctly identified 1979:IV as the peak quarter by the unemployment rate criterion. In their January or February forecasts, two individual forecasters and the Consensus B forecast first correctly identified 1980:I as the cyclical peak by the real GNP criterion.

The problems in predicting the peak of the 1980 recession illustrate that any assessment of turning point forecasts must be a joint evaluation of the criteria chosen to translate the forecast into a binary (expansion or recession) statement as well as the predictive content of the forecast. The failure of the fall 1979 forecasts was less a failure in forecasting real GNP than a failure of the criterion of a half-year decline in real GNP. A false recession signal also emerges when the unemployment rate criterion is employed but only to the extent that this criterion would date the peak in 1979:IV rather than the official date of 1980:I. By any criterion, forecasters had clearly given advance warning of the 1980 recession. The problem was that using either criterion a series of premature false signals had been made for several months, undermining the credibility of the correct calls that were made at about the time of the peak.

The trough of the 1980 recession proved equally difficult to predict. The problem was not in the criterion adopted, as both criteria correctly identify 1980:III as the trough. Rather, the problem was that a long sequence of false trough calls, corresponding to the series of false peak calls, had been made in 1978 and 1979. The correct trough had, in fact, been identified in late 1979 by the individual forecasters and in early 1980 by the consensus forecasts. In 1980, after the recession had been correctly predicted and was under way, all forecasters became overly pessimistic about its duration. The 1980 recession is the shortest on record, and forecasters were either unable or unwilling to predict such an unprecedented event. The Consensus A forecasts in March and June of 1980 correctly called the 1980:III trough. At the same time, Consensus B and three individual forecasters were expecting a trough in 1980:IV. In September, the Consensus A forecast mistakenly joined the more pessimistic majority. It was not until October 1980 that two individual forecasters consistently called the correct 1980:III trough. It was not until late in 1980 that the two consensus forecasts correctly perceived that the string of large increases in the unemployment rate had ended in 1980:III. The problem of overestimating the length of the 1980 recession was most dramatically illustrated by one forecaster who continued to forecast large increases in the unemployment rate until February 1981, more than a half-year after the 1980 trough and less than six months before the next official peak.

9.5   The 1981–2 recession

In sharp contrast to the previous peak, which had been prematurely advertised well before it occurred, the 1981 peak was not widely anticipated. This may reflect the fact that the 1980–1 expansion was the shortest since 1919–20. Like the 1973 peak, the exact dating of the 1981 peak by the real GNP criterion depends on whether preliminary or revised data are used. Unlike the earlier experience, when the preliminary data suggested the officially designated peak date and the revised data did not, the preliminary real GNP data suggested a somewhat different peak date in 1981. One of the earliest recession signs was issued in April but it was largely ignored because (a) it predicted only a one-quarter recession; (b) it came from the same pessimistic forecaster who a few months earlier had been questioning whether the 1980 recession had ended; and (c) this recession call was rescinded the next month. Two forecasters again showed one-quarter recessions in June. (See Table 9.4.) These hesitant recession calls were not confirmed by the unemployment criterion but were reinforced in July, when the preliminary estimates showed real GNP had declined 1.9 percentage points in the second quarter. The four individual forecasters and Consensus B all expected smaller gains in the third quarter and thus, by the real GNP criterion, issued a one-quarter recession call in their July forecasts. The same conclusion appeared in the Consensus A September forecast. Unlike the current revised data, the preliminary data released in October confirmed their expectation that real GNP in 1981:III would fall below 1981:I. On the basis of prior experience, this suggested a peak near 1981:II.[6] In their October forecasts, all of the individual forecasters expected a three-quarter recession starting in 1981:II and ending in 1982:I. Thus, on the basis of the real GNP criterion and preliminary estimates of real GNP, the peak occurred in 1981:II and was first predicted in April, but was not widely recognized until July or September.

The unemployment rate criterion, like the revised real GNP data, correctly dates the peak in 1981:III, as large increases in the unemployment rate occurred in 1981:IV and 1982:I. By this criterion, two individual forecasters first recognized the peak in their September forecasts.

---

[6] It was not until the July 1982 revision that the 1981:I to 1981:III half-year decline in real GNP was eliminated, shifting the cyclical peak back to the official 1981:III date.

Table 9.4. *Forecasting cyclical turning points: 1981–2 recession*

	Consensus A	Consensus B	Forecasters			
			1	2	3	4
1. First called a peak	Sept. 1981	July 1981	April 1981	June 1981	June 1981	July 1981
2. Peak date called[a]	1981:II	1981:II	1981:II	1981:II	1981:II	1981:II
3. Corresponding trough	1981:IV	1981:III[b]	1981:III[b]	1981:III[b]	1981:III[b]	1981:III
4. First called correct peak	Mar. 1982	Dec. 1981	Sept. 1981	Oct. 1981	Sept. 1981	Nov. 1981
5. Corresponding trough	1982:II	1982:I	1982:I	1982:I	1982:I	1982:II
6. First called correct trough	Dec. 1982	Nov. 1982	Oct. 1982	Oct. 1982	Oct. 1982	Oct. 1982
7. Final call of correct trough	Dec. 1982	Nov. 1982	Feb. 1983	Feb. 1983	Oct. 1982	Jan. 1983

[a]Based on preliminary real GNP data, the real GNP criterion places the peak in 1981:II.

[b]Based on real GNP criterion as the peak signal was not confirmed by unemployment rate criterion.

Note: Rows 1 through 3 are based on the real GNP criterion. By that criterion and preliminary GNP data, the peak occurred in 1981:II, so there were no false signals. Rows 4 and 5 are based on the unemployment rate criterion, which accords with the officially designated peak in 1981:III. By this criterion, there were also no false signals. Dates for Consensus A are approximate because monthly forecasts do not exist.

By the end of 1981, all individual forecasters and Consensus B agreed on the correct peak. However, Consensus A did not call the correct peak until March 1982. Thus, while there were no premature false signals of the 1981 peak, there was also no significant prior anticipation. The best that can be said is that many forecasters recognized the peak quite quickly as it was occurring, but that it was not widely acknowledged until several months after it occurred. This optimistic bias may have reflected either support for the incoming President's economic program or disbelief that the 1980–1 expansion would last only a year.

Once recognized, the 1981 recession was generally expected to be brief. In December, views of the trough date ranged from 1981:IV to 1982:II. The view that the recession would last less than a year persisted until July. The first forecasts that the trough would not come until 1982:IV were made in October. By the end of the year, both consensus forecasts shared the view that 1982:IV would be the trough. Unfortunately, as the quarter evolved, three of the four individual forecasts incorrectly extended the recession into 1983:I. It was not until February 1983 that all forecasters consistently agreed that a large increase in the unemployment rate would not occur in 1983:I, the view that only one forecaster had espoused consistently since October 1982.

Thus, despite a belated, unwarranted wave of pessimism that engulfed some, but not most, forecasters, a pattern of undue optimism characterized forecasts of the 1981–2 recession. The recession was a year old before it was first suggested that the recession would match the 1974–5 recession in duration, and this view did not become widespread until the month of the trough. Whether this overly optimistic assessment was due to a misjudging of the stimulative effects of the 1981 tax cuts relative to the impact of monetary restraint or simply to the fact that real GNP increased in 1982:II is not clear.

9.6   Summary and conclusions

The most obvious conclusion to be drawn from the experience in forecasting the three most recent business cycles is the broad similarity between the performances in the two major recessions (1973–5 and 1981–2) and the differences between those experiences and the brief 1980 recession. In both 1973 and 1981, forecasters recognized the peak at about the time that it was occurring. There were few clear prior warnings but also fairly quick, widespread recognition that a recession period had begun. In particular, forecasters gave few false peak signals, early warnings of an earlier or later cyclical peak. The 1980 experience was exactly the opposite. Warnings of a recession – starting in 1979 – were issued as early as late 1978, but it was not until their forecasts in the first quarter of 1980 that most forecasters pinpointed the exact date of the peak. The tradeoff between timeliness and accuracy is striking. These forecasts provided no clear *advance* warnings of the two major recessions but also few false Cassandras. No one could say there were no advance warnings of the 1980 recession. The difficulty in that instance was that the warnings had been so imprecise in dating the peak that they seemed to have been largely ignored.

Whether undue pessimism but with a long lead time is more or less harmful than greater precision with no advance notice depends on the purpose of the forecast user. Those with little flexibility, in the sense that their economic decisions take months to implement, might prefer the unreliable indicator with a long lead time. Those whose decisions can be implemented instantaneouly, such as participants in financial markets, would presumably prefer reliable signals even if they did not come until after the fact.

The same broad conclusion holds for the troughs of the major recessions vis-à-vis the brief 1980 recession. In both 1973–5 and 1981–2, forecasters provided no early warning that these recessions would be the longest of the post-World War II period. That realization sank in gradually in 1982, as they slowly and steadily pushed back the date of the expected trough. The 1974–5 experience was somewhat different. In the spring of 1974, in a wave of enthusiasm after the lifting of the oil embargo, forecasters essentially abandoned their recession forecast. This mistake was corrected before the end of the year when the date of the 1975 trough was, for all practical purposes, established.

This element of overoptimism was absent in the 1980 recession. Once the brief recession was under way, no one expected it to end earlier than it did. Opinion was generally divided between 1980:III, the official trough, and 1980:IV, although a few predicted that the recession would persist into 1981. In a sense, the only mistakes in pinpointing the 1980 trough are those that have also occurred toward the end of other recessions. In each case, just when things neared the bottom, a few forecasters lost confidence in their correct trough prediction and unduly extended the recession an extra quarter. This overly cautious approach may suit forecast users who want to be *sure* an expansion is under way but will never satisfy those who want to be told about the end of a recession before it has occurred.

This review has not focused on determining which individual forecaster was the most or least unreliable. While clear instances of inferior and superior performances can be found, it seems doubtful that reliable generalizations can be drawn from such few and diverse episodes. Some attention was paid to the differences between the consensus and individual forecasts. The general tendencies are not surprising. Because the consensus can never lead its individual constituents, the consensus typically lags. This can be an advantage, as in 1979 when many forecasts were predicting false peaks, or a disadvantage, as in recognizing the 1973 and 1981 peaks as early as possible. By its nature, a consensus forecast can never provide a unique, original forecast. By the same token, the consensus avoids the extreme positions that lead to egregious errors. For example, this review did not discuss the few instances when a forecaster issued false signals far from any turning point. A consensus forecast is unlikely to commit this kind of mistake.

It is important to emphasize that all of the empirical results on which these conclusions are based can be questioned. Forecasters can validly claim that they did not predict a peak or trough that the preceding tables attribute to them. Because forecasts are not typically given in terms of explicit turning point dates, one must adopt a formula or criterion for translating quantitative, quarterly data to turning point signals. A primary motive for this chapter was to demonstrate the difficulty, if not the impossibility, of establishing satisfactory translation criteria. The simplest criterion – the algebraic sign of one, or even two, consecutive changes in real GNP – does not conform at all closely to the official business cycle chronology. Somewhat better, albeit highly imperfect, conformity can be obtained by simple criteria that consider the magnitudes as well as the direction of changes. Undoubtedly, more complex criteria could be constructed that would fit the timing of post-World War II turning points precisely. Any such criterion based on GNP data would still be subject to ambiguities due to the subsequent revisions of these data. A criterion based on unemployment rate data would be less susceptible to this problem, as these data are revised only for seasonal variation. Indeed, the simple unemployment rate criterion used here could easily be modified to become a necessary and sufficient criterion for all turning points. Such an arbitrary modification was not used here out of doubt that it would hold up in future turning points. Any such formula would obscure the basic fact that the NBER's official procedures for establishing turning points are not simple but relatively complex, based on monthly not quarterly data, and ultimately judgmental in that they have not been reduced to a fixed formula. Without such a fixed formula, evaluation of a quantitative, quarterly forecast's performance in predicting turning points must be a joint assessment of the evaluator's criteria and the forecaster's predictive skills.

REFERENCES

Diebold, F. X., and G. D. Rudebusch (1987), "Scoring the Leading Indicators," Special Studies Working Paper No. 206, Board of Governors of the Federal Reserve System, Washington, D.C., February.

Fels, R., and C. E. Hinshaw (1968), *Forecasting and Recognizing Business Cycle Turning Points,* NBER Studies in Business Cycles No. 17. New York: Columbia University Press.

McNees, S. K. (1976), "The Forecasting Performance in the 1970s," *New England Economic Review,* July/August. (An updated version is available from the Research Department – D, Federal Reserve Bank of Boston, 600 Atlantic Avenue, Boston, MA 02106.)

Moore, G. H. (1983), "What Is a Recession?" Chapter 1 in G. H. Moore, *Business Cycles, Inflation, and Forecasting,* 2nd edition, NBER Studies in Business Cycles No. 24. Cambridge, Mass., Ballinger Publishing Company.

(1985), "Forecasting Unemployment with the Leading Employment Index," *Economic Forecasts, 2* (12).

Neftci, S. N. (1982), "Optimal Predictions of Cyclical Downturns," *Journal of Economic Dynamics and Control, 4* (3).

Palash, C. J., and L. J. Radecki (1985), "Using Monetary and Financial Variables to Predict Cyclical Downturns," Federal Reserve Bank of New York *Quarterly Review,* Summer, pp. 36–45.

CHAPTER 10

Turning point predictions, errors, and forecasting procedures

H. O. Stekler

It has long been recognized that there is something special about cyclical turning points and the predictions that are associated with these turns. It has been argued that the procedures for making quantitative forecasts, which are usually derived from minimum mean square error linear prediction theory, are not appropriate for making turning point predictions (Samuelson, 1976; Wecker, 1979). Since the process of detecting changes in regimes is different from making quantitative predictions, forecasting methods designed exclusively to recognize and predict turning points have been developed. These alternative methods, specifically designed for predicting turning points, include individual leading series, indexes of leading series, and rate of change methods.

Yet the problem remains: How do you determine whether a set of quantitative forecasts did or did not predict the onset or end of a recession? This chapter will explore this and related problems. The first section will review the criteria for identifying turning points when indicators are used. Then we will consider the difficulties that may be encountered if one has to determine whether quantitative forecasts predicted turns. The forecast record in the vicinity of turning points will be considered, and hypotheses to explain why the observed errors occurred will be advanced. Finally, there will be suggestions for improving forecasting performance.

10.1 Turning point predictions with indicators

10.1.1 *Calling a turn*

In analyzing the forecasting record of an indicator, it is necessary to develop rules for identifying turning points in the predictor. It was rec-

169

ognized that the rule that would be used for identifying such turns would have to be the one that would actually be employed in a real-time basis (Alexander, 1958). Over the years, experimentation has yielded a number of ad hoc rules.

One such rule, which has proved useful in analyses of indicator performance, is based on the number of months that the predictor is below (above) the peak (trough) (see Alexander and Stekler, 1959). If every movement contrary to the previous trend is counted as a prediction, the "one month up or down" criterion is utilized. A large number of false forecasts are made when this criterion is used. It is, therefore, necessary to use criteria that do not count every reversal of trend as a turning point prediction. The use of an "n or more months up or down" rule is an implicit smoothing device that reduces both the number of false turns and the average forecasting lead. Vaccara and Zarnowitz (1977) suggested an alternative rule: three consecutive declines, for signaling a downturn. There is a difference between the "three-month down" and the three consecutive decline criteria. An indicator may be below peak for three months, but it may not have declined in every one of those months; that is, it may have had a reversal sometime in that three-month period.

For each criterion, it is possible to count the turns, identify the true turns, and in the case of true turns calculate the lead that the predictor had over the predictand.[1] These procedures will be applied to the version of the Index of Leading Series that became available in early 1983. The analysis covers the period 1948–85, and the results are presented in Table 10.1.

The data in Table 10.1 show that the "one month up or down" criterion generates a substantial number of false signals. These diminish if the two- or three-month criteria are applied, but even with the latter there are a significant number of errors. Moreover, the rule that a turn in the Index of Leading Series is identified only if it declines for three consecutive months yields a smaller number of false signals, some of which are, in fact, associated with growth cycles.

Using both three-month rules, the effective leads (lags) at each of the cyclical turns were calculated. At the troughs, except for the 1982 trough, the leads and lags are identical for the two rules, but at peaks the turns identified by the "three consecutive months of declines" have somewhat shorter leads. The reduction in the length of the lead is not

---

[1] The actual forecasting lead that is obtained with any criterion is equal to the actual historical lead minus the number of months lost in identifying the turn. Thus the use of an "n months up or down" criterion involves the loss of $n - 1$ months of the lead.

Table 10.1. *Turning point errors and effective forecast leads or lags of Index of Leading Series, various identification criteria*

	No. of false turns	
Criterion	Peaks	Troughs
One month up or down	37	17
Two months up or down	17	9
Three months up or down	12	6
Three consecutive months of decline or advance	7	1

Effective lead ($-$) or lag ($+$) at turns, in months

Peaks			Troughs		
Date	Three months down	Three consecutive months decline	Date	Three months up	Three consecutive months advance
1948	NA	NA	1949	-1	-1
1953	-1	-1	1954	-3	-3
1957	-9	-5	1958	$+1$	$+1$
1960	-8	-8	1961	$+1$	$+1$
1969	-5	-5	1970	$+2$	$+2$
1973	-3	-3	1975	$+2$	$+2$
1980	-5	-3	1980	$+1$	$+1$
1981	0	0	1982	-5	0

significant enough to offset the substantially smaller number of false turns that this rule has over the three months up or down criterion. It is, as Vaccara and Zarnowitz argued, an appropriate device for identifying turning points in the predictor.

The results of this analysis indicate that the three consecutive months rule provides an effective lead of at least one month at all cyclical peaks except for the 1981 recession. However, there is no effective lead at more than 50 percent of the troughs. The longest lead (five months) occurred at the 1982 trough.

Two objections may be raised to this analysis. First, this historical analysis uses the latest version of the Index of Leading Series, which may have been constructed on the basis of its ability to detect the cyclical turns that already occurred. Second, this analysis does not indicate how the Index would have performed on a contemporaneous basis when preliminary data and/or missing observations may have affected its movements. It was possible to consider the first objection, but time limitations precluded analysis of the second.

The same data that are contained in Table 10.1 were developed for the immediately preceding version of the Index. With some minor exceptions, the results, which are not presented here, were similar to those of Table 10.1. The pre-1983 index had not been developed from data covering the 1981–2 recession. Nevertheless, the effective lead at the 1981 peak was one month (versus zero for the later version) and at the 1982 trough both three months rules had identical leads of six months.

Thus the results of the 1983 version are likely to be representative of the type of forecasting performance that can be expected from using the Index of Leading Series as a cyclical predictor. A more sophisticated set of rules for identifying turns in the leading series was developed by Zarnowitz and Moore (1982). In their approach, a sequential procedure for identifying signals of future cyclical movements is developed using the composite indexes of both the leading and coincident indicators. Their approach correctly predicted all of the cyclical peaks, with sizable leads and with a greatly reduced number of false predictions. However, at the troughs, the signals yielded substantial lags.

Neftci (1982) argued that all of the rules for identifying turning points "lack a precise statistical basis, i.e., optimality." In other words, the procedures are ad hoc. He then developed a statistical procedure for determining when to predict a turning point. The crucial assumption was that a turning point represented a switch in the behavior of the economy from one regime or structure to another.

Neftci applies sequential analysis to the movements of the Index of Leading Series and determines that a turning point will occur when the probability of a switch in regime exceeds a critical level. When the probability is set at a high level, the probability of a false turn is kept low. According to Neftci, if his procedure had been used, in August 1973 it would have predicted that a recession was imminent. This would have yielded a three-month lead. Palash and Radecki (1985) corroborated this result and demonstrated that all the peaks between 1953 and 1980 would have been predicted. Unfortunately, there was no signal for the serious 1981–2 recession. These results may be attributable to two factors.

First, the model was both fitted and tested on the same data for the period 1949–78. This might explain why the turns prior to 1978 were identified so well. Second, Neftci's method requires an estimate of the prior probability of a recession. In these studies the prior is based solely on the length of the expansion, and it must be remembered that the recession of 1981 began only twelve months after the previous one ended.

Diebold and Rudebusch (1987) carried this technique even further, modified the rule for determining the prior probabilities of a recession, and also examined the forecast probabilities of a trough. They also concluded that there was no prediction of the 1981 recession, and their data show that some of the peaks and many of the troughs were "predicted" with a lag.

From these studies, we may conclude that the leading index provides information that is useful for predicting turning points. However, some filter must be developed that will reduce the number of false predictions. These filters could be ad hoc rules or a sophisticated procedure.

10.1.2 When will the turn occur?

According to these studies, the Index of Leading Series is useful in predicting the major turning points of the economy. Although the Index can indicate that a turning point is imminent, the procedures that have been used to identify the turn do not enable us to predict *when* the turn will occur. A number of techniques could be employed to determine when a turn in the economy might occur, given that the leading series have indicated that a turn is likely.

Given the predicted turns in the indicators, Okun (1960) used the median forecast lead to predict the date of the business cycle turn. Dyckman and Stekler (1966) used a different approach and calculated the probabilities that a peak (trough) would occur at a specified time, given the turn in the indicator. Their approach assumed that the length of the leads between the indicator and the business cycle turn was generated by a random process.

It was shown that if X_i ($i = 1 \ldots n$) represents the ith shortest lead obtained in n observations from a population of size N, the expected value of X_i is approximately equal to $(i/n + 1)N$. Thus, the ith shortest lead obtained in the sample was used as an estimate of the $(i/n + 1)$th fractile of the distribution. With nine observations, the shortest lead would be used as an estimate of the lowest decile of the true distribution.

From this procedure, it was possible to estimate the cumulative frequency distribution of leads. First, the observed lead distribution was translated into fractiles. The number of months of lead associated with each observation was plotted against the probabilities associated with each fractile. After this procedure had been applied to all observations, a freehand cumulative distribution was fitted. It was S-shaped because it was assumed that the probability density was unimodal.

The cumulative probability that the peak (trough) would occur within a specified period after the signal in the indicator had been identified can be read off the graph. For example, the cumulative probability that a turn would occur within six months after an indicator had provided a signal would be read off at the six-month point on the graph. Similarly, the probability that a turn would occur in a period four to six months after the signal from the indicator would be the difference between the probabilities at the three- and six-month points.

The results of the Dyckman-Stekler study showed that the largest probabilities that a peak (trough) would occur in a given three-month interval was less than .50 (.36). These were the probabilities given that a true signal had been identified. These probabilities would have to be reduced to account for the fact that in real time it is not possible to know whether a particular movement of the predictor was or was not, in fact, a true signal of a turning point. It was possible to increase the probabilities by using multiple predictors, but the forecasting leads were reduced.[2]

An alternative way of forecasting the date of a turning point is to use the indicators as a quantitative predictor of a composite coincident index or of a particular coincident series. When the coincident series is predicted in this fashion, it is possible to determine both whether a turn was predicted and whether it was forecast contemporaneously or with a lead (lag).

A number of studies have used the Index of Leading Series as a quantitative predictor of coincident series. Such studies include Broder and Stekler (1975), Huth (1985), Hymans (1973), Moore (1969), Stekler and Schepsman (1973), Vaccara and Zarnowitz (1977), and Weller (1979). With the exception of Huth, who used a transfer function methodology, these quantitative analyses have been regression based and have frequently utilized Almon distributed lags of the form:

$$\Delta\log Y_t = \sum_{i=1}^{n} W_i \, \Delta\log ILS_{t-i} \tag{1}$$

The results of the Vaccara-Zarnowitz study, for example, show that, even beyond the period of fit, this approach fairly well replicated movements in the coincident index for the period 1972–6. The later studies have not concentrated on the dating aspect of prediction, nor have

[2] Both Okun and Zarnowitz and Moore made similar points with respect to identifying true turns.

movements for the subsequent two cycles been analyzed, nor has the question of the *effective* forecasting lead been completely addressed.[3]

The preliminary evidence suggests that using an Index of Leading Series as a quantitative predictor of a coincident series can provide a reasonable forecast of the *dates* of the latter's turning points.

10.2   Non-indicator turning point predictions

If a forecaster makes quarterly quantitative estimates of GNP, he or she is, in fact, estimating the timing of a turn and the amplitude and duration of the subsequent movement.

Yet in the preceding chapter, McNees shows how difficult it is to evaluate quantitative forecasts on their ability to predict turning points. McNees indicates that such an evaluation depends not only on the forecaster's record, but also on the criteria that are used for determining what constitutes a turning point or a prediction of a turning point. Part of this problem is that the National Bureau of Economic Research, which officially determines the dates of turns in the economy, uses monthly series for this purpose. The corresponding dates of turns in real GNP, which are available only on a quarterly basis, may not coincide with these NBER turns. Thus it is necessary to develop a methodology for determining what constitutes "a turn in real GNP," before it is possible to conduct this type of evaluation.

McNees shows that a commonly accepted rule for defining a recession, two consecutive quarterly declines in real GNP, is neither valid nor useful. Instead he modifies the rule to call for a two-quarter decline in real GNP from a previous level. This rule is similar to one of the techniques that had been used to identify turns in the leading indicators, that is, months below peak. Using this technique for identifying recessions and predictions of recessions, McNees then shows that the cyclical forecasts for the 1973–82 period had serious flaws. The peaks in 1973 and 1981 were not forecast in advance. Moreover, while some of the predictions recognized these peaks either contemporaneously or with a short lag, other forecasters showed longer lags. The forecasts of the trough in 1975 and 1982 provided "no early warning that these recessions would be the longest of the post–World War II period." The experience in the short 1980 recession differed; there were many false warnings in advance, but the trough was fairly well predicted.

---

[3] When such analyses are undertaken, the problem of using contemporaneous data in a real-time situation and the number of false movements should also be considered.

Some of these results are in accord with previous findings. The failure to recognize cyclical peaks had been documented previously (Zarnowitz, 1979). However, the existence of this overoptimism during a recession is a new result. While these studies report the existence of a variety of turning point errors, most previous research efforts have not attempted to explain why they occurred. The next section will examine possible explanations for the turning point errors.

10.3   Why do turning point errors occur?

Previous studies that have dealt with this problem include the works of Fels and Hinshaw (1968) and Stekler (1972). Fels and Hinshaw developed a system for scoring the statements that business analysts and the Federal Reserve's Open Market Committee made about the economic outlook. The results showed that, as the date of a cyclical turn approached and passed, forecasters' certainty that it would occur increased. However, these authors made no direct comparison of movements in these certainty scores with changes in the objective contemporaneous data, nor is a hypothesis about the forecasting mechanism advanced.

Stekler advanced a preliminary hypothesis and tested it. That study assumed that forecasters begin with some subjective (prior) probability $P(T)$ about the likelihood of a turn. The prior probability that no turn will occur is $P(NT) = 1 - P(T)$. As new information becomes available such as a signal, S, from an indicator, these subjective probabilities are then revised in a Bayesian manner:

$$P(T/S) = \frac{P(S/T) \cdot P(T)}{P(S/T) \cdot P(T) + P(S/NT) \cdot P(NT)} \qquad (2)$$

The probabilities $P(S/T)$ and $P(S/NT)$ come from objective evaluations of the indicator's performance in predicting turns in the economy. This approach was used to examine the probabilities that a forecaster might have experienced prior to the 1957 and 1960 cyclical peaks, if this procedure had been used. The study inferred that a forecaster should have had no difficulty in recognizing the 1957 and 1960 recessions, if the approach had been used and the prior probability had been greater than zero.

The failure to at least recognize these recessions was attributed to the forecasters' priors (for a cyclical turn) that were zero, which meant that they did not "expect" a recession and were "surprised" by its occurrence. Support for this hypothesis is presented by Eckstein (1978, p.

321), who argued that the upper cyclical turn is often associated with credit crunches, and prior to "the crunches, there is no reason to look for the turning point." The performance of the forecasters at the 1973 and 1981 peaks (cited above) does not conflict with this hypothesis. McNees himself suggests that the 1981 peak was not anticipated because forecasters did not expect another recession so soon after the end of the 1980 recession.

This hypothesis is also consistent with the evidence that cyclical upturns are recognized and sometimes forecast in advance. The explanation is that forecasters "expect" the implemented public policies to produce cyclical upturns. This interpretation may also explain why the forecasts of the 1975 and 1982 troughs were overoptimistic.

A further corroboration of this hypothesis comes from an analysis of price forecasts. Studies of the 1969–70 price forecasts (Schnader, 1973; Stekler, 1974) provide a similarly striking asymmetry. In that time period, the inferred prior probabilities that inflation would be controlled quickly were very high.

While there is a persuasive argument that, on the basis of a Bayesian-type approach to forecasting, the turns should have been called, my 1972 model, which was presented above, is too simplistic. First, let us examine the Bayesian updating formula (2). The key probability is $P(S/T)$, the probability that if there is a true turn there will have been a signal. Since every turn had been preceded by a signal, $P(S/T) = 1$ in my 1972 article. However, these indicators, as has been indicated above, can only provide a warning of an impending turn; they cannot indicate when it will occur.

In making quantitative forecasts of GNP, it is necessary to place the turn in a specific period. If this analysis is to be used, it is necessary to determine what a forecaster's probabilities for *a turn in a given quarter* might have been given the information available.[4] Thus to calculate the probability that a turn will occur in a given time period, $P(S/T_t)$ might be calculated from the procedure described in Dyckman-Stekler (1966).

I did not have the time to replicate the 1972 analysis using the data currently available, but it is likely that for $P(S/T_t) < 1$, the posterior probabilities may be lower than what I had obtained earlier. Thus we cannot assert that the failure to predict turning points was primarily attributable to the forecasters' low subjective probabilities of the likelihood of such an event. The variability of indicators' leads may also be a contributing factor.

---

[4] There is still the problem of determining whether any given signal is true or is a false lead.

Moreover, it might be necessary to expand the Bayesian framework to take into account the costs and benefits associated with making the various types of errors and correct predictions. The work of Zarnowitz and Moore (1982) suggests that the costs of predicting false turns may be substantial, for their paper argues that sequential signals from two series be used to predict turns, thus providing confirmation of early (and rejection of possibly erroneous) signals. Schnader and Stekler (1985) have shown that it is possible to derive an optimal decision rule for choosing between the alternative forecasts of turn and no turn. The rule uses a likelihood ratio, derived from observed data, relating the probability that an event occurs when the ith state of the world exists relative to that when the jth state occurs. The events refer to the presence or absence of a signal from the ILS, with a turn in the economy constituting the ith state and no turn the jth state.

This likelihood ratio is then compared with priors multiplied by cost measures associated with the possible outcomes. If there are two alternative forecasts and two states, these are four possible outcomes: two correct forecasts, a false signal, and a failure to predict a true turn. Our theoretical analysis of this forecasting decision process showed that the costs associated with the outcomes clearly may determine whether or not a turn is predicted.

These costs to a forecaster could be loss of reputation, loss of future believability, the losses that may be inflicted upon the forecaster's company, or just some subjective feeling. Business economists indicate that such costs are indeed among the factors considered in making predictions [see, for example, McLaughlin (1980), who indicates (pp. 10–11) that there may be a built in bias against predicting downturns].

This analysis, which takes into account the costs of making various types of errors, has, as yet, not been applied to actual forecasts to determine the influence of these costs on the forecast decision and thus on the observed turning point errors. Such an analysis would have to disentangle the effects of costs, priors, and the variability of forecast leads.

Finally, there is always the possibility that our quantitative forecasting methods cannot predict turning points or that forecasters do not understand the dynamics of the processes being predicted (see Fildes, 1986). A failure to focus on the dynamics may be inferred from the emphasis given to historical patterns (i.e., historically a second recession does not occur shortly after the first has ended). The 1981 peak occurred only twelve months after the 1980 recession ended. Is this the reason why the 1981 turn was missed? Similarly, false turns were predicted after the 1978–9 oil price increases. Were these errors made because a serious recession (which was *not* predicted) occurred after the 1973–4 oil embargo and price increase?

Whatever the cause of the errors, it is important that we learn their cause so that we can improve on past performance. In the meantime, some suggestions for reducing the number of turning point errors are offered in the final section.

10.4   What can be done?

The first suggestion is an old one that bears repeating. Forecasters should pay more attention to the statistical indicators, especially the leading series. Our analysis has shown that the Index of Leading Series predicted all of the major turns in the 1948–85 period. Even the criterion that minimizes the number of false turns, up or down for three consecutive months, yielded some false signals, but the ratio of false to true turns is not excessive. Moreover, many of these errors were associated with growth cycles. This analysis suggests that the leading indicators are indeed useful in predicting turns.

This renewed call for emphasizing the leading indicators is important, for as forecasters have shifted towards quantitative techniques, less attention has been given to the indicators. Since all of the quantitative approaches require some judgmental adjustments, it is just in this area that the indicators are most useful. They can provide qualitative insights into the state of the economy that could influence a forecaster's subjective probabilities of a turn. When the Index of Leading Series signals a turn, a forecaster's prior probability of a recession should rise substantially.

The second task is to develop procedures that would locate the date of the expected turn in the economy, given that a signal has occurred. Obviously, if the *variability* of the forecasting lead were reduced, the date of a turn could be predicted with more precision. In this vein, it might be desirable to explore Wecker's (1979) procedure, which utilizes predictive density functions to identify the date of a turn. Alternatively, techniques based on regression or spectral analysis might yield better estimates of the date of a turn.

Finally, we must improve our evaluation analyses. We must determine why a forecaster did (not) predict a turn. What data were (not) considered? It is difficult to obtain insights about the factors that were taken into account in making a forecast merely by looking at the published numbers. Obviously, most forecasters do not keep a log of the factors that compelled them to issue any particular forecasts. However, the major forecasting organizations do issue a narrative that complements the published quantitative forecast. Analysts could examine this narrative and collate it with the data available at that time. It might then be possible to determine the weight that the forecaster gave to specific information. This analysis could provide useful information both about the forecasting process and the means for correcting errors.

REFERENCES

Alexander, S. S. (1958), "Rate of Change Approaches to Forecasting – Diffusion Indexes and First Differences," *Economic Journal, 68* (June), 288–301.
Alexander, S. S., and H. O. Stekler (1959), "Forecasting Industrial Production – Leading Series versus Autoregression," *Journal of Political Economy, 67* (August), 402–9.
Broder, I., and H. O. Stekler (1975), "Forecasting with a Deflated Index of Leading Series," *New England Economic Review,* September/October, pp. 15–27.
Diebold, F. X., and G. D. Rudebusch (1987), "Scoring the Leading Indicators," *Special Studies Paper No. 206,* Federal Reserve Board, Washington, D.C.
Dyckman, T. R., and H. O. Stekler (1966), "Probabilistic Turning Point Forecasts," *Review of Economics and Statistics, 48* (August), 288–95.
Eckstein, O. (1978), "Discussion on How Have Forecasts Worked?," *American Economic Review, Papers and Proceedings, 68* (May), 320–1.
Fels, R., and C. E. Hinshaw (1968), *Forecasting and Recognizing Business Cycle Turning Points.* New York: National Bureau of Economic Research.
Fildes, R. (1986), "Effective Use of Information in Forecasting – An Evaluation of Construction Industry Forecasting," Working Paper No. 130, Manchester Business School (mimeo).
Huth, W. L. (1985), "A Quantitative Look at the System of Economic Indicators," *Journal of Macroeconomics,* Spring, pp. 195–210.
Hymans, S. (1973), "On the Use of Leading Indicators to Predict Cyclical Turning Points," *Brookings Papers on Economic Activity,* No. 2, 339–84.
McLaughlin, R. L. (1980), "Never, Never-Repeat-NEVER Forecast Recession," *Business Economics,* May, pp. 5–15.
Moore, G. H. (1969), "Forecasting Short-Term Economic Change," *Journal of the American Statistical Association, 64* (March), 1–22.
Neftci, S. N. (1982), "Optimal Prediction of Cyclical Downturns," *Journal of Economic Dynamics and Control, 4,* 225–41.
Okun, A. M. (1960), "On the Appraisal of Cyclical Turning-Point Predictors," *Journal of Business, 33* (April), 101–20.
Palash, C. J., and L. J. Radecki (1985), "Using Monetary and Financial Variables to Predict Cyclical Downturns," *Federal Reserve Bank of New York Quarterly Review, 10* (Summer), 36–45.
Samuelson, P. A. (1976), "Optimality of Sluggish Predictors Under Ergodic Probabilities," *International Economic Review, 17,* 1–7.
Schnader, M. H. (1973), "Forecasting Peaks in the CPI Index," Working Paper No. 116, Economics Department, SUNY, Stony Brook (mimeo).

Schnader, M. H., and H. O. Stekler (1985), "A Hypothesis About a Forecasting Process" (mimeo).

Stekler, H. O. (1972), "An Analysis of Turning Point Forecasts," *American Economic Review, 62* (September), 724–9.

(1974), "An Analysis of Turning Point Forecasts: A Polite Reply," *American Economic Review, 64* (September), 728–9.

Stekler, H. O., and M. Schepsman (1973), "Forecasting with an Index of Leading Series," *Journal of the American Statistical Association, 68* (June), 291–6.

Vaccara, B. N., and V. Zarnowitz (1977), "How Good Are the Leading Indicators?," *Proceedings of the Business and Economic Statistics Section* (American Statistical Association, Washington, D.C.), 41–50.

Wecker, W. E. (1979), "Predicting the Turning Points of a Time Series," *Journal of Business, 52* (January), 35–50.

Weller, B. R. (1979), "Usefulness of the Newly Revised Composite Index of Leading Indicators As a Quantitative Predictor," *Journal of Macroeconomics, 1* (Winter), 141–7.

Zarnotwiz, V. (1979), "An Analysis of Annual and Multi-period Quarterly Forecasts of Aggregate Income, Output, and the Price Level," *Journal of Business, 52* (January), 1–33.

Zarnotwiz, V., and G. H. Moore (1982), "Sequential Signals of Recession and Recovery," *Journal of Business, 55* (January), 57–85.

CHAPTER 11

Forecasting peaks and troughs in the business cycle: On the choice and use of appropriate leading indicator series

Stephen J. Silver

This chapter is the result of attempts to find a way to extract as much information as possible about future economic activity from the twelve time-series commonly referred to as the leading indicators.

Leading indicators are data series that tend to lead business activity. Generally, it is believed that changes in certain economic variables precede, in a causal fashion, other economic variables. Because some of the leading series may produce false signals of future changes, it is also believed that an index composed of several of these leading series, chosen from a variety of economic processes, provides a better indication of future activity than any one series.

The most important of the single series used by business economists to forecast future economic activity is the so-called Index of Leading Indicators. This series is calculated by the Department of Commerce and published in the *Survey of Current Business*. The monthly announcements of the latest Index figure and the changes in the series composing it are major economic events. This chapter is an attempt both to test the forecasting ability of the Index and to create new indices that are more useful in forecasting peaks and troughs in the business cycle.

Section 11.1 is a review of some of the earlier attempts to use leading indicators to forecast economic activity. In section 11.2 I present the theoretical basis for my own research and the results of my attempts to use the indicator series to forecast turning points in the business cycle. Section 11.3 presents my conclusions.

11.1 Review of earlier studies

In this section I review a subset of the voluminous work in the area of leading indicators. My primary concern is not with the theoretical basis

183

for the business cycle, nor with the process of selecting a set of leading indicators; rather, I wanted to focus on the rather meager literature concerned with formal tests of the usefulness of leading indicators in forecasting turning points in economic activity.

Most of the studies reviewed concentrate on developing a rule, or set of rules, by which to forecast whether the economy is at or near a peak or trough. In their attempts to forecast such turning points, researchers at the National Bureau of Economic Research have analyzed literally hundreds of time-series related to macroeconomic activity. These series cover all the major processes of economic activity, including:

1. Employment and unemployment (e.g., length of workweek, unemployment rate, and average duration of unemployment)
2. Production and income (personal income, index of industrial production, and capacity utilization rate)
3. Consumption, trade, orders, and deliveries (value of new orders, vendor performance, and retail sales)
4. Fixed capital investment (business formation rate, contracts, and orders for new plant and equipment)
5. Inventories and inventory investment
6. Prices, costs, and profits (stock price index and index of prices of sensitive materials)
7. Money and credit (M2 and consumer and business credit outstanding)

From among all the series tracked by NBER, twelve have been selected as most relevant to forecasting changes in economic activity. In determining its usefulness as a leading economic indicator, six criteria are applied to a series:

1. Economic significance – how well understood and how important is the role of the variable in business cycles?
2. Statistical adequacy – how well does the series measure the economic variable or process?
3. Timing – how consistently has the series led the economy at turning points?
4. Conformity – how regularly has the indicator conformed to the business cycle at large?
5. Smoothness – how easily can one discriminate between nonrandom movements of the series and the irregular component?
6. Currency (or timeliness) – how promptly is the series available?

A score is awarded for each criterion to each series examined and an overall score for the series is calculated. Series to be included in the com-

Table 11.1. *Definitions of the leading indicators*

Series name	Citibank name	Short definition
AVHRSWK	LPHRM	Hrs. worked, prod. wrkrs.
LAYOFF	LUINC	Ave. wkly. initial unem. claims
NWORDER	MOCM72	Mfg. new orders, cons. GDS/MATS
VENDOR	IVPAC	% Co's reporting slow deliv's
BUSFORM	BUS	Index, net bus. formation
PLANT	MPCON2	Contracts & new orders, plant and equipment
HSSTART	HSBP	Index, new priv. hsing. units
INVENT	IVMUT2	Chg. invent. on hand and order
PMATS	PSMC99	Chg. sensitive mats. prices
S&P	FSPCOM	S&P common stock price index
MONEY	FM2D72	M2 in 72 dollars
CREDIT	FCBCUC	% Chg. bus. & consumer credit

posite index are then chosen on the basis of these overall scores. In selecting the series for the index, the National Bureau also takes into account the desirability of covering a wide range of independent factors that determine the business cycle; that is, an attempt is made to include series covering as many of the various economic processes as possible. In this way the index is a broad measure of what is occurring in the economic arena. Table 11.1 lists the series included in the index as well as the definitions of the series. For a more precise explanation of how the Composite of the Leading Indicators, or CLI, is produced, see *Handbook of Cyclical Indicators* (Department of Commerce, 1984) or Moore and Shiskin (1967).

In order to use the CLI to forecast future economic activity, various rules have been adopted, from casual empiricism, that is, eyeballing the series, to sophisticated statistical techniques. Some researchers have also tried to develop tests of the accuracy of the CLI in predicting future economic changes. Below is a description of three of the rules and tests formulated.

1. The rule of two months of negative and decelerating growth in the CLI:
Howard Keen (1983) observed that each of the last eleven recessions was preceded by two months of negative and decelerating growth in the CLI. Also, on only four occasions was this signal false. Furthermore, the average lead time for the signal was 2.8 months, a relatively long lead time for forecasts this reliable.

2. The sequential rule for recession and recovery: Zarnowitz and Moore (1982) found that, for the seven postwar business cycles, the same sequence of signals would have predicted all seven recoveries and all seven recessions with no false signals. For recessions, the following sequence was used (for recoveries, movements of the CLI are reversed): (a) First signal, a dip in the CLI growth rate to below the 3.3 percent long-term rate. (b) Second signal, a dip in the CLI to negative growth and a dip in the Composite of Coincident Indicators, or CCI, to below 3.3 percent growth. (c) Third signal, a dip in the CCI to negative growth.

While this rule was totally reliable for the period covered, the third signal, on average, occurred one month after a recession actually began. The authors note, however, that this lag in recognition is a great improvement over awaiting the final GNP statistics for the purposes of triggering countercyclical measures, such as public works projects, to combat recession.

3. The Hymans test for predictability: Saul Hymans (1973) developed a strict sequential, ex-ante test of the usefulness of a leading indicator to determine objectively when a turning point is to occur.

In brief, Hymans objected to the determination of turning points in the CLI after the recession or recovery had been well established, as the usefulness of the CLI is in forecasting when such turnarounds will occur. The Hymans test specifies that the CLI must begin signaling a peak, for instance, at most nine periods and at least three periods before the peak and carry over two months into the recession. Furthermore, between the time the peak is predicted and it occurs there must be no reversal, as defined by Hymans, in the signal. If these conditions are not met, the peak was missed. Hymans also specified under what conditions a signal may be considered as false.

On the basis of his criteria, Hymans determined that, during the period 1948–71, which included six peaks and six troughs, 50 percent of the signals given were false, that all the false signals were for peaks, and that the CLI missed 33 percent of the months that should have received peak signals and 24 percent of the months that should have been signaled as troughs.

In additional analysis, Hymans developed an alternative leading indicator series, the Spectral Leading Indicator Index, based on a spectral analysis of the several series in the CLI. This series takes into account the variable lead structure of the series that compose the CLI.

As a general rule, the literature neglects two important facts about the leading indicators. The first is that each indicator forecasts changes in economic activity with its own lead structure rather than with the same lead structure as the other indicators in the Index. Thus, the CLI, as currently constructed, is an imprecise signal for "future" economic activity. A much more realistic composite would lag each series the appropriate number of months before calculating the composite series.

While Hymans's SLI does address this first point, it does not take into account a second issue: that each series has a different lead structure at the peak versus the trough. It makes sense, therefore, to construct two CLIs, one for the peak and the other for the trough. The forecaster would then use the appropriate index as indicated by the current phase of the business cycle.

A final general comment on the value of using indicator series to forecast economic activity relates to the statistical legitimacy of developing ad hoc rules for declaring turning points based on historical precedence. In determining the usefulness of a model, it is a general rule that one loses one degree of freedom for each respecification of the model. Applying this principle to rule making would require the loss of one degree of freedom for each rule tried and rejected before a definitive rule is found.

Given the complexity of rules like those developed by Zarnowitz and Moore (1982) and Keen (1983), it is likely that a great many rules were rejected before they arrived at the ones used. However, chance occurrences of events would assure one of eventually finding a sequence of historical events that preceded every recession (or recovery) and did not precede any other time period. But correlation does not imply causality, and one ought not infer that every future turning point will be preceded by a like sequence of events.

For this reason, I prefer the establishment of a set of guidelines by which any variable, such as an index of leading indicators, is judged effective or ineffective and for all reserachers to abide by that objective standard. In this respect, Hymans has rendered a service, and in this study I will judge the performance of my measures by a fixed standard along the lines of Hymans.

11.2   Methodology

In this section I develop the techniques used to ascertain the proper lead structure of each of the twelve indicator series and to create the two indicator series: the peak leading indicator series (PLI) and trough leading indicator series (TLI).

11.2.1   The lead structure of each series

Preliminary inspection of the component series revealed that the published median leads at turning points were generally longer than those I observed. Before developing my own composite indicator series, I decided, therefore, to investigate further the correct lead structure to incorporate into the PLI and TLI series.

For this purpose, the establishment of a set of guidelines by which any variable, such as a leading indicator series, is judged effective or ineffective has intuitive appeal. In this respect, Hymans's objective rules are ideal, and I judged the performance of each of the twelve constituent series along the lines of Hymans.

In order to evaluate the results, I established a relaxed version of Hymans's ex ante criteria, explained below, to evaluate the appropriateness of each series. I relaxed these criteria because I felt that requiring each series to be as consistent in forecasting turning points as a composite series is not realistic.

For example, if one or two series signal a false positive in any month, so long as the false positives are uncorrelated the composite series would still be dominated by correct negatives and would thus signal correctly. However, if a series persists in giving incorrect signals, it should not be included in the list of leading series. Thus, so long as a series, on balance, signaled correctly for a given turning point, it was given passing marks.

In order to evaluate the performance of a series, I used a revised set of rules to filter out false signals and provide ample lead time for genuine signals. The original rules were as follows:

1. Forecasts are made one month at a time, the possible forecasts being no change in the cycle phase (NC), a peak is coming (P), or a trough is coming (T).
2. The signal obtained as of month t determines the forecast (either NC, P, or T) for month $t + 1$.
3. During an expansion, two consecutive declines in the series lead to the prediction P for the following month.
4. Once two consecutive declines of the series have been observed in an expansion, two consecutive increases in the series are required to define a false peak signal and change the prediction from P to NC.
5. The rules during a downswing phase are precisely symmetric, with two consecutive increases in the series being required for a T prediction, and following a T prediction, two consecutive declines are required to define a false trough and change the prediction from T to NC.

In order to judge the performance of a leading indicator series, Hymans specified the following rules:

1. If a peak occurs in month t, the correct and required predictions for months $t - 3$, $t - 2$, $t - 1$, t, $t + 1$, and $t + 2$ are all P.

2. Since it makes little sense to penalize an early lead, a P prediction is also considered to be correct as early as six months prior to the peak month, provided that it is part of a consecutive string of P predictions continuing at least through a peak month.

3. The trough rules are similar except that the maximum permissible lead is three months rather than six.

4. For all the months not covered under rules 1 through 3, the correct prediction is NC.

In order to evaluate the individual constituent series, I made the following modifications to Hymans's rules:

1. If a peak occurs in month t, the correct and required prediction for months $t - 3$, $t - 2$, $t - 1$, t, $t + 1$, and $t + 2$ are all P. In some cases I relaxed this requirement, so long as the data continued to indicate the correct direction of business activity.

2. A P prediction is also considered to be correct as early as twelve months prior to the peak month provided that it is part of a "nearly-consecutive" string of P predictions continuing at least through the peak month. Again, I was somewhat subjective in deciding whether a series behaved well enough to signal a turning point.

3. The trough rules are similar to those for peaks except that the series need only signal the upturn the first month of the upturn and may lead by six months; thus, the only required T signals at the trough are in periods t, $t + 1$, and $t + 2$. Again, these rules were frequently relaxed.

From examining the performance of the CREDIT series at peaks and troughs, it was decided to revise the criterion for a peak signal to be any month in which consumer credit expanded by less than $10 million. Because of the way the composite indicator series is trend adjusted, any observation that is well below the secular trend growth rate can be considered as signaling a downturn in economic activity.

Apart from these relatively minor changes in criteria, I evaluated the performance of the series as did Hymans. Table 11.2 presents the results of my analysis of the forecast ability of the series.

All the series had a positive median lead time for peaks, but the performance of the series was not uniform; in fact, only five of the series led every downturn (NWORDER, BUSFORM, HSSTART, AVRSWK,

Table 11.2. Performance of the component series of the CLI, 1948–86

A. Leads at peaks, in months

Series	Date of peak								Median	Published median
	Nov. 1948	July 1953	July 1957	April 1960	Dec. 1969	Nov. 1973	Jan. 1980	July 1981		
AVHRSWK	6	2	4	10	2	11	0	1	5	11
LAYOFF	3	7	18	11	7	3	15	2	7	15
NWORDER	4	2	4	13	10	5	12	8	6.5	11
BUSFORM	9+	9	14	2	10	7	14	2	9.5	13
PLANT	4	9	12	6	7	0	1	−1	5	7
HSSTART	6	1	15	12	7	13	3	7	7	15
S&P	4	MISS	−1	8	11	9	MISS	7	5.5	9
MONEY	7	MISS	2	MISS	10	3	23	9	5	16
VENDOR	0	10	11	5	3	−5	7	2	4	9
INVENT	1	−1	5	1	2	−11	3	−3	1	10
PMATS	3	24	6	3	−4	−7	−3	5	3	12
CREDIT	1	1	−3	−3	5	−1	−2	MISS	−1.5	13
CLI	3	3	0	10	2	5	14	2	3	N/A

B. Leads at troughs, in months

Date of trough

Series	Oct. 1949	Aug. 1954	April 1958	Feb. 1961	Nov. 1970	Mar. 1975	July 1980	Nov. 1982	Median	Published median
AVHRSWK	5	4	0	2	2	0	0	2	2	2
LAYOFF	5	-1	0	0	1	0	2	2	1.5	0
NWORDER	3	10	0	1	0	0	2	0	.5	0
BUSFORM	2	5	0	1	3	1	0	2	1.5	2
PLANT	5	8	1	-3	1	0	2	3	1.5	0
HSSTART	8	11	2	0	10	0	3	12	4	5
S&P	3	N/A	4	4	5	6	3	4	4	5
MONEY	9	N/A	8	N/A	7	2	2	5	6	6
VENDOR	4	9	4	11	0	1	1	4	4	4
INVENT	1	-3	-3	-2	7	-11	-7	-6	-2.5	2
PMATS	1	5	-2	1	-3	-1	-1	-2	-1	3
CREDIT	1	-4	-6	-9	-1	-3	0	-1	-1	2
CLI	3	9	2	2	1	1	2	8	2	N/A

LAYOFF), even using the relaxed criteria. Two series, the S&P 500 average and MONEY, missed two of the peaks entirely, and CREDIT missed one downturn. Only MONEY and S&P led every upturn.

Furthermore, the median leads for the twelve series were found to be considerably shorter than those published in the Handbook of Cyclical Indicators, also given in the last column of Table 11.2. Generally, the observed median leads were about half the published medians, averaging 6.5 months at peaks and 2 months at troughs. The published medians averaged nearly 12 and 2.6 months, respectively.

11.2.2 Development of the peak and trough leading indicator indexes

In developing the PLI and TLI indexes, I used the median leads found in the previous section. It was hoped that the new lead structure would generate even better forecasts of turning points in economic activity than were obtained with the published CLI.

I used the same method to construct these indexes as described in the 1984 *Handbook of Cyclical Indicators*. However, I lagged each series in such a way that the composite was constructed with the appropriate lead structure of each indicator. That is, for this month's indicator, I used the value that each indicator had the appropriate number of months before. For instance, for today's CLI for peaks, or PLI, I used the value of AVHRWK five months ago, the value of LAYOFF seven months ago, and so on. In the same way, I calculated the CLI for troughs, or TLI, using the lead structure appropriate at troughs. To forecast the next turning point, one should use the PLI during an expansion and the TLI during a recession.

In my calculations I used all the postwar cycles and an ex ante rule similar to that of Hymans to determine the timing of each series relative to the published turning points. In developing our PLI series, however, I did require the minimum lead to be four months for the three series whose median lead was less than four months. For the TLI, I gave CREDIT a zero-month lead.

In order to evaluate my results, I established a slightly modified version of Hymans's ex ante criteria, explained below, to evaluate the usefulness of the two-series approach. I then compared the predictive ability of the published CLI series and the PLI and TLI series. For this comparision, I did not use the CLI series published by the Department of Commerce because this series was revised for only twelve months beyond the reference month. Consequently, each seasonally adjusted series is based on seasonal factors in effect at most twelve months after the date of each data point. My data series are based on the latest revisions, including seasonal adjustment factors, as of December 1985 and, therefore, are a better challenge for my series.

In order to evaluate the performance of the CLI series, I used the Hymans rules to filter out false signals and provide ample lead time for genuine signals. In order to evaluate the PLI and TLI series, I wanted to recognize the fact that the contemporaneous value of the indicator is constructed with leading series that lead the business cycle by at least four months for peaks. Therefore, the requirements by which the performance of the two series is judged are as follows:

1. If a peak occurs in month t, the correct and required predictions for month t, $t + 1$, and $t + 2$ are all P.
2. A P prediction is also considered to be correct as early as six months prior to the peak month provided that it is part of a consecutive string of P predictions continuing at least through the peak month.
3. The trough rules are similar to those of Hymans' rules because the indicator is constructed with indicators that have a zero-period lead; again, the only required T signals at the trough are in periods t, $t + 1$, and $t + 2$.

When the economy was in a recovery phase, I looked for P signals using the PLI. I counted the number of confirmed and reversed Ps at each peak, as declared by the National Bureau, as well as the number of false Ps. Once the peak was declared, I began looking for Ts using the TLI series, and counted the number of confirmed and false T signals. Table 11.3 shows the results of my analysis.

From Table 11.3 it appears that the PLI/CLI forecasts are an improvement over the published CLI; the two-series approach yielded only fifty-nine false signals compared with eighty-five for the CLI and missed required signals of turning points only eight months compared with eleven months for the CLI.

Inspection of the PLI series reveals that it was remarkably accurate in signaling recessions at or near the declared peaks; except for two of the seven peaks included in the time period covered, the PLI signaled a downturn within two months (early or late) of the reference month. At troughs, the results were quite similar in that the timing of the TLI varied only slightly from the actual troughs.

Table 11.3. *Performance of the CLI and PLI/TLI series, 1948–87*

Period	E/R	False positives		Misses		Lead	
		PLI/TLI	CLI	PLI/TLI	CLI	PLI/TLI	CLI
1949.01–49.10	R	0	0	0	0	2	2
1949.11–53.06	E	13	15	2	1	−2	2
1953.07–54.08	R	0	0	0	0	6	6
1954.09–57.06	E	7	17	0	0	3	−2
1957.07–58.04	R	0	0	0	4	0	1
1958.05–60.03	E	2	4	0	1	0	2
1960.04–61.02	R	2	4	1	0	−1	1
1961.03–69.11[a]	E	14	17	0	2	1	1
1969.12–70.11	R	0	2	1	0	−1	3
1970.12–73.10	E	3	2	0	0	1	5
1973.11–75.03	R	2	0	1	1	−1	−1
1975.04–79.12	E	3	2	0	0	4	11
1980.01–80.07	R	0	0	2	0	−2	0
1980.08–81.06	E	0	2	0	2	1	1
1981.07–82.11	R	6	4	1	0	−1	7
1982.12–87.12	E	7	16	—	—	—	—
Totals	—	59	85	8	11	0[b]	2[b]

[a]Conforming to NBER practice, I did not count as false positives signals for the 1967 "mini-recession."
[b]Medians.

11.3   Results and conclusions

From the results of the preceding section, it seems that the leading indicator series, if used correctly, can still be a valuable tool in forecasting turing points in the business cycle; however, some of the series included in the CLI no longer seem appropriate as leading indicator series. In particular, several of the series were found to lead peaks by less than the six months one would probably consider a minimum standard for a leading indicator. And for some of the series the median leads were negative. Many of the series also do not lead at troughs, and probably should not be included in a TLI series.

ACKNOWLEDGMENTS   I wish to acknowledge the assistance and inspiration of my graduate assistant, Juan Fiori, at Bentley College, without whose inspiration and help this study would not have been completed. Thanks also to the members of the Economics Workshop at Bentley for their helpful comments and suggestions.

REFERENCES

Department of Commerce (1984), Bureau of Economic Analysis, *Handbook of Cyclical Indicators.*

Hymans, S. H. (1973), "On the Use of Leading Indicators to Predict Cyclical Turning Points," *Brookings Papers on Economic Activity, 2,* 339-75.

Keen, H., Jr. (1983), "Leading Economic Indicators Can be Misleading, Study Shows," *Journal of Business Forecasting, 2,* (4), 13-14.

Moore, G. H., and J. Shishkin (1967), *Indicators of Business Expansions and Contractions.* New York: National Bureau of Economic Research, Inc.

Zarnowitz, V., and G. H. Moore (1982), "Sequential Signals of Recession and Recovery," *Journal of Business, 55* (1), 57-85.

CHAPTER 12

Using a consensus of leading economic indicators to find the right ball park for real GNP forecasts

Edward F. Renshaw

There is a practical reason for being interested in consensus forecasts, since they are more accurate than most predictions and will sometimes have a better track record than virtually all forecasting systems based on individual records or parsimonious models (Moore, 1969, McNees, 1987). In this chapter I illustrate the superiority of a consensus approach by using a diffusion index and the downness properties of other leading economic indicators to find the right ball park for real GNP forecasts and improve our ability to identify economic recessions before their occurrence.

12.1 Finding the right ball park

The starting point for what is hoped will be better forecasts is the discovery that the distribution of the average annual growth rates for real GNP has been trimodal. Since 1948 there have been eight instances when the GNP growth rate was zero or negative; seventeen instances when the growth rate was in the 1.7 to 4.1 percent range; and fourteen years when the growth rate was in the 4.7 to 10.3 percent range. The gaps between these poor, mediocre, and super growth rate distributions can probably be attributed to interactions between the multiplier and accelerator principles.

From 1955 to 1980 the average annual percentage change in real gross private fixed domestic investment was approximately equal to three times the average growth rate for real GNP minus six percentage points.[1] This accelerator relationship implies that real GNP must

[1] Where Q is real GNP, K is the flow of productive services for the capital stock, and T is a time trend that represents technology and other resources that have been left out of the production function, this accelerator relationship can be derived from the Cobb

increase at an average rate of about 2 percent per year just to keep investment from falling and having a deleterious feedback effect on the rest of the economy. It thus helps to explain why there have been no cases of positive growth rates for real GNP less than 1.7 percent in the post–World War II period. The instability of the GNP growth rate in this range makes it very difficult for the Federal Reserve to effectively fight inflation without pushing the economy into a recession.

Built-in stabilizers, contracyclical monetary policy, and recessionary tax cuts have moderated post–World War II recessions and kept average annual declines in real GNP in a rather narrow range during business contractions.

Once the economy is recovering from a recession and still possesses excess capacity, inventory rebuilding plus multiplier and accelerator effects will sometimes produce unsustainable growth rates in the 5 to 6 percent range. The purpose of this discussion is not so much to reason why but to try to take advantage of the trimodal distribution of GNP growth rates.

In the 1952–85 period, the seven poorest GNP growth years experienced a mean decline of 1 percent, the mediocre growth years had a mean increase equal to the 2.9 percent growth rate for real GNP over the longer period from 1929–85, and the twelve super growth years had a mean increase of 5.4 percent. If a person had been able to perfectly discriminate between poor, mediocre, and super growth years and had the foresight to assign the appropriate mean growth rate to each type of year, the average absolute forecasting error would have been only .56 percentage points for both the 1952–68 period and the more recent period from 1969–85.

Forecasting next year's GNP growth rate on the assumption that it will be equal to this year's growth rate, by way of contrast, would have yielded a much larger average absolute prediction error: 2.67 percentage points for the 1952–68 period and 2.82 percentage points for the 1969–85 period. When the forecasting game is viewed from this perspective, it would appear that up to 80 percent of the distance to perfect predictions is simply getting in the right ball park.

Whether being in the right ball park is sufficient to insure superior forecasts is less certain, since the mean classification errors are not

Douglas production function, $Q = T^2 K^{1/3}$, which implies that the percentage change in real GNP will be equal to 2 percent plus one-third of the growth rate for the services provided by the capital stock. If the percentage change in fixed investment is assumed to be about equal to the percentage change in the services provided by the capital stock, one can quickly derive an accelerator model by a process of substituting the growth of investment for the growth of capital. For a more extended discussion of this model see, Renshaw (1982).

Table 12.1. *Using the diffusion index for BEA's index of leading economic indicators to forecast average annual percentage changes in real GNP, 1968–87*

Year	Avg diffusion index[a] (1)	Avg annual growth rate for real GNP in the following year		Actual minus predicted growth rate for real GNP	
		Actual (2)	Predicted[b] (3)	Diffusion index[c] (4)	Median professional forecast[d] (5)
1968	59.7	2.4	2.9	−.5	−.9
1969	40.3	−.3	−1.0	.7	−1.4
1970	46.4	2.8	2.9	−.1	−.4
1971	61.8	5.0	5.4	−.4	−.5
1972	68.8	5.2	5.4	−.2	−.9
1973	45.5	−.5	−1.0	.5	−1.6
1974	28.1	−1.3	−1.0	−.3	−.5
1975	60.8	4.9	5.4	−.5	−1.0
1976	61.1	4.7	5.4	−.7	−.3
1977	62.2	5.3	5.4	−.1	1.0
1978	52.4	2.5	2.9	−.4	.1
1979	39.6	−.2	−1.0	.8	1.1
1980	51.7	1.9	2.9	−1.0	.7
1981	37.8	−2.5	−1.0	−1.5	−3.0
1982	54.8	3.6	2.9	.7	1.2
1983	69.4	6.8	5.4	1.4	1.6
1984	48.3	3.0	2.9	.1	−.4
1985	56.9	2.9	2.9	.0	.0
1986	59.0	2.9	2.9	.0	.4
1987	50.0	3.8	2.9	.9	1.6

[a]Percent rising over an one-month span. *Source: Business Conditions Digest*, February 1988
[b]The predicted growth rate for real GNP is assumed to be equal to −1.0 percent if the diffusion index has a value less than 46.0; 2.9 percent if its value is in the 46.0 to 60.0 range; and 5.4 percent if its value is over 60.0.
[c]Column 2 minus column 3.
[d]Based on the median growth rate forecast from the ASA/NBER survey conducted late each year for the following year and published in the *NBER Reporter* each winter.

strictly comparable to the actual errors of professional economists prior to 1986.

When the median real GNP growth rates obtained from the ASA/ NBER survey, which is conducted late each year for the following year, are subtracted from BEA's revised growth rates for real GNP, however, one obtains an average absolute forecasting error of .97 percentage points for the 1969–85 period.[2] (See column 5 of Table 12.1.) This number is 70 percent larger than the mean absolute perfect classification errors in column 4 of Table 12.1 and would suggest that a good system for discriminating between poor, mediocre, and superior growth years might help some economists to improve their forecasting.

Since 1968, one could obtain perfect classification by simply setting the predicted growth rate for real GNP equal to −1.0 percent when the diffusion index for the twelve leading indicator components (percent rising over one-month spans) had an average value less than 46 percent; 2.9 percent when the value for the diffusion index was in the 46 to 60 percent range[3]; and 5.4 percent when the diffusion index had an average value over 60 percent.

All of the super growth years since 1950 can be identified by using the one-month span diffusion index when this statistic is averaged over the year and has a value of 60 percent or more. The only misclassification associated with this transition value is 1968, when the preceding diffusion index had a value of 64.9 percent and real GNP only increased 4.1 percent.

A diffusion index under 46 percent identifies all of the very poor growth years since 1947 but has the disadvantage of predicting four zero or less growth rates that did not occur for the years 1952, 1957, 1961, and 1967. The number of misclassifications can be reduced, however, by taking a census of December down ratios for a more select group of leading indicators.

The down ratio is the December value for the indicator in question expressed as a proportion of its preceding cyclical high. Cutoff ratios can then be found for the various indicators that minimize the number of false signals or misclassifications when the indicator is required to correctly identify at least six of the eight years when the GNP growth rate was zero or negative.

Cutoff ratios of .610 or less for residential building permits, .950 for stock prices, and .450 for the inverted yield on 91-day Treasury bills would have enabled one to correctly identify all of the poor growth years since 1947 and provide only one false signal for December 1966, when

---

[2] Forecasts from the ASA/NBER survey are published in the *NBER Reporter* each winter. This average and other comparative statistics are based on information as of December 1986.

[3] It should be noted, however, that the average growth rate for real GNP has slumped to only 2.5 percent since 1969. At some point in the not too distant future it will probably make sense to lower the expected growth rate for mediocre years to this figure to better reflect a slump in the natural growth rate for the U.S. eocnomy.

the United States was involved in the Vietnam War and the Federal Reserve was trying to curb inflation with tight money (Renshaw, 1987). A more diverse five-indicator model that assigns a cutoff ratio of .975 to hours worked in manufacturing and a ratio of .981 to M2 expressed in 1982 dollars was even more optimistic about the prospects for a reasonably good economic year for 1988. This model correctly predicts all eight poor growth years since 1947 and misclassifies only one good year.

The emphasis to this point has been on a consensus of individual indicators. The consensus approach can also be applied to a hodgepodge of time-series such as the index of leading indicators and some of its more interesting components (Renshaw, 1984, 1988a) or to an individual time-series, where the down ratios are based on differencing intervals of varying duration.

A December to December decline of 4 percent or more for BEA's composite index of leading economic indicators correctly identifies six of the eight following years when the real GNP growth rate was zero or negative. A June to December decline of 1.9 percent or more identifies all eight poor growth years but has the disadvantage of signaling one bad year that did not occur. A September to December decline of 1.5 percent or more identifies seven of the eight poor growth years and predicts two no-growth years that never materialized. A consensus of the down ratios for these three differencing intervals correctly identifies all of the poor growth years since 1947, and there are no false signals (Renshaw, 1988d).

Why does the consensus approach work so well? Part of the answer is random distortions in the individual series that drop out of a consensus forecast but can adversely affect the short-term forecasting accuracy of a structural model or a composite index of leading indicators.[4]

Stock prices provide a very good illustration of this point. Although the S&P stock price index is a superb predictor of economic recoveries, it has never been a very reliable predictor of economic recessions without some confirmation on the part of other leading indicators (Renshaw, 1988b, 1988e, 1988f). A December down ratio of .950 for this index correctly identifies seven of the eight poor growth years since 1947 but has the disadvantage of signaling four poor growth years that did not occur.

---

[4] A superior consensus forecast may simply imply that there is a more complex multivariate model that would provide even better forecasts. There are some population distributions with long tails, however, where the median value for a small sample will provide a better estimate of the population mean than the sample mean or composite index based on a weighted sum of individual predictors (Brown and Tukey, 1946).

During the forty-year period from 1946–86 there were fourteen major declines in the S&P index amounting to 13.9 percent or more on a daily basis and only eight recessions. If the economy was not already in a recession by the time the index declined by this percentage, there was only a one-in-four chance that it would slip into another recession before recovering to a new cyclical high (Renshaw, 1987). After a big decline and a rally of 15 percent or more, the odds of slipping into another recession in the following year are reduced to about one-in-ten (Renshaw, 1988c).

12.2   Identifying recessions before they occur

Forecasting economic recessions at or near their occurrence is a particularly difficult matter since most of the components of the index of leading economic indicators are not very well behaved at business peaks.

Table 12.2 shows the composite index of leading indicators and its twelve components as of 1984 when their values at business peaks are expressed as a proportion of their own previous peak values for the cycle in question. Two additional indicators are included in this table to reflect monetary tightness: M1, which was briefly included in BEA's index in the late 1970s, and the inverted yield on new 91-day Treasury bills. Nonsmoothed values for changes in inventories and sensitive material prices are used to provide one with a more precise picture of their peak values and volatility.

Since the great depression of the 1930s, economic expansions have ranged in duration from 12 to 106 months. The great variation in duration would suggest that about the only property of leading indicators that can be used to predict recessions is downness.[5]

One of the characteristics of down ratios at business peaks that should be of concern to forecasters is their correlation with respect to time. An index of leading indicators containing numerous components with down ratios that trend upward over time increases the risk of a surprise recession similar to the one experienced in July 1981 when the composite index was down only 1.2 percent.

One of the most interesting findings to emerge in connection with the peak ratios in Table 12.2 is the discovery that those indicators which are probably affected the most by monetary policy come closest to possess-

---

[5] In their 1938 discussion of "Statistical Indicators of Cyclical Revivals," Mitchell and Burns note, "The duration of business cycles as shown in the table differ so much and so irregularly that they give little help in judging when the next cyclical turn may occur." Reprinted in Moore (1961).

Table 12.2 Leading economic indicators at business peaks: *Value of the indicator at the business peak expressed as a proportion of its own previous peak*

Type of indicator	Month and year of business peaks								Rank order correlation with respect to time (9)
	Nov. 1948 (1)	July 1953 (2)	Aug. 1957 (3)	Apr. 1960 (4)	Dec. 1969 (5)	Nov. 1973 (6)	Jan 1980 (7)	July 1981 (8)	
M2 in 1972 dollars	.920	1.001	.985	.998	.981	.977	.932	.981	-.24
M1 in 1972 dollars	.907	.996	.960	.972	.970	.965	.926	.978	-.17
Residential building permits	.729	.546	.610	.713	.773	.579	.645	.630	-.02
Change in sensitive material prices	.213	-.031	-.234	.110	.089	.664	.378	-.086	.14
Stock prices	.909	.928	.940	.933	.856	.862	1.021	.952	.38
T-bill rate inverted	.333	.467	.191	.272	.295	.404	.361	.476	.40
Vendors performance	.762	.312	.472	.438	.744	.989	.615	.821	.48
Index of 12 leading economic indicators	.934	.968	.959	.956	.968	.977	.947	.988	.48
Average hours worked in manufacturing	.975	.985	.971	.978	.974	.995	.983	.993	.51
New unemployment insurance claims inverted	.573	.802	.868	.830	.852	.888	.772	1.000	.57
Net business formation	.834	.962	.932	.973	.992	.960	.983	.963	.57
Plant and equipment orders	.810	.582	.803	.924	.878	1.006	.843	.906	.63
New orders for consumer goods	.858	.869	.845	.843	.956	.990	.916	.976	.67
Change in inventories	-.426	-.228	-.215	-.636	.111	.851	-.126	.183	.74
Change in business and consumer credit	-.040	.244	.270	.612	.325	.449	.797	.884	.93

Source of basic data: U.S. Department of Commerce, *Handbook of Cyclical Indicators*, 1984.

Table 12.3. *Some adjusted lead times for monetary indicators at business peaks, 1947–84*

Business peak	M1 in 1972 dollars[a] (1)	M2 in 1972 dollars[a] (2)	Residential building permits[b] (3)	Inverted T-bill yield[c] (4)	Median lead time[d] (5)
Nov. 1948	20	20	2	14	14
July 1953	NS[e]	NS	29	7	7
Aug. 1957	12	0	12	29	12
Apr. 1960	6	NS	6	19	6
Dec. 1969	5	4	1	47	5
Nov. 1973	7	3	1	5	5
Jan. 1980	12	12	2	14	12
July 1981	7	7	4	7	7

[a]Months to the business peak after the money supply has declined 1.5 percent from its peak.
[b]Months to the business peak after the permit index has declined 20 percent if the permit peak was less than 150 and 35 percent if the permit peak was over 150.
[c]Months to the business peak after a cyclical doubling of the discount rate on 91-day Treasury bills.
[d]The median lead time for M1, residential building permits, and the inverted T-bill yield.
[e]No signal.

ing peak ratios that are not time dependent. In Table 12.3 some rules of thumb are formulated for some of these indicators that may be of value both for forecasting purposes and in providing some clue as to how tight monetary policy can be without tipping the economy into a recession. It should be noted, however, that most of the leading indicators have peak ratios that are not inconsistent with the hypothesis that a greater degree of downness can be tolerated if its occurrence is gradual.

The money supply, M2 expressed in 1972 dollars, has peak ratios with the lowest rank order correlation with time ($-.24$). This would suggest that monetary policy may have become somewhat tougher over time and/or that the lead times for this variable have become somewhat longer on the average.

Column 2 of Table 12.3 shows the adjusted lead times for M2 after it has declined 1.5 percent or more from its own cyclical peak. Although this criterion was not a good predictor of economic recessions when the CPI inflation rate was 2 percent or less (as was the case in 1953 and 1960 when no recessionary signals are indicated), economic theory implies that one should keep a wary eye on the money supply when inflation is a problem.

An attractive feature of this rule of thumb for predicting recessions is a dearth of false signals. From 1947–86 there was only one period during the Korean War when M2 in constant dollars declined 1.5 percent and then recovered to a new cyclical high before the occurrence of another recession.

M1 expressed in 1972 dollars has the second lowest rank order correlation with time $(-.17)$. There were three occasions from 1948–86, however, when this measure of the money supply declined by 1.5 percent and then recovered to a new high before another recession.

The slow growth of demand deposits during 1987 has caused some analysts to suggest that multinational corporations are now moving their cash balances more aggressively from country to country in response to fluctuations in the value of the dollar. If this hypothesis is correct, false signals for M1 may be more common in the future.

Residential building permits, which are known to be very sensitive to changes in monetary policy, have a rank order correlation with time that is closest to zero $(-.02)$. In column 3 of Table 12.3 a 20 percent decline in the building permit index is used to signal a recession if the preceding permit peak was less than 150 and a decline of 35 percent if the permit peak was over 150. The lead times for this signaling system are all positive and for the most part are in the comparatively narrow range of from one to six months.

From 1948–87 there was only one extended period during the Vietnam War when residential building permits declined by more than 20 percent and then recoverd to a new cyclical high before another recession.

The change in sensitive material prices has a rank order correlation of .14. Although the quantity theory of money might lead one to suppose that this variable should be directly influenced by monetary policy, its peak ratios are so variable as to be of little value as a stand-alone predictor of economic recessions.

Stock prices, which a number of studies have shown to be directly influenced by the growth of the real money supply,[6] have the fifth lowest rank order correlation with time (.38).

---

[6] There were nineteen years from 1947–86 when M1 expressed in constant dollars was allowed to increase by 1.6 percent or more. The financial returns associated with the S&P index were always positive and have an average value of 22.5 percent. During the twenty years when the real money supply declined or increased less than 1.6 percent, the average return was only 4.2 percent. For those eight years when the real money supply declined by more than 2 percent, the average financial return was -1.1 percent.

The inverted yield on new 91-day Treasury bills has a rank order correlation with time of .40. The adjusted lead times for this indicator are presented in column 4 of Table 12.3 for all those cases where the peak ratios are down 50 percent or more from their recessionary peaks. While some of the adjusted lead times are rather long, there are no cases where this variable declined more than 50 percent and then recovered to a new cyclical peak before another recession.

Column 5 of Table 12.3 shows the median adjusted lead times for inverted Treasury bills, building permits, and real M1. The lead times are all in the comparatively narrow range of from five to fourteen months. When M2 is substituted for M1, the median minimum adjusted lead time is reduced from five to three months.

There are two false (or very premature) signals associated with these median forecasting systems. They occurred during the early build-up phases of the Korean and Vietnam Wars. Since the United States has never experienced an official recession during the early stages of any of the six major wars it has been engaged in since 1854, these false signals can perhaps be dismissed as not being very important.

The most interesting finding to emerge in connection with the non-monetary indicators in Table 12.2 is their relatively high rank order correlations with time. The eight components of the index of leading indicators that may be affected only indirectly by tight money have correlations in the .48 to .93 range. The upward trend in the peak ratios for these indicators may imply that the U.S. economy is now more resistant to economic recessions than it used to be, if monetary policy is the same.

Before World War II there were only two peace-time expansions of the U.S. economy with a duration of three or more years, the 36-month expansion from March 1879 to March 1882 and the 50-month expansion from March 1933 to May 1937. In the post–World War II period there was a 37-month peace-time expansion from October 1945 to November 1948, a 39-month expansion from May 1954 to August 1957, a 36-month expansion from November 1970 to November 1973, a 58-month expansion from March 1975 to January 1980, and the most recent expansion, which is already more than 65 months old.

In his book *The Business Cycle in a Changing World,* Arthur Burns (1969) commented on some of the structural changes that have occurred in the U.S. economy since the depression of the 1930s and suggested:

> It is possible that in the future a "recession" will mean merely a reduced rate of growth of aggregate activity instead of an actual and sustained decline, but there is as yet insufficient ground for believing that economic developments will generally conform to this model in

the near future. Hence, the wise course for economists is to continue basic research on the nature and causes of business cycles, to remain watchful of developments that seem likely to bring on a slump in activity, and extend the search for acceptable pathways of prosperity without inflation.

One of the less appreciated problems with the index of leading economic indicators is that it attempts to accomplish too much. The component series in BEA's present index are evaluated on the basis of six major characteristics: economic significance, statistical adequacy, consistency of timing at both business cycle peaks and troughs, conformity to business expansions and contractions, smoothness, and prompt availability (Zarnowitz and Boschan, 1975). This host of desired characteristics has produced an index that is not as useful as it might be in explaining specific developments such as the next economic recession.

One of the advantages of the consensus approach is that it does allow one to focus a reserach effort on a very specific objective such as the identification of a recession before it occurs. In pursuing such a narrow objective it may be possible to make better use of some indicators, such as the inverted yield on Treasury bills or the volume of trading on the New York Stock Exchange,[7] that are too volatile or otherwise misbehaved to be included in a composite index of leading indicators.

One of the more troubling aspects to the down ratios for the leading indicators at business peaks in Table 12.2 is the discovery that most of the indicators do not have very consistent down ratios when they are needed the most. This would suggest that economic forecasters using the consensus approach may be well advised to be quite selective in the choice of leading indicators. This will be especially desirable if some of the indicators have the specialized ability to forecast a particular event better than most of the other indicators.

If a consensus is based on a relatively small number of important indicators, the analyst is more likely to become familiar with their idiosyncrasies and may be in a better position to spot and interpret abnormal behavior that should be disregarded in forecasting a particluar outcome.

---

[7] It is not very well appreciated that trading activity is a more reliable predictor of economic recessions than stock prices. In the 100-year period from 1885 to 1985 there are four cases where stock prices achieved a new cyclical high when the U.S. economy was experiencing a business peak and thirteen cases where the lead time for the S&P index was four months or less. There have only been three cases where the lead time for NYSE volume was less than five months and only one case (January 1980) when the average number of shares traded on this exchange did not decline before a business peak.

12.3   Some concluding observations

In his review of *Measuring Business Cycles* by Burns and Mitchell (1946), Koopmans (1947) criticized the atheoretical approach of the National Bureau of Economic Research and suggested that without resort to theory, "conclusions relevant to the guidance of economic policies cannot be drawn." If Thurow (1986) and others are correct in contending that there have been no accidental recessions since 1960–1 and that every recession since then has been deliberately or inadvertently created by the Federal Reserve to stop inflation, however, there is a possibility that some of the leading indicators in Table 12.3 will be valued not only for their forecasting ability but also as a means of providing the Board of Governors of the Federal Reserve with some time-tested clues as to how tight U.S. monetary policy can be without risking the trauma of another recession.

REFERENCES

Brown, G., and J. Tukey (1946), "Some Distributions of Sample Means," *Annuals of Mathematical Statistics, 17,* 1–12.
Burns, A. (1969), *The Business Cycle in a Changing World.* New York: Columbia University Press for the NBER, pp. 50–1.
Burns, A., and W. Mitchell (1946), *Measuring Business Cycles.* New York: National Bureau of Economic Research (Studies in Business Cycles, No. 2).
Koopmans, T. (1947), "Measurement Without Theory," *Review of Economics and Statistics, 29* (August), 167.
McNees, S. (1987), "Consensus Forecasts," *New England Economic Review,* November (1961), pp. 15–21.
Moore G. (1961), *Business Cycle Indicators.* Princeton, N.J.: Princeton University Press.
    (1969), "Forecasting Short-term Economic Change," *Journal of the American Statistical Association,* March, pp. 1–22.
Renshaw, E. (1982), "Monetary Policy, Inflation and the Aggregate Accelerator Principle," in *The Future of Monetary Policy,* Hearings Before the Joint Economic Committee, Congress of the United States, June 2–15, pp. 137–42.
    (1984), "Forecasting GNP: The Revised US Index of 12 Leading Economic Indicators," *Futures,* December, pp. 627–33.
    (1987), "Stock Market Shows No Recession," *The Journal of Commerce,* November 5, p. 8A.
    (1988a), "Better Indicator for Determining Where the U.S. Economy is Headed," *The Market Chronicle,* January 28, pp. 1 and 5.
    (1988b), "Investors in Equities Will Wind Up with Better 1988 Than 1987," *The Market Chronicle,* February 18, pp. 1 and 9.
    (1988c), "Absent Recession in 1988 Means a Decent Year for Stocks," *The Market Chronicle,* March 10, pp. 1 and 3.

(1988d), "Checking Up on Investors' North Star – Index of Leading Economic Indicators," *The Market Chronicle,* May 5, 1 and 15.

(1988e), "Stock Prices and Economic Activity," *The Market Chronicle,* June 2, pp. 1 and 9.

(1988f), "Housing, Money, Interest Rates and Economic Activity: How to Determine When the US Economy is in Danger of Slipping Into Another Recession," *The Market Chronicle,* October 13, pp. 1 and 7.

Thurow, L. (1986), "Creating a World Class Team," in D. Obey and P. Sarbanes, ed., *The Changing American Economy.* (New York: Basil Blackwell, pp. 169–79.

Zarnowitz, V., and C. Boschan (1975), "Cyclical Indicators: An Evaluation and New Leading Indexes," *Business Conditions Digest,* May, pp. v–xiv.

CHAPTER 13

Some Australian experience with leading economic indicators

Allan P. Layton

In Australia the leading and coincident indexes of economic activity, computed monthly by the Columbia University-based Center for International Business Cycle Research (CIBCR) in collaboration with Dr. Ernest Boehm of Melbourne University, have been gaining increasing prominence in economic debate. Movements in the indexes are the subject of many newspaper articles, and government and business economists alike use them to gauge the performance of the macroeconomy.

In this chapter several applications of the use of these two important economic indexes are discussed. Firstly, the degree to which movements in the leading index reliably anticipate fluctuations in the coincident index is investigated. Secondly, the usefulness of the leading index in forecasting fluctuations in telecommunications traffic is statistically evaluated. Finally, the Australian and U.S. coincident indexes are used to clarify the question of whether there is any empirical support for the view that Australia's economy is systematically led by cyclical fluctuations in the U.S. economy.

13.1 A statistical analysis of the relationship between the leading and coincident indexes

In this section the results of two related statistical analyses are presented. The relationship between the two indexes is first investigated using the technique of cross-spectral analysis; subsequently, a Granger causality analysis is conducted on the two series. [Full details of these two studies may be found in Layton (1986a, 1987a).]

211

13.1.1   *The cross-spectral analysis*

The choice of the technique of cross-spectral analysis is motivated by the possibility that the strength of the association between the two indexes is likely to vary according to whether swings in the leading index are short term or long term in nature. (For technical details of cross-spectral analysis, see Appendix A.) What we are interested in here is ascertaining the coherence (strength of association) between the two indexes at different cycle lengths (short, medium, and long term).

The component series of the two indexes are given in Table 13.1. The data consist of 408 monthly observations on the leading index (LEAD) and the coincident index (COIN) extending from January 1950 to December 1983 inclusive.

For the purposes of the spectral analysis, LEAD will be considered the input variable and COIN the output. This seems a natural selection in this instance. A graph of the two series is supplied in Figure 13.1.[1]

The actual analysis is conducted in two parts, first using the initial 204 observations (1/1950–12/1966) and then using the last 204 observations. This two-part approach was motivated because it has been suggested that the duration of cycles may have become shorter in recent years.

Results (January 1950 to December 1966): Before the cross-spectral analysis is conducted, each series is (first) differenced and the two resulting series aligned such that the largest cross-correlation occurs at lag zero. This avoids bias in the cross-spectral estimates (Makridakis and Wheelright, 1978).

The estimated spectrum of COIN is given in Figure 13.2. Clearly, cycles of long duration dominate the series, with the peak in the spectrum actually occurring at fifty-one months ($f = .0196$). This suggests the average length of the growth cycle during this period to be a little over four years. Coherence at these long cycle-lengths is very high as is evident from Figure 13.3. At the cycle-length of fifty-one months coherence is in fact 81 percent.

Results (January 1967 to December 1983): Again, each series was (first) differenced and the pair aligned before cross-spectral analysis was conducted. A pattern very similar to that found for the earlier period was

---

[1] Each index has been trend adjusted using the phase average trend method of Boschan and Ebanks (1978).

Table 13.1. *Australian leading and coincident indicators*[a]

Indicators	Unit	Monthly or quarterly	Starting date
Leading			
1. Factory overtime	Hours	M	1961:1
2. Net demand for new telephone services	No.	M	1951:1
3. Value of private non-residential building approved in 1979–80 prices	$	M	1949:1
4. Total new residential building approved	No.	M	1948:1
5. Change in price index of materials used in manufacturing, all groups, six-months smoothed	%	M	1949:1
6. Australian Stock Exchange share price index, "all ordinaries"	Index	M	1948:1
7. Gross operating surplus in 1979–80 prices	$	Q	1951:1
8. Ratio of implicit price deflator to unit-labor cost	Ratio	Q	1951:1
9. Overdraft limits outstanding in 1979–80 prices	$	M	1962:1
Roughly coincident			
1. Household income in 1979–80 prices	$	Q	1951:1
2. Gross nonfarm product in 1979–80 prices	$	M	1951:1
3. Quantity of factory production	Index	M	1950:1
4. Retail sales, all items (excluding motor vehicles, etc.) in 1979–80 prices	$	M	1951:1
5. Total employed civilian labor force	No.	M	1948:1
6. Unemployment rate, inverted	%	M	1949:1

[a]For greater detail of the series see Boehm and Moore (1984).

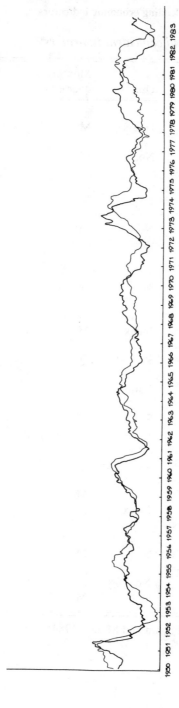

Figure 13.1. Australia's growth cycle and leading indicator index, 1950–83. (Lead: dark black).

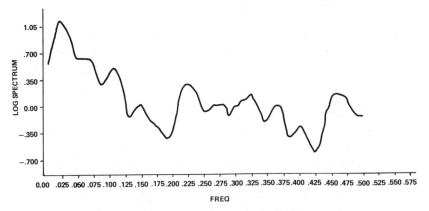

Figure 13.2. Spectrum of Australia's growth cycle, 1950–66. The cycle length, in time periods per cycle, may be computed as 1/FREQ. The spectrum peaks at frequency .0196 or at a cycle length of fifty-one months per cycle.

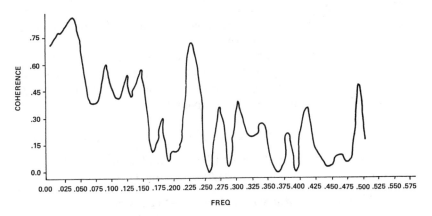

Figure 13.3. Coherence of Australia's growth cycle and leading indicator index, 1950–66. At the frequency .0196 (fifty-one months per cycle) the coherence is 81 percent (coherence has a maximum possible value of 100 percent).

evident in the spectrum of COIN. (To save space, graphs for this later period are omitted.) The spectrum actually peaked at the cycle-length of forty months (f = .0253), and the coherence at the cycle-lengths around this peak was still quite high (75 percent), although less than in the case of the earlier data. Also, the finding of a dominant forty-month cycle-length in the spectrum of the coincident index for this later period of the data is consistent with the well-known "forty-month cycle" in evidence in the United States (Burley, 1960, p. 195).

Taking the two sets of spectral results together provides considerable support for the usefulness of the leading index in anticipating pronounced and protracted swings in direction in the coincident index.

13.1.2 *A Granger causality analysis*

The results in the previous section lend substantial support to the view that information provided by the leading index may be useful in forecasting future movements in the coincident index. To realize this possibility, it is necessary to specify and estimate an econometric forecasting model for COIN using LEAD as an explanatory variable. The procedure followed in identifying an appropriate model is that due to Haugh and Box (1977). (See Appendix B.) To assess the success of the resulting econometric model, its forecasting performance is compared with the performance of an ARIMA model for COIN (Box and Jenkins, 1976). Using post-sample mean square error (PSMSE) as the metric, Granger causality (see Appendix B) may be said to be absent if the econometric model fails to outperform the ARIMA model.

For the purpose of this modeling exercise 204 observations are employed spanning the period January 1967 to December 1983. The first 168 are used for specification and estimation, and the remaining 36 observations are retained for post-sample testing.

Results: The estimated ARIMA models for the two series are as follows:

$$\text{Coincident series: } (1 - 0.1810B - 0.2107B^2)Y'_t = a_{1t}$$
$$(0.0763) \quad (0.0774)$$

$$\text{Leading indicator series: } (1 - 0.3451B)X'_t = a_{2t}$$
$$(0.0727)$$

where Y' and X' are first differences of the original data, and coefficient standard errors are in parentheses.

Positive and negative lag residual cross-correlations are presented in Table 13.2. The picture conveyed by these correlations is remarkably clear. All negative lag correlations, except lag 11, are insignificant at the two standard error level. This single correlation can be regarded as being due to sampling error and so the results suggest the absence of any empirical feedback from the growth cycle to the leading index. Concerning the positive lags, only correlations at lags 5 and 6 are statistically significant at the 2 SE level and are of the appropriate sign theoretically.

Table 13.2. *Cross-correlations to lag 24 between ARIMA residuals of the leading indicator and coincident series*

	LEAD (t) and COIN ($t + K$)							
Lag $K =$	1	2	3	4	5	6	7	8
	0.104	0.057	−0.022	0.044	0.251	0.197	0.027	0.129
	9	10	11	12	13	14	15	16
	−0.032	0.100	0.155	0.095	0.073	−0.027	−0.037	0.114
	17	18	19	20	21	22	23	24
	−0.058	0.086	−0.005	−0.004	−0.151	−0.038	−0.006	−0.164
Lag $K =$	−1	−2	−3	−4	−5	−6	−7	−8
	0.097	−0.113	−0.062	−0.058	0.108	−0.133	−0.072	−0.133
	−9	−10	−11	−12	−13	−14	−15	−16
	−0.041	−0.065	−0.175	−0.119	−0.033	−0.138	−0.054	−0.056
	−17	−18	−19	−20	−21	−22	−23	−24
	−0.036	−0.063	−0.116	−0.021	−0.000	−0.047	−0.006	−0.007

Correlations at lags 11 and 24 are ignored in the interests of sensible model specification.

This all suggests the rather simple residual bivariate distributed lag regression model:

$$a_{1t} = p_1 a_{2t-5} + p_2 a_{2t-6} + N_t \tag{1}$$

where a_{1t} and a_{2t} denote the ARIMA residuals of COIN and LEAD, respectively, and N_t represents noise in the model.

Amalgamation of this model with the two ARIMA forms yields:

$$Y'_t = b_1 Y'_{t-1} + b_2 Y'_{t-2} + b_3 X'_{t-5} + b_4 X'_{t-6} + b_5 X'_{t-7} + N_t \tag{2}$$

where Y'_t, for example, $= (1 - B)Y_t$ and Y_t and X_t denote COIN and LEAD respectively.

Estimation of equation (2) indicated b_5 to be less than its standard error and so it was dropped. The final estimated model is

$$\hat{Y}_t = .070 Y_{t-1} + .1711 Y_{t-2} + .1839 X_{t-5} + .1012 X_{t-6} \tag{3}$$
$$(.0775) \quad\quad (.0745) \quad\quad (.0517) \quad\quad (.0544)$$

Model (3) was subjected to residual autocorrelation and cross-correlation checks. On the basis of these residual diagnostic checks, the model was accepted. Forecasts for the period January 1981 to December 1983 using model (3) were then compared (in terms of MSE) with those obtained from the ARIMA model for COIN. The bivariate model was found to yield a 13 percent reduction in PSMSE compared with the univariate model. Given this in combination with the adequate within-sample diagnostic checks reported above, and the statistical significance of X'_{t-5} and X'_{t-6}, the sample evidence suggests that the data do not reject the existence of Granger causality from the leading index to the growth cycle.

13.2   Analyzing cyclical response of telecommunications traffic using the leading index

Results presented in the previous section suggest that the leading index is indeed useful in anticipating future movements in overall economic activity as measured by the coincident index. It is natural to ask whether the leading index holds any information for forecasting fluctuations in important subsectors of the Australian economy. One such subsector that is of growing importance is Australia's overseas telecommunications industry.

Australia's telecommunications services have in general exhibited several pronounced cycles over the time period 1965–84. If telecommunications traffic is responsive to fluctuations in economic activity, then it follows that such fluctuations in traffic may be anticipated by movements in the above-mentioned leading index. Such an association, if established, would suggest the inclusion of the leading index in the construction of a forecasting model with a view to providing management with early warning of traffic turning points and facilitating financial planning.

To ascertain the degree to which movements in overseas telecommunications traffic are concurrent with contemporaneous economic activity, Layton (1986b), among other things, carried out a Granger (1980) causality analysis of Australian outgoing telephone telecommunications traffic and Australia's coincident index as constructed by CIBCR. The method employed was that due originally to Haugh (1976) and, without details, the end result of the detection technique is summarized in Table 13.3. Using a significance criterion of twice the standard error, the only significant link between the two series occurs at lag zero. This empirical finding supports the hypothesis that telecommunications demand is a coincident indicator of current economic activity or, if one prefers, current economic activity is a coincident indicator of outgoing telecommunications demand.

If overseas telecommunications outgoing traffic is sensitive to changes in the general level of domestic aggregate economic activity, it follows that movements in leading indicators of such activity may be useful in anticipating changes in traffic data. Thus there is sufficient a priori evi-

Table 13.3. *Causality analysis of Australian outgoing traffic and Australia's coincident indicator*

	COIN TRAFFIC							TRAFFIC COIN					
Lag	−6	−5	−4	−3	−2	−1	0	1	2	3	4	5	6
Cross-corre-lation	.05	−.13	.07	.08	.01	−.04	.22	−.12	−.14	.03	−.04	−.08	−.05

Notes: The cross-correlations are between ARIMA residuals for the two series. The sampling frequency is monthly over the period 1969–80. If the two series are independent, the standard error of each quantity is .09.

dence to suggest that telecommunications traffic may be strongly associated with earlier movements in the leading index. If such an association exists, it is of interest to see whether a similar finding is in evidence in other industrialized countries. With this in mind, U.S. outgoing telephone traffic to Australia[2] and the U.S. leading index are similarly analyzed. The technique employed is again that of cross-spectral analysis. [Full details of this study may be found in Layton, Defris, and Zehnwirth (1986).]

The following traffic series (monthly 1970–83) were examined:

Series 1 Total Australian outgoing telephone (in paid minutes)
Series 2 U.S. outgoing to Australia telephone (in paid minutes)

This period was chosen because in an earlier study (see Defris, Layton, and Zehnwirth, 1986) a structural break was evident between 1965 and 1970 in the U.S. data.

The level of aggregation used is such that both business calls (a factor of production) and social calls (a consumer good) are included together. If could be argued that, as a factor of production, business calls may be likely to be more sensitive to economic cyclical fluctuations and should therefore be treated separately. This course was not followed for two reasons:

1. Disaggregated data from the United States were not available to the author.
2. Australian disaggregated data are not recorded at all.

To obtain some feel for the likely seriousness of this unavoidable level of aggregation, the following result offers some assistance. On the basis

---

[2] It was not possible for me to obtain total telephone outgoing for the United States on a monthly basis as was preferable for this analysis.

of a market survey, OTC[3] has elected to regard a particular subset of destinations as "business"; i.e., calls to those countries are *predominantly* business in nature. Similarly, it regards another subset of destinations (these two subsets are mutually exclusive but not exhaustive) as "social." In their study Defris et al. (1986) found traffic to each subset of destinations to be quite coherent with the leading index. In fact "social" traffic was found to have a greater coherence than "business" traffic.

Volume data were re-expressed in terms of monthly annual growth rates: for example, January 1983/January 1982 and so on. Thus, the analysis is conducted on Series 1 and 2 expressed in these terms. Little or no long-term trend or seasonality was evident in the Australian rates of growth series. However, the U.S. traffic growth rates series depicted a slight upward trend that was removed by regressing the series on time. Graphs of the two series and the corresponding leading indexes are given in Figure 13.4. The vertical axis is not labeled to preserve confidentiality of OTC and U.S. data.

Results: An inspection of the aligned cross-plots between Lead and Traffic for both countries (see Fig. 13.4) indicates that overall longer-term upturns and downturns in Traffic are reflected in Lead. Systematic association between the two series is not so strong if the shorter-term fluctuations in Traffic are considered. Cross-correlation analysis identified the average lead time between movements in Lead and Traffic to be around six months for Australia and seven months for the United States.

The important cross-spectral diagnostic for present purposes is the coherence between the two aligned series. As noted earlier, it is only meaningful to examine the coherence at cycle-lengths that have relatively large power in the spectrum of Traffic. Inspection of the spectra showed that most of the power occurred at long cycle-lengths, and in fact at cycle-lengths around two to three years coherence between Traffic and Lead was about 0.60 for both countries. (To save space, graphs of these data are omitted.)

The analysis implies, perhaps not surprisingly, that the indicators are most useful for anticipating the medium- to longer-term movements in the traffic data rather than the very short (less than 1 year) fluctuations.

---

[3] Overseas Telecommunications Commission. In Australia there is a government monopoly of the overseas telecommunications industry.

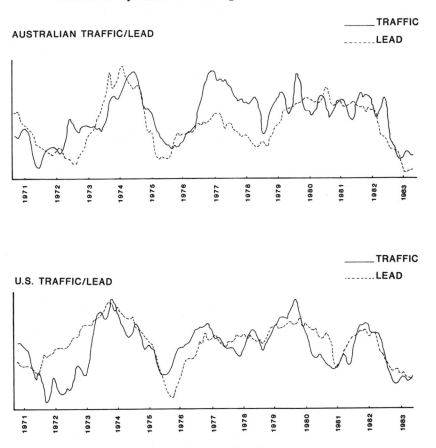

Figure 13.4 Cross plots traffic/lead (aligned).

The average lead time between shifts in the indicator and shifts in the traffic ranges from six to seven months. It is emphasized that the indicators provide a warning of the longer-term swings in direction of the traffic series rather than warnings of short-term fluctuations.

These findings suggest the appropriateness of including the leading index as a putative explanatory variable in the construction of a forecasting model for telecommunications traffic. This has been demonstrated for the Australian case in Layton (1986b). Using the methodology of Haugh and Box (1977), a dynamic distributed lag vector autoregressive model was specified, estimated, evaluated, and tested on post-sample data. Relevant modeling results are as follows:

Regression model:

$$Z_{2t} = .010 + .490Z_{2t-12} + .742Z_{1t-5}$$
$$(.002)\quad (.083)\qquad\quad (.376)$$
$$-1.063Z_{1t-6} + .741Z_{1t-7} + (1 - .794B)a_t$$
$$(.558)\qquad\quad (.334)\qquad\qquad (.060)$$

ARIMA model for traffic:

$$(1 - .461B^{12})Z_{2t} = (1 - .722B)v_t + .011$$
$$(.082)\qquad\qquad\quad (.059)\qquad (.002)$$

ARIMA model for LEAD:

$$(1 - .479B)Z_{1t} = u_t$$
$$(.075)$$

$$Z_{2t} = (1 - B)\ln X_{2t}\qquad Z_{1t} = (1 - B)\ln X_{1t}$$
$$Z_{2t} = \text{Traffic}\qquad\qquad X_{1t} = \text{Lead}$$

The performance of the bivariate model can be judged by comparing the post-sample mean square forecast error (PSMSE) of the model with that of the ARIMA model for Traffic used to forecast the same period. Such a comparison revealed an improvement in MSE of 19 percent over the ARIMA model.

Now it may be argued that economic activity in the country of destination of telecommunications traffic may be a useful leading indicator of outgoing traffic. To test this possibility a Sims-type (1980) reduced-form causality test was conducted using U.S. outgoing telephone traffic to Australia as the response variable and the Australian leading and coincident indexes as alternative putative "causal" variables. Without details the null hypothesis of independence between U.S. outgoing traffic and Australian economic activity was rejected at the 1 percent level of significance.

13.3   Australian and U.S. cyclical economic linkages

In recent years increasing attention is being paid in the literature to the impact of international influences upon the economic performance of Australia. More particularly, discussion has centered upon the transmission of world inflation to Australia's shores. In a related vein there exists theoretical support for the view that the U.S. economy, because of its sheer size and the fact it is a fiat reserve currency country, may play a dominant role in determining world monetary growth and inflation in general, and the monetary growth and inflation rates of smaller, dependent economies in particular.

Despite this increased awareness of the influence on Australia of the rest of the world, particularly the United States, little effort has been made to systematically analyze the impact of international cyclical activity on Australian economic fluctuations. Most studies have concentrated on domestic factors.

Thus, in the current section, Australia's cyclical economic history, as measured by the coincident index (ACOIN), is compared statistically with that of the United States, using the U.S. coincident index as the measure of cyclical economic activity (USCOIN). The analytical procedure used is the construction of a forecasting model for the Australian growth cycle incorporating the U.S. cycle as an explanatory variable. The procedure employed to obtain this model is the dynamic transfer function empirical specification approach of Box and Jenkins (1976) followed by a post-sample causality evaluation in the spirit of Granger (1980). [Full details of this investigation have been published elsewhere (Layton, 1987b).]

The data consist of monthly observations on trend-adjusted ACOIN and USCOIN spanning the period January 1967 to December 1983 inclusive. Again, the last thirty-six observations are used for post-sample causality evaluation. A graph of the two series is given in Figure 13.5. Modeling details are as follows:

ARIMA model for U.S. coincident index:

$$(1 - 0.6355B)Z_t = a_{1t}$$
$$(0.0604)$$

$$Z_t = (1 - B)X_t \quad X_{1t} = \text{USCOIN}$$
$$BX_{1t} = X_{1t-1}$$

ARIMA model for Australian coincident index:

$$(1 - .1810B - .2107B^2)Y_t = a_{2t}$$
$$(.0763) \quad (.0774)$$

$$Y_t = (1 - B)X_{2t} \quad X_{2t} = \text{ACOIN}$$

Dynamic regression model for Australian coincident index:

$$(1 - .2151B)Y_t = .3178Z_{t-8} + a_{3t}$$
$$(.0761) \quad (.1208)$$

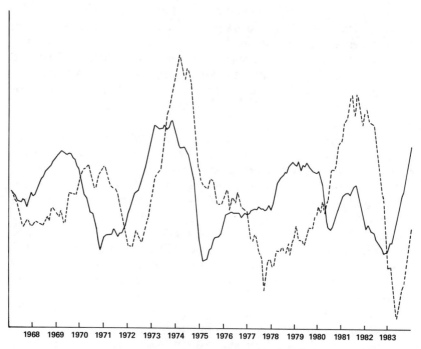

1968 1969 1970 1971 1972 1973 1974 1975 1976 1977 1978 1979 1980 1981 1982 1983

Figure 13.5. The U.S. (solid line) and Australian (dashed line) growth cycles, 1967–83.

Model comparisons for Australian coincident index:

	WSMSE	% reduction	PSMSE	% reduction
ARIMA	1.069		2.604	
Regression	1.036	3.0	2.409	7.5

The forecasting performance of the econometric model was evaluated by comparing its PSMSE with that of the ARIMA model for ACOIN referred to earlier. There was a reduction, but the improvement was a marginal 7.5 percent. In fact, the reduction proved to be statistically insignificant.

In summary, the estimated model indicates that U.S. cyclical activity had a statistically significant influence (by usual t tests) on Australian cyclical activity during the historical period under study. Moreover, U.S. cyclical activity is found to lead on average by about eight months. These within-sample findings complement and support the work of Boehm and Moore (1984). Using a turning point analytical approach, they found the U.S. growth cycle to be a consistent leader of the Australian cycle. The present analysis reinforces this finding in that the strength and consistency of the association is examined at all points not just at turning points. Furthermore, the empirically identified lead of eight months bears a close similarity both to the earlier Australian finding of Barry and Guille (1976), who found the lead to be about two quarters, and also to the eight- to ten-month lead found by Klein and Moore (1979) in the case of Italy.

However, using PSMSE as a metric, the estimated model only marginally outperforms a corresponding ARIMA model for the Australian cycle in a thirty-six period post-sample forecasting evaluation. In fact, the reduction in MSE (just over 7 percent) is found to be statistically insignificant at usual levels of significance. Given this post-sample performance, Granger (1980) causality may be said to be absent between the two series.

Taking the within-sample and post-sample results in combination, the present analysis therefore provides only little empirical support for the existence of a systematic linkage between cyclical movements in the economies of the two countries.

13.4   Future research

From this and other research it seems reasonably clear that pronounced swings in the leading index provide reliable information regarding future swings in the course of economic activity as measured by the coincident index. Once a turning point in the leading index has been identified, one is fairly secure, given the historical record, in expecting an imminent turn in the coincident index. The timing of this turn is less definite. If one follows the traditional turning point approach, the historical median (or mean) lead may be chosen and amended subjectively in light of any current special circumstances.

However, even if this estimated lead proves accurate, the approach gives no information on the amplitude of the future swing in the coincident index. Additionally, of course, the estimated lead may itself be quite wide of the mark. From both government policy and business forecasting standpoints it would be useful not only to know a turning point in economic activity is imminent but also to have an estimate of the size of the swing (upturn/downturn). In fact it would be useful to be able to make objective probability statements as to whether current economic activity has peaked or troughed given the most recent turning point in the leading index. Research into optimal methods of providing such information could be meaningfully conducted.

Appendix A: Theory of spectral and cross-spectral analysis

If a series exhibits an oscillatory behavior over time, it may be fitted by a sum of cosine waves. Each cosine wave (cycle) represents a particular frequency (or wavelength) and possesses an amplitude. For example, in the model:

$$Y(t) = A \cos(wt + \theta) \tag{1}$$

w represents the angular frequency (in radians), A the amplitude, and θ the phase. The frequency, f, is given by $f = w/2\pi$, which is in terms of cycles per unit of time. The wavelength, p, is given as $p = 1/f$, which is in terms of time periods per cycle. In practice the total variation in a time-series may be explained by cycles of several different wavelengths and the aim of spectral analysis is to assess how much of the total variation arises from various wavelength bands. Thus, if the series $Y(t)$ has k different frequencies, it may be represented as:

$$Y(t) = \sum_{j=1}^{k} (a_j \cos w_j t + b_j \sin w_j t) + Z_t$$

where $a_j = A_j \cos \theta_j$, $b_j = -A_j \sin \theta_j$, and Z_t is some stationary stochastic process. In obtaining the above decomposition the trigonometric identity $\cos(wt + \theta) = \cos wt \cos \theta - \sin wt \sin \theta$ was used.

This leads to the so-called Fourier representation of a time-series. Specifically, suppose there are available N data points, $y(1), \ldots, y(N)$. Then they can be fitted perfectly by

$$y(t) = \hat{a}_0 + \sum_{j=1}^{N/2-1} (\hat{a}_j \cos w_j t + \hat{b}_j \sin w_j t) + \hat{a}_{N/2} \cos t \tag{2}$$

where the Fourier frequency w_j is $2\pi j/N$. The choice of this set of discrete frequencies is essentially computational.

The quantity $N(a_j^2 + b_j^2)/2$ is the estimate of the contribution to the variation in the series due to the frequency w_j. Furthermore, a plot of $I(w_j) = N(a_j^2 + b_j^2)/4$ against w_j is called a periodogram and is an estimate of the spectrum which itself measures the true contribution to the total variance in the time-series accounted for by frequency w_j.

An alternative and very useful representation of the periodogram is in terms of the more familiar autocovariance function. Specifically:

$$I(w_j) = \left(\hat{c}_0 + 2 \sum_{k=1}^{N-1} \hat{c}_k \cos w_j k \right) / \pi$$

where $\hat{c}_0$ is the variance of the data, and $\hat{c}_k$ is the calculated autocovariance at lag k. Thus the periodogram (spectrum) is an exact transformation of the sample (true) autocovariance function, the information contained in the autocovariance function simply being recast into a different picture of the time-series properties of the series.

The raw periodogram is an inconsistent (in the statistical sense) estimator of the spectrum. Essentially this is because, as the sample size (N) increases, more parameters are being estimated. This is evident in equation (2) above. Thus the periodogram needs to be smoothed so as to provide a consistent estimator of the spectrum.

One simple approach for obtaining the smoothed periodogram is by grouping the raw periodogram ordinates in sets of m and finding their average; that is,

$$I(w) = \frac{1}{m} \sum_j I(w_j)$$

(see Chatfield, 1975) where j varies over m consecutive integers. The larger m is the smaller the variance of the estimates will be but bias will increase, and if m is too large interesting features of the spectrum, such as peaks, may be smoothed out. The quantity $2\pi m/N$ is called the bandwidth.

Pairs of variables may be similarly analyzed. Suppose the two series of interest are denoted $X(t)$ and $Y(t)$ and that X can be thought of as input and Y as output. A prime concern is often to see in which frequency bands X and Y have high coherence, a measure of linear association analogous to squared correlation (or R^2) in regression. The closer the coherence is to one, the more closely related are X and Y at the corresponding frequency. It should be emphasized that two series can be highly coherent at some frequency bands while having little or no coherence at others.

Most important is the coherence between X and Y at the frequency bands which account for much of the variation in the output series (Y), that is, at the frequencies for which there are large, dominant, sharp peaks in the spectrum of Y. After all, since it is variation in the output variable that is ultimately to be explained, it is of little interest if X is highly coherent with Y at some frequencies that account for little or no variation in Y.

Also of some interest in cross-spectral analysis is the phase at the frequencies of interest. If two series are exactly synchronized (in terms of peaks and troughs), they have a phase of zero. Phase can take values of zero up to π (where peaks of one correspond to troughs in the other). A final statistic that is often reported is the gain. This essentially refers to the difference in amplitude between the input and output series at various frequencies. In the present context this is of less interest than coherence and is therefore not reported.

Digressing somewhat, it is worth noting that, after differencing to remove trend, the output variable here (the coincident index) is likely to have, by its very construction, a spectrum peak within the so-called band of business cycle frequencies. In Australia's case this band is thought to roughly correspond to cycle-lengths of between three and five years. Hence, the current emphasis on coherence around the spectrum peak of the output series is virtually synonomous with investigating the coherence between the leading index and the coincidence index in the business cycle frequency band.

Appendix B: Causality analysis

Granger causality is in terms of predictability (Granger, 1969). In the bivariate case X is said to cause Y if the use of X improves the forecasts of Y. Thus, the testing procedure is to first specify and estimate a univariate model for Y incorporating only the information contained in its own past. The forecasts from this model are then compared with forecasts obtained by specifying and estimating a model for Y that incorporates not only its own past but also that of X. It is important that this comparison be carried out post-sample (Granger, 1980). The metric used for comparison purposes in this chapter is that of post-sample mean square error (PSMSE).

To specify the appropriate bivariate model, the empirical specification procedure of Haugh and Box (1977) is used here. Briefly this amounts to first independently prewhitening both series using ARIMA filters (Box and Jenkins, 1976). A distributed lag regression model for the prewhitened residual series is then specified by analyzing the ARIMA residual cross-correlations at positive and negative lags. A final model specification is achieved by amalgamating the ARIMA models with this dynamic residual regression model.

Causality testing is carried out by comparing the post-sample forecasting performance (using MSE) of the estimated bivariate model for the output variable Y with that of the corresponding univariate model for Y. It is worth reiterating that many other approaches to testing for Granger causality [e.g., those listed in Nelson and Schwert's (1982) Monte Carlo work] are not conducted in the post-sample arena. Granger (1980) has criticized such tests on the grounds that they are not compatible with the spirit of his definition. Thus the prewhitening technique used here is employed more as a specification tool rather than as a causality test. Ultimate causality conclusions are based on the forecasting power of a dynamic distributed lag reduced-form model for Y in terms of the input X.

REFERENCES

Barry, P. F., and C. W. Guille (1976), "The Australian Business Cycle and International Cyclical Linkages, 1959–74," *The Economic Record, 52* (June), 137–65.
Boehm, E. A., and G. H. Moore (1984), "New Economic Indicators for Australia, 1949–84," *Australian Economic Review*, 4th Quarter, 34–56.
Boschan, C., and W. E. Ebanks (1978), "The Phase-Average Trend: A New Way of Measuring Economic Growth," *Proceedings of Business and Economic Statistics Section of American Statistical Association*, pp. 332–5.
Box, G. E. P., and G. W. Jenkins (1976), *Time Series Analysis: Forecasting and Control*. San Francisco: Holden Day.
Burley, S. P. (1960), "A Spectral Analysis of the Australian Business Cycle," *Australian Economic Papers*, December, pp. 193–218.
Chatfield, C. (1975), *The Analysis of Time Series: Theory and Practice*. London: Chapman and Hall.
Defris, L. V., A. P. Layton, and B. Zehnwirth (1986), "Impact of Economic Cycles on Telecommunications Demand," *Information Economics and Policy, 2*, 105–17.
Granger, C. W. J. (1969), "Investigating Causal Relations by Econometric Models and Cross-spectral Models," *Econometrica, 37*, 424–38.
(1980), "Testing for Causality: A Personal Viewpoint," *Journal of Economic Dynamics and Control, 2*, 329–52.
Haugh, L. D. (1976), "Checking the Independence of Two Covariance-Stationary Time Series: A Univariate Residual Cross-correlation Approach, *Journal of the American Statistical Association, 71*, 378–485.
Haugh, L. D., and G. E. P. Box (1977), "Identification of Dynamic Regression (Distributed Lag) Models Connecting Two Time Series," *Journal of American Statistical Association, 72*, 121–30.
Klein, P. A., and G. H. Moore (1979), "A Growth Cycle Chronology for Post-War Italy," CIBCR, Columbia University (cyclostyled).
Layton, A. P. (1986a), "A Causality Analysis of Australia's Growth Cycle and the Composite Index of Leading Indicators," *Australian Economic Papers*, June, 57–66.
(1986b), "A dynamic regression forecasting model of Australian telecommunications traffic," Research Paper No. 306. School of Economic and Financial Studies, Macquarie University.
(1987a), "A Spectral Analysis of Australia's Leading and Coincident Indexes of Cyclical Economic Growth," *The Australian Economic Review*, 1st Quarter, 39–45.
(1987b), "Australian and U.S. Growth Cycle Linkages, 1967–1983," *Journal of Macroeconomics*, 31–44.
Layton, A. P., L. V. Defris, and B. Zehnwirth (1986), "An International Com-

parison of Economic Leading Indicators of Telecommunications Traffic," *International Journal of Forecasting, 2,* 413–25.

Makridakis, S., and S. C. Wheelwright (1978), *Forecasting: Methods and Applications.* New York: John Wiley.

Nelson, C. R., and G. W. Schwert (1982), "Tests for Predictive Relationships Between Time Series Variables: A Monte Carlo Investigation," *Journal American Statistical Association, 77,* 11–18.

Sims, C. A. (1980), "Macroeconomics and Reality," *Econometrica, 48,* 1–48.

CHAPTER 14

Turning point prediction with the composite leading index: An ex ante analysis

Francis X. Diebold and Glenn D. Rudebusch

On the day of its release, the preliminary estimate of the Department of Commerce composite index of leading indicators (CLI) is widely reported in the popular and financial press. Although declines in the composite leading index are often regarded as a potential signal of the onset of a recession, evaluations of the ability of the CLI to predict turning points have been limited in most previous studies by the use of final, revised CLI data. However, the composite leading index is extensively revised after each preliminary estimate; not only are revisions made as more complete historical data become available for the components, but ex post, the statistical weights are updated and components are added or eliminated to improve leading performance. Forecasts constructed with an ex post, recomputed CLI may differ from real-time forecasts based on the contemporaneous, original construction CLI. In this chapter, we perform a completely ex ante, or real-time, evaluation of the ability of the CLI to predict turning points by using the original preliminary estimates and revisions as they became available in real time.

In section 14.1, we describe revisions in the CLI and our procedure for generating ex ante turning point probability forecasts from the CLI. The methodology is the Bayesian procedure described in Diebold and Rudebusch (1989a), adapted to a newly constructed ex ante dataset. This new dataset, which has over 70,000 elements, contains every preliminary, provisionally revised, and final estimate of the CLI since the inception of the index in 1968. This allows us to reproduce the precise

We would like to thank Bill Nelson, Suzanne Nace, and Gerhard Fries for research assistance, and Barry Beckman, Frank de Leeuw, Jim Hamilton, Kajal Lahiri, Johannes Ledolter, Geoffrey Moore, Jim Stock, Mark Watson, and Victor Zarnowitz for useful comments at various stages of this research program. The views expressed in this paper are not necessarily those of the Board of Governors of the Federal Reserve System or its staff.

information content in the CLI available to forecasters at any point in time. Our implementation also incorporates results on the nature of duration dependence in U.S. expansions and contractions. While these results, which are examined in an appendix, are of independent interest to students of the business cycle, they also provide requisite inputs for the turning point probability forecasts.

In section 14.2, we evaluate the ex ante forecasts in terms of Brier's (1950) quadratic probability score (QPS), the probability-forecast analog of mean squared error. We also examine an informative factorization of the joint density of forecasts and realizations. The performance of the ex ante Bayesian probability forecast is compared with that of a range of alternatives, including a naive "no change" forecast, the optimal constant probability forecast, and the well-known rule of three consecutive declines.

In section 14.3, to facilitate interpretation of the results, we describe the stochastic properties of the preliminary CLI release and subsequent revisions, both within the across definitional regimes. Particular attention is paid to the information content of the preliminary estimate relative to the final revised value. A characterization of the statistical properties of the revisions is given relative to the polar cases of efficient forecast error and classical measurement error.

14.1   Ex ante CLI probability forecasts

While the information content of preliminary estimates is a consideration in any real-time forecasting situation, it is especially important when evaluating the performance of the composite index of leading indicators. The CLI is extensively revised from its preliminary estimate to its final form, undergoing both statistical and definitional revisions. Toward the end of each month, the Bureau of Economic Analysis (BEA) produces a preliminary estimate of the previous month's composite leading index on the basis of incomplete and preliminary source data, and it may also revise the index for any or all of the preceding eleven months. Thus, each initial estimate is subject to up to eleven revisions within the first year. These *statistical* revisions in the CLI occur because of statistical revisions in the component indicators (due to larger and/or more representative samples as time passes, etc.) and also because of late-arriving data that are included, for example, in the first revision but not in the preliminary estimate.

However, the currently available CLI data are not only of a revised statistical form, but the components have also been reweighted and reselected ex post to improve the performance of the index over the sample.

These *definitional* revisions in the composite leading index have several different forms:

1. Compositional changes due to changes in data availability, data timing, or cyclical lead performance
2. Changes in weights assigned to component indicators due to statistical updating as more data become available
3. Definitional changes in component indicators, which may be due to changes in component definitions or coverage, and so on.

A substantial number, about one every two years, of these definitional revisions have occurred since the first presentation of the index of leading indicators in the November 1968 *Business Conditions Digest (BCD)*. Compositional changes in the CLI occurred in August 1969, April 1975, February 1979, January 1982, January 1983, and January 1987. For example, a major revision occurred in January of 1983 when the BEA updated statistical factors, incorporated historical revisions in the component data, and replaced two of the components (crude materials price inflation and the change in liquid assets) with series that were broadly similar but produced a more consistent ex post leading performance.

Given these extensive revisions, it is of interest to recreate a real-time forecasting environment for predictive evaluation. For forecasting cyclical turning points, a leading index is only as good as the rule used to interpret its movements and map these movements into turning point predictions.[1] The classic example of a turning point filter associated with the CLI is the "three consecutive declines" rule for signaling a downturn (e.g., Vaccara and Zarnowitz, 1977), but many other methods have been proposed (e.g., Hymans, 1973; Wecker, 1979; Zarnowitz and Moore, 1982). More recently, a class of sequential-analytic event-oriented leading indicator prediction rules has gained popularity. The approach originates in Neftci's (1982) ingenious application of Shiryayev's (1978) results on optimal detection of changes in the probability generating process. Neftci uses this technique in a business cycle context to forecast turning points, that is, the dates of transition between "expansion" and "contraction" regimes. This approach, which we denote as the sequential probability recursion (SPR), has been refined recently by Diebold and Rudebusch (1989a) and Hamilton (1989). Evaluation of real-time turning point forecasts produced via the SPR methodology, as well as various other simpler methodologies, is the subject of this chapter.

---

[1] For an ex ante analysis that considers the standard problem of forecasting the level of an economic series, such as aggregate output, see Diebold and Rudebusch (1989b).

Assume that the behavior of the economy differs during expansions and contractions. Given this nonlinearity, it is advantageous to forecast both the expected future value of an economic variable and the form of its future probability structure as delineated by turning points (see Neftci, 1982; Diebold and Rudebusch, 1989a). To formalize this forecasting procedure, let Y_t be a coincident time-series that moves with general economic activity and switches probability distribution at turning points, and let X_t be a leading time-series with turning points (i.e., changes in distribution) that occur before the turning points in the coincident series. Let Z be an integer-valued random variable that represents the time index date of the first period after the turning point in X_t. For example, in the prediction of a downturn:

$$X_t \sim F_t^u(X_t) \qquad 1 \le t < Z$$
$$X_t \sim F_t^d(X_t) \qquad Z \le t \tag{1}$$

where F_t^u and F_t^d are the respective upturn and downturn distributions. Time-sequential observations on the leading indicator are received, so at time t, there are $(t + 1)$ observations denoted $\bar{x}_t = (x_0, x_1, \ldots, x_t)$. At time t, we calculate a probability for the event $Z \le t$, that is, that by time t a turning point in X has occurred.

The probability of $Z \le t$ after observing the data $\bar{x}_t$ at time t can be decomposed by Bayes's formula:

$$P(Z \le t \mid \bar{x}_t) = \frac{P(\bar{x}_t \mid Z \le t)P(Z \le t)}{P(\bar{x}_t)} \tag{2}$$

Define $\Pi_t = P(Z \le t \mid \bar{x}_t)$ as the posterior probability of a turning point given the data available. Then, as shown in Diebold and Rudebusch (1989a), a very convenient recursive formula for the posterior probability of a downturn is available:

$$\Pi_t = \frac{[\Pi_{t-1} + \Gamma_t^u(1 - \Pi_{t-1})]f_t^d(\bar{x}_t)}{\{[\Pi_{t-1} + \Gamma_t^u(1 - \Pi_{t-1})]f_t^d(\bar{x}_t) + (1 - \Pi_{t-1})f_t^u(\bar{x}_t)(1 - \Gamma_t^u)\}} \tag{3}$$

where $\Gamma_t^u = P(Z = t \mid z \ge t)$, the probability of a peak in period t given that one has not already occurred, and f_t^u and f_t^d are the probability densities of the latest (tth) observation if it came from, respectively, an upswing or downswing regime (in X_t). (To use this formula in the prediction of troughs, exchange f_t^u with f_t^d and use the transition probability Γ_t^d, the probability of a trough in t given a continuing contraction.) With this formula, the probability Π_t can be calculated sequentially by using the previous probability Π_{t-1}, the "prior" (independent of $\bar{x}_t$) turning point probability that $Z = t$ (i.e., Γ_t^u or Γ_t^d), and the likelihoods of the most recent observation x_t based on the distribution of X_t in upswings and downswings. Given Π_t, a probability forecast about the value of Z, the forecaster maps this into the occurrence of a turning point in Y_t. In practice, the probability of a turning point in X_t is related to the probability of an imminent turning point in Y_t over a fixed horizon decided upon by the investigator.

To apply the above sequential probability recursion, we must first estimate the densities f_t^d and f_t^u, as well as the turning point transition probabilities Γ_t^u and Γ_t^d, and we must specify an initial condition Π_0. The specification of these elements has been explored to some degree in Diebold and Rudebusch (1989a), and we adopt their final specification with one crucial modification: we consider an ex ante forecasting exercise with rolling creation of the CLI upswing and downswing densities based only on observations that would have been available in historical time.

The sequential probability formula requires the probability densities of the leading series conditional on an expansion regime and conditional on a contraction regime. The leading series is assumed to have two stochastic generating structures, expansion and contraction, and this division of the leading series into regimes depends upon the underlying classification of economic activity. We have followed the *Business Conditions Digest* (see chart A in various issues) in denoting peaks and troughs of the CLI that correspond to the NBER business cycle. The procedure used to construct f_t^u and f_t^d involved fitting a normal density function to previous observations in each regime. In particular, if $\bar{x}_t = (x_0, x_1, \ldots, x_t)$ is the vector of sequential observations on the leading indicator observed up to time t, let $\bar{x}_t^u$ be the vector of those observations from the upswing regime and $\bar{x}_t^d$ be those observations from the downswing regime. Then f_t^u is a normal density with mean and variance equal to the sample mean and variance of $\bar{x}_t^u$, and f_t^d is a normal density with mean and variance equal to the sample mean and variance of the elements of $\bar{x}_t^d$. The composite leading index was first reported in the *BCD* in 1968 and was reported ex post back to 1948. Our scoring sample runs from December 1968 to December 1986, and for each month a new set of densities is computed based on previous data back to 1948. A twelve-month data lag is also built in, so that the last twelve observations are not used in constructing the densities. This is to allow a real-time forecaster sufficient time to recognize regime changes and classify observations.[2]

---

[2] For general references to the use of preliminary data in forecasting, see Howrey (1978). Three exceptions to the use of final, revised data in CLI evaluation are Stekler and Schepsman (1973) and Zarnowitz and Moore (1982), who find that the use of preliminary data increases false signals, and Hymans (1973), who finds little difference.

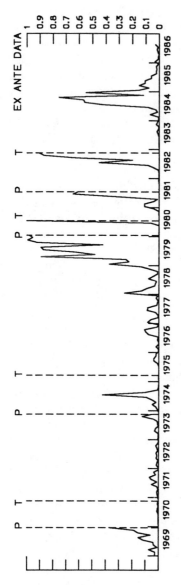

Figure 14.1. Ex ante CLI recession probabilities.

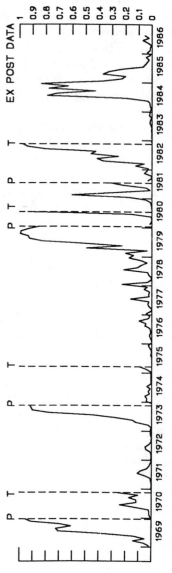

Figure 14.2. Ex post CLI recession probabilities.

236

The appendix provides evidence that, for the postwar period, the probability of a peak or a trough does not change significantly as the current regime progresses [also see the more sophisticated analysis in Diebold and Rudebusch (1990)]. For example, a long expansion is no more likely to end than a short one. Thus, we limit ourselves to time-invariant specifications of the transition conditional probabilities, that is, $\Gamma_t^u = \Gamma^u$ and $\Gamma_t^d = \Gamma^d$.

The final element in the recursive probability formula is last period's posterior probability of a turning point. There are two corrections made to this probability in practice. First, at the start of a new regime, a start-up probability of zero is used as the previous period's probability. Also, as is clear from the formula, if the posterior probability reaches one at any point, it will force all remaining probability forecasts to be one in the regime. Thus, we put an upper bound of 0.95 on the previous posterior probability as it enters the recursive probability formula.

Examples of turning point probability forecasts based on ex ante and ex post CLI data are given in Figures 14.1 and 14.2. (The forecasts shown use constant prior transition probabilities that are optimal in an average accuracy sense, to be defined rigorously in the next section, at a forecast horizon of seven months for expansions and three months for contractions.) The ex post probability forecasts perform quite well. Using an arbitrary critical probability of 0.9 [as advocated in Neftci (1982)] to signal turning points, the ex post forecasts would have signaled in advance three of the four peaks (missing the very sudden 1981 peak) and two of the four troughs with no false alarms. Using the real-time data, only one of the peaks is predicted and two of the troughs, again with no false alarms. While these results are indicative, they depend upon the critical probability value (.9) chosen. In the next section, we consider a more rigorous evaluation procedure that makes use of the information contained in the entire range of probability forecasts.

14.2   Evaluation of the probability forecasts

Accuracy refers to the closeness, on average, of predicted probabilities and observed relative frequencies. Consider a time-series of T probability forecasts $\{\Pi_t\}_{t=1}^T$, where Π_t is the time-t probability forecast of a turning point over horizon H. Let $\{R_t\}_{t=1}^T$ be the corresponding time-series of realizations; R_t equals one if a turning point occurs within the horizon (i.e., between times t and $t + H$) and equals zero otherwise. The quadratic probability score (Brier, 1950) is given by:

$$QPS = 1/T \sum_{t=1}^{T} 2(\Pi_t - R_t)^2 \qquad (4)$$

The QPS ranges from 0 to 2, with a score of 0 corresponding to perfect accuracy. The QPS is the unique strictly proper scoring rule that is a function of the divergence between predictions and realizations; extended discussion and motivation, as well as consideration of alternative loss functions and evaluation measures, may be found in Diebold and Rudebusch (1989a).

The quadratic probability scores for a variety of probability forecasting methods are presented in Table 14.1. The forecasts are scored separately in the prediction of peaks and troughs, and scoring horizons range from one to thirteen months. Three different applications of the SPR are scored. Two are produced with the final, revised CLI data as of January 1987: SPR^a uses upswing and downswing CLI densities formed with the complete sample of data, while SPR^b rolls through the final data sample and creates densities only with data temporally prior to the forecast. The third SPR forecast, SPR^c, is truly ex ante and is formed with precisely the information set that would have been available to a real-time forecaster. At each horizon, we present the QPS of these SPR forecasts optimized with respect to the constant transition probabilities. Thus, the forecasts are completely ex ante, conditional upon Γ^u and Γ^d.

Other non-leading-indicator turning point probability forecasts are also scored. The forecasting methods include a no-change, NAIVE forecast, which amounts to a constant zero probability forecast, $\Pi_t = 0$, of a downturn or upturn. This is the probability forecast analog of a random walk (in this case, QPS $= 2\bar{R}$). More generally, one can search in the zero–one interval for the number that is the most accurate as a probability prediction of turning points. Such optimal, CONSTANT probability forecasts are of the form $\Pi_t = \kappa^u$ during expansions and $\Pi_t = \kappa^d$ during contractions, where the constants are chosen to minimize QPS. In the fifth row of Table 14.1, for example, at a forecast horizon of five months, a 12 percent probability forecast of a downturn ($K^u = .12$, given in parentheses below the score) is the most accurate constant probability forecast. Finally, two variants on the "three consecutive declines" theme for the prediction of downturns were evaluated for expansions. A recession signaling rule of three consecutive declines (3CD) was applied that translates three declines in the CLI into successive probability forecasts of 1.0, .8, .6, .4, .2, and 0.0 (unless, of course, three more consecutive declines occur, at which time the probability forecast returns to 1.0). This was applied to both the final data (3CD^b) and the real-time data (3CD^c). We attach no particular importance to this "rule-of-three," but rather take it to be indicative of various rules of thumb that have appeared in the literature. No similar rule of thumb for the

Table 14.1. *QPS as a function of horizon for various forecasting methods*

Method	Forecast horizon (in months)						
	1	3	5	7	9	11	13
Prediction of peaks							
SPR[a]	.05	.09	.12	.14	.22	.29	.36
(Γ^u)	(.00001)	(.003)	(.007)	(.02)	(.03)	(.04)	(.11)
SPR[b]	.05	.08	.12	.14	.21	.29	.36
(Γ^u)	(.00001)	(.002)	(.006)	(.02)	(.03)	(.04)	(.10)
SPR[c]	.04	.11	.19	.25	.31	.37	.42
(Γ^u)	(.00002)	(.0005)	(.003)	(.01)	(.03)	(.04)	(.05)
NAIVE	.05	.15	.25	.35	.45	.56	.66
CONSTANT	.05	.14	.22	.29	.35	.40	.44
(κ^u)	(.02)	(.07)	(.12)	(.18)	(.23)	(.28)	(.33)
3CD[b]	.14	.13	.08	.11	.21	.32	.41
3CD[c]	.11	.17	.24	.29	.39	.47	.55
Prediction of troughs							
SPR[a]	.10	.30	.45	.49	.56		
(Γ^d)	(.005)	(.05)	(.18)	(.29)	(.42)		
SPR[b]	.10	.30	.46	.48	.52		
(Γ^d)	(.005)	(.05)	(.21)	(.33)	(.51)		
SPR[c]	.10	.35	.60	.71	.57		
(Γ^d)	(.0001)	(.001)	(.005)	(.34)	(.61)		
NAIVE	.16	.49	.82	1.10	1.35		
CONSTANT	.15	.37	.48	.50	.44		
(κ^d)	(.08)	(.25)	(.41)	(.55)	(.67)		

The scoring sample is Dec. 1968–Dec. 1986. For each CONSTANT and SPR score, the associated constant prior transition probability is given beneath in parentheses. Superscripts on the forecasting methodologies refer to: (a) Based on the final revised CLI data as of January 1987, with SPR densities formed from final revised data. (b) Based on the final revised CLI data as of January 1987, with rolling SPR densities. (c) Based on ex ante real-time CLI data, with rolling SPR densities.

prediction of troughs appears in the literature; we therefore construct and score this forecast only for expansions. The linear decay that we adopt prevents abrupt dropoffs of Π_t from 1.0 to 0.0 and improves the performance of the "raw" rule of three at most horizons.

The results in Table 14.1 indicate that there is clearly information in the final revised CLI data for the prediction of both peaks and troughs. Both the simple 3CD rule-of-thumb and the more rigorous SPR substantially outperform, in an average accuracy sense, the naive and constant probability forecasts at a variety of horizons. The use of rolling densities formed from the ex post data in the construction of SPR forecasts (SPR^b) does not change this result.

The situation shifts dramatically, however, when the CLI data contemporaneous to the forecast are used in forming forecasts (SPR^c and 3CD^c). With preliminary data, the simple rule-of-thumb 3CD^c never outperforms the constant probability forecast. The SPR^c does improve upon the constant probability forecast, though the enhancement at most horizons is not as great as for the ex post forecast SPR^b. Furthermore, during downswings, SPR^c performance is worse than CONSTANT at the longer forecasting horizons.

The deterioration of the SPR forecasts from ex post to ex ante can be decomposed into (a) that due to different ex ante and ex post densities f^u and f^d characterizing upswings and downswings, and (b) that due to different preliminary and revised CLI values. Comparing the SPR^a, SPR^b, and SPR^c rows of Table 14.1, we conclude that use of ex ante CLI data, as opposed to real-time density estimates, is responsible for most of the forecast divergence.

14.3   Characterization of revisions in the CLI

It was noted earlier that differences in ex ante and ex post turning point forecasting performance can be traced to one or both of the following: use of real-time CLI data and use of real-time estimated densities in the SPR. We saw that the first of these, not the second, was responsible for most of the difference; as such, we now study the properties of both intra- and inter-definitional revisions in the CLI.

We first consider the nature of revisions across definitional and compositional changes. The size of revisions to the CLI provides an indication of the information content of the preliminary estimates. Over the entire sample from December 1968 to January 1987, the standard deviation of the revision from the preliminary estimate of the CLI percentage change to the final estimate as given in January 1987 is .86 percentage points. Thus, for example, if the preliminary increase is 1.0 percent, one can only be 80 percent confident that the final estimate will be greater than −.10 and less than 2.10 percent (assuming normality). Within the most recent subsample of January 1983 to February 1986 (this allows for a final, eleventh revision through January of 1987), where definitional revisions are not a factor, the standard deviation from the preliminary estimate to eleventh revision is .49, and the corresponding 80 percent confidence interval is ±.63 percent.

We now examine statistical revisions *within* two recent definitional regimes, in particular, the periods February 1979 to December 1981 and January 1983 to January 1987. These represent timely and comparatively long regimes, and they provide an interesting contrast in terms of aggregate economic activity. For each date in each sample, we have twelve estimates available, which we denote Y1, Y2, . . . , Y12, where Y1 is the preliminary number and Y12 is the final revised number. We therefore have eleven non-overlapping revisions for each calendar date, defined by Y2Y1 = Y2 − Y1, . . . , Y12Y11 = Y12 − Y11.

It may be useful to classify the stochastic properties of revisions relative to the polar cases of classical measurement error and efficient forecast error, as in Mankiw, Runkle, and Shapiro (1984) and Mankiw and Shapiro (1986). The intuition behind the dichotomy is simple: If a provisional estimate differs from the revised value by only measurement error, then the revision is uncorrelated with the revised value but correlated with the provisional information set. On the other hand, if a provisional estimate represents an efficient forecast (i.e., rational, or minimum mean squared error conditional on available information), then the revision is correlated with the revised value but uncorrelated with the provisional information set. By determining where the CLI revisions lie within this spectrum, we can gain insight into the potential for achieving improvement in the preliminary numbers. If the intra-definitional-regime revisions behave as efficient forecast errors, then they are optimal estimates of the final, revised numbers. To the extent that the final numbers produce the better forecasts, then, efficient forecast error revisions are desirable.

We consider first the January 1983–January 1987 sample. Descriptive statistics, for varying degrees of revision collapse, are shown in Table 14.2. Note that the standard deviations of Y1, . . . , Y12 are all in the neighborhood of .86 percent, whereas the standard deviations of the revisions begin around .5 (for the earliest revisions) and eventually decrease to around .1 (for the last revisions). Thus, the standard deviation of the revisions (particularly the early revisions) is quite large rela-

Table 14.2. *Revisions in the composite leading index,*
1983–7

Variable	N	Mean	SD	T ratio
Y1	49	0.52	0.86	4.26
Y2	48	0.60	0.92	4.48
Y3	47	0.55	0.83	4.57
Y4	46	0.54	0.85	4.34
Y5	45	0.54	0.85	4.27
Y6	44	0.55	0.86	4.23
Y7	43	0.57	0.88	4.26
Y8	42	0.57	0.88	4.16
Y9	41	0.60	0.87	4.41
Y10	40	0.60	0.89	4.28
Y11	39	0.58	0.88	4.12
Y12	38	0.56	0.88	3.92
Y3Y1	47	0.03	0.45	0.49
Y5Y3	45	0.00	0.16	0.00
Y7Y5	43	0.01	0.16	0.29
Y9Y7	41	0.01	0.09	0.70
Y12Y9	38	−0.03	0.13	−1.46
Y5Y1	45	0.04	0.48	0.53
Y9Y5	41	0.02	0.18	0.86
Y12Y9	38	−0.03	0.13	−1.46
Y6Y1	44	0.04	0.47	0.58
Y12Y6	38	−0.01	0.16	−0.21
Y12Y1	38	0.07	0.49	0.82

Note: YmYn denotes the revision from the nth estimate to the mth
estimate of the percent change in the CLI.

tive to the standard deviation of the percent-change CLI estimates. This
implies that all of the CLI growth rate estimates, and particularly that
of Y1, have large associated confidence intervals. The t-tests detect no
bias in any of the revisions.

If revisions are efficient forecast errors, then the variances of Y1
through Y12 should be monotonically increasing, because an efficient
forecast is necessarily smoother than the series being forecast. Conversely, if revisions are measurement errors, then the variances of Y1,
..., Y12 should be decreasing. The data do not distinguish these two

Table 14.3. *Revisions and revised values: correlations and P-values, 1983–7*

	Y1	Y5	Y9	Y12
Y5Y1	−0.23	0.33	0.28	0.28
	0.12	0.03	0.08	0.09
Y9Y5	0.00	−0.11	0.09	0.07
	0.98	0.48	0.56	0.69
Y12Y9	−0.06	−0.09	−0.15	−0.01
	0.72	0.60	0.35	0.97

Note: YmYn denotes the revision from the nth estimate to the mth estimate of the percent change in the CLI.

cases, as the estimated standard deviations of Y1, ..., Y12 display little variation.

Correlations between levels and three broad revisions are given in Table 14.3. Under the null of efficient forecast errors, the above-diagonal entries should be significant, while the below-diagonal entries should be insignificant. The table appears roughly consistent with the rational forecast error scenario; in particular, the entries of the first above-diagonal row of the table are significant at the 10 percent level and large in absolute value; for a more detailed analysis, see Diebold and Rudebusch (1988). The other above-diagonal entries are insignificant, perhaps because revisions after the fourth estimate contain little information, and the correlations cannot be estimated with precision.

The results for the earlier sample (1979–81) are quite different. There is a dropoff in variance as we move from Y1 to Y2 (Table 14.4) that is not consistent with forecast efficiency, and the correlations reported in Table 14.5 indicate a measurement error component, as evidenced by the lack of significant above-diagonal correlations as well as a highly significant below-diagonal correlation.

We interpret these results as indicating that the definitional change implemented in January 1983 significantly enhanced the statistical properties of the CLI revisions. One obvious source of measurement error in the preliminary estimate is that it is based on incomplete data, for not all component indicators are included in the preliminary (and sometimes even the second and third) releases. To the extent that better forecasts for the missing component indicators can be found, an element

Table 14.4. *Revisions in the composite leading index, 1979–81*

Variable	N	Mean	SD	T ratio
Y1	35	−.32	1.77	−1.07
Y2	34	−.24	1.55	−.88
Y3	33	−.26	1.57	−.96
Y4	32	−.23	1.56	−.84
Y5	31	−.15	1.57	−.53
Y6	30	−.17	1.60	−.58
Y7	29	−.20	1.62	−.68
Y8	28	−.20	1.61	−.64
Y9	27	−.14	1.64	−.44
Y10	26	−.14	1.61	−.45
Y11	25	−.16	1.61	−.48
Y12	24	−.21	1.64	−.63
Y3Y1	33	.08	.59	.79
Y5Y3	31	.01	.24	.15
Y7Y5	29	−.07	.13	−2.68
Y9Y7	27	−.01	.14	−.41
Y12Y9	24	.01	.21	.19
Y5Y1	31	.07	.57	.73
Y9Y5	27	−.08	.19	−2.03
Y12Y9	24	.01	.21	.19
Y6Y1	30	.04	.57	.42
Y12Y6	24	−.03	.27	−.61
Y12Y1	24	−.02	.74	−.14

Note: YmYn denotes the revision from the nth estimate to the mth estimate of the percent change in the CLI.

of measurement error is immediately introduced into the revisions. In the 1979–81 sample, two components, net business formation and the change in inventories, were not available for any of the preliminary numbers, and inventory change was also omitted from twenty-six of thirty-five first revisions and from one second revision. For the more recent sample from 1983–7, only the preliminary numbers suffer from omitted components.[3]

[3] After the most recent compositional redefinition of the CLI (see Hertzberg and Beckman, 1989), only components that will be available for the preliminary estimate were included in the newly reconstructed CLI.

Table 14.5. *Revisions and revised values: correlations and P-values, 1979–81*

	Y1	Y5	Y9	Y12
Y5Y1	−0.54	−0.25	−0.25	−0.23
	0.00	0.17	0.20	0.28
Y9Y5	−0.12	−0.13	−0.01	−0.03
	0.55	0.53	0.97	0.88
Y12Y9	−0.39	−0.37	−0.37	−0.26
	0.06	0.08	0.07	0.22

Note: YmYn denotes the revision from the nth estimate to the mth estimate of the percent change in the CLI.

14.4. Summary and conclusions

We have used a Bayesian algorithm to produce ex ante probability forecasts of peaks and troughs from the CLI. Most notably, the forecasts were constructed using the original preliminary data and revisions as they became available in real time. The forecasts were evaluated, and compared with ex post forecasts and forecasts generated by alternative methods, using proper probability forecast scoring rules. Finally, in order to better understand the differences between ex ante and ex post forecast performance, we characterized the properties of CLI revisions. Our main findings include the following:

1. A deterioration in turning point forecasting performance occurs when ex ante data are used, regardless of the forecasting method adopted. In the prediction of peaks, the real-time SPR maintains a small margin of superiority over its competitors. The deterioration in ex ante SPR forecast performance is relatively more severe for the prediction of troughs, leading to mixed results for comparative predictive ability, depending on the forecast horizon. The real-time SPR appears to maintain slight superiority at short horizons, but fares slightly worse than less sophisticated methods at longer horizons. This may be due simply to the short lengths of most contractions, so that good forecasting at long horizons is trivially simple (but not useful) merely by setting Π to a large enough value.

2. Deterioration in SPR forecast performance is due mostly to the move to ex ante data, as opposed to the use of rolling probability densities in the SPR. Examination reveals that the size and volatility of CLI revisions, both within and across definitional regimes, are high relative

to the magnitude of the revised percentage change in the CLI. Moreover, the CLI revisions appear to contain a measurement error component, which may be partially explained by the missing indicators in the preliminary CLI estimate. The measurement error component does not appear to be too severe in practice, however, and may be becoming less pronounced over time, due to beneficial definitional revisions.

3. There is no indication that turning point probabilities increase with the age of an expansion or contraction, in the period since World War II. Overall, postwar expansions and contractions show only weak, if any, duration dependence. This means that the transition probabilities used in the SPR, Γ_t^u and Γ_d^t, may be taken as approximately constant.

Appendix: Duration dependence in U.S. business cycles

Key elements of the SPR procedure for forecasting peaks and troughs are the probabilities of a turning point conditional only upon the expansion or contraction length-to-date. These probabilities, denoted by Γ_t^u during upswings and Γ_t^d during downswings, are the prior probabilities for the Bayesian recursion. Figure 14A.1 shows two examples of the possible relationship between the probability that an ongoing expansion will reach a peak and the age of that expansion.[4] The linear upward sloping hazard function (solid line, λ_2), which corresponds to a process with positive duration dependence, indicates that as an expansion progresses, the probability of a peak increases. The horizontal hazard (dashed line, λ_1), on the other hand, for which the transition probability is constant, corresponds to an absence of duration dependence. The resulting distributions of lengths of expansions and contractions are illustrated in Figure 14A.2. The duration distribution associated with the constant hazard is exponential. In discrete time, the distribution is geometric, with the probability of a regime of duration τ given by:

$$P(\text{duration} = \tau) = (1 - p)^{\tau-1}p \qquad (0 < p < 1) \qquad (A1)$$

where the probability p of a turning point is a constant. This is shown as the monotonically declining dashed line in Figure 14A.2. The duration distribution corresponding to the increasing hazard, on the other hand, is non-geometric; its explicit shape will depend on the explicit nature of the hazard. In general, however, its probability mass will be more concentrated than that of the geometric, an implication of the

---

[4] This same duration analysis applies to the probability of a trough and the age of the preceding contraction. However, the slope and position of the lines will differ across expansions and contractions to reflect different average regime lengths.

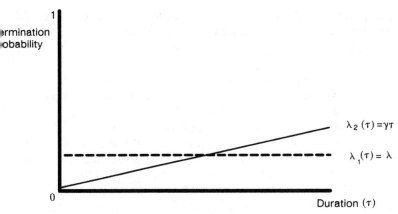

Figure 14.A1. Increasing and constant hazard functions.

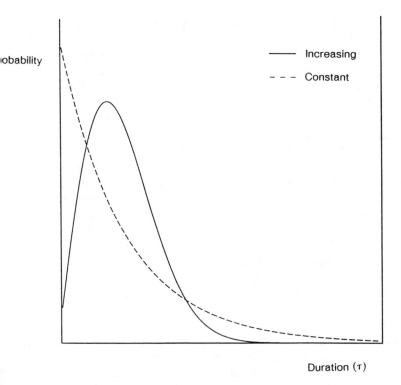

Figure 14.A2. Duration distributions associated with increasing and constant hazards.

turning point probability rising with duration length.[5] Consider, for example, the case of $p_\tau = \tau/100$; then the resulting density is

$$P(\text{duration} = \tau) = (1 - p_\tau)^{\tau-1} p_\tau \tag{A2}$$

which was used to generate the solid curve in Figure 14A.2. The hazard probability begins at .01 and rises by steps of .01 per period, leading to regime durations clustered around an intrinsic period.

We examine directly whether a histogram of historical duration lengths conforms to a geometric distribution, as it must under the non-periodic null hypothesis of constant turning point probabilities. Similar tests have been applied by McCulloch (1975), Savin (1977), and de Leeuw (1987). These studies are limited by the choice of a particular set of assumptions used in the construction of the histograms for the tests, which may account for the somewhat conflicting results obtained. We provide a sensitivity analysis exploring the whole range of possible assumptions.

We proceed as follows. For any given vector of expansion or contraction durations x, the data are first transformed by a minimum duration factor t_0 as $x^* = x - (t_0 - 1)$, which shifts the origin to reflect the length of the shortest possible regime. Minimum allowable expansion and contraction durations arise from definitional aspects of the NBER reference cycle dating procedure. Moore and Zarnowitz (1986), for example, indicate that expansions and contractions of less than six months would be very unlikely to qualify. (Note that under the geometric null, the unconditional distribution of τ is the same as the distribution of τ conditional on τ taking on a value greater than or equal to t_0.) Given the number of histogram bins K to be used, the bin width W is defined by $(x^*_{max} - x^*_{min})/K$, where x^*_{max} and x^*_{min} are the largest and smallest elements of the observed duration sequence x^*. The element, x^*_i, is grouped in bin n if $(x^*_{min} + (n - 1)W) \leq x^*_i < (x^*_{min} + nW)$. The histogram bin heights are computed by dividing the number of bin members by $N \cdot W$, that is, the duration sample size multiplied by the bin width.

We also compute exact finite sample confidence intervals under the geometric null. The maximum likelihood estimate of the hazard parameter of the best-fitting geometric distribution is $\hat{\lambda} = 1/\bar{x}^*$, where $\bar{x}^* = \sum_{i=1}^{N} x^*_i/N$ is the sample mean. A sample of N pseudorandom deviates is drawn from this geometric distribution, and the histogram with cell boundaries identical to the original is computed. (Generated deviates falling below x^*_{min} or above x^*_{max} are classified as members of bin 1 or bin

---

[5] This insight provides a link between the concepts of duration dependence and periodicity. See Diebold and Rudebusch (1990) for detailed discussion.

K, respectively.) This procedure is replicated 5,000 times. This allows construction of confidence intervals around individual bin heights. The goodness-of-fit test statistic also can be calculated as

$$S = \sum_{i=1}^{K} [(O_i - E_i)^2/E_i] \qquad (A3)$$

where O_i is the observed number of elements of bin i and E_i is the expected number of elements of bin i under the geometric null (the average across simulations). Using the 5,000 simulated samples as observations allows construction of the exact distribution of the test statistic, which for our small sample sizes typically deviates from its asymptotic χ^2 distribution.

The lengths of expansions and contractions (in months) are derived from the business cycle turning dates as designated by the National Bureau of Economic Research. The entire sample of thirty-one expansions and thirty contractions, every business cycle since 1854, is given in Table 14A.1. Nine different subsamples are considered, including pre- and post–World War II expansions and contractions, as well as peacetime expansions. We generally favor the entire expansion and contraction samples since, as pointed out by Romer (1986), the evidence of structural shift between the pre- and postwar economies is not completely convincing. The choice of a proper sample depends upon which cycles are considered part of the intrinsic structure of the economy and which are attributed to special non-cyclical events (e.g., wars). We also consider the sensitivity of our results to the number of histogram cells (K), two through five. Statistical theory provides some guide in the construction of a histogram as to the correct number of cells to be distinguished. Terrell and Scott (1985) show that the minimum number of cells required for an optimal histogram is[6]

$$K^* = \{(2N)^{1/3}\} \qquad (A4)$$

where the special brackets indicate rounding up to the nearest integer.[7] Histograms formed with this optimal minimum cell number have been shown to perform very well in practice. Finally, we consider a variety of

[6] The optimality is in terms of minimum deviation [in the Kullback-Liebler (1951) sense] of the estimated histogram cell heights from the true, but unknown, values of the probability distribution.

[7] The choice of cell number is important; too coarse a partition yields an uninformative distribution estimate, while too fine a partition yields a very jagged (and hence equally uninformative) estimate.

Table 14.A1. *NBER business cycle reference dates and durations*

Trough	Peak	Contraction	Expansion
December 1854	June 1857	NA	30
December 1858	October 1860	18	22
June 1861	April 1865	8	$\overline{46}$
December 1867	June 1869	32	$\overline{18}$
December 1870	October 1873	18	34
March 1879	March 1882	65	36
May 1885	March 1887	38	22
April 1888	July 1890	13	27
May 1891	January 1893	10	20
June 1894	December 1895	17	18
June 1897	June 1899	18	24
December 1900	September 1902	18	21
August 1904	May 1907	23	33
June 1908	January 1910	13	19
January 1912	January 1913	24	12
December 1914	August 1918	23	$\overline{44}$
March 1919	January 1920	7	$\overline{10}$
July 1921	May 1923	18	22
July 1924	October 1926	14	27
November 1927	August 1929	13	21
March 1933	May 1937	43	50
June 1938	February 1945	13	$\overline{80}$
October 1945	November 1948	8	$\overline{37}$
October 1949	July 1953	11	$\overline{45}$
May 1954	August 1957	10	$\overline{39}$
April 1958	April 1960	8	24
February 1961	December 1969	10	$\overline{106}$
November 1970	November 1973	11	$\overline{36}$
March 1975	January 1980	16	58
July 1980	July 1981	6	12
November 1982	?	16	72[a]

[a]The 72-month duration of the expansion beginning in November of 1982 is intended as a conservative estimate, implying that it ended in November 1988.
Note: Wartime expansions are underlined.

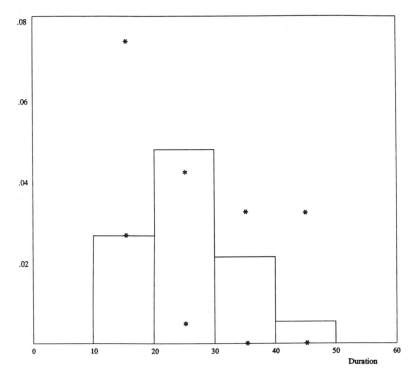

Figure 14.A3. Pre–World War II, peacetime expansions (E6).

minimum duration values. For each subsample, t_0 values up to the shortest expansion or contraction duration in that subsample are considered; in this way, we ensure that all values of x^* remain positive.

Probability-values (p-values) for the goodness-of-fit test statistic based on nonparametric distribution estimates are shown in Table 14A.3, and selected corresponding histograms are shown in Figures 14A.3, 14A.4, and 14A.5. The p-values represent the likelihood of obtaining the value of the test statistic actually obtained, under the geometric null of no duration dependence; large p-values therefore imply that the transition probabilities Γ^u and Γ^d should be invariant to the age of the ongoing regime. The range of samples investigated, denoted E1 through E6 and C1 through C3 for expansions and contractions, respectively, is identified in Table 14A.2.

In Table 14A.3 our choice for a single preferred p-value for each sample is underlined, though our conclusions based on these preferred prob-

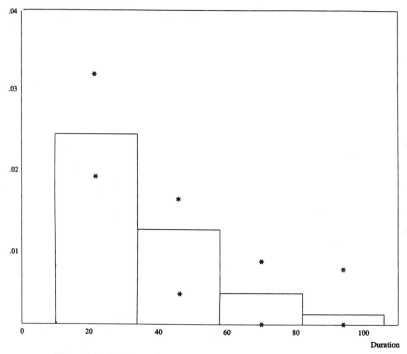

Figure 14.A4. Expansions, complete sample (E1).

abilities will always be tempered by their sensitivity to the number of histogram cells (K) used to characterize the distribution and the minimum duration values (t_0).[8] A reasonable choice for t_0 is the actual shortest observed duration, which is six months for contractions, the length of the 1980 contraction, and ten months for expansions. Our preferred cell number is the Terrell-Scott optimal bin number. Setting $K = K^*$ for our samples implies that observations should be grouped into four cells for all samples except the postwar ones, where three cells should be used.

Of the underlined p-values for the nine samples investigated in Table 14A.3, only one indicates significant duration dependence at the 5 percent level. This is sample E6, the set of all prewar, peacetime expansions. However, for the sample of all prewar expansions, duration dependence

---

[8] Previous researchers, such as McCulloch, Savin, or de Leeuw, have essentially focused on only a few of the entries in Table 14A.3, without an examination of the sensitivity of the results to their assumptions.

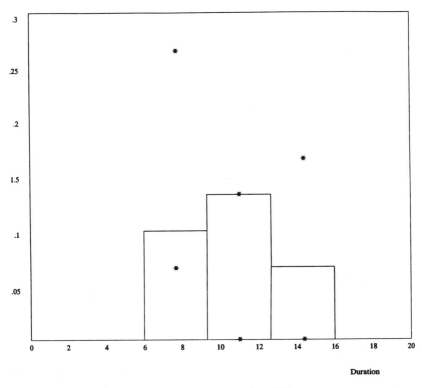

Figure 14.A5. Post–World War II contractions (C2).

Table 14.A2. *Business cycle subsamples investigated, with associated size*

Sample	Sample size
Expansions	
E1. Entire sample	31
E2. Entire sample, excluding wars	26
E3. Post–World War II	9
E4. Post–World War II, excluding wars	7
E5. Pre–World War II	21
E6. Pre–World War II, excluding wars	19
Contractions	
C1. Entire sample	30
C2. Pre–World War II	21
C3. Post–World War II	9

Table 14.A3. *Goodness-of-fit tests, expansion, and contraction samples (probability values under the geometric null)*

		Sample								
K	t_0	E1	E2	E3	E4	E5	E6	C1	C2	C3
2	4	.47	.17	.47	.71	.82	.80	.77	.49	.77
2	5	.47	.15	.47	.70	.82	.80	.76	.51	.76
2	6	.47	.14	.46	.70	.82	.79	.77	.51	.75
2	7	.62	.13	.47	.70	.82	.80	NA	NA	.77
2	8	.61	.21	.46	.71	.82	.80	NA	NA	NA
2	9	.62	.21	.72	.70	.82	.80	NA	NA	NA
2	10	.80	.21	.71	.69	.64	.79	NA	NA	NA
2	11	NA	NA	.72	.69	NA	NA	NA	NA	NA
2	12	NA	NA	.71	.69	NA	NA	NA	NA	NA
3	4	.78	.40	.60	.25	.14	.03	.48	.04	.63
3	5	.78	.48	.60	.25	.17	.06	.59	.06	.65
3	6	.85	.49	.64	.25	.26	.07	.63	<u>.20</u>	.64
3	7	.85	.58	.66	.33	.27	.09	NA	NA	.74
3	8	.91	.62	.66	.33	.35	.14	NA	NA	NA
3	9	.91	.65	.65	.38	.46	.14	NA	NA	NA
3	10	.96	.75	<u>.73</u>	<u>.37</u>	.50	.21	NA	NA	NA
3	11	NA	NA	.72	.37	NA	NA	NA	NA	NA
3	12	NA	NA	.74	.41	NA	NA	NA	NA	NA
4	4	.55	.15	.05	.23	.01	.00	.82	.60	.98
4	5	.61	.18	.05	.25	.01	.00	.84	.79	.98
4	6	.68	.22	.08	.28	.02	.01	<u>.77</u>	.91	<u>.96</u>
4	7	.72	.27	.09	.30	.03	.01	NA	NA	.96
4	8	.75	.32	.10	.33	.05	.02	NA	NA	NA
4	9	.79	.38	.11	.35	.09	.03	NA	NA	NA
4	10	<u>.85</u>	<u>.44</u>	.13	.40	<u>.13</u>	<u>.04</u>	NA	NA	NA
4	11	NA	NA	.13	.47	NA	NA	NA	NA	NA
4	12	NA	NA	.14	.45	NA	NA	NA	NA	NA
5	4	.45	.59	.34	.09	.00	.00	.95	.01	.93
5	5	.51	.67	.39	.10	.00	.00	.97	.04	.92
5	6	.58	.72	.43	.13	.00	.00	.97	.11	.92
5	7	.64	.79	.45	.15	.00	.00	NA	NA	.87
5	8	.69	.85	.51	.18	.01	.00	NA	NA	NA
5	9	.74	.90	.55	.18	.02	.01	NA	NA	NA
5	10	.80	.95	.59	.21	.04	.02	NA	NA	NA
5	11	NA	NA	.67	.23	NA	NA	NA	NA	NA
5	12	NA	NA	.70	.26	NA	NA	NA	NA	NA

Note: The definition of samples and sample key is given in Table 14.A2. Our preferred (K, t_0) combination for each sample is underlined. NA = not applicable.

is also significant at the 5 percent level when a slightly smaller t_0 value is used or when observations are placed into five cells. The nonparametric duration distribution estimate for sample E6 is shown in Figure 14A.3 (where $K = 4$ and $t_0 = 10$). For each histogram cell, the high and low points of the 95 percent confidence interval for that individual cell height under the geometric null are indicated by asterisks (*). The distribution of prewar, peacetime expansions shows a clear peak, representing a clustering of durations, unlike a steadily declining geometric distribution. In contrast, for the sample of all expansions, shown in Figure 14A.4, the cell heights are not significantly different from their values under the geometric null, as suggested by the associated p-value of .81; a similar distributional shape is found for the sample of all contractions (not shown). The p-value for postwar contractions is rather small, especially for slightly smaller t_0 values, although the null is not rejected at conventional significance levels. The nonparametric distribution estimate for this sample (with $K = 3$, $t_0 = 6$), given in Figure 14A.5 shows a small, insignificant peak, though our ability to discriminate between alternatives is limited by the small sample.

The sample period that is relevant for our forecasting evaluation is the postwar period, and there is little evidence of duration dependence in postwar expansions and contractions.[9] Obviously, our failure to reject the geometric null hypothesis does not imply its acceptance; nevertheless, if duration dependence is present, it would appear to be a very weak phenomenon.

---

[9] This result does not necessarily imply, however, that business fluctuations amount to "Monte Carlo cycles," as claimed by McCulloch. In particular, entire business cycles (peak-to-peak or trough-to-trough) may display strong duration dependence even though expansions and contractions do not. See Diebold and Rudebusch (1990) and Zarnowitz (1987).

REFERENCES

Brier, G. W. (1950), "Verification of Forecasts Expressed in Terms of Probability," *Monthly Weather Review, 75*, 1–3.
de Leeuw, F. (1987), "Do Expansions Have Memory?," Discussion Paper No. 16, U.S. Department of Commerce, Bureau of Economic Analysis.
Diebold, F. X. and G. D. Rudebusch (1988), "Stochastic Properties of Revisions in the Index of Leading Indicators," In *Papers and Proceedings of the American Statistical Association, Business and Economic Statistics Section, 1987*. Washington, D.C.: American Statistical Association.
(1989a), "Scoring the Leading Indicators," *Journal of Business, 62*, 369–91.
(1989b), "Forecasting Output with the Composite Leading Index: An Ex Ante Analysis," FEDS Working Paper, Federal Reserve Board.

(1990), "A Nonparametric Investigation of Duration Dependence in the American Business Cycle," *Journal of Political Economy 98*, 596–616.

Hamilton, J. D. (1989), "A New Approach to the Economic Analysis of Non-stationary Time Series and the Business Cycle," *Econometrica, 57*, 357–84.

Hertzberg, M. P., and B. A. Beckman (1989), "Business Cycle Indicators: Revised Composite Indexes," *Business Conditions Digest, 29*, 97–102.

Howrey, E. P. (1978), "The Use of Preliminary Data in Econometric Forecasting," *Review of Economics and Statistics, 60*, 193–200.

Hymans, S. H. (1973), "On the use of Leading Indicators to Predict Cyclical Turning Points," *Brookings Papers on Economic Activity, 2*, 339–84.

Kullback, S., and R. A. Liebler (1951), "On Information and Sufficiency," *Annals of Mathematical Statistics, 22*, 79–86.

Mankiw, N. G., D. E. Runkle, and M. D. Shapiro (1984), "Are Preliminary Estimates of the Money Stock Rational Forecasts?," *Journal of Monetary Economics, 14*, 15–27.

Mankiw, N. G., and M. D. Shapiro (1986), "News or Noise? An Analysis of GNP Revisions," *Survey of Current Business*, May.

McCulloch, J. H. (1975), "The Monte Carlo-Cycle in Business Activity," *Economic Inquiry, 13*, 303–21.

Moore, G. H., and V. Zarnowitz (1986), "The Development and Role of the National Bureau of Economic Research's Business Cycle Chronologies," in R. J. Gordon, ed., *The American Business Cycle*. Chicago: University of Chicago Press.

Neftci, S. N. (1982), "Optimal Prediction of Cyclical Downturns," *Journal of Economic Dynamics and Control, 4*, 225–41.

Romer, C. D. (1986), "Is the Stabilization of the Postwar Economy a Figment of the Data?," *American Economic Review, 76*, 314–34.

Savin, N. E. (1977), "A Test of the Monte Carlo Hypothesis: Comment," *Economic Inquiry, 15*, 613–17.

Shiryayev, A. N. (1978), *Optimal Stopping Rules*. New York: Springer-Verlag.

Stekler, H. O., and M. Schepsman (1973), "Forecasting with an Index of Leading Series," *Journal of the American Statistical Association, 68*, 291–6.

Terrell, G. R., and D. W. Scott (1985), "Oversmoothed Nonparametric Density Estimates," *Journal of the American Statistical Association, 80*, 209–14.

Vaccara, B., and V. Zarnowitz (1977), "How Good are the Leading Indicators?," *Proceedings of the American Statistical Association, Business and Economic Statistics Section, 1976*. Washington, D.C.: American Statistical Association.

Wecker, W. E. (1979), "Predicting the Turning Points of a Time Series," *Journal of Business, 52*, 35–50.

Zarnowitz, V. (1987), "The Regularity of Business Cycles," National Bureau of Economic Research Working Paper No. 2381.

Zarnowitz, V., and G. H. Moore (1982), "Sequential Signals of Recession and Recovery," *Journal of Business, 55*, 57–85.

CHAPTER 15

Forecasting recessions under the Gramm-Rudman-Hollings law

Victor Zarnowitz and Geoffrey H. Moore

The Gramm-Rudman-Hollings (GRH) law passed by the Congress in December 1985 establishes a process whereby the Federal budget deficits are to be gradually phased out by the fiscal year (FY) 1991. A series of targeted ceilings on the unified budget deficit is instituted, beginning with $172 billion for FY 1986 and $144 billion for FY 1987 and proceeding by decrements of $36 billion per year to zero in FY 1991. The planned reductions are to be achieved by spending and tax measures agreed upon by the legislative and executive branches of the U.S. government. However, if an agreement is not reached, the target for any FY is to be achieved through an automatic across-the-board spending cut in all eligible defense and nondefense categories. Early in 1986 a lower court ruled that the sequestering provision of GRH is unconstitutional; this ruling was confirmed by the Supreme Court on July 7, 1986. This does not pertain to the issues discussed in this paper.

Section 254 of the GRH law provides for "Special Procedures in the Event of a Recession." It states that the Congressional Budget Office (CBO) Director shall notify the Congress at any time (a) if the CBO or the Office of Management and Budget (OMB) "has determined that real economic growth is projected or estimated to be less than zero with respect to each of any two consecutive quarters" within a period of six successive quarters starting with the one preceding such notification, or

We are indebted to Jean Tesche for statistical assistance on this paper and to Christine Verhaaren for typing. A grant from the Sterling National Bank and Trust Co. to the Center for International Business Cycle Research helped to support the work. An earlier version of the paper was presented at the Sixth International Symposium on Forecasting in Paris on June 16, 1986. The research reported here is part of the NBER's research program in Economic Fluctuations. Any opinions expressed are those of the authors and not those of the National Bureau of Economic Research.

(b) "if the Department of Commerce preliminary report of actual real economic growth (or any subsequent revision thereof) indicates that the rate of real economic growth for each of the most recent reported quarter and the immediately preceding quarter is less than one percent."

Upon receiving the CBO Director's notification, both houses of Congress commit themselves to procedures designed to suspend several GRH provisions. These concern the maximum deficits for the current and the next fiscal year, and the corresponding spending and revenue levels.

In short, the targeted deficit reductions are to be suspended when a recession is either (a) forecasted by CBO or OMB or both, or (b) reported as being under way by the Bureau of Economic Analysis (BEA) in the U.S. Department of Commerce. This is important since the spending cuts and/or tax increases needed to produce the deficit reductions might seriously aggravate the recession. And the probability that a recession will occur at some time during the long period between the present and the end of FY 1991 must certainly be viewed as rather high.

This chapter addresses three questions in the following order:

1. How accurately and promptly has the Department of Commerce report that real GNP growth fell below 1 percent in two consecutive quarters identified previous business recessions? This is an attempt to trace the implications of provision (b) above with the aid of historical data.
2. What can reasonably be expected from the past record of economic forecasters with respect to their ability to predict a recession defined as two consecutive quarters of decline in real GNP? This is a similar attempt to trace the implications of provision (a) above.
3. How do the foregoing results compare with alternative signals of recession based upon leading indicators and employment data?

15.1   Defining and recognizing recessions

The conditions under which the deficit reductions otherwise mandated under GRH would be suspended imply two alternative definitions of a business recession. One of these requires at least two consecutive quarters during which "real economic growth" stays below zero: this refers to the CBO or OMB forecasts. The other, used with reference to the BEA reports, is a sequence of at least two quarters with growth rates of less than 1 percent. It is clear from the language employed in some earlier sections of the law that the criterion in both cases is growth of GNP in constant dollars.[1] The difference between the two definitions suggests that the legislators may have thought that forecasts of negative growth were more likely to identify actual recessions than forecasts of very low but still positive growth.

We abstract for the time being from forecasting and address the problems of defining and recognizing recessions from data limited to the quarterly series on output of the U.S. economy (GNP in constant dollars). One difficulty here is that some generally recognized recessions have not been marked by two consecutive declines in this series. Thus in 1960 total U.S. output fell in the second and fourth quarters but not in the third quarter, and in 1980 it fell in the second quarter only (Table 15.1). In these cases, then, the criterion of two successive declines in real GNP would have produced no recognition of a recession at all. However, in both these instances the criterion of two quarters of less than 1 percent growth was met, which may account for the alternative definition in GRH. Nevertheless, any individual indicator series, even one as comprehensive and important as GNP, can measure only some of the aspects of aggregate economic activity. Also, all such series contain measurement errors that are in part independent and revealed by data revisions. For these reasons, business cycles are better identified from the consensus of key macroeconomic indicators for employment, production, real income, and real sales than from any single one of these series. The National Bureau of Economic Research (NBER) has always relied on this principle in developing its much tested and widely accepted chronology of recessions and recoveries. The peak and trough dates in our tables are those determined by NBER.

Table 15.1 compares the recessions as dated by NBER (columns 1–3) with periods of two or more consecutive quarters during which the economy grew less than 1 percent (seasonally adjusted annual rate). Ten such sequences of low or negative growth rates occurred in the presently available (June 1986) series of real GNP for 1948–82 (part A, column 4), whereas the number of concurrent business cycle contractions is eight. Thus the GRH definition that counts low rises along with declines in total output yields two additional "recessions." One of these relates

---

[1] Both the House Amendment and the Senate Amendment in section VI ("Economic Conditions") of GRH contain similar provisions regarding the predicted and actual real growth rates. The House version also referred to the event that the average rate of unemployment for two consecutive months is 1 percent above the same two months for the previous year, but this particular trigger was dropped in the Conference Agreement (see Congressional Record-House, December 10, 1985, p. H-11710).

Table 15.1. *Lags in recognizing recessions under the GRH criterion for real GNP growth (two consecutive quarters below 1 percent)*

Business cycle recession		Recession duration (months)	Growth in real GNP (1982 $) from preceding quarter[b]	Peak signal date[c]	Data release date[d]	Lead (−) or lag (+), months	
Peak (1)	Trough (2)	(3)	(4)	(5)	(6)	Signal[e] (7)	Recognition[f] (8)
A. Based on the present historical real GNP data[a]							
11/48	10/49	11	I49 II49 −4.6 −2.3	11/48	7/49	0	+8
7/53	5/54	10	III53 IV53 I54 II54 −1.9 −3.2 −5.4 −1.6	5/53	1/54	−2	+6
8/57	4/58	8	IV57 I58 −6.1 −7.9	8/57	4/58	0	+8
4/60	2/61	10	II60 III60 IV60 −1.1 0.4 −3.4	2/60	10/60	−2	+6
12/69	11/70	11	IV69 I70 II70 −1.6 −2.4 −0.3	8/69	4/70	−4	+4
11/73	3/75	16	III74 IV74 I75 −5.1 −3.5 −7.6	5/74	1/75	+6	+14
1/80	7/80	6	I79 II79[g] 0.0 −0.4 II80 III80 −9.1 0.3	11/78	7/79	−14[i]	−6[i]
				2/80	10/80	+1	+9

7/81	11/82	16	IV81 I82[h] −5.5 −5.9 / III82 IV82 −3.2 0.6	8/81	4/82	+1	+9
				5/82	1/83	+10[i]	+18[i]
Mean (SD)	11 (4)					0 (3)	+8 (3)

B. Based on the earliest available preliminary data[j]

I. Nominal GNP[k]

11/48	10/49	11	I49 II49 III49 IV49 / −12.0 −10.1 −5.2 1.0	11/48	7/49	0	+8
7/53	5/54	10	III53 IV53 I54 II54 / −2.1 −6.7 −6.4 0.2	5/53	1/54	−2	+6
8/57	4/58	8	IV57 I58 / −6.9 −10.2	8/57	4/58	0	+8
4/60	2/61	10	II60 III60 IV60 / −1.2 0.0 −3.0	2/60	10/60	−2[i]	+6[i]

II. Real GNP[k]

4/60	2/61	10	III60 IV60 I61 / −3.8 −0.9 −3.5	5/60	1/61	+1	+9
12/69	11/70	11	IV69 I70 II70 / −0.4 −1.6 −1.4	8/69	4/70	−4	+4
11/73	3/75	16	I74 II74 III74 IV74 I75 II75 / −6.1 −1.9 −2.6 −9.5 −11.1 −1.5	11/73	7/74	0	+8
1/80	7/80	6	II80 III80 / −9.6 +0.3	2/80	10/80	+1	+9

Table 15.1. (cont.)

Business cycle recession Peak (1)	Trough (2)	Recession duration (months) (3)	Growth in real GNP (1982 $) from preceding quarter[b] (4)	Peak signal date[c] (5)	Data release date[d] (6)	Lead (−) or lag (+), months Signal[e] (7)	Recognition[f] (8)
7/81	11/82	16	IV81 I82[l] −4.5 −3.9	8/81	4/82	+1	+9
			III82 IV82 0.0 −1.1	5/82	1/83	+10[i]	+18[i]
Mean (SD)		11 (4)				0 (2)	+8 (2)

[a] From the February 1986 issue of *Business Conditions Digest* (BCD).

[b] The identified periods include all those with at least two consecutive quarters of growth less than 1 percent at seasonally adjusted annual rate (SAAR).

[c] Mid-month of the quarter preceding the quarter with real growth rate of less than 1 percent (see the first listing in column 4).

[d] Assumed to be the first month following the second quarter with real growth of less than 1 percent (see the second listing in column 4).

[e] Measured from the monthly business cycle peak date (column 1) to the peak signal date (column 5).

[f] Measured from the monthly business cycle peak date (column 1) to the data release date (column 6).

[g] The intervening quarters, III79, IV79, and I80, had growth rates of 3.7 percent, −0.8 percent, and 4.1 percent, respectively.

[h] The intervening quarter, II82, had a growth rate of 1.2 percent.

[i] Excluded from the averages shown below.

[j] Compiled from successive issues of the *Survey of Current Business* (SCB) and BCD.

[k] Real GNP estimates were first published in SCB October 1959 and in the biennial supplement to SCB *Business Statistics*, 1959 edition. Hence nominal GNP estimates only are used here for the period 1948–58. For 1960 and 1961 both nominal and real GNP estimates are used. See text.

[l] The intervening quarter, II82, had a growth rate of 1.7 percent according to preliminary data (from BCD, July 1982).

to a mild two-quarter slowdown that preceded the downturn of January 1980 by about a year, a serious discrepancy. The other merely involves a single-quarter interruption of the 1981–2 decline in real GNP. When the two episodes are excluded, the peak signal dates from the historical series (mid-months of quarters preceding the low-growth periods, see column 5) are found to be on the average coincident with the business cycle peaks. The range of these timing comparisons is from a lead of four months to a lag of six months; the standard deviation is three months (column 7).

For a time, the earliest estimates for GNP were published in the last month of the quarter as the "flash report," based on very incomplete data and often subject to large revisions. Now the first report is published in the first month of the following quarter, and in the earlier years the publication lags were longer. In Table 15.1, the effective data release dates are taken to fall in the month following the second quarter with real growth of less than 1 percent (column 6). The recognition lags, measured from the reference peak dates to these data release dates, are listed in the last column of the table; excepting the two false signals noted before, their range is +4 to +14, with a mean of +8 and standard deviation of three months. For six of the seven recessions, the recognition lag was at least six months. These results are about what one would expect, given the requirement of at least two successive quarters of very low or negative growth, the roughly coincident cyclical timing of real GNP, and the informational delays involved.

Of course, the data used in Table 15.1, part A were not available to anyone who would have tried to recognize recessions at the time they occurred. Part B of the table is based on preliminary data that would have been available to contemporary observers. Quarterly estimates of real GNP began to be published regularly in 1959, and so for 1948–58 only the rates of change in current-dollar GNP are used. Price changes were moderate in this period (except in 1950), and indeed the results are identical with those based on the present data for real GNP (compare the first four lines, columns 5–8, in parts A and B of the table). Preliminary data based on incomplete information often have large extrapolative components, and they share with forecasts the tendency to underestimate actual change (Cole 1969; Zarnowitz 1982), but here the early estimates produce results that are very close to those obtained with the last revised estimates. The mean signal and recognition lags in part B are 0 and +8, respectively, the same as in part A; the standard deviations are somewhat smaller.

To sum up, mere monitoring of the data on real GNP growth cannot produce prompt recognition of recessions. The typical range of the delays involved in the process is about six to nine months, by which time the recession itself may nearly be over. (Business cycle contractions since 1948 ranged from six to sixteen months and averaged eleven months.) The length of the recognition lags is very little affected by whether a recession is defined as two consecutive quarterly declines in real GNP or as two quarters of growth below 1 percent. Also, the conclusion that the lags tend to be long relative to the length of recessions holds regardless of whether preliminary or revised data are used.

The events that must occur for the deficit cuts to be suspended are exactly stipulated in GRH, but there appears to be nothing specific in the law about the mechanism for ending a decreed suspension. Presumably, the deficit reductions will resume when the legislators recognize that the conditions which triggered the suspension no longer exist, but how promptly would this happen in response to what signals? Suppose that the recognition that a recession is over required two consecutive quarters of positive growth in real GNP to follow each of the sequences listed in Table 15.1, column 4. Then substantial delays in recognizing a recovery would be likely; for the eight business cycle troughs of 1949–82 such lags would have ranged from five to ten months and averaged eight months, using the present data. A better rule to follow would be to assume that the recovery is on as soon as it is known that output increased at an annual rate of more than 1 percent for a single quarter after a period of a recognized recession. This criterion would have come fairly close to most of the trough dates of recessions, reducing the average recognition lag to three months. However, some false signals of troughs would have resulted, as illustrated by the rise of real GNP in II82 (see Table 15.1, footnotes *h* and *l*).

15.2   Forecasting recessions

The meaning of the long recognition lags listed in Table 15.1 is that any signals from the actual data on real GNP growth would have been much too tardy for the purposes envisaged in the recession-related provisions of GRH. If Congress had to rely on such signals, it would be likely to suspend the deficit cuts at best only late in a recession. By then the fiscal tightness required by GRH would have already done its harm in contributing to the business contraction. The suspension might still help in hastening the end of the decline, but it could also be sufficiently mistimed to overstimulate the economy during the following recovery and expansion.

Clearly, it is only timely and accurate forecasts of an approaching recession that could provide the right warnings when needed. Studies have repeatedly shown that combining predictions from diverse sources and methods often results in significant gains in accuracy. That is, the consensus forecasts from surveys are typically more accurate than most of the individual forecasters polled (Zarnowitz, 1984), when accuracy is measured over a considerable period of time. The record of such group averages in predicting the major macroeconomic variables is often as good as or better than that of the principal econometric forecasting models (McNees, 1973, 1979). These research findings are based on the median forecasts from the surveys conducted quarterly since 1968 by the American Statistical Association (ASA) and NBER. For this chapter we shall use the consensus forecasts of real GNP growth both from the ASA-NBER quarterly survey and from the well-known Blue Chip Economic Indicators monthly survey. The results should compare reasonably well with what might be expected from the CBO and OMB forecasts that are required under the GRH law.

Fifteen of the quarterly ASA-NBER surveys since 1968 can be linked to recessions as defined by GRH (Table 15.2). Six of these predicted that real GNP would turn down and fall for at least two consecutive quarters during the year ahead, while nine predicted that a decline shown by the preliminary data for one or more previous quarters would continue for at least one more quarter. Estimates of actual change are listed for two quarters (Q_{-1}, Q_0) preceding the quarter Q_1 in which the survey was taken (columns 4–6). The median survey forecasts of real growth in the five successive quarters covered by each survey $(Q_1–Q_5)$ are shown next (columns 7–11). Signal leads or lags (column 14) measure the intervals between the peak dates implied by the configurations of the estimates and forecasts (column 12) and the business cycle peak dates determined by NBER (column 1). Recognition leads or lags (column 15) measure the intervals between the survey release dates (column 13) and the business cycle peak dates.[2]

The *first* signals of peaks that did subsequently occur and the corresponding recognition lags are included in the averages shown on the bottom line. The other entries in the last two columns are put in parentheses and excluded from the averages. Most of these are *secondary* signals that merely confirm the initial ones, but in 1979 a recession was repeatedly predicted that did not happen in that year and these signal and recognition leads, marked F, are also excluded. It is important to note, however, that these false warnings could not be readily recognized as

---

[2] The survey questionnaire is mailed by the ASA in the middle month of each quarter to a list of persons who are professionally engaged in forecasting the course of the economy. The replies are sent to and examined by the NBER, and regular reports on the results are released in the third month. This survey was discontinued in 1990.

Table 15.2. *Forecasting recessions under the criterion of two consecutive declines in real GNP, ASA-NBER survey medians, 1969–82*

Business cycle recession		Recession duration (months) (3)	Preliminary actual changes[a]			Forecasts of changes in successive quarters[b]					Peak signal date[c] (12)	Survey release date[d] (13)	Lead (−) or lag (−), months	
Peak (1)	Trough (2)		2nd previous quarter (Q_{-1}) Date (4)	Percent (5)	Previous quarter (Q_0) (6)	Q_1 (7)	Q_2 (8)	Q_3 (9)	Q_4 (10)	Q_5 (11)			Signal[e] (14)	Recognition[f] (15)
12/69	11/70	11	IV69	−0.4	−1.6	−1.2	2.8	4.5	3.2	13.0	8/69	6/70	−4	+5
11/73	3/75	16	III73	3.4	1.3	−2.4	−0.4	2.4	3.6	4.5	11/73	3/74	0	+4
			IV73	1.6	−5.8	−0.4	2.0	4.1	3.2	3.6	11/73	6/74	(0)	(+7)
			II74	−1.6	−2.9	−4.5	−2.4	1.6	2.8	4.9	11/73	12/74	(0)	(+13)
			III74	−1.9	−9.1	−6.6	0.0	3.2	5.3	5.7	11/73	3/75	(0)	(+16)
			IV74	−9.6	−11.2	−1.2	3.6	6.1	5.3	6.1	11/73	6/75	(0)	(+19)
1/80	7/80	6	III78	2.6	6.1	2.4	1.2	−1.2	−0.8	2.8	5/79	3/79	(−8)F	(−10)F
			IV78	6.9	0.7	1.6	−1.2	−1.6	1.6	0.4	5/79	6/79	(−8)F	(−7)F
			I79	1.1	−3.3	−1.6	−3.2	−1.2	2.0	3.6	2/79	9/79	(−13)F	(−4)F
			II79	−2.3	2.4	−1.6	−4.1	−2.8	1.6	3.2	8/79	12/79	−5	−1
			III79	3.1	1.4	0.4	−2.8	−0.8	1.2	2.0	2/80	3/80	(+1)	(+2)
			IV79	2.0	1.1	−5.3	−4.1	−1.2	2.4	3.2	2/80	6/80	(+1)	(+5)
			I80	1.2	−9.1	−4.5	−0.8	3.2	3.2	4.1	2/80	9/80	(+1)	(+8)
7/81	11/82	16	II81	−1.6	−0.6	−3.6	−0.8	3.6	4.9	4.9	2/81	12/81	−5	+5
			III81	1.4	−5.2	−2.8	2.4	4.5	4.9	2.8	8/81	3/82	(+1)	(+8)
Mean (SD)		12 (5)											−4 (2)	+3 (3)

[a] Based on the data available to the forecasters. Q_0 = quarter preceding the survey quarter (Q_1). Entries in columns 5–6 are at annual rates.

[b] Taken from ASA-NBER quarterly forecast releases. Quarterly percentage changes given in the source are converted to compound annual rates.

[c] Mid-month of the quarter preceding the first quarter in which real GNP declined.

[d] Last month of the survey quarter (Q_1).

[e] Measured from the business cycle peak date (column 1) to the peak signal date (column 12). The leads or lags in parentheses refer to secondary signals and are excluded from the averages below. F = false signal.

such at the time and might have been seriously misleading, although a brief recession did occur in 1980.

The forecasters as a group did not perform well in predicting the 1969–70 recession, according to the present criteria. In November 1969 their average forecast for IV69 was − 1.2% which correctly captured the timing of the peak, but the predicted decline was to last one quarter only. In February 1970 no further downward movement was anticipated. The May 1970 survey is the first to qualify under the criterion of two consecutive quarterly declines. Hence the recognition lag was six months, whereas the corresponding recognition lag in Table 15.1 was 4 months.

The survey taken in February 1974 predicted negative growth rates for both I74 and II74. Hence the forecast yields a lag of four months at the business cycle peak of November 1973, much less than the recognition lag of eight months based on preliminary actual data (Table 15.1, part B). Moreover, according to the presently available revised data the recognition lag was fourteen months (Table 15.1, part A).

This brings up an important point. The GNP data are subject to long series of revisions which are frequently large relative to the quarterly changes. Compared with the "final" figures, the preliminary estimates of growth in the nation's output are sometimes about as much in error as the earlier forecasts of growth. In large part, the measurement errors involved are occasioned by major benchmark revisions related to censuses taken at intervals of several years or by changes in the base year of the constant price estimates. Neither the forecasters nor the data compilers themselves can reasonably be expected to predict such revisions. Since the final data may not be known for years, they can hardly be of much help on a current basis to economic analysts and forecasters.

During 1979, when economic activity ceased to grow after four years of expansion, many economists repeatedly predicted a downturn too soon. Thus the surveys of February, May, and August 1979 produced median forecasts of declines that did not happen (F). But the same episode also produced the earliest correct peak forecasts in the November 1979 survey as the long-anticipated downturn materialized at the beginning of 1980. The signal and recognition *leads* of five and one months, respectively, contrast with *lags* of one and nine months in Table 15.1.[3]

Finally, the downturn of July 1981 was not anticipated earlier that

---

[3] Recall that real GNP declined only in one quarter (II80) during the short recession of January–July 1980 so that the "less than 1 percent growth" rule must be invoked in Table 15.1 to identify this particular peak. But the same rule, when applied to the present revised data, yields in this case a lead of six months (Table 15.1, part A)! This is because these data show zero growth in I79 and a slight decline in II79.

Table 15.3. *Forecasting recessions under the criterion of two consecutive declines in real GNP, Blue Chips survey means, 1979–82*

| Business cycle recession | | Recession duration (months) | Preliminary Actual Changes[a] | | | Forecasts of changes in successive quarters[b] | | | | | Peak signal date[c] | Survey release date[d] | Lead (−) or lag (+), months | |
| Peak (1) | Trough (2) | (3) | 2nd previous quarter (Q_{-1}) | | Previous quarter (Q_0) | Q_1 | Q_2 | Q_3 | Q_4 | Q_5 | | | Signal[e] | Recognition[f] |
			Date (4)	Percent (5)	(6)	(7)	(8)	(9)	(10)	(11)	(12)	(13)	(14)	(15)
1/80	7/80	6	III78	2.6	6.9	2.5	1.4	−0.9	−0.6	0.3	5/79	4/79	(−8)	(−9)F
			III78	2.6	6.9	1.5	2.7	−0.2	−0.7	0.4	5/79	5/79	(−8)	(−8)F
			IV78	6.9	0.4	1.7	−0.5	−1.3	−0.1	1.9	5/79	6/79	(−8)	(−7)F
			IV78	6.9	0.8	−0.9	−1.2	−1.5	0.3	1.9	2/79	7/79	(−11)	(−6)F
			I79	1.1	−3.3	−1.2	−2.4	−0.1	2.1	3.5	2/79	8/79	(−11)	(−5)F
			I79	1.1	−2.4	−1.5	−2.7	−0.2	1.9	3.3	2/79	9/79	(−11)	(−4)F
			I79	1.1	−2.3	0.4	−2.3	−1.6	1.0	3.2	8/79	10/79	(−5)	(−3)F
			II79	−2.3	2.4	−1.4	−3.3	−1.7	1.6	3.1	8/79	11/79	−5	−2
			II79	−2.3	3.5	−1.5	−3.8	−2.1	1.2	3.0	8/79	12/79	(−5)	(−1)
			II79	−2.3	3.1	0.3	−3.4	−2.9	0.3	2.3	11/79	1/80	(−2)	(0)
			III79	3.1	1.4	−1.5	−2.4	−0.3	2.1	NA[a]	11/79	2/80	(−2)	(+1)
			III79	3.1	2.1	0.4	−1.9	−0.9	0.7	NA	2/80	3/80	(+1)	(+2)
			III79	3.1	2.0	1.3	−2.1	−3.1	−0.7	1.0	2/80	4/80	(+1)	(+3)

IV79	2.0		1.1		−3.5	−4.0	−1.9	0.2	NA	2/80	5/80	(+1) (+3)
IV79	2.0		0.6		−7.0	−4.4	−1.2	1.3	2.9	2/80	6/80	(+1) (+5)
IV79	2.0		1.2		−8.2	−4.8	−1.2	1.9	3.3	2/80	7/80	(+1) (+6)
I80	1.2		−9.1		−4.4	−0.8	2.3	3.3	4.0	2/80	8/80	(+1) (+7)
I80	1.2		−9.0		−3.3	0.1	2.1	3.4	4.4	2/80	9/80	(+1) (+8)
I81	8.6		−1.9		−0.7	2.6	3.8	4.1	4.7	2/81	8/81	−5 +1
I81	8.6		−2.4		−0.5	1.7	3.3	4.1	4.8	2/81	9/81	(−5) (+2)
I81	8.6		−1.6		−0.8	0.5	2.6	3.6	4.8	2/81	10/81	(−5) (+3)
II81	−1.6		−0.6		−2.6	0.6	3.2	5.0	5.0	2/81	11/81	(−5) (+4)
II81	−1.6		0.6		−4.9	−0.8	2.8	5.5	5.4	7/81	12/81	(0) (+5)
III81	1.4		−5.2		−1.1	2.9	5.4	5.2	4.2	7/81	1/82	(0) (+6)
III81	1.4		−5.2		−2.1	2.4	5.0	5.1	4.3	7/81	2/82	(0) (+7)
III81	1.4		−4.7		−2.8	1.7	4.2	4.7	3.5	7/81	3/82	(0) (+8)
III81	1.4		−4.7		−4.0	1.5	4.5	4.6	3.6	7/81	4/82	(0) (+9)

7/81 11/82 16

Mean (SD) 11 (7) −5 (0) 0 (2)

[a] Based on the data available to the forecasters. Q_0 = quarter preceding the survey quarter (Q_1). Entries in columns 5–6 are at annual rates.
[b] Averages of forecasts published monthly in Blue Chip Economic Indicators by Eggert Economic Enterprises, Inc., Sedona, Arizona. All entries are at annual rates.
[c] Mid-month of the quarter preceding the first quarter in which real GNP declined.
[d] Taken from the Blue Chip monthly release.
[e] Measured from the business cycle peak date (column 1) to the peak signal date (column 12). The leads or lags in parentheses refer to secondary signals and are excluded from the averages below. F = false signal.
[f] Measured from the business cycle peak date (column 1) to the survey release date (column 13). See footnote e.
[g] NA = not available.

year, although in May the forecasters as a group predicted zero growth for II81 and in August predicted zero growth for III81. The first forecast of at least two successive quarters of decline was issued in November and then showed negative growth for three quarters, starting with II81. The signal and recognition lags for this recession are -5 and $+5$ months, respectively, which is still much better than the corresponding lags of $+1$ and $+9$ months recorded in Table 15.1.

The overall averages in Table 15.2 are a signal lead of four months and a recognition lag of three months. The corresponding measures yielded by the actual data for the same period are mean lags of one and nine months in Table 15.1A and of two and eight months in Table 15.1B. This suggests a significant gain from the forecasts, which, however, is qualified by the false signals that on balance weigh much more heavily against the forecasts than against the data.

The Blue Chip surveys, initiated in 1978, cover only the recessions of 1980 and 1981–2, but they have the advantage of being monthly and hence very up-to-date. The twenty-seven surveys that produced average predictions of recessions as defined by GRH are listed in Table 15.3, which follows the same rules and has the same format as Table 15.2.

Although their sources as well as frequency are quite different, the two sets of forecasts show similar patterns. In Table 15.3 again there is a sequence of false signals of peaks in 1979 that ends in November when both surveys gave the earliest correct warning of the January 1980 downturn (the recognition lead is here slightly longer for Blue Chips because of faster processing). Blue Chips then produced a somewhat longer sequence of timely signals. Both surveys erred in August–September 1980 in forecasting that the recession would continue in the second half of the year. Blue Chips issued a correct prediction of the July 1981 peak in August, that is, with a lag of one month only, whereas ASA-NBER did so in December, with a recognition lag of five months. For the two recessions of the early 1980s, the averages of the earliest signals are -5 and 0 for Blue Chips and -5 and $+2$ for ASA-NBER.

Finally, let us note that neither group predicted any two-quarter declines in real GNP since the end of the last recession in November 1982. This may be counted as a significant plus for the forecasters since the slowdown from mid-1984 through 1985 was accompanied by severe difficulties in several important economic sectors, much uncertainty, and large revisions of the GNP data.

15.3   Alternative approaches

Table 15.4 compares the above results with some alternatives. Signals of recession from reported data on real GNP growth under the GRH def-

Table 15.4. *Five sets of recession signals from data and forecasts, timing comparisons, 1948–81*

		Recognition lead (−) or lag (+) in months				
Business cycle peak (1)	Preliminary GNP data[a] (2)	ASA-NBER Survey forecasts[b] (3)	Blue Chip survey forecasts[c] (4)	Leading and coincident indicators[d] (5)	Unemployment rate forecasts[e] (6)
November 1948	+8	NA[f]	NA	NA	+2
July 1953	+6	NA	NA	+2	+6
August 1957	+8	NA	NA	+1	−1
April 1960	+9	NA	NA	+5	+3
December 1969	+4	+5	NA	+4	+7
November 1973	+8	+4	NA	+4	+2
January 1980	+9	−1	−2	+2	0
July 1981	+9	+5	+1	+3	+6
		Means (standard deviations)			
1948–81 (8 peaks)	+8(2)	NA	NA	NA	+3(3)
1953–81 (7 peaks)	+8(2)	NA	NA	+3(1)	+3(3)
1969–81 (4 peaks)	+8(2)	+3(3)	NA	+3(1)	+4(3)
1980–81 (2 peaks)	+9(0)	+2(4)	0(2)	+2(1)	+3(4)

[a]From Table 15.1, part **B**, column 8.
[b]From Table 15.2, column 15.
[c]From Table 15.3, column 15.
[d]From Moore (1983, Chapter 4, Table 4-7 and page 54). The signals used are P3, based on first revised data prior to October 1976, preliminary data since then. See text.
[e]From Moore (1985, Table 3). See text.
[f]NA = not available.

inition are very tardy (column 2). The evidence from surveys of fore-casters looks reasonably good, suggesting that some recessions can be predicted at about the time of their occurrence or with short lags (columns 3 and 4). But this result must be tempered by the recognition that (a) the time-series of forecasts cover few recessions and so are not very informative on this point; (b) the variation of the leads and lags obtained is relatively large (see the reported standard deviations); and (c) the fore-casters produced some potentially misleading false signals.

It is therefore of interest to consider also some other possible approaches to signaling recessions, which could provide inputs into the forecasts by the agencies involved in the GRH process. A few years ago, we developed a system of recession and recovery signals based upon smoothed rates of change in the government indexes of leading and coincident indicators (Zarnowitz and Moore, 1982; reprinted with an update in Moore, 1983, chapter 4). This system produces sequentially, on a current monthly basis, early warnings and confirmations of busi-ness cycle turning points. The first signal of a peak (P1) is observed when the smoothed rate of growth in the leading index falls below 2.3 percent, while the corresponding rate for the coincident index is nonnegative (L < 2.3; C ≥ 0); the second (P2) is defined by L < -1.0, C < 2.3; and the third and last (P3) by L < 0, C < -1.0. The P1 criterion results in very early signals, which, however, turn out fairly often to be false (F); P2 substantially reduces both the lead times and the frequency of the Fs; and P3 is associated with short or intermediate lags but seems to elimi-nate the Fs altogether. Table 15.4, column 5, lists the lags for P3 and shows them to average two or three months. A particular advantage of this approach is the low variability of the lags over time.

Each of the post–World War II business cycle downturns in the United States was accompanied by increases in the overall unemploy-ment rate of at least 0.5 percent averaged over spans of six months. An index combining six selected series published by the Bureau of Labor Statistics relating to marginal employment adjustments (e.g., average work week, layoffs, initial unemployment claims) is compiled monthly by the Columbia Center for International Business Cycle Research (CIBCR). Smoothed rates of growth in this index produce relatively accurate semiannual (January and July) forecasts of changes in the aver-age rate of unemployment over the ensuing six-month periods (Moore, 1985). A by-product of these CIBCR projections is a set of signals of recessions reproduced in Table 15.4, column 6. Five of these are timely (-1 to $+3$ months) and three are lags of six to seven months; two fore-casts, dated 7/56 and 1/67, gave false peak warnings. The averages are lags of three to four months. The unemployment criterion of recession has two advantages: the unemployment rate is not subject to revision, and it is a concept widely understood by the public.

15.4   Summary

Our results lead to the following conclusions:

1. There are serious problems with the definition of recessions adopted in the Gramm-Rudman-Hollings law. Business cycles are best identified by the consensus of movements in the principal economic aggregates, as is done in the widely used chronology maintained by the National Bureau of Economic Research. Not all recessions are associated with, or well identified by, real GNP either declining or growing less than 1 percent (seasonally adjusted annual rate) for two consecutive quarters. GNP estimates are subject to long sequences of revisions that are often large, which aggravates the situation.

2. The record of preliminary estimates of real GNP published by the Department of Commerce shows that most recessions would have been at least half over by the time they would be recognized by the criterion of slow growth specified in the GRH law. Hence the suspension of deficit cuts according to this criterion may come too late to play an effective anti-recession role.

3. Tests of the alternative criterion based upon forecasts of two successive declines in real GNP, using records of consensus forecasts by economists, yield more satisfactory results. Most recessions would have been recognized just a few months after they began. Occasionally, however, premature or false warnings have occurred.

4. Leading indicators of aggregate economic activity can also assist the makers and users of forecasts in reducing the length and variability of the lags in recognizing recessions. Indicators that are specifically designed to anticipate changes in employment and unemployment may provide additional services of this type.

5. Although no criteria for recognizing *recoveries* from recessions are specified in the GRH law, tests of two possible procedures show that most recoveries could be identified shortly after they began.

REFERENCES

Cole, R. (1969), *Errors in Provisional Estimates of Gross National Product.* New York: National Bureau of Economic Research (NBER).
McNees, S. K. (1973), "The Predictive Accuracy of Econometric Forecasts," *New England Economic Review,* September/October, pp. 3–27.
     (1979), "The Forecasting Record of the 1970s," *New England Economic Review,* September/October, pp. 1–21 (corrected version).

274   Victor Zarnowitz and Geoffrey H. Moore

Moore, G. H. (1983), *Business Cycles, Inflation, and Forecasting,* 2nd ed. Cambridge, Mass.: Ballinger Publishing Co. for NBER.

(1985), "Forecasting Unemployment with the Leading Employment Index," *Economic Forecasts: A Worldwide Survey,* December, pp. 268–73.

Zarnowitz, V. (1982), "On Functions, Quality, and Timeliness of Economic Information," *Journal of Business,* January, pp. 87–119.

(1984), "The Accuracy of Individual and Group Forecasts from Business Outlook Surveys," *Journal of Forecasting,* January–March, pp. 11–26.

Zarnowitz, V., and G. H. Moore (1982), "Sequential Signals of Recession and Recovery," *Journal of Business,* January, pp. 57–85.

CHAPTER 16

Leading indicators of inflation

Howard L. Roth

Sharp increases in both the average level and the variability of inflation in the 1970s focused the attention of economists on the inflationary process. Outside the mainstream of academic research, a number of economists have proposed leading indicators of inflation. These indicators, it is hoped, will warn of impending significant changes in the rate of inflation. An underlying assumption is that inflation, like economic output, is cyclical, with peaks and troughs in the rate of inflation defining inflation cycles. The inflation indicators are designed to "predict" as accurately as possible past peaks and troughs in inflation. Thus, the development of leading indicators of inflation extends the indicator approach long associated with business cycle research to inflation forecasting.

This chapter evaluates five leading indicators of inflation. Three are composite indexes that use the methodology employed by the Department of Commerce in computing the composite indexes for the business cycle. Another is the growth rate of M1. The fifth is based on the ratio of capacity utilization to the foreign exchange value of the dollar. In general, the indicators show promise, but it is too early to embrace them wholeheartedly. The indicators are new, and while they "predict" past turning points in inflation quite well, there is no guarantee that they can warn of future turning points in inflation – the task for which they were developed.

This chapter is structured as follows. Section 16.1 describes the five leading indicators of inflation, section 16.2 assesses how useful the indi-

The views expressed herein are solely those of the author and do not necessarily represent the views of the Federal Reserve Bank of Kansas City or of the Federal Reserve System. Michael Grace provided ample research assistance.

275

cators may be in predicting inflation, and section 16.3 summarizes the study.

16.1 Five inflation indicators

As in predicting economic growth, anticipating turning points is the most difficult part of forecasting inflation. The difficulty in predicting turning points in economic output led to a search for economic variables with turning points correlated with turning points in the business cycle. Since the 1930s, the National Bureau of Economic Research (NBER) has identified numerous economic variables with turning points that lead, coincide with, or lag turning points in the business cycle. The Department of Commerce has taken the identification of indicator variables a step farther by combining the best of each category in composite indexes.

Interest in finding indicator variables for inflation has been a recent development. The low and stable inflationary environment of the post–Korean War 1950s and the 1960s provided little incentive to find inflation indicators. But sharp increases in both the level and the variability of inflation in the 1970s focused attention on the inflationary process. A number of leading indicators of inflation have been proposed in the last five years, including at least three composite leading indexes.

Several characteristics are sought in choosing indicator variables, whether for the business cycle or for inflation. First, the indicator should represent an important economic process and accurately measure it. Second, a variable used as a leading indicator should not be subject to major revisions. Third, the indicator should bear a consistent relationship over time to movements and turns in the business cycle or inflation, as the case may be. Thus, leads or lags should be fairly constant in length and anticipate or echo a high percentage of the turning points in the process being studied. Fourth, the indicator should not be dominated by irregular and noncyclical movements. A common fault of indicators is the presence of "noise," fluctuations of very short duration that tend to mask important cyclical movements. And fifth, measurements of the indicator need to be promptly available and frequently reported.

Three composite indexes and two simpler indicators make up the five leading indicators of inflation analyzed in this chapter.[1] Two of the composite indexes were developed by Geoffrey H. Moore of the Center for International Business Cycle Research at Columbia University, one for

[1] The three composite indexes have been constructed with the Department of Commerce's methodology for compiling the business cycle composite indexes.

use by the center and the other for the *Journal of Commerce*.[2] The third composite index was put together by Michael Niemira of PaineWebber.[3] A fourth indicator, the Morosani index, is computed by Cyrus J. Lawrence Inc.[4] The fifth indicator is the rate of growth of the narrowly defined money supply, M1.[5]

The index Moore and his co-workers developed for the *Journal of Commerce* is an index of spot prices for eighteen industrial materials.[6] All of the materials included in the index are widely used in further processing. Thus, changes in the prices of these materials would tend to be reflected in the prices of finished products. Furthermore, all the materials in the index are freely traded in open markets that tend to be affected by changing economic conditions. Thus, increased demand for products and services in the economy would tend to increase demand for industrial materials, pushing industrial materials prices, and thus the index, higher.

The leading inflation index developed by Moore for the Center for International Business Cycle Research is a composite of five economic series: the percentage of the working-age population that is employed; growth of the *Journal of Commerce* industrial materials spot price index; growth of total business, consumer, and federal government debt outstanding; the growth rate of an index of import prices; and a Dun and

---

[2] Sources: Center for International Business Cycle Research, Graduate School of Business, Columbia University, and *Journal of Commerce,* Knight-Ridder, Inc.

[3] Source: PaineWebber, New York City.

[4] Source: Cyrus J. Lawrence Inc., New York City. The Morosani index was constructed by John Morosani while he was an economist at Cyrus J. Lawrence Inc.

[5] The inflation indicator properties of the pre-1980 measure of M1, which does not include other checkable deposits (OCDs), were also studied. The results for "Old M1" are not presented. The two measures of M1 had identical indicator properties until the mid-1970s because OCDs were negligible until then. Subsequently, the current M1 measure predicted inflation turning points marginally better than did Old M1.

[6] The eighteen industrial materials are burlap, cotton, polyester, printcloth, scrap steel, copper scrap, aluminum, zinc, lead, tin, hides, rubber, tallow, plywood, corrugated boxes, red oak, benzene, and crude oil. This index is a revision of an earlier *Journal of Commerce* price index that covered fifteen industrial materials. In the revision, the prices of turpentine, linseed oil, and silk were deleted and the prices of crude oil, aluminum, plywood, red oak, benzene, and corrugated boxes were added. The most important addition in the current environment is crude oil. The original index was developed by J. Roger Wallace when he was associate editor and economist of the *Journal of Commerce.* For additional information on the revision of the *Journal of Commerce's* industrial materials price index, see the August 28, 1986, and September 2, 1986, editions of the *Journal of Commerce* or "The *Journal of Commerce* Guide to Inflational Trends – Summary Description of the New Industrial Materials Price Index," *The Journal of Commerce,* New York, 1986.

Bradstreet compiled index of the consensus among businessmen regarding changes they expect in their selling prices.[7]

The first three components of the Moore index are intended to reflect the intensity of demand pressures in the labor, commodities, and capital markets, respectively.[8] The percentage of the working age population that is employed has a direct bearing on how intensely employers have to compete for workers. When the percentage is high, competition for workers tends to be high, and wage inflation is likely to increase. As wage costs are generally reflected in the prices of products and services, the percentage of the working-age population employed should be positively correlated with the prices of products and services.

The Moore index uses the *Journal of Commerce*'s index of industrial materials prices to measure demand pressures in commodities markets and growth in total debt to measure demand pressures in capital markets. As indicated above, changes in prices of industrial materials are likely to be reflected in the prices of final goods. Growth in total debt generally reflects spending plans, as new borrowing is often undertaken to finance the purchase of goods and services. Thus, more rapid growth of total debt might well be an early symptom of inflationary pressures stemming from increased demand for goods and services.

The two remaining components of Moore's composite index were incorporated early in 1986.[9] One is the growth rate of an index of import prices, included because of the greater effect import prices have on consumer prices. The other component – the Dun and Bradstreet index giving the percentage of surveyed businessmen expecting their prices to be higher in the coming quarter than a year earlier – was added because

---

[7] Sources: U.S. Department of Commerce, Bureau of Economic Analysis (percentage of working age population employed); *Journal of Commerce,* Knight-Ridder, Inc. (index of industrial materials prices); Board of Governors of the Federal Reserve System (growth of total debt); Bureau of Labor Statistics (import prices); Dun and Bradstreet, Inc. (survey of businessmen regarding anticipated selling prices).

[8] For additional detail on the development of the Moore index, see Moore and Kaish (1983) and Moore (1983b).

[9] See Moore (1986). The Moore composite index was revised a second time in September 1986 to reflect changes in three of its components. The revised *Journal of Commerce* industrial materials price index, which includes crude oil, replaced its predecessor in the Moore composite index. A Bureau of Labor Statistics import price series that excludes crude oil replaced the earlier series, which included crude oil. And the growth rate of debt was revised upward as a result of revisions in the mortgage debt of savings and loan associations. The Moore index analyzed in this chapter is the first revision. The empirical work presented here was completed before the second revision of the Moore index.

businessmen presumably have an advantage in predicting where their prices are headed.

The leading indicator of inflation developed by Michael Niemira is a composite of four economic series: vendor performance, the ratio of employment to population, the National Association of Purchasing Management's (NAPM) price survey index, and the Federal Reserve's trade-weighted dollar index.[10] The vendor performance series measures the percentage of purchasing agents in the Greater Chicago area experiencing slower deliveries than a month earlier.[11] Slower deliveries often reflect a higher volume of business and, therefore, can presage price increases. The NAPM price survey index summarizes recent price experiences and expectations of 250 purchasing managers concerning the prices they face.[12] In many instances, changes in input prices are later reflected in the prices of output. The trade-weighted value of the dollar summarizes in one number the individual exchange rates of the dollar against ten major foreign currencies.[13] The exchange rate of the dollar is a direct determinant of the costs of imports to domestic consumers, as well as a constraint on the prices set by domestic producers of import-competing goods. When the dollar appreciates, as it did in the early 1980s, the prices of imports and domestically produced import-competing goods tend to rise more slowly, and perhaps even decline. Thus, an appreciating dollar has a restraining effect on consumer price inflation. Conversely, a falling dollar can lead to higher inflation – the current concern.

The Morosani index, computed by Cyrus J. Lawrence Inc., is based on the ratio of the Federal Reserve's capacity utilization measure to the trade-weighted value of the dollar. This ratio is used in predicting the inflation rate twelve months in the future. The rate of capacity utilization is intended to capture the effect of demand pressures in the economy, and the trade-weighted value of the dollar is intended to measure the delayed effects of changes in the dollar's value on consumer price

---

[10] See Niemira (1984). Niemira revised his index after the work reported in this chapter was begun, adding three new series – the Federal Reserve's measure of capacity utilization in manufacturing, the *Journal of Commerce* index of spot prices of industrial materials, and a U.S. Department of Agriculature series on agriculture prices – and replacing the Federal Reserve Board's trade-weighted measure of the dollar with the X131 measure of the dollar developed at the Federal Reserve Bank of Dallas. For details on the revision, see Niemira (1986).

[11] Source: Purchasing Management Association of Chicago.

[12] Source: National Association of Purchasing Managers.

[13] Source: Board of Governors of the Federal Reserve System.

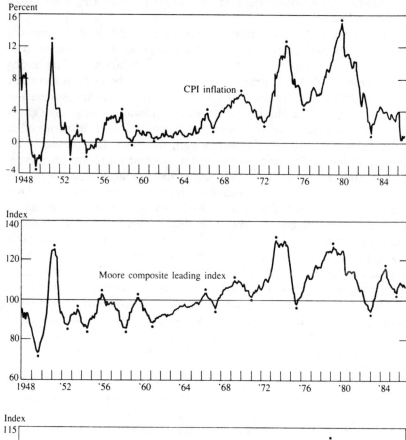

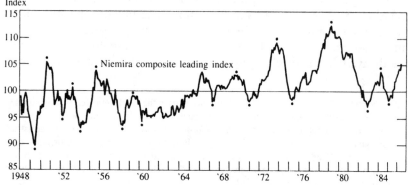

Figure 16.1. Consumer price index (CPI) inflation and five leading indicators. *Source:* Federal Reserve Bank of Kansas City.

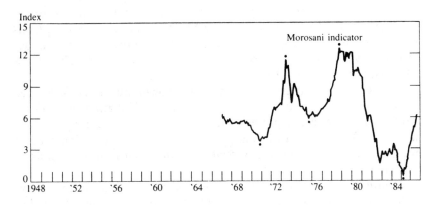

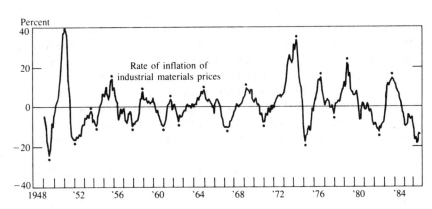

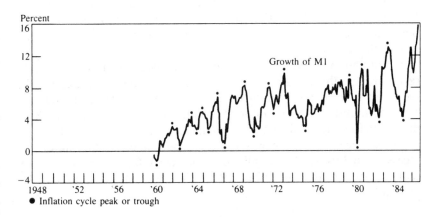

● Inflation cycle peak or trough

Figure 16.1. *(cont.)*

inflation. Increases in capacity utilization and decreases in the trade-weighted value of the dollar push the Morosani indicator higher. Conversely, declines in capacity utilization and increases in the trade-weighted value of the dollar lower the indicator. For details on the Morosani indicator, see Roth (1986).

The remaining inflation indicator is the growth rate of M1. Reference to this measure is frequently made in support of inflation predictions. To be sure, what is being predicted is typically a change in the average level of inflation, not a turning point. Nevertheless, M1 is included in the study to see how well its growth rate anticipates turning points in inflation.

Figure 16.1 brings together the five leading inflation indicators and CPI inflation. All the indicators except M1 were specifically designed to anticipate changes in the rate of inflation as measured by the CPI, all urban. For this reason, growth of the CPI, all urban, is used throughout this study to measure inflation. As can be seen in Figure 16.1, the Moore and Niemira indexes extend back to January 1948, the *Journal of Commerce* index begins in January 1949, monthly data on M1 start in January 1959, and the Morosani index begins even later, in January 1967. Peaks and troughs in the series are marked. In general, the indicators and the CPI inflation measure show broadly similar fluctuations. Similarities between M1 growth and CPI inflation, though, are the most difficult to discern, particularly after 1979.

The identification of peaks and troughs in Figure 16.1 for CPI inflation and the five inflation indicators reflects the maintained hypothesis that inflation as well as economic output is cyclical. The behavior of inflation in post–World War II business cycles can be seen in Figure 16.2, where the CPI inflation graph of Figure 16.1 has been superimposed on the business cycle recessions of the post–World War II era, shown shaded.

Examination of Figure 16.2 suggests that recessions slow inflation. In seven of the eight recessions shown, inflation was lower at the end of the recession than at the beginning. The brief 1957–8 recession was the exception. But it was a minor exception, as inflation began a sharp decline before the 1958 recovery began. The behavior of inflation during the most recent recession was more typical. At the beginning of this recession in July 1981, the inflation rate was 10.6 percent. By the subsequent trough in November 1982, the rate had dropped to 4.3 percent.[14]

---

[14] Two studies of the behavior of inflation during economic slowdowns are Miller (1981) and Moore (1983a).

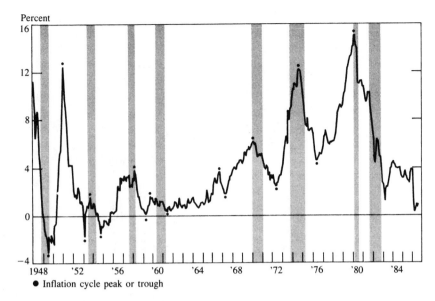

Figure 16.2. Growth rate of consumer price index, all urban. Shaded bars show business cycle recessions.

Not only was inflation lower at the end of all but one recession, but in most cases, the rate of inflation continued to fall after business had begun to recover. Most recently, inflation continued to fall after the trough of the business cycle in November 1982.[15]

Figure 16.2 also suggests that expansions fuel inflation. In five of the seven expansions since 1948, inflation was higher at the end of the expansion than at the beginning. The two exceptions were the 1958–60 expansion and the recent expansion in 1981. However, the 1981 expansion was the shortest of the post–World War II expansions, which may help explain why inflation did not increase.

These regularities support the notion that inflation is related to the business cycle. Table 16.1 tabulates the inflation peaks and troughs

[15] This description of inflation since November 1982 does not accord perfectly with Figure 16.2. The figure shows inflation rising between March 1983 and February 1984 and then steadily declining after February 1984. The eleven-month upturn in inflation beginning in March 1983 is most likely a statistical artifact. The Bureau of Labor Statistics changed the way homeownerhip costs are computed in the CPI in January 1983. Other consumer price inflation measures, including an experimental CPI measure using the new methodology, show no upturn in inflation in 1983.

Table 16.1. *Inflation turning points, 1948–86*

Trough[a]		Peak[a]		Change in inflation during preceding		Duration in months of preceding	
Month	Rate[b]	Month	Rate[b]	Expansion	Contraction	Expansion	Contraction
7/49	−3.1	2/51	12.7	15.8	—	19	—
1/53	−1.6	10/53	1.8	3.4	−14.3	9	23
10/54	−1.2	3/58	4.0	5.2	−3.0	41	12
4/59	0.2	10/59	1.9	1.7	−3.8	6	13
6/61	0.6	10/66	3.8	3.2	−1.3	64	20
5/67	2.1	2/70	6.3	4.2	−1.7	33	7
6/72	2.9	9/74	12.4	9.5	−3.4	27	28
6/76	4.9	3/80	15.2	10.3	−7.5	45	21
Average				6.7	−5.0	30.5	17.7

[a]See text footnote 16.
[b]Rate of inflation expressed as six-month, smoothed growth rate of CPI, all urban (annualized).

marked in Figures 16.1 and 16.2.[16] As shown in Table 16.1, expansionary phases of inflation cycles lasted an average of 30.5 months, during which the inflation rate rose an average of 6.7 percentage points. Contractionary phases of inflation cycles were shorter, lasting an average of 17.7 months. The rate of inflation declined an average of 5.0 percentage points during these contractions.

16.2 Performance of the indicators

How well do the five indicators perform? It is difficult to give a definitive answer because most of the indicators are too new to have established a track record. Nonetheless, this section provides some assessment by first examining how closely turns in the indicators would have corresponded to past turns in inflation and then measuring how well the indicators perform in estimated inflation equations.

16.2.1 Correlation with inflation turning points

With respect to how closely turns in the indicators correspond to past turns in inflation, a perfect indicator would turn before each turn in inflation, lead inflation the same number of months every time, and turn only before turns in inflation. Table 16.2 documents how well the indicators meet these criteria.

The data in the upper half of Table 16.2 show how consistently the indicators turn before turns in inflation. For example, the Moore index turns one month before the July 1949 inflation trough. In fact, the Moore index and the other indicators almost always turn before inflation, as is evident from the predominance of minus signs. None of the indicators misses an inflation turning point.

Data in the lower half of Table 16.2 show the average number of months that turns in the indicators lead or lag turns in inflation and the standard deviations of these leads and lags. The average lead of the Moore composite index is 7.7 months, and the average lead of the Niemira composite index is 9.8 months. The other three inflation indicators

---

[16] The criteria used in specifying peaks and troughs were the size of the change in the rate of inflation and the length of time over which the change took place. Generally, a change of at least 1.5 percentage points was required over a period of at least six months.

To be sure, identification of inflation troughs and peaks is somewhat arbitrary. The 1959 expansion and the 1967 contraction listed in Table 16.1 barely meet the criteria. And the rise in inflation in 1983 appears to be a statistical artifact and is not listed as an inflation expansion in Table 16.1, even though inflation increased almost 3 percentage points over an eleven-month period.

Table 16.2. *Turning points of inflation indicators*

| Inflation troughs (T) and peaks (P)[a] | No. of months that indicator turning points lead (−) or lag (+) inflation turning points | | | | |
	Moore	Niemira	Morosani	Industrial materials prices	M1
July 1949 (T)	−1	−1	NA	−1	NA
Feb. 1951 (P)	+1	−6	NA	−3	NA
Jan. 1953 (T)	−7	−10	NA	−14	NA
Oct. 1953 (P)	−3	−7	NA	−2	NA
Oct. 1954 (T)	−3	−9	NA	−8	NA
Mar. 1958 (P)	−27	−30	NA	−30	NA
Apr. 1959 (T)	−11	−12	NA	−17	NA
Oct. 1959 (P)	−2	−6	NA	−11	NA
June 1961 (T)	−4	−15	NA	−6	−14
Oct. 1966 (P)	−4	−7	NA	−23	−6
May 1967 (T)	0	−2	NA	−5	−4
Feb. 1970 (P)	−5	−6	NA	−11	−13
June 1972 (T)	−19	−18	−19	−18	−29
Sep. 1974 (P)	−15	−11	−14	−6	−20
June 1976 (T)	−11	−15	−9	−17	−14
Mar. 1980 (P)	−12	−2	−17	−12	−7

	Mean lead (−) or lag (+) in months				
All turning points	−7.7	−9.8	−14.8	−11.5	−13.4
Troughs	−7.0	−10.3	−14.0	−10.8	−15.3
Peaks	−8.4	−9.4	−15.5	−12.3	−11.5
	Standard deviation of leads and lags in months				
All turning points	7.4	7.1	3.8	7.8	7.7
Troughs	6.0	5.7	5.0	6.1	8.9
Peaks	8.6	8.1	1.5	9.1	5.6
	Number of extra turning points[b]				
	2	2	0	6	8

NA: Data not available.

[a] Six-month smoothed growth rate of CPI, all urban (annualized).

[b] No corresponding turning points in the CPI growth rate. The Moore composite index has extra turning points in December 1982 (T) and June 1984 (P). The Niemira composite index has extra turning points in November 1982 (T) and March 1984 (P). The industrial materials prices index has extra turning points in September 1961 (P), July 1962 (T), July 1976 (P), September 1977 (T), June 1982 (T), and September 1983 (P). M1 has extra turning points in November 1961 (P), September 1962 (T), November 1964 (P), June 1965 (T), May 1980 (T), October 1980 (P), July 1982 (T), and May 1983 (P).

turn earlier than the composites. The Morosani index leads CPI inflation an average of 14.8 months, but this average is based on only four
observations. The average lead of the industrial materials index is about
12 months. M1 leads inflation by 13.4 months, on average. None of the
indicators have constant leadtimes, as indicated by the standard deviations listed in Table 16.2. The Morosani indicator has the least variable
leadtime, but again, this statistic is based on only four observations. The
variabilities of the leads of the other four indicators are broadly similar.

The bottom line of Table 16.2 reveals that the Morosani indicator
has no "extra" turning points – turning points that do not correspond
to turning points in CPI inflation.[17] The two composite indexes each
have two extra turns, the industrial materials price index has six, and
M1 has eight.

16.2.2 Predictions of inflation turning points

A second way of evaluating the inflation indicators is according to how
well they can be used in generating early warning signals of cyclical
swings in inflation. How this criterion differs from the criterion used in
Table 16.2 can be illustrated by a hypothetical example. Suppose an
inflation indicator declined one month after having climbed steadily
over the preceding year. Suppose further that inflation also had been
increasing steadily, with no signs of moderating. Generally, a one-
month decline in the indicator would not justify a warning that inflation
was about to fall. One-month declines in indicators are often reversed
the following month.

What would warrant a prediction of falling inflation, generally, is any
behavior of the indicator that has been associated in the past with downturns in inflation. This behavior might be a number of consecutive
monthly declines of the indicator when inflation had been increasing.
Or it might be a critical percentage decline of the indicator. These are
only two of many possible rules for determining when the behavior of
the indicator justifies warning that inflation is about to fall. If, in fact, a
warning signal is given and inflation actually falls, three events will have
taken place: the indicator will have turned, the indicator will have given
a warning signal that inflation is about to fall, and inflation will have
fallen. In terms of these three events, the criterion used in the analysis

---

[17] Extra turning points are also a problem of the composite business cycle indicators.
Efforts have been made to alleviate this problem in the case of composite index of leading business cycle indicators. See Saul H. Hymans (1973), Stephen Beveridge and
Charles R. Nelson (1981), and Carl J. Palash and Lawrence J. Radecki (1985), and the
references therein.

underlying Table 16.2 was how well turns in the indicator correlate with turns in inflation. The criterion used in this section is how well the indicator signals the turns in inflation.

In a sense, the second criterion is an extension of the first. The ability to signal cyclical swings in inflation depends on how closely the turning points of the indicator are correlated with turning points in inflation. But the ability to signal cyclical swings in inflation also depends on how strongly the indicator moves in anticipation of a cyclical swing in inflation and how well the conditions under which the indicator anticipates a turning point in inflation can be summarized by a rule for signaling turning points.

Of the five indicators, only Moore's index has a turning point rule specified for it. The rule is based on growth of the index. A peak is signaled the first month growth falls below −1.0 percent. Similarly, a trough is signaled the first month growth exceeds 1.0 percent. As can be seen, this rule allows the Moore index to signal all the inflation turning points in Table 16.1, although frequently signaling only after the fact.

Turning point rules were developed in this study for the other four indicators. The objective was to find rules that allowed the indicators to signal past turning points accurately, the hope being that the rules will continue to work well in the future. Developing good rules for some of the indicators was quite involved. Fortunately, this was not the case with the Niemira index. The rule developed for the Moore index works well for the Niemira index.

The rule developed for the Morosani index compares the predicted change in the rate of inflation in the next twelve months with the change in the rate of inflation in the preceding twelve months.[18] A trough is signaled the first month the predicted change in inflation in the next twelve months is positive, the change in the preceding twelve months is negative, and the difference between the two changes exceeds 2 percentage points. The peak signal is the mirror image of the trough signal.

The rule for the M1 indicator compares current growth of M1 with its average growth in the previous twelve months. A trough is signaled the first month that growth exceeds the average by at least 2 percentage points. A peak is signaled the first month M1 growth falls below the average by at least 2 percentage points.

The rule for the raw industrial materials index is also based on the difference between the growth of the index and its average growth in the previous twelve months. But because prices of raw industrial materials

---

[18] The most recent data used in computing the Morosani index were from the period in which the predictions would have been made.

Table 16.3. *Turning point signals given by inflation indicators*

Inflation troughs (T) and peaks (P)[a]	No. of months that indicator turning point signals lead (−) or lag (+) inflation turning points				
	Moore	Niemira	Morosani	Industrial materials prices	M1
July 1949 (T)	4	2	NA	NA	NA
Feb. 1951 (P)	4	2	NA	1	NA
Jan. 1953 (T)	−2	−6	NA	−5	NA
Oct. 1953 (P)	0	−3	NA	2	NA
Oct. 1954 (T)	0	−2	NA	−5	NA
Mar. 1958 (P)	−21	−25	NA	−26	NA
Apr. 1959 (T)	−7	−8	NA	−10	NA
Oct. 1959 (P)	3	3	NA	4	NA
June 1961 (T)	2	3	NA	−3	M
Oct. 1966 (P)	−1	2	NA	−16	−3
May 1967 (T)	3	4	NA	4	1
Feb. 1970 (P)	−2	0	−11	−4	−8
June 1972 (T)	−13	−6	−23	−10	−21
Sep. 1974 (P)	−3	−3	−8	−4	−13
June 1976 (T)	−5	−8	−4	−9	−12
May 1980 (P)	−7	−7	−4	−7	0

Mean lead (−) or lag (+) in months

All turning points	−2.8	−3.3	−10.0	−5.9	−8.0
Troughs	−2.3	−2.6	−7.7	−5.4	−10.7
Peaks	−3.4	−3.9	−13.5	−6.3	−6.0

Standard deviation of leads and lags in months

All turning points	6.5	7.0	7.0	7.6	7.4
Troughs	5.4	4.7	2.9	4.6	9.0
Peaks	7.4	8.6	9.5	9.5	5.0

Number of false signals[b]

	2	4	0	6	4

M: Indicator fails to signal turning point in CPI: NA: Data not available.

[a] Six-month smoothed growth rate of CPI, all urban (annualized).

[b] Signaled turning point did not materialize. The Moore composite index gives false signals in March 1983 (T) and September 1984 (P). The Niemira composite index gives false signals in June 1962 (P), April 1963 (T), April 1983 (T), and August 1984 (P). The industrial materials price index gives false signals in March 1962 (P), April 1963 (T), October 1976 (P), June 1978 (T), December 1982 (T), and February 1984 (P). And M1 gives false signals in September 1980 (T), July 1981 (P), October 1982 (T), and November 1983 (P).

can swing widely, a trough is not signaled until the index exceeds the average by at least 2.5 percentage points for three consecutive months. A peak is not signaled until the index falls below the average by at least 2.5 percentage points for three consecutive months.

In signaling turns in inflation, a perfect indicator signals every turn in inflation, gives its signal the same number of months ahead or behind every time, and does not give false signals. Table 16.3 documents how well the indicators meet these criteria.

The data in the upper half of Table 16.3 indicate how successfully the indicators signal past turns in inflation. For example, the Moore index signals the July 1949 trough in inflation four months later, in November 1949. This signal only confirms a turn in inflation, as do almost half of the signals recorded in Table 16.3. But confirming signals can be useful. In practice, it takes time to determine whether a change in the rate of inflation is temporary or is the beginning of a new phase. An indicator that signals at or soon after turning points in inflation can help make the distinction. A confirming signal is at least more informative than no signal. Missed signals are not a problem, however. The only miss is committed by the M1 index.

Data in the lower half of Table 16.3 report the average number of months of advanced warning given by the indicators and the variability of these warnings. The average warnings range from 2.8 months for the Moore composite index to 10 months for the Morosani indicator. The Niemira composite index signals slightly earlier, on average, than the Moore index. The Moore index has the least variable leadtime, although no major differences were found in the variabilities of the indicators, as indicated by the standard deviations listed in Table 16.3.

The bottom line of Table 16.3 shows that only the Morosani indicator succeeds in giving no false signals. The Moore composite index makes two false signals. The Niemira composite index and the M1 indicator each give four false signals. The industrial materials price index gives six false signals.

Of the five inflation indicators, the Moore index and the Niemira index best meet the criteria underlying Tables 16.2 and 16.3. Both of these composite indexes match every turn in inflation. Both composites make only two extra turns, and both signal every turning point in inflation. The Moore index gives two false signals and the Niemira index gives four. The performance of the Morosani index is exemplary. This index makes no errors, but its record is very short. The industrial materials price index and M1, on the other hand, are considerably less promising. Both the industrial materials price index and M1 make too many extra turns and give too many false signals.[19] In addition, M1 fails to signal one inflation turning point.

16.2.3 Tests of the indicators' ability to explain past inflation

Inflation and the inflation indicators as bivariate random processes: A more sophisticated way of evaluating the inflation indicators is to measure how well they perform in estimated inflation equations. The methodology employed here is that of Granger causality tests (see Granger, 1969). The statistical test is whether past values of an indicator along with past values of inflation better explain inflation than past values of inflation alone.

Inflation and each indicator are assumed to compose a bivariate autoregressive process

$$\text{inf}_t = a + \sum_{i=1}^{k} b_i \cdot \text{inf}_{t-i} + \sum_{i=1}^{k} c_i \cdot \text{ind}_{t-i} + \epsilon_t \tag{1}$$

$$\text{ind}_t = d + \sum_{i=1}^{k} f_i \cdot \text{ind}_{t-i} + \sum_{i=1}^{k} g_i \, \text{inf}_{t-i} + v_t \tag{2}$$

wher inf_t and ind_t are the values of inflation and the indicator at time t, and ϵ_t and v_t are serially uncorrelated random variables, possibly contemporaneously correlated with each other.

Equation 1 is the relevant equation for measuring the usefulness of an indicator in predicting inflation. The null hypothesis to be tested is

$$H_0: c_1 = c_2 = \cdots = c_k = 0 \tag{3}$$

The test of H_0 is carried out by estimating equation 1 by ordinary least squares, first unconstrained and then with the c_i constrained to be zero. The test statistic employed is

$$F = \frac{(\text{SSE}_c - \text{SSE}_u)/k}{\text{SSE}_u/[T - (2k + 1)]} \tag{4}$$

where SSE_c and SSE_u are the residual sum of squares from the constrained and unconstrained estimations, and T is the number of observations in the sample. (Note that $2k + 1$ is the number of parameters

---

[19] Salih N. Neftci (1982) suggests an approach to formulating indicator rules based on sequential analysis that may reduce the number of false signals given off by indicators.

estimated in the unconstrained case.) If ϵ_t and v_t are normally distributed and certain other conditions hold, F converges in distribution to X_k^2/k as T grows large (see Schmidt, 1976).

Table 16.4 lists the tests results for the value of the indicators in explaining past inflation. Monthly data were used to estimate equation 1, as they were throughout the study. To obtain an indication of the effect of the number of lags, k, in equation 1, two sets of tests were made: one with the number of lags equal to twelve and another with the number of lags equal to twenty-four.[20]

The null hypothesis that the indicator does not help explain past inflation can be rejected at a 1 percent level of significance for four of the indicators when the number of lags is twelve and for all five indicators when the number of lags is twenty-four. The only exception is growth of M1 with twelve lags. When twelve lags are used, growth of M1 is not significant at the 10 percent level. A result not discernible in Table 16.4 is that increasing the number of lags to twenty-four reduces the predictive usefulness of all of the indicators except growth of M1.

Adding money as a third variable in the vector autoregression: Theory predicts that growth of money determines the rate of inflation in the long run. For this reason, a series of tests were conducted to determine whether the indicators other than M1 explain inflation beyond what is explained by past inflation and past growth of M1. Each of the inflation indicators other than M1 was modeled with inflation and growth of M1 as a three-variable vector autoregression. The inflation equation in this formulation is

$$\inf_t = a + \sum_{i=1}^{k} b_i \cdot \inf_{t-i} + \sum_{i=1}^{k} f_i \cdot mg_{t-i-24} + \sum_{i=1}^{k} c_i \cdot \text{ind}_{t-i} + \epsilon_t \quad (5)$$

where mg_t is the rate of growth of M1 at time t.

The ability of the inflation indicators to explain inflation is evaluated in the same way as in the preceding section. Equation 5 is estimated twice: first unconstrained and then with the c_i constrained to be zero. The null hypothesis is again that in equation (3), and the statistic used to test this hypothesis is equation (4) with $T - (3k + 1)$ replacing $T - (2k + 1)$ as the number of degrees of freedom in the denominator.

---

[20] Preliminary tests showed that growth of M1 lagged twenty-four months is a better predictor of inflation than is contemporaneous growth of M1. For this reason, growth of M1 is lagged twenty-four months throughout this study. For example, when the indicator in equation 1 is growth of M1, the third term on the right hand side is $c_1 mg_{t-25} + c_2 \cdot mg_{t-26} + \cdots + c_k \cdot mg_{t-24-k}$.

Table 16.4. *Value of the inflation indicators in explaining inflation: bivariate case*

| | No. of lags | | | |
| | 12 | | 24 | |
	Test statistic	Sample period	Test statistic	Sample period
Moore index	9.12[a]	1949:1–1986:7	3.92[a]	1950:1–1986:7
Niemira index	6.58[a]	1949:1–1986:5	2.99[a]	1950:1–1986:5
JOC index of commodity prices	6.66[a]	1950:1–1986:8	2.29[a]	1951:1–1986:8
Morosani index	3.72[a]	1969:1–1986:5	1.94[a]	1970:1–1986:5
M1	1.00	1963:1–1986:7	1.80[a]	1964:1–1986:7

[a]Significant at the 1 percent level.

Table 16.5 lists the results of the new tests. The null hypothesis is rejected at the 1 percent level in three cases and at the 5 percent level in the other case. That is, the ability of the inflation indicators to explain inflation is significant even when lagged inflation and lagged M1 growth are included as explanatory variables. In one way, these results are conservative. The number of lags used in the tests was twenty-four, a number favoring growth of M1 and not the other indicators in attempting to explain inflation.

An obvious question is how valuable is growth of M1 in explaining inflation in equation 5. That is, can the null hypothesis

$$H_0: f_1 = f_2 = \cdots = f_k = 0$$

be rejected? Table 16.6 lists the results of the tests of the new null hypothesis. In two cases, growth of M1 was significant at the 1 percent level. In another case, growth of M1 was significant at the 5 percent level. In the remaining case, growth of M1 was significant at the 10 percent level.

Value of the inflation indicators in a theoretical model of inflation: Another way of evaluating the inflation indicators is in the context of a theory-inspired reduced-form model of inflation. In a framework developed by Kahn (1985), changes in inflation are divided into three cate-

Table 16.5. *Value of the inflation indicators in explaining inflation when lagged money growth is included*

	Test statistic	Sample period
Moore index	3.40[a]	1964:1–1986:5
Niemira index	2.35[a]	1964:1–1986:5
JOC index of commodity prices	2.64[a]	1964:1–1986:5
Morosani index	1.60[b]	1972:1–1986:5

Note: Number of lagged values of explanatory variables was twenty-four in all cases.
[a]Significant at the 1 percent level.
[b]Significant at the 5 percent level.

Table 16.6. *Predictive usefulness of money growth beyond that of the other inflation indicators*

	Test statistic	Sample period
Moore index	1.79[a]	1964:1–1986:5
Niemira index	1.41[c]	1964:1–1986:5
JOC index of commodity prices	2.04[a]	1964:1–1986:5
Morosani index	1.65[b]	1972:1–1986:5

Note: Number of lagged values of explanatory variables was twenty-four in all cases.
[a]Significant at the 1 percent level.
[b]Significant at the 5 percent level.
[c]Significant at the 10 percent level.

gories: changes that are lingering effects of past changes in inflation (inertia), changes caused by shocks to aggregate demand, and changes caused by shocks to aggregate supply. To test the importance of the inflation indicators in explaining inflation, the indicators are appended to a reduced-form equation of inflation implied by the above framework, and the significance of the indicators is determined.

Two reasons are typically cited for persistence or inertia in inflation. First, long-term nominal contracts, such as union wage contracts, might cause costs of production and product prices to adjust slowly to changing economic conditions. If this is so, inflation would most likely display more inertia than if contracts were shorter or wages were indexed to a general index of prices in the economy. Decentralized or asynchronous wage bargaining would tend to add to the inflation inertia caused by long-term contracts.

The second theory of inflation inertia relies on gradual adjustment of expectations by economic agents. If inflation depends on expected inflation and expected inflation depends, in turn, on past inflation, inflation will display inertia. Actual inflation will depend on expected inflation if, for example, actual inflation is not known when labor contracts are bargained or when businesses set the prices of their products, and workers' willingness to supply labor depends on their expectations of inflation-adjusted wages or firms price according to their expectations for general inflation. Then, if workers' or firms' expectations of inflation are based primarily on past inflation, inflation will also depend on past inflation.[21]

Aggregate demand shocks originate from the spending of consumers, firms, and the government. Other things equal, an increase in growth of aggregate demand places upward pressure on inflation. For example, increased consumer or business confidence or more stimulative policy action may lead to demand pressures that raise inflation. There are many ways to model aggregate demand pressure for use in an inflation equation. A simple way, and the way used in the empirical work below, is to measure aggregate demand pressure with the GNP gap.

The GNP gap is the ratio of natural (potential) output to actual real GNP. Values of the GNP gap greater than one reflect an economy not producing up to its potential. Resources are unemployed or underemployed, and there is generally little upward pressure on inflation, at least from the demand side. On the other hand, a value of the GNP gap less than one reflects an economy operating at greater than its (long-run) potential. At such times, upward pressure on inflation could be quite intense.

Aggregate supply represents the production of goods and services by firms using labor and other inputs. Changes in the supplies of inputs, whether domestic or international in origin, and government-imposed restraints on the pricing of products by businesses are examples of aggregate supply shocks. A beneficial aggregate shock decreases inflation and increases growth of real output, other things equal. Plunging crude oil

---

[21] Of course, inflation expectations based on past inflation are generally not "rational" in the sense used by rational expectations theorists.

prices early in 1986 were a beneficial aggregate supply shock. Adverse supply shocks increase inflation and decrease growth of real output. The oil price shocks of 1973–74 and 1979–80 are examples of adverse aggregate supply shocks. If the decline in the exchange value of the dollar since February 1985 makes imported factors of production more costly, it will be an adverse aggregate supply shock.

These considerations when incorporated within a vector autoregressive framework lead to the following kind of inflation equation

$$\text{inf}_t = a + \sum_{i=1}^{k} b_i \cdot \text{inf}_{t-i} + \sum_{i=1}^{k} d_i \cdot \text{gap}_{t-i} + \sum_{i=1}^{k} f_i \cdot \text{oil}_{t-i}$$

$$+ \sum_{i=1}^{k} g_i \cdot \text{doll}_{t-i} + h \cdot \text{NIXON} + \sum_{i=1}^{k} c_i \cdot \text{ind}_{t-i} + \epsilon_t \quad (6)$$

The lagged inflation terms on the right-hand side represent inflation inertia. The GNP gap, gap_t, measures aggregate demand pressures. Relative oil prices, oil_t, the trade-weighted value of the dollar, doll_t, and the price controls of the Nixon administration, NIXON, represent aggregate supply shocks.

The null hypothesis is again that given by equation (3), and the statistic used to test this hypothesis is

$$F = \frac{(\text{SSE}_c - \text{SSE}_u)/k}{\text{SSE}_u/[T - (5k + 2)]} \quad (7)$$

Results from tests of H_0 are presented in Table 16.7. The indicators continue to help explain inflation, although perhaps to a lesser extent than in the simpler models of inflation. The Moore index and the *Journal of Commerce* index are significant at the 1 percent level, the Morosani indicator is significant at the 5 percent level, and the Niemira index and M1 are significant at the 10 percent level.

16.2.4   Qualifications

The empirical results obtained above might put the inflation indicators in too favorable a light. A few qualifications should be made. First, except for M1, the indicators were specifically designed to anticipate past turning points in the rate of inflation. That they perform this task well should not be surprising. But this ability to predict past turning points in inflation does not ensure success in anticipating future turning points in inflation. The underlying economic processes that led to the correlations between the indicators and inflation could change. As cases in point, the Niemira composite leading inflation index has been revised

Table 16.7. *Predictive usefulness of the inflation indicators in a theory-derived reduced-form inflation equation*

	Test statistic	Sample period
Moore index	2.34[a]	1969:1–1986:5
Niemira index	1.66[c]	1969:1–1986:5
JOC index of commodity prices	2.22[a]	1969:1–1986:5
Morosani index	1.77[b]	1969:1–1986:5
M1	1.62[c]	1969:1–1986:5

Note: Number of lagged values of explanatory variables was twelve in all cases.
[a]Significant at the 1 percent level.
[b]Significant at the 5 percent level.
[c]Significant at the 10 percent level.

once and the Moore composite index has been revised twice in the past two years to reflect the growing importance of imports on consumer price inflation. The composite indexes are new, and it is reasonable to expect that some initial refinement may be needed. But if they continue to need modifying every two or three years, the indexes will be of little use.

This point is part of a more general criticism – that the indicator approach is really measurement without theory (see, for example, Auerbach, 1982). The root of this criticism is that the indicators do not emerge naturally from a rigorous theoretical model of the economy.[22] Rather, the variables used as indicators or as components of composite indexes simply make sense.[23] Without a theoretical model, it is difficult to explain or predict changes in the relationships between variables. This shortcoming can lead to problems. Suppose, for example, that two economic variables have been highly correlated and that, as a result, one of the variables has been an excellent indicator of the other. The two variables need not be directly related. Their correlation could arise from

[22] Much of the applied macroeconomics is subject to this criticism, which might say as much about the state of theoretical macroeconomics as it does about the practice of applied macroeconomics.

[23] The good performance of the Morosani index does not make sense in one respect. The index relies on the level rather than the growth rate of the trade-weighted value of the dollar. Intuitively, the growth rate of the dollar would be expected to be more closely correlated to inflation than is the level of the dollar.

their being related to a third variable. If a change in the economy resulted in the third variable being no longer related to either of the two original variables, the correlation observed between the two original variables might disappear.

A second criticism of the inflation indicators is that completely revised data were used in evaluating their performances. In practice, many of the data are preliminary and subject to revision. Reliance on preliminary data could degrade the performance of the indicators. An analysis of the indicators' performance based on originally published data is beyond the scope of this study, but the possibility cannot be dismissed that the results reported here are biased favorably by use of revised data.

16.3   Summary and conclusions

Five leading indicators of inflation have been examined in this chapter. Three are composite indexes patterned after the composite leading index of the business cycle. A fourth indicator is based on the ratio of capacity utilization to the trade-weighted value of the dollar. The fifth is the growth rate of M1.

All of the indicators, particularly the Moore and Niemira composite indexes, anticipate past turning points in consumer price inflation quite well. The growth rate of M1 and to a lesser extent the commodity price index turn more frequently than consumer price inflation and are, therefore, too prone to predict turns in inflation that never materialize. In a variety of contexts, the indicators are significant explanatory variables in inflation equations.

On the basis of the empirical evidence presented here, the inflation indicators warrant increased attention and additional study.

REFERENCES

Auerbach, A. J. (1982), "The Index of Leading Indicators: 'Measurement Without Theory,' Thirty-Five Years Later," *The Review of Economics and Statistics*, November, pp. 589–95.
Beveridge, S., and C. R. Nelson (1981), "A New Approach to Decomposition of Economic Time Series with Attention to Measurement of the 'Business Cycle,'" *Journal of Monetary Economics, 7* (March), 151–74.
Granger, C. W. J. (1969), "Investigating Causal Relationships by Econometric Models and Cross Spectral Methods," *Econometrica, 37* (July), 424–38.
Hymans, S. H. (1973), "On the Use of Leading Indicators to Predict Cyclical Turning Points," *Brookings Papers on Economic Activity*, Feburary, pp. 339–84.

Kahn, G. A. (1985), "Inflation and Disinflation: A Comparison Across Countries," *Economic Review,* Frederal Reserve Bank of Kansas City, *70* (2, February), 23–42.

Miller, G. H. (1981), "Slowdowns in Economic Activity and the Rate of Inflation," *Economic Review,* Federal Reserve Bank of Kansas City, *66* (8, September/October), 18–27.

Moore, G. H. (1983a), "Recession Slows Inflation," reprinted in *Business Cycles, Inflation, and Forcecasting,* 2nd edition. Cambridge, Mass.: Ballinger Publishing Co.

(1983b), "Inflation Barometer: Rougher Weather Ahead," *The Morgan Guarantee Survey,* December.

(1986), "A Revised Leading Index of Inflation," Center for International Business Cycle Research, Graduate School of Business, Columbia University, Feburary.

Moore, G. H., and S. Kaish (1983), "A New Inflation Barometer," *The Morgan Guarantee Survey,* July.

Neftci, S. N. (1982), "Optimal Predictions of Cyclical Downturns," *Journal of Economic Dynamics and Control,* pp. 225-241.

Niemira, M. P. (1984), "A Multiple Stage Decision Model for Forecasting Inflation," PaineWebber, July.

(1986), "Updated PW Leading Indicator of Inflation," PaineWebber, New York, December 26.

Palash, C. J., and L. J. Radecki (1985), "Using Monetary and Financial Variables to Predict Cyclical Downturns," *Quarterly Review,* Federal Reserve Bank of New York, Summer, pp. 36–45.

Roth, Howard L. (1986), "Leading Indicators of Inflation," *Economic Review,* Frederal Reserve Bank of Kansas City, *71* (9, November), 3–20.

Schmidt, P. (1976), *Econometrics.* New York: Marcel Dekker, Inc.

PART III
NEW ECONOMIC INDICATORS

CHAPTER 17

Commodity prices as a leading indicator of inflation

James M. Boughton and William H. Branson

Changes in commodity prices have long played an important indicative role in analyses of global economic conditions, principally because of their importance for developing countries. More than seventy countries derive at least 50 percent of their export earnings from nonfuel primary commodities; another twenty derive the majority of their export earnings from fuels (see IMF, 1988, pp. 104–5). Changes in the terms of trade for these countries typically arise largely from changes in world commodity prices. Recently, however, attention has also been drawn to the importance of changes in commodity prices as indicators of changes in inflationary conditions affecting industrial countries. For example, the *World Economic Outlook* recently began to include an analysis comparing percentage changes in an index of forty primary commodity prices with the aggregate inflation rate of the seven largest industrial countries (see IMF, 1988, p. 11). The task of this chapter is to examine the usefulness of commodity prices as a leading indicator of inflation in the large industrial countries as a group.

An early exponent of focusing on commodity prices in this context was Robert Hall. In his 1982 book, Hall argued in favor of basing U.S. monetary policy on a commodity standard, with the commodities chosen on the basis of the closeness of their historical fit against the cost of

Mr. Branson's work on this paper was completed in part while he was a Visiting Scholar at the IMF and in part while a Visiting Scholar at the Banca d'Italia. We are grateful to Tom Walter, who carried out the empirical tests for this paper; to a number of colleagues at the IMF, especially Blair Rourke and Alphecca Muttardy, who helped prepare and interpret the data; to Mark Watson, for a number of suggestions; and to participants at seminars at the IMF and the Banca d'Italia. The views expressed herein are those of the authors and should not be attributed to any institution.

living.[1] Bosworth and Lawrence (1982) also emphasized the role of commodity prices as a contributor to the rise in inflationary pressures during the 1970s. More recently, Federal Reserve Board Governor Wayne Angell (1987) noted the close qualitative link between turning points in a broad index of commodity prices and turning points in the U.S. consumer price index (CPI). Other, notably Klein (1986) and Roth (preceding chapter), have examined the performance of commodity prices as one component of overall predictions of inflation.

Figure 17.1 presents inflation rates for the U.S. CPI and a world export-weighted index of commodity prices; this chart is similar to one presented by Angell (1987). Two stylized facts emerge clearly. First, there is a similarity in the cycles for commodity and consumer prices, with the commodity-price cycles often turning ahead of turns in the CPI. Second, the amplitudes of these cycles are very different (note the differences in the two scales). There is thus a presumption that the relationship is more qualitative than quantitative. Figure 17.2 presents the same type of information except that CPI inflation is a weighted average of inflation rates in the seven largest industrial countries, as in the *World Economic Outlook*. The qualitative relationships are generally similar in the two sets of data. These stylized facts are discussed more critically in the empirical sections that follow.

This chapter begins (section 17.1) by discussing the theoretical relationship between commodity and consumer prices and the conditions under which, in general, one would expect commodity prices to be a leading indicator of inflation. Section 17.2 then presents some tests of the relationships between conventional broad indexes of commodity prices and consumer prices. In section 17.3, the question of using the data to generate the optimum weights in a commodity price index is taken up. Conclusions are summarized in section 17.4.

17.1   A dynamic model of commodity and industrial prices

This section presents a dynamic model of the relationship between commodity and industrial prices as a theoretical motivation of the idea of movements in commodity prices as a leading indicator of general price level fluctuations. The model treats commodities as either final goods or inputs, and emphasizes the role of expectations in determining movements of commodity prices.

---

[1] The index favored by Hall at that time was limited to four commodities: ammonium nitrate, copper, aluminum, and plywood (Hall, 1982, p. 112). Hall (1987) later emphasized the limitations of that index.

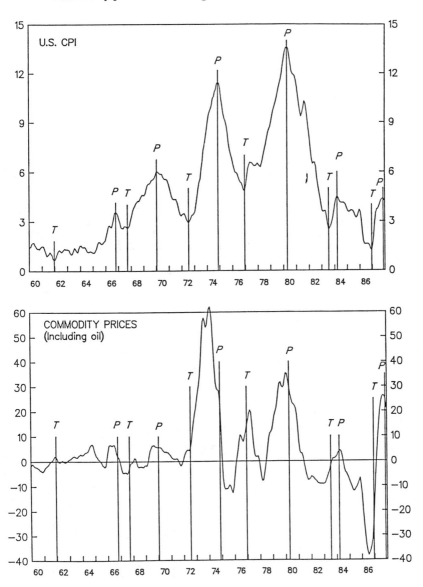

Figure 17.1. Rates of change of commodity prices and U.S. consumer prices, in U.S. dollars, 1960–87 (in percent). Three-month centered moving average of twelve-month inflation rates. T and P denote troughs and peaks, respectively, in the CPI.

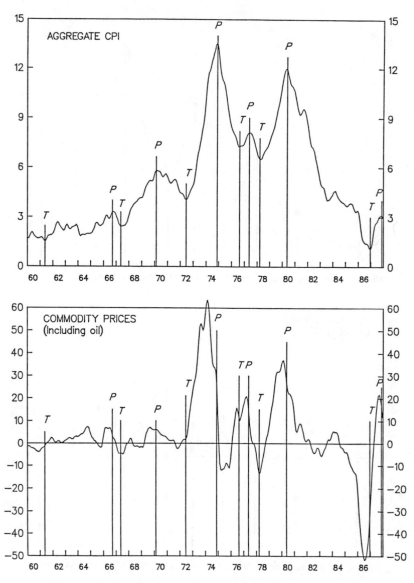

Figure 17.2. Rates of change of commodity prices and industrial-country consumer prices, in an aggregate currency basket, 1960–87 (in percent). Three-month centered moving average of twelve-month inflation rates. T and P denote troughs and peaks, respectively, in the CPI.

An important feature of the model is that commodity prices are determined in "auction" markets, actually financial markets that trade commodity contracts, whereas industrial prices are set by sellers and adjusted gradually. This permits commodity prices to react immediately to "news" about future inflation, and to lead adjustment of industrial prices. The two cases of commodities as final goods or as inputs are treated separately, but the basic results are the same in both cases. With unanticipated monetary disturbances, commodity prices overshoot and lead industrial prices, but with real disturbances, the relationship is less clear. For example, with a supply shock and no monetary accommodation, commodity prices would lead industrial prices, but the two would move in opposite directions.

17.1.1 Commodities as final goods

This subsection discusses a basic dynamic model of the interaction of commodity and industrial prices in which the two are final goods entering the CPI, and commodity prices are determined in flexible markets with forward-looking expectations. The model can be interpreted as one country with two sectors, or as two countries, one producing commodities and the other a perishable industrial output. The model includes a monetary sector, in which expectations of commodity price movements are important, and an industrial sector, in which prices adjust gradually following excess demand. To focus attention on price dynamics, the level of real output in the industrial sector is held constant. The model is an extension of Frankel (1986), which applies the Dornbusch (1976) overshooting model to the case of commodity price dynamics.

Equilibrium in the money market is described in the standard form of equation (1):

$$m - \alpha p_m - (1 - \alpha)p_c = \phi y - \lambda i \qquad (1)$$

Here m, p_m, p_c, and y are the logarithms of nominal money, the price of manufactures, the price of commodities, and real output; i is the nominal short-term interest rate; and α is the share of manufactures in the CPI. Commodity price inflation and the interest rate are related by an arbitrage condition:

$$i = \dot{p}_c + b \qquad (2)$$

where b is the real return to holding commodities for final use, net of storage costs, and $\dot{p}_c$ is the *expected* rate of change of the commodity

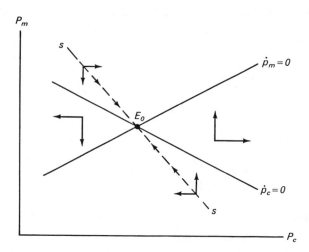

Figure 17.3. Commodity and manufactures prices: market equilibrium and dynamics.

price. Substitution of equation (2) into (1) yields the first dynamic equation:

$$m - \alpha p_m - (1 - \alpha)p_c = \phi y - \lambda(\dot{p}_c + b) \tag{3}$$

The locus of points where $\dot{p}_c = 0$ is shown in Figure 17.3; its slope is $-(1 - \alpha)/\alpha$.

For a point above the $\dot{p}_c = 0$ line to be consistent with money market equilibrium, the level of the commodity price (P_c) must be expected to rise. This is because above the line the CPI is higher, and real balances lower, than on it. This makes the interest rate higher than b above the $\dot{p}_c = 0$ line, so commodity prices must be expected to rise. If expectations exhibit perfect foresight, P_c must actually be rising above the $\dot{p}_c = 0$ line. In other words, a commodity price level above that consistent with zero expected inflation must be supported by a positive rate of commodity price inflation. Similarly, at any point below the $\dot{p}_c = 0$ line, commodity prices would be falling. These dynamics of P_c are shown by the horizontal arrows in Figure 17.3.

The supply of the industrial good (y_m) is assumed to be constant. Demand is assumed to be an increasing function of the price of commodities relative to industrial goods, P_c/P_m, and a decreasing function of the real interest rate in terms of the industrial good. Thus demand is given by

$$d = \delta(p_c - p_m) - \sigma(i - \dot{p}_m) \tag{4}$$

The price of the industrial good is assumed to adjust slowly to eliminate excess demand:

$$\dot{p}_m = \pi[\delta(p_c - p_m) - \sigma(i - \dot{p}_m) - y_m] \qquad (5)$$

The terms on $\dot{p}_m$ can be consolidated to yield the second dynamic equation:

$$\dot{p}_m = \eta[\delta(p_c - p_m) - \sigma_i - y_m] \qquad (6)$$

where $\eta = \pi/(1 - \pi\sigma)$. This term must be positive if a positive shock to excess demand is to raise the price of industrial goods.

The positively sloped $\dot{p}_m = 0$ line in Figure 17.3 shows the relationship between the two prices that would maintain zero excess demand in the market for industrial goods for a given value of the money stock. The slope of the line is positive because an increase in the commodity price creates excess demand for industrial output, requiring an increase in the industrial price to eliminate it. The slope is less than unity because as prices rise, the interest rate also rises, reducing the demand for industrial goods.[2] So as the price of commodities rises, the increase in industrial goods prices needed to eliminate excess demand is less than proportional. At points above the $\dot{p}_m = 0$ line, there is excess supply of industrial goods and the price is falling, assuming $\eta > 0$. Below the line, there is excess demand and the price is rising. The dynamics of adjustment of the industrial price are summarized by the vertical arrows in Figure 17.3.

The two equilibrium lines in Figure 17.3 show the equilibrium pair of prices at E_0 for a given money stock and real commodity supply conditions. The dynamic adjustment to equilibrium is along the stable saddle path ss. This path has two essential properties. It leads to the equilibrium, and along it the expected rate of change of the commodity price is realized. All other paths explode away from the equilibrium; they are speculative bubbles. The assumption that the market seeks out the stable ss path is equivalent to assuming that speculative bubbles are unsustainable. Eventually they collapse, and the market moves back to the stable path.

The model of Figure 17.3 can be used to illustrate two properties of commodity price behavior that are important for constructing a leading indicator for inflation: following an unanticipated increase in the money supply, commodity prices overshoot, and they lead the adjustment in prices of industrial goods. In a situation in which the signals from the

---

[2] Upward movement along the $\dot{p}_m = 0$ locus implies $\dot{p}_c > 0$; from equation (2), this requires a rise in the interest rate.

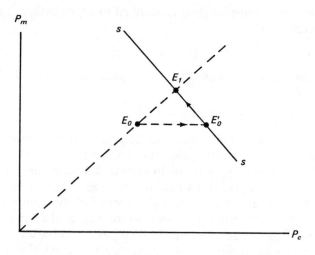

(a) Monetary Disturbance (Overshooting)

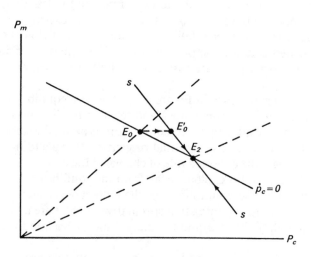

(b) Real Disturbance (Undershooting)

Figure 17.4. Price adjustments with commodities as final goods.

various monetary aggregates are unclear, the movements in commodity prices can be interpreted as distilling the information in the aggregates into a clearer signal.

The role of commodity prices as a leading indicator of the inflationary effects of a monetary disturbance is illustrated in panel (a) of Figure 17.4, which shows the effects of an unanticipated increase in the money supply. If the model is interpreted as representing two countries, this would involve a proportional increase in both countries' money supplies. The original equilibrium from Figure 17.1 is at E_0 in Figure 17.4. An increase in the money supply shifts both the $\dot{p}_c = 0$ and $\dot{p}_m = 0$ lines, and the new long-run equilibrium moves proportionately out to E_1. In the long run, both prices rise by the same proportion as the money supply. In the short run, the gradually adjusting industrial price does not move, but the flexible commodity price jumps to the new ss path at E_0'. Then gradually the industrial price rises and the commodity price falls along the ss path to the new equilibrium at E_1.

The initial jump in the commodity price is consistent with an initial decline in the interest rate. In the original equilibrium at E_0, the expected rate of commodity price increase is zero, and the interest rate is equal to b. The rise in the money supply increases real balances initially, reducing the interest rate below b. This is consistent with equilibrium only if commodity prices are expected to fall. So initially the commodity price must rise by enough to create the expectation that it will fall during the adjustment period. This generates the jump onto the new ss path, along which the commodity price falls as expected as the economy moves toward E_1. At that point, real balances and the interest rate are back to their original levels, and the expected rate of commodity price inflation is again zero.

The reaction of the model to a real disturbance that alters the equilibrium relative price of commodities is shown in panel (b) of Figure 17.4. As one would expect, it is substantially different from the reaction to a monetary disturbance. Suppose that a supply shock raises the equilibrium relative price of commodities. This shifts the $\dot{p}_m = 0$ line down along the $\dot{p}_c = 0$ line to a new long-run equilibrium at E_2, which lies on a ray from the origin that characterizes the new higher ratio of commodity prices to industrial prices. With no monetary accommodation, the $\dot{p}_c = 0$ line does not move. The result is that commodity prices jump onto the new ss path at E_0' and then continue to rise, gradually, as industrial prices fall toward the new equilibrium E_2. As is usual in this type of model, the commodity price undershoots in response to a real disturbance. The industrial price must fall if there is no monetary accommodation. So in this case commodity prices lead, but industrial prices move in the opposite direction.

It appears that commodity prices would not be a reliable indicator of future price developments in the presence of unaccommodated supply shocks, unless reliable information were available about the nature and the effects of those shocks. This problem can be minimized, although probably not eliminated, by using an index of commodity prices that are subject to supply shocks from different, preferably independent, sources. Such an index would resemble a portfolio of commodities with a minimum aggregate variance from supply disturbances, since at any point in time positive and negative disturbances would be offsetting. Presumably movements in this index would be dominated by demand disturbances, actual or expected, which would be a desirable property of an inflation indicator.

17.1.2 Commodities as inputs

The case of commodities as inputs can be discussed more briefly, since only two minor modifications need to be made to the model, and the results are essentially the same. In the money market, the deflator is now simply the price of industrial goods, so the dynamic equation (3) reduces to

$$m - p_m = \phi y - \lambda(\dot{p}_c + b) \tag{3'}$$

This change makes the $\dot{p}_c = 0$ line in the top panel of Figure 17.5 horizontal at the level of the industrial price that clears the money market with zero expected commodity price inflation.[3] At points above the $\dot{p}_c = 0$ line, real balances are lower than on it, so the interest rate is higher than b, and commodity prices are expected to rise. Below the $\dot{p}_c = 0$ line, commodity prices are falling. These dynamics are illustrated by the horizontal arrows in the top panel of Figure 17.5.

The market for industrial output is slightly more complicated. The demand for industrial goods is a decreasing function of the real interest rate. The supply of industrial goods is an increasing function of their price relative to commodites. Therefore, excess demand is a decreasing function of the relative price of industrial goods and the real interest rate. This gives a new equation for $\dot{p}_m$:

$$\dot{p}_m = \eta[\beta(p_c - p_m) - \sigma i] \tag{6'}$$

Here β represents the supply effect, and η is defined as before.

The $\dot{p}_m = 0$ locus is the positively sloped line in the top panel of Figure 17.5. To hold excess demand equal to zero in the market for

---

[3] Movement to the right along the $\dot{p}_c = 0$ line in Figure 17.5 implies falling value added in the industrial sector, since input prices are rising against constant output prices. Therefore, if the vertical axis in Figure 17.5 measured the price of industrial-sector value added instead of the price of final output, the $\dot{p}_c = 0$ line would be downward-sloping, as before.

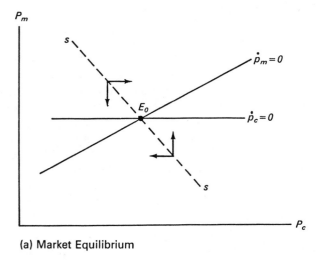

(a) Market Equilibrium

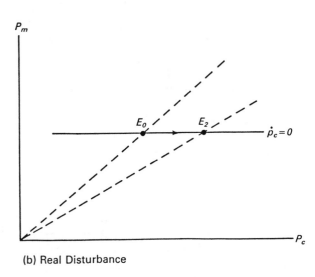

(b) Real Disturbance

Figure 17.5. Price adjustments with commodities as inputs.

industrial goods with a given increase in the commodity price, the industrial price would increase less than proportionately because the interest rate rises. Thus, the $\dot{p}_m = 0$ line along which excess demand for the industrial good is zero has a slope less than unity in the top panel of

Figure 17.5. Above this line, there is excess supply and p_m is falling. Below it, p_m is rising. The stable dynamic adjustment path is ss in Figure 17.5, as in the case of commodities as final goods.

The analysis following an unanticipated increase in the money supply is the same as that in panel (a) of Figure 17.4, discussed above. Adjustment to a supply shock that raises the equilibrium price of commodities relative to that of industrial output is illustrated in the bottom panel of Figure 17.5. The $\dot{p}_m = 0$ line shifts out to intersect the $\dot{p}_c = 0$ line at the new equilibrium price ratio. The commodity price rises, but with no monetary accommodation, the price of industrial goods remains unchanged. The price of value added in the industrial sector or country falls. As before, it may be noted that a broad index of commodity prices might essentially average out supply shocks, leaving monetary disturbances to dominate movements of the index.

In these two models, commodity prices play the role of an inflation hedge. With gradual adjustment of industrial prices, agents can protect themselves against an anticipated inflation by buying commodities or, more generally, commodity futures contracts. The result falls naturally out of an analysis with two prices, one that adjusts gradually and one that can jump. The latter becomes the hedge against inflation in the former. A richer model would include more prices, such as foreign exchange or domestic equities, that can adjust instantaneously to inflationary expectations. In such a model, several variables can play the role of inflation hedge, with a wide variety of overshooting and undershooting behavior. This was shown in Frenkel and Rodriguez (1982). Which price is the best indicator of future inflation then becomes an empirical question. The conclusion to be drawn from the analysis in this section is that commodity prices are a reasonable candidate.

17.2   Empirical tests using conventional indexes

This section evaluates the empirical relationships between commodity prices and general price movements in industrial countries. In order to simplify the discussion, tests will be presented only for consumer rather than output prices as the objective variable, and only for the large industrial countries as a group.[4] These decisions are somewhat arbitrary, but there is likely to be a stronger empirical link from commodity prices to consumer prices than to output prices, especially in countries that are net importers of primary commodities. Focusing on the aggregate inflation rate for a broad group of countries may also enhance the measured

---

[4] The countries are the United States, Japan, the Federal Republic of Germany, France, the United Kingdom, Italy, and Canada.

importance of commodity prices as a leading indicator; changes in inflation in individual countries may be relatively more affected by policy actions and exogenous domestic events and less by international variables.

17.2.1 Construction of data

The first empirical task is to construct a data series for the aggregate CPI for the large industrial countries. How best to do this is not obvious, because national price data are in different currencies. One approach would be to convert the time-series data on price levels into a common currency (say, U.S. dollars or special drawing rights, SDRs) and then construct an average index using GNP, consumption, or some other set of weights. One would then have a direct estimate of the aggregate price level measured in that currency. An alternative would be to average the logarithms of the price levels in local-currency terms. This procedure would give a more accurate measure of the average inflation experience in the countries concerned. Which procedure to choose depends on the intended purpose, but in the present case the choice is complicated because of the diverse international structure of the markets for primary commodities.

The problem may be illustrated as follows. If the national price indexes are averaged directly, the aggregate price level is described by

$$p_t = \sum_{i=1}^{7} w_i p_{i,t} \qquad (7)$$

where p_t is the logarithm of the aggregate CPI, p_i is the logarithm of the CPI for country i (denominated in the currency of that country), and the w_i are the weights. Alternatively, if the aggregate CPI is to be denominated in the currency of (say) the first country, then the formula may be written as

$$p'_t = w_1 p_{1,t} + \sum_{i=2}^{7} w_i(e_{i,t} + p_{i,t}) \qquad (7')$$

where e_i is the logarithm of the exchange rate for country i, expressed as the cost of local currency in terms of the currency of country i.

The difference between these two measures of the aggregate CPI constitutes an exchange rate between the currency of country 1 and the weighted geometric average of the other countries as a group:

$$p'_t - p_t = \sum_{i=2}^{7} w_i e_{i,t} \equiv e_t \qquad (8)$$

For the tests in this chapter, the aggregate CPI is constructed according to equation (7); for convenience, the implicit currency basket in which the data are thereby denominated will be referred to as the "group currency unit" or GCU.[5]

The difficulty posed by this choice is that the relationship between commodity and consumer prices is not invariant with respect to the currency in which the data are denominated. In order to isolate the effects of commodity price movements on inflation from those of exchange rate changes, it is desirable not only that commodity and consumer prices be denominated in the same currency or basket, but also that the denomination used correspond as closely as possible to the currency or basket that is most relevant for the various markets concerned. This last concept, however, is quite vague and difficult to judge empirically. Most commodity prices are quoted in U.S. dollars, but a number of them are quoted in other currencies, most notably pounds sterling, deutsche marks, and Japanese yen. Furthermore, the currency in which prices are quoted does not necessarily indicate the currency that is most relevant for that particular market; for a price quoted in U.S. dollars, for example, it is possible that movements in the effective exchange rate for the dollar could systematically induce corresponding changes in the dollar price.

The consequences of choosing an inappropriate denomination may be demonstrated by reference to a simple bivariate model. First, letting c denote an index of commodity prices, note that the dollar-denominated index (c') may be converted into GCUs:

$$c_t = c'_t - e_t \tag{9}$$

corresponding to the relationship described for the aggregate CPI in equation (8). Now suppose that the "true" relationship between commodity and consumer prices, free of exchange rate effects, holds when the data are denominated in GCUs, expressed as

$$p_t = a + bc_t + \epsilon_t \tag{10}$$

Obviously, if one were to estimate, instead of equation (10), a regression in which commodity prices were denominated in dollars (or another currency), a spurious exchange rate effect would be introduced. Perhaps less obviously, a spurious effect would be introduced even if *both* indexes were denominated in dollars. Suppose one were to estimate

$$p'_t = \alpha + \beta c'_t + \mu_t$$

[5] This procedure is equivalent to the methodology used in Fund publications such as the *World Economic Outlook* for constructing aggregate inflation rates for groups of countries.

which is equivalent to

$$p_t = \alpha + \beta c_t + (\beta - 1)e_t + \mu_t \qquad (10')$$

Unless $\beta = 1$, the exchange rate now enters the implicit equation in GCUs, in contrast to equation (10).

In the absence of detailed knowledge about the nature of the individual markets, the best that one can do is to use a broad index of major currencies and to be sure that all data are measured commensurately. Since the aggregate CPI is constructed according to equation (7), it is appropriate to measure commodity prices in GCUs, converting dollar prices by the exchange rate described in equation (8).

The commodity price index to be used for these tests uses a total of forty prices, weighted according to 1979–81 shares in world exports.[6] It is the same index that is used in the *World Economic Outlook,* as noted in the introduction. Preliminary tests suggested that similar results (though generally not quite as favorable) would obtain using other weighting methods such as imports or consumption rather than exports. A major decision is whether to include oil prices, since in 1979–81 oil accounted for roughly 50 percent of world exports of primary commodities. The inclusion of oil did somewhat improve the statistical properties in preliminary tests, and it was therefore included in the final index.

17.2.2   Long-run relationships

The first empirical question to be analyzed is whether there exists a stable long-run relationship between the level of commodity prices and the level of consumer prices. If so, then it may be possible to make quantitative inferences about future CPI inflation from observations of commodity prices. In the absence of a long-run relationship between these levels, there may still be qualitative linkages between changes in inflation rates in the two data series, but one would want to avoid arguing that any given change in commodity prices would be expected to be followed (eventually) by a specified change in consumer prices.

A very simple heuristic approach to this question is to examine the stationarity of the relative price of commodities. As may be seen from Figure 17.6, there has been a general downward trend in this relative price; the extent of the drift, however, has not been uniform, and it was starkly interrupted by a sudden and large rise in 1972–3. The hypothesis that the relative commodity price is unbounded in the long run would seem to be a reasonable one to entertain.

---

[6] For a description of prices, see IMF (1986, Appendix II). The export weights are listed in Table 17.4, below.

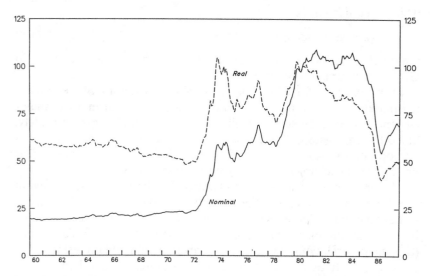

Figure 17.6. Commodity prices: nominal and real, 1960–87 (in GCUs; 1980 = 100). The real price is obtained by deflating by the seven-country consumer price index.

One test of this hypothesis is to run augmented Dickey-Fuller regressions for commodity and consumer prices:

$$\Delta x_t = \beta x_{t-1} + \Sigma_i \lambda_i \Delta x_{t-i} \tag{11}$$

where x is the difference of order j (for a test of stationarity of order j) in the logarithm of the variable, and the null hypothesis (no stationarity) is that $\beta = 0$. As shown in Table 17.1, the tests have been conducted over three sample periods, all ending in 1987. In addition to the full-sample estimates, regressions have been run for samples beginning in 1972, when commodity prices first began to show substantial fluctuations, and beginning in 1974, after the apparently unique jump in commodity prices that occurred in 1972–3.

In the case of commodity prices, the null hypothesis of nonstationary first differences is rejected, regardless of the sample period. For consumer prices, however, the hypothesis that $\beta = 0$ cannot be rejected, although the second differences appear to be stationary. The implication of these tests is that commodity prices are integrated of order 1, whereas consumer prices are integrated of order 2. In these circumstances, the two data sets cannot be cointegrated, and the standard cointegration tests are not applicable [see, for example, Granger (1986)]. It is thus pos-

Table 17.1. *Stationarity tests for commodity and consumer prices*[a]

	Commodity prices	Consumer prices
Tests for first-order stationarity		
1960–87	−4.54**	−0.86
1972–87	−3.5*	−0.73
1974–87	−4.49**	−1.37
Tests for second-order stationarity[b]		
1960–87		−5.82**
1972–87		−3.94**
1974–87		−4.07**

[a]The numbers in this table are *t*-statistics from estimates of equation (11) over the indicated sample periods using monthly data. The distribution of these statistics is not standard; the 95 percent confidence level for the rejection of nonstationarity (*) is approximately 3.17, and the 99 percent level (**) is approximately 3.77. See Engle and Granger (1987).
[b]These tests are relevant only where the hypothesis of first-order nonstationarity has not been rejected.

sible to turn to tests of shorter-run relationships, ignoring the long-run constraints that might otherwise have been imposed by the data.[7]

17.2.3 Short-run relationships

The next step is to evaluate the relationship between shorter-run movements in commodity and consumer prices. For this purpose, it is helpful to render the data stationary, which may be accomplished simply by taking second differences of the data. As noted above, commodity prices are reasonably stationary in first differences, but second differencing is required to make the full data set stationary. In addition, in order to reduce the importance of seasonal fluctuations, inflation rates have been calculated as 12-month changes. Thus, the following tests relate to monthly changes in twelve-month inflation rates:

$$z_t = (x_t - x_{t-1}) - (x_{t-12} - x_{t-13})$$

[7] The absence of cointegration in these data was also documented in Durand and Blöndal (1988).

Table 17.2. *Commodity prices and industrial-country inflation:*
Granger causality tests[a]

	Non-oil commodities		All commodities	
	Commodity prices cause CPI	CPI causes commodity prices	Commodity prices cause CPI	CPI causes commodity prices
With data in U.S. dollars				
1960–87	—	**	—	**
1972–87	—	—	—	—
1974–87	—	—	—	*
With data in GCUs				
1960–87	**	—	**	—
1972–87	—	—	**	—
1974–87	—	—	*	—

[a]For the test of whether commodity prices cause (in Granger's sense) the CPI, the CPI has been regressed on eighteen lagged monthly values of the commodity price index plus eighteen lagged values of itself. For the test of reverse causation, the two series are switched. Industrial-country inflation is measured by the average change in consumer prices for the seven largest countries; the construction of the data is described in the text. All data have been made stationary by taking monthly changes in twelve-month inflation rates. A single asterisk indicates that the null hypothesis – that the aggregate effect of the lagged values of the independent variable is zero – is rejected with 95 percent confidence. A double asterisk indicates rejection of the null with 99 percent confidence.

where x is the logarithm of the relevant index and z is the whitened form of the data.

Causality tests: Table 17.2 summarizes the results of tests of whether commodity prices "cause," in Granger's sense, consumer prices for the large industrial countries as a group. The null hypothesis is that the lagged values of commodity prices contribute nothing to predictions of aggregate CPI inflation, given the predictions from lagged values of the CPI. In addition, tests of reverse causation are also included. In view of the ambiguities associated with the currency denomination of the data, discussed above, the tests have been conducted both with the data expressed in U.S. dollars and with the data denominated in GCUs. Finally, given the rather different behavior of both consumer and commodity prices before and after the early 1970s, the tests have been run over three overlapping samples. The full sample runs from 1960 through 1987; the second sample drops all data before 1972, when commodity prices first displayed a rise in variability; the third begins after the major commodity price inflation of 1972–3.

For the full sample (1960–87), the direction of estimated causation depends entirely on the currency denomination. In terms of U.S. dollars, it appears that consumer prices lead commodity prices; in terms of GCUs, the reverse is true. For the shorter samples, there is no evidence of causation in either direction for non-oil commodity prices. When oil prices are included in the index, and the data are denominated in GCUs, there appears to be causation running from commodity to consumer prices. Given the lack of robustness of the results, it is difficult to draw any firm conclusions from this exercise. Nonetheless, it does seem warranted to conclude that if commodity prices are to serve as a leading indicator of industrial-country inflation, it is preferable to denominate the data in terms of a broad currency basket rather than in terms of U.S. dollars.

Full-sample relationships: As a fairly simple test of whether commodity prices contribute to predictions of inflation, the changes in the aggregate CPI inflation rate have been regressed on lagged changes in itself plus lagged changes in commodity-price inflation, using polynomial distributed lags (PDLs).[8] The null hypothesis for this test is that the contribution of the PDL on commodity prices does not add to the in-sample explanatory power of the regression.

The baseline regression, omitting commodity prices, is estimated (1962–87, monthly data) as

$$
\begin{array}{ll}
& \overline{R}^2 = .292 \\
.479 \sum_{i=1}^{36} w_i p_{t-i} & DW = 1.60 \\
(3.39) & SEE = .224
\end{array}
\qquad (12)
$$

and the expanded regression result is

$$
\begin{array}{lll}
& & \overline{R}^2 = .393 \\
p_t = .315 \sum_{i=1}^{36} w_i p_{t-i} + .108 \sum_{i=1}^{36} v_i c_{t-i} & DW = 1.59 \\
(1.74) & (2.95) & SEE = .207
\end{array}
$$
$$(13)$$

---

[8] The specific functional form is a thirty-six-month, fourth-order PDL, constrained to zero at the far end of the distribution.

The F statistic for the additional contribution of the commodity price index (c) is 13.8, which implies rejection of the null hypothesis with more than 99 percent confidence.

An interesting comparison may be made against predictions using an aggregate measure of monetary growth in the large industrial countries.[9] The data series for money stocks has been extended back only to January 1964; using three-year lags on twelve-month inflation rates and taking moving averages, the regressions for this comparison therefore start in February 1968. For this sample, a regression using only past inflation (as in equation 12) has $\overline{R}^2 = .345$; the addition of a PDL on current and lagged money growth has $\overline{R}^2 = .361$. The F statistic for the significance of this improvement is 2.5 (significant with 95 percent confidence), compared with 13.8 for commodity prices. It is, of course, possible that other models – allowing for other influences or developing different lag structures – might alter these comparisons. Nonetheless, there is a prima facie case for the value of commodity prices as an inflation predictor.

Post-sample tests: Table 17.3 presents information on the out-of-sample predictive ability of commodity prices, with broad-money equations also included for comparison. For this exercise, regressions such as those in equations (12) and (13) were run over a series of six sample periods, starting with 1968–77 and then extending by two years up to 1968–85. In each case, the estimated equations were used to generate dynamic predictions for the aggregate CPI inflation rate over the twenty-four months following the end of the sample. During the prediction period, commodity price inflation and broad-money growth were projected on the basis of their own prior history. As shown in the table, three comparisons were made. First, did the inclusion of commodity prices reduce the standard error of the estimate within the sample period? Second, did the equations that include commodity prices reduce the forecast error for the average inflation rate over the two-year horizon? Third, did they reduce the root mean squared error (RMSE) for the twenty-four monthly inflation forecasts?

Perhaps the most striking feature of Table 17.3 is that the RMSE is reduced by the inclusion of commodity prices in only two of the six forecast periods: 1984–5 and 1986–7. Throughout these four years, the prior weakness in commodity prices provided useful information about

---

[9] Money stocks in each country are broadly defined (money plus quasi-money, as defined in *International Financial Statistics*). These stocks are aggregated using the same procedure as the CPIs; thus the data are implicitly denominated in GCUs.

Table 17.3. *Inflation predictions, 1976–87 (in percent)*

	1976–7	1978–9	1980–1	1982–3	1984–5	1986–7
Actual inflation	7.5	9.5	10.3	4.9	3.7	2.1
Baseline prediction	8.1	7.7	11.0	6.6	4.9	2.8
Baseline prediction error	0.6	−1.8	0.7	1.7	1.2	0.7
Predictions using commodity prices						
Predicted inflation	6.6	5.5	12.0	7.5	4.9	2.7
Reduction in:						
In-sample error	16.8	14.6	12.2	10.5	9.5	9.5
Prediction error[b]	—	—	—	—	—	0.1
RMSE	—	—	—	—	2.3	60.9
Prediction using Broad Money Balances						
Predicted inflation	7.5	7.5	10.2	7.5	5.3	2.7
Reduction in:						
In-sample error	2.9	2.2	1.5	1.3	1.0	0.6
Prediction error[b]	0.6	—	0.6	—	—	0.1
RMSE	—	12.0	96.2	—	—	41.0

[a]Post-sample twenty-four-month dynamic predictions of the aggregate CPI from equations as described in the text. The estimation sample is from February 1968 (plus prior lagged data to December of the year preceding the listed forecast period).
[b]In percentage points.

how rapidly consumer prices would decelerate. In the earlier periods, the predictions are worsened somewhat in comparison with those made only on the basis of the history of the CPI itself. The equations using broad money do somewhat better in the earlier periods, but less well in the last two.

Overall, the inclusion of neither commodity prices nor broad money could be said to have improved the post-sample inflation forecasts. In contrast, within each sample period, there is a substantial improvement in the fit when commodity prices are included, and only a small improvement when money balances are included. It thus appears that the quantitative linkages between commodity and consumer prices are significant, but are not stable enough to permit one to draw quantitative inferences about the extent to which consumer prices might respond to a given change in commodity prices.

17.3   Empirical estimates of weights

The tests in section 17.2 took as given the weights assigned to each commodity in the price indexes. The purpose of this section is to examine the feasibility of estimating optimum weights (optimum in the sense of generating the best predictions of the aggregate CPI) for a commodity price index through regression analysis.

17.3.1   *Estimation of indexes*

Two basic approaches have been used to estimate commodity price indexes on the basis of their relationship with the aggregate CPI. One is to allow the data to determine the weights freely, with all commodity prices as contenders for inclusion in the index. The other involves constraining the data, by eliminating negative weights and, in the final set of estimates, by initially aggregating commodities that have small weights in industrial-country trade or consumption into somewhat broader categories. The second approach was intended to check whether the efficiency of the estimates might be improved by the constraints.

Estimation using all available commodity price data: The objective of the first approach is to allow the maximum freedom for the data to "speak" in determining the "best" weights for commodities for the purpose of predicting CPI inflation. This approach uses the prices that are incorporated into the available IMF commodity price indexes, plus the prices of gold and petroleum, in an unconstrained regression framework. There are some thirty years of monthly observations on the forty commodity price series, extending from January 1958 through September 1987. With a forecast horizon chosen to run from one to thirty-six months, the problem is to devise a procedure that narrows quickly to the most important explanatory variables over different forecast horizons with a minimum of loss in efficiency in utilizing the information in the data.

The procedure that was employed to estimate "optimum" indexes was as follows. First, the aggregate CPI and all forty series, expressed as logarithms of GCU-denominated indexes, were transformed by taking the first differences of their twelve-month differences (i.e., changes in inflation rates). Second, the forty principal components were extracted from the data matrix of the transformed commodity price data, to produce orthogonal regressors. Third, a multiple regression was estimated over the period February 1962 to December 1982 with the transformed CPI as the dependent variable and the forty principal components as independent variables (with the constant suppressed) separately at each lag length from one to thirty-six months. The termination of the sample at the end of 1982 was chosen so as to leave a reasonably long postsample period for testing the stability of the results.

These regression results were used to select significant principal components for the remaining analysis. Two selection criteria were used to narrow the set of principal components. The first was to rank them by average absolute t-ratio across lags. The second was to select principal components with coefficients that were significant at the 1 percent level for at least four different lags, of which at least one was longer than twelve months. The second criterion yielded eight principal components, of which six coincided with those in the highest eight on the average absolute t-ratio criterion. Thus the two criteria together yielded a list of ten candidate principal components for the next stage.

Next, a regression was estimated with the transformed CPI as the dependent variable and fourth-order PDLs with length thirty-six months (constrained to zero at the far end only) on the candidate principal components as independent variables along with a similar PDL on the lagged transformed CPI. This regression (over the 1962–82 period) had an adjusted R^2 of .57, compared with .32 for a regression of the transformed CPI only on its own lags. Each of the ten selected principal components contributed significantly to this regression. Finally, the coefficient on the weighted (and normalized) lag distribution on each principal component was taken as an estimate of the contribution of that component to the index being derived.

Table 17.4. *Econometrically estimated weights for commodity price indexes (in percent)*[a]

Commodity[b]	Unconstrained	Eliminating negative weights	Using prior aggregation	Memorandum: world export weights[c]
Cereal	−21.9	7.3	10.3	10.6
Wheat	−4.8	—	5.0	5.1
Maize	60.8	7.3	3.7	3.8
Rice	−77.8	—	1.6	1.6
Vegetables	−4.7	12.1	4.9	5.7
Soybeans	16.0	10.9	3.9	4.5
Other	−20.6	1.2	1.0	1.2
Meat	−6.3	3.9	—	3.3
Beef	−38.7	—	—	2.8
Lamb	32.4	3.9	—	0.5
Sugar	27.2	5.2	1.0	1.6
Bananas	−9.7	—	—	0.4
Beverages	38.2	19.0	—	6.0
Coffee	−19.7	12.1	—	3.8
Cocoa	42.5	5.1	—	1.6
Tea	15.5	1.9	—	0.6

328

Agricultural raw materials	59.0	26.3	52.2	12.0
Timber	60.0	7.2	15.6	5.4
Cotton	−88.7	—	—	2.0
Wool	−39.1	—	—	1.2
Rubber	25.9	3.1	11.9	1.3
Tobacco	54.5	6.5	24.7	1.3
Other	46.4	9.4	—	0.7
Metals	−7.6	23.1	2.1	14.9
Copper	24.3	2.9	0.4	3.0
Aluminum	−0.5	—	0.3	2.3
Gold	5.0	0.6	0.5	3.7
Iron ore	62.6	7.6	0.3	2.1
Other	−99.1	12.1	0.6	3.8
Petroleum	25.8	3.1	29.4	45.5
Total	100.0	100.0	100.0	100.0

[a]Detail may not add to totals because of rounding.
[b]Several of the listed commodities are divided into two or more components in the full data set. When negative weights were reset to zero for the second index, the calculations were made at that disaggregated level.
[c]Based on 1979–81 data. *Source*: IMF, Commodities Division.

The lag distributions on the ten principal components in the final regression differ in length and shape. Therefore, when the implied weights on the commodity prices are retrieved, a weighting matrix is obtained, which in principle would have a different set of weights for each lag length. Thus the distributed lag coefficients on the final principal components equation could be used to estimate a different set of weights for the commodity prices at each forecast horizon, reflecting differences in the information in the various commodity prices for explaining aggregate CPI inflation at different forecast horizons. This step was not taken at this stage. Instead, a single set of weights was calculated, reflecting the average information in the commodity price series across forecast horizons. These are the weights shown in the second column of Table 17.4.

The most notable feature of the weights in the unconstrained index is that about half of the commodities have negative weights. In particular, within most groups, some commodities have positive and some negative weights. The reason for the negative weights is not that a rise in the price of a particular commodity, by itself, would be expected to lead to a fall in consumer prices; it is rather that the regression essentially computes the weights for an optimal portfolio of commodity prices that minimizes the residual error vis-à-vis the CPI. This procedure assigns negative weights to some prices that have positive covariance with the others. Small changes in specification could easily reverse the signs on individual commodities. The individual weights therefore should not be assigned much intrinsic value.

The time path of this index is shown in the far left panel of Figure 17.7. It is apparent that this is a much more volatile index than the others. In 1974 it even took on negative values, reflecting rapid increases in prices – especially certain metals – that have negative weights in the index. Nonetheless, a moving average of this index would have a time profile reasonably similar to those of the other indexes shown in the figure.

A regression of the transformed aggregate CPI on its own history plus a thirty-six-month PDL on this first index yielded an adjusted R^2 of .32. The reduction from .57 is a measure of the cost of time aggregation into a single index; in fact, it may be seen that most of the improvement over equation (12) has been lost through time aggregation. The out-of-sample performance of this index is examined in the next subsection.

Estimation subject to constraints: The second index was derived from the first by simply eliminating all of the commodities whose prices had

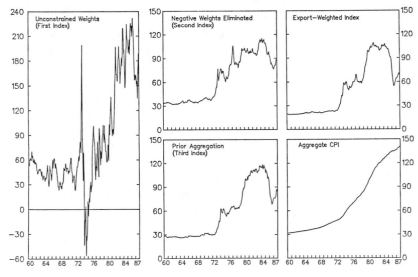

Figure 17.7. Econometrically estimated indexes, the export-weighted index, and consumer prices, 1960–87 (in GCUs; 1980 = 100).

negative coefficients in the first index. The weights for this index are shown in the third column of Table 17.4. As may be seen by comparing these weights with the export weights in the last column of the table, and by examining the movements in the index as shown in Figure 17.7, this index looks more like a conventional price index than does the unconstrained version.

A regression of the transformed aggregate CPI on itself lagged, plus a PDL on the transformed version of this second index, yielded an adjusted R^2 of .33, which is slightly higher than that for the first index but still well below the performance of the conventional export-weighted index (equation 13, above).

The third index (fourth column of Table 17.4 and lower middle panel of Figure 17.7) was derived by a procedure that differed in two major respects from that used for the first two indexes. First, most of the prices in the original set of forty were aggregated into broader categories, in order to reduce the amount of detailed information required for the estimation process and to eliminate the possibility that a commodity with relatively little importance in trade or consumption might have a large weight in the estimated index. This aggregation procedure, using world export weights, produced six aggregates (cereals, vegetable oils, beverages, meat, metals, and fibers) and five single commodities (sugar, petroleum, rubber, tobacco, and timber).[10]

When these eleven prices were converted into stationary series by taking changes in twelve-month rates of change, there was very little multicollinearity in the data matrix. Therefore, it was decided to compute the regressions using these transformed prices rather than their principal components. Thus the second stage of the procedure was to regress the transformed aggregate CPI on PDLs of the eleven transformed price series, plus the PDL on its own lagged values.[11] That regression yielded an adjusted R^2 of .52, compared with .57 for the unconstrained estimation of the first index. As before, the coefficients on the sums of the lag distributions from this regression were normalized to sum to unity and were used as the weights for the third index. The time profile for this index (Figure 17.7) is quite similar to that of the export-weighted index, although there are periods when they move independently. A regression using a PDL on this index had an adjusted R^2 of .43; this is the best in-sample result for any of the four indexes.

17.3.2   Evaluation of the estimated indexes

The properties of a leading indicator are, of course, not well defined by how well they fit within the sample period. This subsection therefore examines the post-sample properties of the estimated indexes. These properties are summarized in Table 17.5, which may be compared with the results presented earlier in Table 17.3.

As with the full-sample results, it may be seen that the third index does much better than the other two estimated indexes, and a little better than the export-weighted index, in terms of reducing the standard error of the estimate for in-sample CPI predictions. Post-sample, however, the unconstrained index does quite a bit better: the average prediction error is reduced in three of the six periods, and the RMSE is reduced in four of six cases.

The apparently poor overall quantitative performance of commodity

---

[10] The prices of bananas, hides, jute, and sisal, which did not fit neatly into the subaggregates and which had a small weight in both consumption and trade, were eliminated from this data set. The price of sugar for this exercise is a weighted average of the three prices in the full data set (a free market price and the U.S. and European Community import prices).

[11] In order to further simplify the procedure, the lag lengths in this regression were shortened to twelve months (except for petroleum, whose effect ran out to twenty-four months), the polynomials were constrained to third rather than fourth degree, and the end-point constraint was dropped.

Table 17.5. *Inflation predictions using estimated commodity price indexes, 1976–87 (in percent)* [a]

	1976–7	1978–9	1980–1	1982–3	1984–5	1986–7
Actual inflation	7.5	9.5	10.3	4.9	3.7	2.1
Baseline prediction	8.1	7.7	11.0	6.6	4.9	2.8
Baseline prediction error	0.6	−1.8	0.7	1.7	1.2	0.7
Predictions using first (unconstrained) index						
Predicted inflation	7.9	8.4	11.0	6.3	4.9	3.3
Reduction in:						
In-sample error	4.8	5.0	5.3	4.3	4.7	4.3
Prediction error	0.2	0.7	—	0.3	—	—
RMSE	32.8	27.0	—	21.1	19.0	—
Prediction using second (positive-weight) index						
Predicted inflation	8.3	6.0	11.2	7.3	6.4	4.3
Reduction in:						
In-sample error	8.0	8.5	6.5	6.5	6.3	5.3
Prediction error	—	—	—	—	—	—
RMSE	—	—	—	—	—	—
Prediction using third (prior-aggregation) index						
Predicted inflation	3.8	6.2	11.8	7.5	3.8	3.2
Reduction in:						
In-sample error	18.2	16.4	15.2	14.7	12.5	12.6
Prediction error	—	—	—	—	1.1	—
RMSE	—	—	—	—	94.6	12.7

[a]Post-sample twenty-four-month dynamic predictions of the aggregate CPI from equations as described in the text. The estimation sample is from February 1962 (plus prior lagged data) to December of the year preceding the listed forecast period.

prices as additional inflation predictors is attributable in part to the difficulty of forecasting commodity prices during the forecast period. When actual commodity prices are used in the post-sample period, the prediction errors drop sharply. The use of a twenty-four-month dynamic forecast period is a harsh standard, and the choice is to some extent arbitrary. Given the strong in-sample performance – especially for the third estimated index as well as for the export-weighted index – it is likely that better results would be obtained for shorter horizons.

Qualitative relationships may be as important as quantitative ones if commodity prices are to serve as a leading indicator. That is, one may be at least as interested in predicting turning points in CPI inflation as in predicting the value of the future inflation rate. It was already noted (see Figure 17.1) that there is an observed tendency for inflation in the export-weighted commodity price index to display cyclical patterns that are similar to those of the aggregate CPI inflation (though with differing amplitudes) and that frequently lead CPI turning points. This tendency is examined more closely in Table 17.6.

The first three columns of Table 17.6 list the turning points in the aggregate CPI inflation (denominated in GCUs) since the beginning of 1970.[12] These turning points are defined by a shift in direction that is sustained for at least three months. For a peak, it is also required that it exceed the previous trough by at least seventy-five basis points; troughs must be at least fifty basis points below the previous peak. These requirements are obviously rather arbitrary, but they do capture the major turns in CPI inflation, taking account of the general upward drift in the data.

The remaining columns of Table 17-6 indicate the lead times that one would have obtained from various commodity price indexes, or from monetary growth. These lead times are shorter than the actual lead times, usually by three or four months, in order to take account of the need for identifying a turning point. For example, when commodity price inflation reaches a trough, one cannot immediately identify it as such; only after it has risen for two or three months can one know that a trough has occurred. These turning points are defined as for the CPI, except that the required magnitudes are larger and are symmetric, reflecting the different patterns in the data.[13] A lead time of zero months

---

[12] The 1960s were eliminated from this test because the aggregate CPI displayed very little cyclical behavior during that decade.

[13] For the first estimated index, which is highly volatile, the required swing is 50 percentage points. For the other commodity price indexes, the required swing is 5 percentage points. For broad money, the requirement is the same as that for the CPI.

Table 17.6. *Prediction of turning points in aggregate CPI inflation*

Turning points in aggregate CPI inflation			Lead time for prediction (in months)[a]				
Date	Peak or trough	Inflation rate	Export weights	First index	Second index	Third index	Broad money
Feb. 1970	P	6.0	—	4	—	—	1
June 1972	T	3.9	—	6	6	4	—
Nov. 1974	P	13.7	7	—	0x	7	—
July 1976	T	7.1	6	—	5x	6	—
June 1977	P	8.2	1x	15	2	2	—
April 1978	T	6.4	—	—	—	—	7
April 1980	P	12.1	0	16	6	—	—
Dec. 1986	T	1.0	2x	—	11x	1x	—
Nov. 1987	P	3.1	0	—	—	—	—

[a] x indicates that a false signal preceded the correct one. — indicates (a) that the index was pointing in the wrong direction at the time of the turning point in the CPI or (b) that the index called the turning point more than eighteen months in advance or before the preceding turning point.

is treated as a successful prediction, because the commodity price data are available a few weeks earlier than the CPI data.

The main conclusion to be drawn from Table 17.6 is that the commodity price indexes – with the exception of the first (unconstrained) estimated index – are reasonably successful predictors of turning points. The conventional export-weighted index predicted six of the nine turning points, as did the second estimated index. These indexes gave from one to three false signals over the eighteen-year period. The third estimated index predicted five turns, while the first predicted four.[14] In contrast, growth in the aggregate stock of money predicted only two of the nine turning points in the aggregate CPI.

17.4   Conclusions

This chapter has argued that commodity prices might serve as a useful leading indicator of inflation, based on the relative importance of flexible auction markets for the determination of these prices. They thus may have a tendency to respond relatively quickly, especially in response to monetary disturbances. This conclusion holds regardless of whether primary commodities serve mainly as final goods or as industrial inputs.

Empirical evaluation of conventional trade-weighted commodity price indexes leads to several conclusions. First, commodity and consumer prices are not cointegrated; the hypothesis that the relative price of primary commodities is bounded, or that there is a reliable long-run relationship between the level of commodity prices and the level of consumer prices, may be rejected. Second, there is a tendency for changes in commodity prices to lead those in consumer prices, at least when the data are denominated in a broad index of major-country currencies. When the data are denominated in U.S. dollars, consumer prices appear to lead commodity prices. This conclusion underscores the importance of making appropriate allowances for exchange rate changes in analyzing these relationships. Third, although the inclusion of commodity prices significantly improves the in-sample fit of regressions of an aggregate (multi-country) consumer price index, the results may not be sufficiently stable to improve post-sample forecasts. The prediction record, however, improves in the most recent period.

[14] The results for the estimated indexes are hypothetical and illustrative, because the indexes were constructed using data through 1982 and so could not have been used to predict the earlier turning points.

Estimation of alternative commodity-price indexes, in which the weights are chosen so as to minimize the residual variance in aggregate inflation regressions, was not fully successful. The derived indexes do track the behavior of the aggregate CPI reasonably well in-sample. On the other hand, the weights are not robust with respect to changes in the methodology, and the indexes work only moderately well in post-sample predictions. Overall, the estimated indexes do not appear to offer significant advantages over the conventional export-weighted index.

The bottom line is that commodity prices do have a useful role to play in this context, but one must be careful to interpret the relationships correctly. The ratio of consumer to commodity price movements changes over time, and the relative price of commodities undergoes long sustained swings; nonetheless, the qualitative linkages are quite evident in the data. Perhaps most important, turning points in commodity-price inflation frequently precede turning points in consumer-price inflation for the large industrial countries as a group.

REFERENCES

Angell, W. D. (1987), "A Commodity Price Guide to Monetary Aggregate Targeting," paper prepared for Lehrman Institute, December 10.

Bosworth, B. P., and R. Z. Lawrence (1982), *Commodity Prices and the New Inflation.* Washington, D.C.: The Brookings Institution.

Dornbusch, R. (1976), "Expectations and Exchange Rate Dynamics," *Journal of Political Economy, 84,* 1161–76.

Durand, M., and S. Blöndal (1988), "Are Commodity Prices Leading Indicators of OECD Prices?," OECD Department of Economics and Statistics, Working Paper No. 49, February.

Engle, R. F., and C. W. J. Granger (1987), "Co-Integration and Error Correction: Representation, Estimation, and Testing," *Econometrica, 55* (March), 251–76.

Frankel, J. A. (1986), "Expectations and Commodity Price Dynamics: The Overshooting Model," *American Journal of Agricultural Economics, 68* (May), 344–8.

Frenkel, J. A., and C. A. Rodriguez (1982), "Exchange Rate Dynamics and the Overshooting Hypothesis," *Staff Papers,* International Monetary Fund, 29 (March), 1–30.

Granger, C. W. J. (1986), "Developments in the Study of Cointegrated Economic Variables," *Oxford Bulletin of Economics and Statistics, 48* (August), 213–28.

Hall, R. E. (1982), *Inflation: Causes and Effects.* Chicago: The University of Chicago Press.

   (1987), "Choice of Indicators for Monetary Policy," testimony before the Subcommittee on Domestic Monetary Policy and the Subcommittee on International Finance, Trade, and Monetary Policy, U.S. House Committee on Banking, Finance, and Urban Affairs, November 17.

International Monetary Fund (1986), *Primary Commodities: Market Developments and Outlook.* Washington, D.C.: IMF, May.

International Monetary Fund (1988), *World Economic Outlook: A Survey by the Staff of the International Monetary Fund.* (Washington, D.C.: IMF, April.

Klein, P. A. (1986), "Leading Indicators of Inflation in Market Economies," *International Journal of Forecasting, 2,* 403–12.

CHAPTER 18

A leading indicator of inflation based on interest rates

Susmita Dasgupta and Kajal Lahiri

Correct prediction of the inflation rate and its turning points is an important problem for businesses and households alike. An early signal for a major turn in the inflation rate will allow economic agents to redo their economic calculations for the forthcoming environment. Because inflation rates are highly cyclical, Moore (1983a, 1983b) adapted the leading indicator approach, long associated with the National Bureau of Economic Research (NBER) studies of business cycles, to specifically forecast the inflation rate. Klein (1986) successfully extended this methodology of inflation forecasting to a number of major market-oriented economies. Moore (1986) reported that the composite inflation indicator has a better ex post record in forecasting next year's inflation rate than the consensus of economists has achieved. In Chapter 16, Roth evaluated five different leading indicators of inflation and found that composite indicators have a very impressive track record.

The main purpose of this chapter is to propose another predictor of inflation obtained by extracting information about future inflation from nominal interest rates of various maturities. For the sake of comparison, we will analyze these forecasts in the context of the existing leading indicator literature. Since the nominal interest rate, which is known at the beginning of a period, can be written as expected real interest rate plus expected rate of inflation, a reasonable estimate of the ex ante real rate will yield an equally reasonable estimate of the inflation component. Thus, in the extreme case in which the real rate is taken to be approximately constant, the variation in the nominal rate will reflect one-for-

We are grateful to Michael Niemira, who kindly sent us the data necessary for reconstructing his inflation index, and to Robert Flood, for giving us a program to compute the GMM estimates reported in this chapter. We thank Terrence Kinal and Geoffrey Moore for many helpful conversations.

one the variation in the expected inflation rate (see Fama 1975; Fisher 1930). Several recent studies have utilized this framework to forecast inflation by modeling the expected real interest rate appropriately.[1] On the whole, the results show that the derived price forecasts are unbiased and efficient and perform better than many survey forecasts. This is potentially promising, since the leading indicator based on interest rates will have many of the desirable characteristics of a good indicator variable.[2] The indicator is based on solid yet simple economic theory representing a very important economic process and will not be sensitive to official data revisions.

The plan of this chapter is as follows: In section 18.1, we set out the model and explain how monthly values of the leading inflation indicator will be calculated once prices and yields on Treasury bills are known for that month. In section 18.2, we present the empirical results and compare our results with a composite leading indicator developed by Niemira (1986). Finally, concluding remarks are presented in section 18.3.

18.1   The model

The nominal rate of interest for a k-period bond can be decomposed as

$$R_{t+k,k} = i_{t+k,k} + \Pi^e_{t+k,k} \tag{1}$$

where $R_{t+k,k}$ is the nominal return for holding a bond for k periods realized at time $t + k$, $\Pi^e_{t+k,k}$ is the expected rate of inflation formed at point t to prevail over the ensuing k periods, and $i_{t+k,k}$ is the expected (ex ante) real rate of interest for the same period.[3] Note that at time t, $R_{t+k,k}$ is known to both the economic agent and the econometrician. However, $i_{t+k,k}$ and $\Pi^e_{t+k,k}$ are unknown to the econometrician, but not to the economic agent. Our aim is to get an estimate of $i_{t+k,k}$ in order to identify $\Pi^e_{t+k,k}$.

The expected inflation rate $\Pi^e_{t+k,k}$ is obtained as the mathematical expectation of the inflation rate $\Pi_{t+k,k}$, conditional on the information set I_t available at time t. This is the so-called rational expectations hypothesis (REH), which states that

$$E(\Pi_{t+k,k} - \Pi^e_{t+k,k} \mid I_t) = 0 \tag{2}$$

---

[1] See Mishkin (1981), Lahiri (1981), Lahiri and Lee (1981), Fama and Gibbons (1984), Huizinga and Mishkin (1984), Hafer and Hein (1985), Hamilton (1985), Burmeister, Wall, and Hamilton (1986), Rosengren (1987), Kinal and Lahiri (1988), Lahiri and Zaprowski (1988), etc.

[2] See Roth (1986) and Chapter 16.

[3] See Lahiri and Zaprowski (1988).

where $E(\cdot)$ is the expectation operator. One of the implications of equation (2) is that

$$\Pi_{t+k,k} = \Pi^e_{t+k,k} + \epsilon_{t+k,k} \tag{3}$$

where $\epsilon_{t+k,k}$ is the price forecast error having zero expectation and a finite variance σ^2_ϵ.

We define the realized (ex post) real interest rate as

$$R_{t+k,k} - \Pi_{t+k,k} = r_{t+k,k} = i_{t+k,k} - \epsilon_{t+k,k} \tag{4}$$

Note that $r_{t+k,k}$ is known only at time $t + k$. Recent research on real interest rates has established that they are not constant.[4] The following general autoregressive (AR) model, which we use to describe the movement in the ex ante real rate, incorporates the random walk model as a special case.

$$i_{t+k,k} = a_0 + \sum_{j=1}^{l} a_j i_{t+k-j,k} + W_{t+k,k} \tag{5}$$

Any set of variables known to the economic agent at time t that may affect $i_{t+k,k}$ can be introduced in equation (5) without affecting the analysis that follows. However, a number of justifiable macroeconomic variables, such as supply shocks, exogenous demand, and liquidity, were found to be redundant by Kinal and Lahiri (1988). By using equations (3), (4), and (5), we obtain an equation in terms of observables as

$$r_{t+k,k} = a_0 + \sum_{j=1}^{l} a_j r_{t+k-j,k} + V_t \tag{6}$$

where

$$V_t = -\epsilon_{t+k,k} + W_{t+k,k} + \sum_{j=1}^{l} a_j \epsilon_{t+k-j,k}$$

Thus, equation (6) is an autoregressive (AR) model with moving average (MA) errors. Efficient estimation of such models can be achieved by using the generalized method of moments (GMM) technique due to Hansen (1982). (See also Kinal and Lahiri, 1988.) Note that when the holding period (k) is larger than the observation interval the data are overlapping. This introduces a moving average build up of errors of order k, in addition to the MA(l) errors in V_t that we have due to the AR(l) real rate process. This makes the final structure of V_t more complicated and, a priori, indeterminate. Fortunately, it is our empirical

[4] Mincer and Zarnowitz (1969) discuss this point. See also Pesando (1975).

experience that in the final analysis V_t can become serially uncorrelated, thereby making the estimation process particularly simple. Ordinary least squares will yield consistent a_j parameters in equation (6).

At time t, CPI_t arrives, and hence we can compute $\Pi_{t,k}$ as $(\ln CPI_t - \ln CPI_{t-k}) \times 100$. Hence $r_{t,k} = R_{t,k} - \Pi_{t,k}$ can be obtained. Thus, we can run the regression

$$r_{t,k} = a_0 + \sum_{j=1}^{l} a_j r_{t-j,k} + V_t \tag{6a}$$

to estimate a_j ($j = 0, 1, 2, \ldots$), and use these a_j to predict the ex ante real rate as

$$\hat{r}_{t+1,k} = \hat{a}_0 + \sum_{j=1}^{l} \hat{a}_j\, r_{t-j,k} \tag{6b}$$

Note, however, that $r_{t+1,k}$ is an estimate of the expected real rate over the period $(t - 11, t + 1)$, but the real rate over $(t, t + 1)$ is unknown at time t. In order to get $\Pi^e_{t+k,k}$ in equation (1), we need to estimate $i_{t+k,k}$ by estimating $r_{t+k,k}$, which is the expected real rate over the appropriate holding period $(t, t + k)$. Rationality requires that an optimal forecast at t for k periods ahead is achieved by substitution of the as yet unknown magnitudes in the autoregression [equation (6)] by their forecast values recursively as

$$\hat{r}_{t+2,k} = \hat{a}_0 + \hat{a}_1\hat{r}_{t+1,k} + \hat{a}_2 r_{t,k} + \hat{a}_3 r_{t-1,k} + \ldots \tag{7}$$
$$\hat{r}_{t+3,k} = \hat{a}_0 + \hat{a}_1\hat{r}_{t+2,k} + \hat{a}_2\hat{r}_{t+1,k} + \hat{a}_3 r_{t,k} \ldots$$
$$.$$
$$.$$
$$.$$
$$\hat{r}_{t+k,k} = \hat{a}_0 + \hat{a}_1\hat{r}_{t+k-1,k} + \hat{a}_2\hat{r}_{t+k-2,k} + \hat{a}_3\hat{r}_{t+k-3,k} + \ldots + \hat{a}_k r_{t,k}$$

Once we have an estimate of the agents' expected real rate for holding the bond over $(t, t + k)$, the expected rate of inflation over the same period can be obtained simply as

$$\Pi^e_{t+k,k} = R_{t+k,k} - \hat{i}_{it+k,k} \tag{8}$$

where $\hat{i}_{t+k,k} = \hat{r}_{t+k,k}$. Since it is reasonable to assume that economic agents in the financial markets will try to predict the forthcoming inflation rate in the best possible manner given whatever information is available as of time t, $\Pi^e_{t+k,k}$ can be taken as the market's best guess about future inflation.

When additional information arrives at the end of each month, we can go through the steps (6)–(8) repeatedly to generate a sequence of k-

period ahead forecasts $\Pi_{t+k+j,k}$($j = 1, 2, \ldots$). These forecasts are truly ex ante in the sense that in generating a historical prediction for $\Pi^e_{t,k}$, no information after t was utilized. Note that in order to generate k-period ahead forecasts we should in principle use a k-period bond whose returns are market determined in nominal terms at the beginning of the period.

18.2 Empirical results

One advantage of using the interest rate as an indicator of inflation is that by choosing a bond of appropriate maturity we can predetermine the lead time for turning point predictions. The empirical analysis uses monthly data for January 1954 through September 1986. Data on the consumer price index (CPI) were seasonally adjusted. For the nominal interest rate variable, we use the yield on new issues of twelve-month Treasury bills sold at the last week of the last month.

We have experimented with three alternative estimates of the ex ante real rate to generate price forecasts. The first is based on full rationality using the chain rule of forecasting, and is given in equation (7). We used a twelve-order autoregressive model where the residuals were found to be serially uncorrelated. The second option used the same twelve-order AR process for the ex ante real rate, but rather than generating a forecast for $r_{t+k,k}$ recursively by chain rule, it used $\hat{r}_{t+1,k}$ as a proxy for $r_{t+k,k}$ as in equation (6b). The third alternative assumes that the real rate is a random walk, that is, $r_{t+1,k} = r_{t,k} + V_{t+1}$.[5] This simplifies the process of generating price forecasts very significantly, since now the latest observed real rate is used as an estimate of $i_{t+k,k}$. Thus $\hat{\Pi}^e_{t+k,k}$ is obtained as $R_{t+k,k} - r_{t-1,k}$. Over our sample period, the real rate process was estimated as

$$r_{t,k} = .979r_{t-1,k} + U_t + .267U_{t-1} \tag{9}$$

The standard error of the autoregressive parameter was .0107. Using the Phillips (1987) statistic for testing for a unit root, we could not reject the null hypotheses. Note that because of overlapping data with the autoregressive model, the MA coefficient was estimated to be only .267. In Fama and Gibbons (1984) and Huizinga and Mishkin (1984), the same parameter was very close to one because their data were non-overlapping. For the first two alternatives, we generated ex ante price forecasts by estimating the AR(12) real rate model recursively from December

---

[5] These last two options are very similar in spirit to what Fama and Gibbons (1984) have utilized; however, their use was not in the context of multispan forecasts with overlapping data.

Table 18.1. *Inflation forecast errors for alternative real rate models*

Real rate model	Mean error	RMSE
Random walk, 1953:01–1986:08	−.0716	2.596
Random walk, 1963:01–1986:08	−.0726	2.961
AR(12) model without chain rule, 1963:01–1986:08	.0804	2.672
AR(12) with chain rule, 1963:01–1986:08	−.0390	3.077

1962 to September 1986.[6] The model is first estimated over January 1954 to December 1962. Using these parameter values, forecasts are made for January 1963 to December 1963. This forecast value, when subtracted from the relevant nominal rate, will yield our estimate of the inflation forecast for the one-year horizon January–December 1963. Monthly one-year ahead forecasts are then generated recursively by updating the original sample period by one additional observation at a time. In this way, the updated structural parameters and the forecasts will reflect all the up-to-date information. Out-of-sample prediction errors associated with these three alternative real rate models are given in Table 18.1. We find that the mean error is very close to zero for all of them. Since no regression estimation is necessary for the random walk alternative, we could generate ex ante forecasts from January 1953. Overall, we find that in terms of root mean squared prediction errors the complicated alternatives do not perform any better than the simple random walk model. Thus, in the remainder of the chapter, we will report and analyze results obtained using this option only.

By regressing $\Pi_{t+12,k}$ on $\Pi^e_{t+12,k}$ we obtained the following results[7]

$$\Pi_{t+12,12} = 1.49 + .648\,\hat{\Pi}_{t+12,12}, \ \bar{R}^2 = .63. \tag{10}$$
$$\quad\ \ (.15)\quad (.024)$$

[6] See Lahiri and Zaprowski (1988) for calculational details.

[7] The numbers in parentheses are asymptotically correct standard errors obtained by using formula given in Hansen (1982). The errors, as expected, were serially correlated having an MA(11) process. In a different context Hodrick and Hansen (1989) have recently suggested a simpler procedure to test a relationship like equation (10). The idea is to regress $12 \times \Pi_{t+1,1}$ on $(\hat{\Pi}^e_{t+12,12} + \hat{\Pi}^e_{t-11,12} + \cdots + \hat{\Pi}^e_{t+1,12})/12$. This way one is expected to avoid the moving-average buildup of errors due to overlapping data, and the estimation is achieved by ordinary least squares. The results were very similar to equation (10), and the residuals were almost serially uncorrelated.

Thus more than 60 percent of the variation in yearly inflation rate is explained by our interest rate predictor. Given that here we are dealing with twelve-period ahead ex ante forecasts, the record is quite impressive. Moreover, the explanatory power of more than 60 percent was true over various subperiods. In order to test whether nominal interest has any causal effect on inflation rate in the Granger sense, we regressed $\Pi_{t+12,k}$ on $\Pi_{t,12}$, $\Pi_{t-1,12}$, . . . $\Pi_{t-32,12}$ and $R_{t,12}$, $R_{t-1,12}$ . . . $R_{t-32,12}$ and tested whether the coefficients corresponding to $R_{t-j,12}$ ($j = 0, 1, . . .$) are jointly zero. The null hypothesis was resoundingly rejected at the 5 percent level of significance.

18.2.1 Turning point predictions

Another way of evaluating the inflation predictor is to find out how well it can be used as an early signal for cyclical swings in inflation. Our indicator will be perfect if it turns exactly twelve months before a turn in inflation rate and turns only before turns in inflation. Table 18.2 documents how well the indicator meets this criterion. It always turned before a turn in inflation, as is evident from the last column, and it never missed an inflation turning point. However, rather than the expected mean lead time of twelve months, the average lead is little over seven months. For troughs the mean lead time is slightly higher (8.25 months) than that for peaks (6 months). Thus, given the record over last thirty-six years, the inflation predictor extracted solely from interest rates can have nearly six to seven months of lead time to predict an impending turn in the inflation rate with considerable persistence. In Figure 18.1, we have plotted our inflation predictor against the six-month inflation rate. We find that the cyclical movements of the two series are remarkably similar. The only exception is the early 1980s, where actual inflation was grossly mispredicted by the forecasts. The U.S. economy was subjected to a number of shocks in the early 1980s. A new chairman took the helm of the Federal Reserve system (Fed) in 1979 and almost immediately the Fed announced a change in its operating procedure from controlling interest rates to targeting the money supply. The Fed then returned to its pre-1979 operating procedure in October 1982. Kinal and Lahiri (1988) found evidence for a significant break in the real rate process during 1980–2. They also found evidence that this was a short-lived specification shift, since after 1982 the process seems to have returned to its pre-1980 formulation. Thus, in the future our inflation predictor is expected to perform as well as its pre-1980 record. In addition, one can argue that prediction errors during 1980–2 could be genuine "surprises" since the period was in real flux and the economic

Table 18.2. *Twelve-month inflation forecasts: turning point signals*

Inflation troughs (T) and peaks (P)	Predicted troughs and peaks	Timing of signals
Oct. 1954 (T)	Aug. 1955	−2
Mar. 1958 (P)	Feb. 1958	−13
Apr. 1959 (T)	July 1959	−9
Oct. 1959 (P)	July 1960	−3
June 1961 (T)	Sept. 1961	−9
Oct. 1966 (P)	May 1967	−5
May 1967 (T)	May 1968	0
Feb. 1970 (P)	Sept. 1970	−5
June 1972 (T)	Mar. 1972	−15
Sept. 1974 (P)	Aug. 1974	−13
June 1976 (T)	June 1976	−12
Mar. 1980 (P)	Mar. 1981	0
Mar. 1983 (T)	May 1983	−10
Feb. 1984 (P)	May 1985	3
Apr. 1986 (T)	July 1986	−9
Mean lead (−) or lag (+)		
All turning points		−7.12
Troughs		−8.25
Peaks		−6.00

[a]Number of months that indicator turning point signals lead (−) or lag (+) actual turning points.

agents were going through a serious learning experience about the regime change.

We have also conducted a similar turning point analysis after generating three-month ahead forecasts based on three-month Treasury bill rates. The real rate model was a simple random walk. Results are given in Table 18.3, where we find that the interest rate-based predictor could anticipate all turning points. The average lead length for troughs was three months, as expected. However, the average for peaks was a lag of 0.17 months. This result is similar to the twelve-month results; the lead length to anticipate troughs seems to be longer than that for peaks. Since anticipating troughs is in many ways more critical for inflation predic-

347

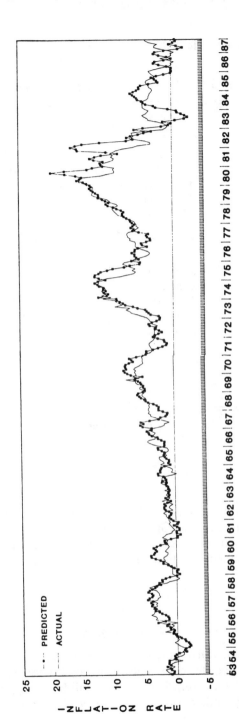

Figure 18.1. Six months ahead inflation forecasts.

Table 18.3. *Three-month inflation forecasts: turning point signals*

Inflation troughs (T) and peaks (P)	Predicted troughs and peaks	Timing of signals
Oct. 1959 (P)	Jan. 1960	0
June 1961 (T)	July 1961	−2
Oct. 1966 (P)	Jan. 1966	0
May 1967 (T)	May 1967	−3
Feb. 1970 (P)	Apr. 1970	−1
June 1972 (T)	Feb. 1972	−7
Sept. 1974 (P)	Jan. 1975	+1
June 1976 (T)	July 1976	−2
Mar. 1980 (P)	June 1980	0
Mar. 1983 (T)	Feb. 1983	−4
Feb. 1984 (P)	June 1984	+1
Apr. 1986 (T)	July 1986	0
Mean lead (−) or lag (+)		
All turning points		−1.42
Troughs		−3.0
Peaks		+.17

[a]Number of months that indicator turning point signals lead (−) or lag (−) actual turning points.

tion, this feature of the interest-based inflation indicator seems to be particularly useful. Also in terms of Granger's causality test, we found that the direction of causality goes strictly from the generated forecasts to the subsequently observed inflation rates and not the other way around.

18.2.2 Comparison with a composite leading indicator

In Chapter 16, Roth evaluated five different leading indicators of inflation. Two of these are composite indexes developed by Moore (1983b, 1986), one for use by the Center for International Business Cycle Research (CIBCR) and the other for the *Journal of Commerce*. The third inflation indicator, developed by Niemira (1986), is a composite of seven economic series: vendor performance (VP), the ratio of employment to population (EP), the National Association of Purchasing Managers' (NAPM) buying price survey, Dallas Federal Reserves trade-weighted dollar index (DEXR), the Federal Reserve's measure of capacity utilization in manufacturing (CUM), the *Journal of Commerce* index of spot prices of industrial raw material (JSPI), and the U.S. Department of Agriculture series on agricultural prices (AGP).[8]

Since the Niemira index is essentially a careful elaboration of Moore's CIBCR index using the same Department of Commerce/NBER methodology, and seems to be more comprehensive, we shall compare the inflation predictor from interest rates ($\hat{\Pi}_{t+k,k}$) with the Niemira composite index (NCI). In order to be directly comparable, we reconstructed the Niemira index as a six-month ahead predictor by optimally choosing the lead-lengths of individual indices following the R^2 rule suggested by Holmes (1986). Since DEXR and AGP were added as two additional indexes later, two separate sets of weights were calculated, one for January 1953–February 1971 and the other for March 1971–September 1986. These are given in Table 18.4. Some of the weights changed remarkably from one subperiod to another, which is one of the reasons composite indicators often need reexamination. On the other hand, the corresponding values for the interest rate-based predictor were .729 and .642, respectively. We have done turning point calculations using the Niemira index similar to those in Table 18.2 and found that it anticipated all turning points correctly. As constructed, the average lead length was very close to six months. However, it gave two false signals for peaks in February 1954 and August 1970. These results are very similar to those found by Roth (1986) and Niemira (1986).

In order to judge the relative predictive capabilities of the alternative leading indicators, we used a procedure recently suggested by Fair and Shiller (1989). The information content of different competing forecasts can be compared by regressing the actual *change* in a variable to be forecasted on alternative forecasts of the *changes,* following the econometric literature on encompassing tests of non-nested hypotheses. Since we can not directly compare the RMSE of the two indicators, this procedure is particularly suitable for our situation. Ordinary least squares regression

---

[8] The other two indicators evaluated by Roth were (a) the ratio of the Federal Reserve's Capacity Utilization measure to the trade-weighted value of dollar and (b) the growth rate of the narrowly defined money supply. The track records of these two indicators were either too short or not as good as the composite indicators.

Table 18.4. *Weights for the Niemira index*[a]

	1953:01–1971:02			1971:03–1986:09	
	R^2	Weights		R^2	Weights
NAPM			NAPM		
(−5)	.397	.318	(−5)	.548	.328
EP			EP		
(−1)	.298	.245	(−1)	.006	.003
VP			VP		
(−9)	.198	.163	(−9)	.265	.158
CUM			CUM		
(−7)	.007	.006	(−7)	.388	.232
JSPI	.324	.266	JSPI	.021	.013
			DEXR		
			(−3)	.406	.243
			AGP		
			(−12)	.033	.019

[a]Numbers in the parentheses are the leads in the component series that maximized the correlation with the six-month inflation rate.

over the sample period January 1953–September 1986 for a total of 405 observations gave the following results.

$$\Pi_{t+k,k} - \Pi_{t+k-1,k} = \begin{matrix} -.007 \\ (-.082) \end{matrix} + \begin{matrix} .483 \\ (6.85) \end{matrix} (\Pi_{t+k,k} - \Pi_{t+k-1,k})$$
$$+ \begin{matrix} .112 \\ (3.58) \end{matrix} (\text{NCI}_{t+k,k} - \Pi_{t+k-1,k}) \quad (11)$$

The numbers in parentheses are t-ratios that have been adjusted following Hansen (1982). Since the units of the two predictors are quite different, in order to compare the relative importance of the two, we computed what are known as beta or standardized coefficients based on the above regression results. A beta coefficient is obtained by multiplying the regression coefficient by the ratio of the standard deviation of the particular explanatory variable to that of the dependent variable. The resulting standardized coefficients then measure the change in the dependent variable corresponding to a unit change in the respective explanatory variable, holding the other explanatory variables constant, and measuring all changes in standard deviation units. Beta-coefficients for $\hat{\Pi}_{t+k,k}$ and $\text{NCI}_{t+k,k}$ were calculated to be .355 and .174, respectively. Thus we find that even though both predictors have independent information in explaining inflation, the interest rate-based predictor ($\hat{\Pi}^e$) dominates the composite leading indicator (NCI). The interest rate predictor seems to have almost two times more predictive power than the composite index. More important, our results suggest that the Niemira index will benefit by incorporating the interest rate-based predictor as one of its major components.

18.3   Conclusion

Because of the cyclical nature of inflation rates, the leading indicator approach seems to be useful in predicting both the level and the turning points of the inflation rate. In this chapter, we have analyzed an inflation indicator based solely on nominal interest rates. We have extended the analysis of Fama (1975), Lahiri and Lee (1981), Mishkin (1981), Fama and Gibbons (1984), Hafer and Hein (1985), Hamilton (1985), Kinal and Lahiri (1988), and others to develop a multiperiod leading indicator of inflation with overlapping observations. We found that a simple random walk model for the real interest rate performs as well as the more complicated recursively generated forecasts based on a chain rule of forecasting. We experimented with twelve- and three-months ahead forecasts, and found that over 1953–86 they anticipated all turning points, much like the comprehensive composite leading indicators developed by Moore (1983b, 1986) and Niemira (1986). Moreover, by using a recent test proposed by Fair and Shiller (1989), we found that the simple interest rate-based inflation predictor is two times more efficient in predicting the six-month ahead inflation rate than the composite leading indicator developed by Niemira (1986). However, the test results also imply that the Niemira index has significant independent information about future inflation not contained in the simple interest rate-based inflation predictor. This suggests that the usefulness of a composite leading indicator of inflation can be greatly enhanced if price forecasts extracted from the bond market are carefully included as one of its components. This is left for future research.

REFERENCES

Burmeister, E., E. D. Wall, and J. D. Hamilton (1986), "Estimation of Unobserved Expected Monthly Inflation Using Kalman Filter," *Journal of Business and Economic Statistics, 4* (2, April), 147–60.

Fair, R. C., and R. J. Shiller (1989), "The Information Content of Ex Ante Forecasts," *Review of Economics and Statistics, 71*, 325–31.

Fama, E. F. (1975), "Short-term Interest Rates as Predictors of Inflation," *American Economic Review, 75*, 68–87.

Fama, E. F., and M. R. Gibbons (1984), "A Comparison of Inflation Forecasts," *Journal of Monetary Economics, 13*, 327–48.

Fisher, I. (1930), *The Theory of Interest.* New York: Macmillan (reprinted by A. M. Kelly, Clifton, N.J., 1965).

Hafer, R. W., and S. E. Hein (1985), "On the Accuracy of Time-Series, Interest Rate and Survey Forecasting of Inflation," *Journal of Business, 58*, 377–98.

Hamilton, J. D. (1985), "Uncovering Financial Market Expectations of Inflation," *Journal of Political Economy, 93*, 1224–41.

Hansen, L. P. (1982), "Large Sample Properties of Generalized Method of Moments," *Econometrica, 50*, 1029–54.

Hodrick, R. J., and L. P. Hansen (1989), "Dividend Yields and Expected Stock Returns: Alternative Procedures for Inference and Measurement," Mimeo, October.

Holmes, R. A. (1986), "Leading Indicators of Industrial Employment in British Columbia," *International Journal of Forecasting, 2* (1), 87–100.

Huizinga, J., and F. S. Mishkin (1984), "Inflation and Real Interest Rates on Assets of Different Risk Characteristics," *Journal of Finance, 39*, 699–712.

Kinal, T., and K. Lahiri (1988), "A Model for Ex Ante Real Interest Rates and Derived Inflation Forecasts," *Journal of the American Statistical Association, 83*, (September), 665–73.

Klein, P. A. (1986), "Leading Indicators of Inflation in Market Economies," *International Journal of Forecasting, 2* (4), 403–12.

Lahiri, K. (1981), *The Econometrics of Inflationary Expectations.* Amsterdam: North-Holland Publishing Co.

Lahiri, K., and J. S. Lee (1981), "On the Constancy of Real Interest Rates and the Mundell Effect," *Journal of Banking and Finance, 5*, 557–73.

Lahiri, K., and M. Zaprowski (1988), "A Comparison of Alternative Real Rate Estimates," *Oxford Bulletin of Economics and Statistics, 50* (August), 303–12.

Mincer, J., and V. Zarnowitz (1969), "The Evaluation of Economic Forecasts," in J. Mincer, ed., *Economic Forecasts and Expectations.* New York: NBER, Columbia University Press.

Mishkin, F. S. (1981), "The Real Interest Rate: An Empirical Investigation," in K. Brunner and L. Metzer, eds., *Carnegie-Rochester Conference Series on Public Policy,* autumn, pp. 152–200.

Moore, G. H. (1983a), *Business Cycles, Inflation and Forecasting.* Cambridge, Mass: Ballinger.

(1983b), "Inflation Barometer: Rougher Weather Ahead," *The Morgan Guaranty Survey,* December 6–10.

(1986), "A Revised Leading Index of Inflation," Center for International Business Cycle Research, Graduate School of Business, Columbia University, February.

Niemira, M. P. (1986), "Updated PW Leading Indicator of Inflation," PaineWebber, New York, December 26.

Pesando, J. (1975), "A Note on the Rationality of Livingston's Price Expectations Data," *Journal of Political Economy, 89*, 849–858.

Phillips, P. C. B. (1987), "Time Series Regression with a Unit Root," *Econometrica, 55,* 277–301.

Roth, H. L. (1986), "Leading Indicators of Inflation," *Economic Review,* Federal Reserve Bank of Kansas City, *71* (9, November), 3–20.

Rosengren, E. S. (1987), "Forecasting Changes in Inflation Using the Treasury Bill Futures Market," *New England Economic Review,* Federal Reserve Bank of Boston, March/April, pp. 41–8.

CHAPTER 19

Using composite leading indicators of consumption to forecast sales and to signal turning points in the stock market

Michael P. Niemira

Consumption represents two-thirds of the nation's output. Although consumption is so important, economists generally explain consumer spending patterns with little more than Keynes's fundamental psychological law. Keynes (1936) observed that people "increase their consumption as income increases, but not by as much as the increase in their income." Following this line of reasoning, consumption is passive and dances to the tune of income. Even widely accepted theories of consumption, such as the permanent income hypothesis or the relative income hypothesis, continue this myth by viewing income as the main *cyclical* force behind consumption. If income declines, the consumer draws down savings, which initially acts as a consumption-smoothing mechanism, to maintain a more or less constant growth rate in consumer spending. But is consumption truly passive? Gardner Ackley (1961) asked the pertinent question regarding the relationship of income and consumption: *Which is the direction of causation?* While Ackley correctly observed that a high correlation between income and consumption was due to the "double relationship" that income determines consumption while consumption also drives income, he did not go far enough in his analysis.[1]

As shown in Figure 19.1, business cycle history supports the view that at cyclical turning points, consumption declines prior to a decline in income. Indeed, Robert E. Hall (1987) recently set out to show that the

This is based on work done at PaineWebber and published in association with Ann Knight, Steve Girsky, Linda Kristiansen, and Pat McCormack. Thanks to Margo McGlade and Jack Schwager for their helpful comments and suggestions on various aspects of the work. Also thanks to Hope Flammer, Nancy Parish, and April Brady.
[1] This should not be viewed as suggesting that income is unimportant at cyclical turning points; however, it is argued that other dynamics are more important at turning points.

355

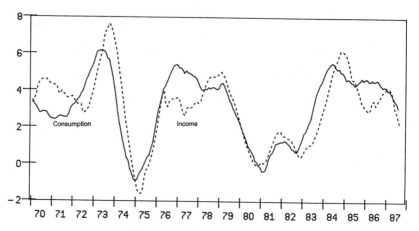

Figure 19.1. Cyclical relationship between consumption and income. Real dollars, twelve-month growth rates.

role of the consumer has been incorrectly subjugated in business cycle theories. His approach was criticized on methodology grounds (and maybe correctly so), but the conclusion is more defensible than his critics granted him. Furthermore, Mengarelli (1986) argued theoretically that while the *pure* underconsumption theory alone is not sufficient to produce a recession, it can be a significant factor leading to one.

It is not the intent of this paper to develop a cyclical theory of consumption,[2] but it is important to recognize that although employment and income growth are key determinants of spending, fluctuation in those aggregates generally does not lead cyclical fluctuation in consumer spending. Therefore, monitoring the economic fundamentals, while important, does not provide advance warning of the cyclical direction of future retail sales. Nonetheless, advance warning is still possible. Using the National Bureau of Economic Research (NBER) leading indicator approach, I have compiled a barometer of future sales activity for automotive and nonautomotive retail sales. I then show that these leading indicators can be helpful for spotting cyclical changes in their specific industry stock market cycles.

[2] It does not take a major deviation from accepted theory to argue this point. For example, if the consumption function is defined as: $c_t = f(c_{t-1}, y_t)$ where c is the rate of change in consumption and y is the rate of change in income, this suggests that lagged consumption growth can cause a further slowdown (or increase) in the current period's consumption rate. This begs the question of why the lagged consumption rate declined (increased), but it does provide a logical model of the process.

19.1   Leading indicator of automotive sales[3]

Automobile industry sales have traditionally been driven by two components, one demographic and one economic. The demographic component is based on factors such as cars per household, scrappage rates, and the age distribution of cars on the road. The economic component is affected by factors such as personal income, installment debt, and interest rates. While the demographics drive long-term auto sales trends, economic factors influence the short-term contours of the auto cycle.

19.1.1   *Formulation of the leading indicator of auto sales*

The NBER methodology was used to formulate a "leading indicator" of the automotive sales cycle. The advantage of the NBER method over more elaborate econometric models is that a leading indicator is easy to understand, easy to communicate, and easy to monitor.[4] While the leading indicator approach does not have a rigid theoretical structure, it is based on a theory of index models (Sargent and Sims, 1977). Although this "theory" provides a solid mathematical framework for the NBER's research method, it does not provide, in and of itself, the economic rationale for the selection of the individual components to include in the composite. Judgment and empirical testing of numerous indicators led to the final form of the *PaineWebber Leading Indicator of Automotive Sales*. The *PW Leading Indicator of Auto Sales* is a composite of five components:

1. The Federal funds rate (the only interest rate that leads business cycle upper turning points) is used as a gauge of future auto loan rates.
2. The University of Michigan's consumer confidence index is an indicator of the consumer's willingness to spend.[5]

---

[3] This material is drawn from work done at PaineWebber in association with Ann C. Knight and Stephen J. Girsky (Knight, Niemira, and Girsky, 1986).

[4] For a nontechnical discussion of the difference between econometric models and leading indicators, see Robert Jacobson (1981).

[5] Breuss and Wuger (1986) reviewed the use of consumer survey information to forecast turning points in consumer spending. They noted that work by Katona in the United States found that inclusion of consumer sentiment indicators into models of consumer spending improved the prediction of turning points. However, their own work on Austrian consumer spending models using survey indicators found only a modest improvement in their predictive ability.

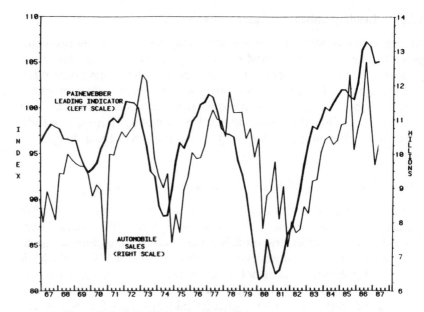

Figure 19.2. PaineWebber leading indicator versus auto sales.

3. The ratio of used car to new car prices, as measured by the Bureau of Labor Statistics (BLS), is used as a proxy for the relative stock of new and used cars. As the stock of used cars grows relative to new car inventories, there is downward pressure on used car prices. As used car prices continue to decline relative to new car prices, there is likely to be a substitution of used cars for new cars.
4. The relative price of gasoline to the nonenergy, nonfood consumer price index (CPI-U) is used to pick up price shocks (both increases and decreases) and moves inversely with car sales.
5. Sensitive employment is calculated as the ratio of voluntary and new entrant unemployment to total employment. An increasing number of individuals voluntarily leaving their jobs indicates growing confidence in the economy (and future job prospects). This ratio also includes new entrants to the workforce as a proxy for the return of discouraged workers.

Although there may not be an elegant theory behind the selection of these indicators, the variables used in the composite leading indicator are often found in auto sector econometric models. However, this approach starts with a "reduced-form" equation or direct specification.

The final step in forming a composite index is to weight each component according to its volatility and correlation with auto sales.[6] Figure 19.2 shows the performance of this composite in forecasting moves in car sales.

19.1.2 *Performance of the indicator and its components*

An auto industry sales cycle chronology was developed (this could be viewed as a "target" or "coincident" indicator of auto sector activity) to compare turning points in the sales cycle with similar turns in the individual components used in the composite and with the composite itself. The selection of turning point dates for the auto industry cycle was rather straightforward, using visual inspection. It is interesting to observe, however, that the auto industry tends to lead business cycle turning points. Therefore, using existing leading indicator composities for the overall economy will not help predict the path of future car sales. This highlights the importance of developing a unique and specialized set of indicators for this industry.[7] This also seems to reinforce the old saw that "as the auto industry goes, so too goes the economy."

Table 19.1 lists the components of the indicator and documents how well each component has corresponded to turns in the auto sales cycle. It also shows the timing of this lead–lag relationship. As Table 19.1 also indicates, the Federal funds rate and the consumer confidence index have the most consistent lead times, with median leads of four quarters and two quarters, respectively.

Table 19.2 documents the performance of the PW leading indicator over the past twenty years. The indicator has never missed a significant turn and has a very respectable average lead time of 3.5 quarters over the sales cycle. Moreover, it also has a similar lead time over *all* points in the cycle (not just turning points). While this composite indicator has been reliable and is reasonably accurate, no leading indicator is 100 percent perfect; the ideal indicator simply does not exist. For instance, the PW indicator cannot account for demographic changes, such as changes in cars per household or auto price incentives. This means that judgment on these issues must be used in combination with this barometer to forecast the path of car sales.

---

[6] The weighting of components by their relative correlations is an idea suggested in R. A. Holmes (1986). For a discussion of the "standard" methods of putting together composite indexes, see Boschan and Zarnowitz (1977).

[7] For a discussion of the merits of developing specialized industry leading indicators, see Niemira (1982).

Table 19.1. *Turning point signals given by indicator components*

| Auto sales troughs (T) and peaks (P) | No. of quarters that components turning point signals lead (−) or lag (+) auto sales turning points | | | | |
	Fed funds[a]	Consumer confidence[b]	Gas price[c]	Car price ratio[d]	Sensitive employment[e]
Q3 1968 (P)	−4	−4	−5	−2	−3
Q4 1970 (T)	−5	−2	−1	−3	−7
Q1 1973 (P)	−4	−2	NCT	+1	−4
Q4 1974 (T)	−1	+1	NCT	−3	−3
Q2 1978 (P)	−5	−4	−5	−5	−5
Q2 1982 (T)	−2	0	+2	−6	−8
Highest correlation for all observations	−3	−2	−3	−7	−7

NCT = no corresponding turn.
[a]Federal funds rate (inverted).
[b]University of Michigan's consumer confidence index.
[c]Relative price of gasoline to the nonenergy, nonfood consumer price index (CPI-U).
[d]Ratio of used car prices to new car prices, as measured by the Bureau of Labor Statistics (BLS).
[e]Sensitive employment is calculated as the ratio of voluntary and new entrant unemployment to total employment.

Table 19.2. *Turning points of PW leading indicator of car sales versus auto sales cycle*

Auto sales troughs (T) and peaks (P)	Lead time (in quarters)[a]
Q3 1968 (P)	−4
Q4 1970 (T)	−4
Q1 1973 (P)	−4
Q4 1974 (T)	−1
Q2 1978 (P)	−5
Q4 1981 (T)	−3
Average	−3.5
Standard deviation	−1.4
Median	−4.0

[a]Minus sign implies lead time.

19.1.3   *PW Leading Indicator of Auto Sales leads industry stock prices too*

In addition to leading the automobile sales cycle, the PW indicator tends to lead the S&P auto group stock index (see Figure 19.3). The correlation between the *PW Leading Indicator of Automobile Sales* and the S&P auto stock price index is slightly better than the correlation between the leading indicator and auto industry sales (80.8 percent versus 77.5 percent). However, the average lead time is much less (1 quarter versus 3.5 quarters).

19.2   Leading indicator of retail sales[8]

The *PaineWebber Leading Indicator of Retail Sales (PWLIRS)* is a composite index of four sensitive economic measures of future sales activity. The selection of the individual components is based on a screening process to determine: (a) which series lead the turning points in the year-over-year pace of general merchandise, apparel, and furniture (GAF) sales,[9] (b) which series have a general lead over GAF sales

---

[8] This material is drawn from work done at PaineWebber in association with Linda T. Kristiansen and Patrick F. McCormack (Kristiansen, Niemira, and McCormack, 1987).

[9] The key barometer of activity used by the industry is GAF sales in nominal dollars. Because this is the "industry norm", the coincident measure of activity is year-over-year percentage changes in nominal GAF sales.

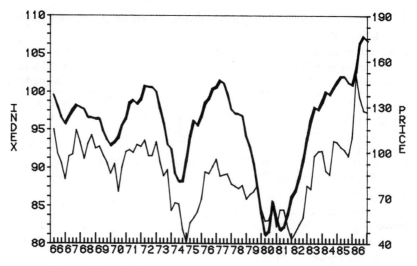

Figure 19.3. PaineWebber leading indicator (bold line) versus S&P auto price index (light line).

with respect to *all* data observations, and (c) which series make economic sense for inclusion as leading indicators. The four components that passed this screen are total home sales, consumer confidence, the Federal funds rate, and debt payments. Total home sales is the sum of new and existing home sales. Between 1970 and early 1987, home sales had an average lead time of four months over all observations in the GAF sales cycle. The Federal funds rate had the second best track record in anticipating changes in GAF sales; it had an average lead of seven months over sales. Consumer confidence had a meager two-month average lead time in forecasting the changes in the sales cycle, though from a conceptual standpoint it scored high as a series for inclusion. The final series included in the turning point indicator is debt payments. This Commerce Department series is a monthly estimate of consumer installment and mortgage debt payments; it had an average lead of twelve months, the longest lead time of any component. Once the indicator selection was completed, the composite index was formed using the same methodology as that used to put together the leading indicator of auto sales. This retail sales turning point indicator has historically forecast the direction of GAF sales with an average lead time of five months over all observations but a slightly longer nine-month average lead time at cyclical turning points.

The selection of these four components used in the PW barometer implies a *causal* lead with GAF sales and not just "good luck" in finding some indicators. The logic behind the individual selection of these indicators is:

1. *Home sales:* Home sales are a leading indicator of non-auto consumption since many new or replacement purchases accompany the purchase of a home.
2. *Consumer confidence:* The consumer's state of mind can determine whether or not the consumer spends. This is a very short-term lead indicator.
3. *Federal funds rate:* This is the only interest rate classified by the Department of Commerce as a leading indicator at peaks of business cycles. This "policy" rate can set the tone for other interest rates, including mortgage rates, which influence the home buying behavior by the consumer. But even beyond that, swings in the Fed funds rate can influence consumer psychology.
4. *Debt payments:* This series measure the aggregate monthly mortgage and consumer credit payments by the consumer. When these debt payments rise as a result of higher interest rates and/or additional debt being taken on, this has a depressant effect on future consumption, and vice versa when debt is declining.

19.2.1 *Performance of turning point indicator*

How well has the *PWLIRS* worked in calling directional changes in sales? The initial step in assessing the accuracy of the *PWLIRS* is to determine the turning points in the sales cycle. The sales cycle is defined as the year-over-year percentage change in current dollar GAF sales. It is measured in current dollars and not in real or inflation-adjusted dollars (or volume terms) for two reasons: (a) sales are reported that way and (b) company earnings (and stock prices) are in current dollars. Thus this is the most appropriate way to measure industry activity despite the fact that inflation, at times, can hide underlying weakness in volume. Table 19.3 presents this monthly sales cycle chronology. The sales cycle has an average length of three years with an equal span of time during expansions and contractions.

The *PWLIRS* has an average lead time of nine months at high and low points in this sales cycle (see Table 19.4). At peaks the lead time is ten months, and at troughs in the sales cycle the lead averages 7.8 months. Overall, the performance has been quite respectable in calling

Table 19.3. *GAF sales growth cycle, 1968 to present*

			Duration, months	
High	Low	Value[a]	High to low	Low to high
July 1968		+16.6%		—
	Aug. 1970	+2.5	25	
Apr. 1973		+16.3		32
	Nov. 1974	+0.7	19	
Dec. 1975		+14.3		13
	May 1976	+2.9	5	
June 1978		+15.3		23
	June 1980	+3.0	24	
Apr. 1981		+13.4		10
	Sept. 1982	−0.1	17	
Nov. 1983		+13.9		14
	June 1985	+4.4	19	
Feb. 1987[b]		+9.4		20
Average duration			18.2	18.7

[a]Year-over-year percentage changes.
[b]Tentative.

the major turning points in the sales cycle. Figure 19.4 shows the relationship between the leading indicator and the sales cycle.

19.3   From sales to stock prices

What is the relationship between the sales cycle and the retail group's stock price cycle? As shown in Figure 19.4, the cycle in the industry's composite stock price tends to lead major upturns in the sales cycle (which are usually associated with business cycles). Investors generally anticipate sales and earnings improvement as a recession draws to an end, and they bid up the price of the retailers' stock in advance of this event. While the link between sales and stock price movement is well established, actual sales cannot, in and of themselves, be used to anticipate stock movement.

Fortunately, the PW leading indicator of sales can be a guide to the longer-term direction of retailers' stock prices. But even the *PWLIRS,* which attempts to capture fundamental shifts in the consumer sector as

Table 19.4. *PaineWebber leading indicator of retail sales (PWLIRS) vs. GAF sales cycle, 1968 to present*

Sales cycle High	Sales cycle Low	PWLIRS High	PWLIRS Low	Timing[a] (months)
July 1968		Aug. 1967		−13
	Aug. 1970		Feb. 1970	−6
Apr. 1973		Mar. 1971		−25
	Nov. 1974		Aug. 1973	−15
Dec. 1975		Feb. 1976		+2
	May 1976		May 1976	0
June 1978		Mar. 1977		−15
	June 1980		Apr. 1980	−2
Apr. 1981		Sept. 1980		−7
	Sept. 1982		July 1981	−14
Nov. 1983		Mar. 1983		−8
	June 1985		Aug. 1984	−10
Feb. 1987[b]		Oct. 1986[b]		−4
			Average	−9

[a]Minus indicates lead time and plus indicates lag time with respect to sales turning point.
[b]Tentative.

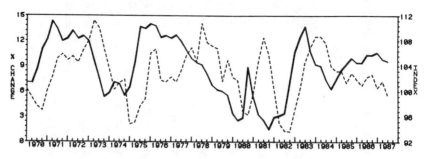

Figure 19.4. PaineWebber leading indicator of retail sales versus GAF sales. Quarterly data through Q2, 1987. Solid line: Leading indicator (right scale). Dashed line: Change in GAF sales (left scale).

reflected through various key economic indicators, has its problems. For example, recent tax law changes – which have no "leading indicators" – can dominate short-term movement in the retail group stock prices. This explains why, during the "severe" 1981 recession, retailers' stock prices declined only 15.9 percent compared with an average of more than twice that decline for the previous four downswings in the retail stock price cycle. Sales activity is not the whole story behind stock price movement, but it is a very powerful force: knowing when sales are turning can be profitable.

19.3.1   *Combining the technical and fundamental into a trading system*

Although the purpose of the *PWLIRS* is to forecast the future direction of GAF sales, it also can be used in a "trading system" to determine when to buy or sell stock of the retailers. However, it is extremely important to recognize that no trading system is 100 percent effective, and any buy/sell signal should be considered as only one input into the buy/sell decision process.

A momentum indicator has been derived from the PW leading indicator of sales using trailing three- and twelve-month year-over-year growth rates. This momentum indicator is intended to signal when to buy or sell the retailers' group stock relative to the S&P 400 composite stock price index. A buy signal occurs when the shorter-term growth rate of the momentum index exceeds the longer-term growth rate by more than 1.75 percentage points (this is used to eliminate statistical noise and is calculated as the average absolute deviation around the mean – which provides a "normal" range of fluctuation). A sell signal occurs when the

Table 19.5. *Buy/sell signals for the retailers stock price[a] and S&P 400 stock price changes, 1970–July 1987*

Buy/sell action using PWLIRS		% change in retail stock price index[a]	S&P 400 % change	Difference
Buy	Sell			
May 1970		—		
	July 1971	+67.8	+32.2%	+35.6%
Mar. 1974		−37.6	−0.1	−37.5
	Mar. 1976	+34.9	+4.4	+30.5
July 1980		−10.2	+18.9	−29.1
	June 1981	+23.8	+10.0	+13.8
Jan. 1982		−15.9	−11.8	−4.1
	Aug. 1983	+129.2	+39.7	+89.5
Nov. 1984		0.0	+1.9	−1.9
	July 1987[b]	+118.4	+94.2	+24.2

[a]The PaineWebber retail composite stock price index is an equally weighted geometric average of monthly stock price movement for: Sears, K Mart, J. C. Penney, May, Zayre, Woolworth, Carter Hawley Hale, Federated, Dayton Hudson (from October 1969), and Wal-Mart (from February 1972). January 1968 base set equal to the S&P 400 for same time period. All these calculations exclude dividend reinvestment.
[b]Through most recent data, not a sell signal.

shorter-term growth rate declines faster than the longer-term growth rate such that the difference declines below −1.75 percentage points. Historically, the buy/sell signals occurred, on average, about two months prior to the absolute high or low in the relative stock price series. Since 1970, during periods when the buy signals were in force, the retail stocks would have outperformed the market by an average 39 percent; when sell signals were in force, retail stocks would have underperformed the market by about 13 percent (see Table 19.5).

The major difference between this system and other more traditional technical systems, which generally use only a moving average or combination of moving averages on the stock price series itself, is that the buy/sell decision is tied to a *fundamental* industry leading economic indicator—the *PWLIRS* and not the stock price. Logically, this system blends a technical and a fundamental approach.

One further comment on trading systems: Numerous systems could have been used for determining when to buy or sell the retailer's stock. Jack Schwager (1984) has shown that (a) the optimal historical system for calling a turning point may not be the best performing system in the future, (b) optimized results used to evaluate the track record bias the evaluation, and (c) little is gained by using a sophisticated optimization scheme versus a simple decision rule. Therefore, using Schwager's conclusions, the method discussed here for a buy or sell decision should stand or fall on the basis of the *fundamental* logic and not on the basis of which technical decision rule is used to call a turn.

19.4   Forecasting relative stock price performance: A track record

Over the last two decades, the PW retail sales barometer has led turns in the relative stock performance of the retail composite stock price index versus the S&P 400 stock price index (see Figure 19.5). It is helpful to consider each turning point call and determine what else was occurring that could have reinforced the call or questioned it.

May 1970 – buy: The economy was in a recession that began in late 1969. Momentum in the *PWLIRS* began to pick up, which anticipated the November 1970 business cycle trough. The buy signal was flashed two months prior to the low in the relative stock price.

July 1971 – sell: This sell signal anticipated the relative stock price high by five months. The retail group's stock performance was aided by the December 1971 enactment of the Revenue Act of 1971. This Federal tax law change accelerated the scheduled increases in personal exemptions and the standard deduction by one year.

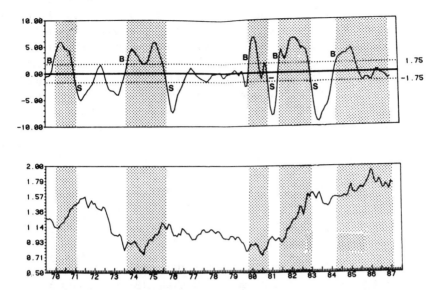

Figure 19.5. Top: Retail stock price momentum indicator. Monthly data through July. B = buy; S = sell. Bottom: Relative stock price performance for ten retail companies. Retail companies include Carter Hawley Hale (CHH), Dayton Hudson (DH), Federated (FDS), K mart (KM), J.C. Penney (JCP), Sears (S), Wal-Mart (WMT), Woolworth (Z), and Zayre (ZY).

March 1974 – buy: The economy entered a recession in November 1973, but consumption weakened much earlier than this business cycle turning point. The economy went through a two-phase slowdown; first consumption slowed and then weakness in the industrial sector developed about six months later. In March 1975, Congress passed the Tax Reduction Act of 1975, which provided a 10 percent rebate on 1974 taxes up to a maximum of $200 for individuals, cut taxes retroactive to January 1975 through increased standard deductions, and provided an earned income credit for low-income families. This kept the momentum going for the retailers.

March 1976 – sell: A sell signal was called four months after the relative stock price peaked. This signal remained in force despite the passage of the Revenue Act of 1978, which did little for the retailers.

July 1980 – buy: A buy signal occurred five months prior to the relative stock price high. The peak in the relative stock price coincided with the business cycle trough. Credit controls and oil prices hikes were instrumental in causing the 1980 recession, which lasted a mere six months – matching the record for the shortest recession.

June 1981 – sell: This sell signal anticipated the July 1981 peak in the business cycle by one month and was coincident with the peak in the relative price. The subsequent relative price decline was modest by historical standards, since Congress passed a sweeping tax reduction package in August 1981. The Economic Recovery Tax Act of 1981 contained provisions to cut individual taxes by 5.0 percent on October 1, 1981, an additional 10 percent on July 1, 1982, and another 10 percent on July 1, 1983.

January 1982 – buy: By early 1982, forecasters were already calling the end of the 1981 recession, which turned out to be too early since the economy had a second down phase. Nonetheless, this buy signal came one month after the relative stock price low; this signal turned out to be the start of a major upsurge in the retailers' group stock. The overall economy continued in recession through November 1982.

August 1983 – sell: This sell signal occurred one month after the high in the relative stock price. This signal was associated with a continuing recovery in the economy.

November 1984 – buy: A buy signal came seven months after the relative stock price low. The high value of the dollar was taking a toll on the manufacturing sector; the manufacturing sector, in many respects, entered its own industry recession. However, the economy in general was more fortunate as a shift toward greater service sector employment cushioned the economy on the downside. Congress passed the Tax Reform Act of 1986, which provided yet another modest cut in individual taxes and cut corporate tax rates. Passage of this legislation provided another incentive to own retailers' stock, given expectations of a pickup in consumer spending and company profits.

On balance, the trading system presented here works reasonably well but clearly should be viewed in context with other instutitional changes.

19.5   Conclusion

A "quantitative-historical" or an "institutional" approach to forecasting has been taken in this chapter. Philip A. Klein (1983, p. 873) described this "neglected" approach as "explaining the world as it is. . . . [A] principal charge of institutionalists against mainstream economic theorizing has always been that the abstractions are often too extreme." But clearly the mainstream may argue that the approach used to develop these composite leading indicators of auto and non-auto retail sales is simply "measurement without theory" – which was a well-echoed phrase from the early days of the NBER's empirical work. Fortunately, the record has shown that the traditional NBER cyclical indicator techniques are useful, are easy to interpret and communicate, and work well for forecasting.

REFERENCES

Ackley, G. (1961), *Macroeconomic theory*. New York: Macmillan Company, pp. 233–6.

Boschan, C., and V. Zarnowitz (1977), "Composite Indexes: A Brief Explanation and the Method of Construction," *The Handbook of Cyclical Indicators*, U.S. Department of Commerce, pp. 73–6.

Breuss, F., and M. Wuger (1986), "Consumer Sentiments as an Indicator for Consumption Behaviour," in K. H. Oppenlander and G. Poser, eds., *Business Cycle Surveys in the Assessment of Economic Activity*. Aldershot, England: Gower Publishing House, pp. 319–352.

Hall, R. E. (1986), "The Role of Consumption in Economic Fluctuations," in Robert J. Gordon, ed., *The American Business Cycle*. Chicago: University of Chicago Press, pp. 237–266.

Holmes, R. A. (1986), "Leading Indicators of Industrial Employment in British Columbia," *International Journal of Forecasting, 2* (1), 87–100.

Jacobson, R. (1981), "Foretelling the Future," *FRB SF Weekly Letter*, Federal Bank of San Francisco, March 27.

Keynes, J. M. (1936), *General Theory of Employment, Interest and Money*. New York: Harcourt, Brace & Co., p. 96.

Klein, P. A. (1983), "The Neglected Institutionalism of Wesley Clair Mitchell: The Theoretical Basis for Business Cycle Indicators," *Journal of Economic Issues, 17* (4, December) 867–99.

Knight, A. C., M. P. Niemira, and S. J. Girsky (1986), PaineWebber Leading Indicator of Automobile Sales, PaineWebber, New York, December 15.

Kristiansen, L. T., M. P. Niemira, and P. F. McCormack (1987), The Paine-Webber Leading Indicator of Retail Sales, PaineWebber, New York, August 31.

Mengarelli, G. (1986), "Business Cycle Theory and Structural Changes in the 1970s," *Review of Economic Conditions in Italy*, Banco di Roma, No. 3 (September–December), pp. 455–84.

Niemira, M. P. (1982), "Developing Industry Leading Economic Indicators," *Business Economics*, January, pp. 5–16.

Sargent, T., and C. Sims (1977), "Business Cycle Modeling without Pretending to Have Too Much A Priori Economic Theory," *New Methods in Business Cycle Research: Proceedings from a Conference*, Federal Reserve Bank of Minneapolis, October, pp. 45–100.

Schwager, J. D. (1984), "Optimization: A Search That May Not Pay Off," *Futures*, August, pp. 64–6.

CHAPTER 20

Economic indicators for Australia's service industries

Ernst A. Boehm

The growing importance of the service industries justifies more attention being devoted to the development of indicators that reflect their part in economic fluctuations. In this chapter an attempt is made to apply to the service industries the indicator techniques that are well developed for analysis of the total economy. Leading, roughly coincident, and lagging indicators are identified for Australia's service industries. Composite indexes are constructed of five leading and four coincident indicators of the service industries. Both indexes are compared with the leading and coincident composite indexes that reflect the economic fluctuations in the total economy for Australia. The problems encountered in identifying service industry indicators are discussed.

One interesting finding is that the leading index for the service sector foreshadows equally as well as does our leading index for the total economy the pending changes in the pace and level of business activity. On the other hand, the coincident index for the service industries does not perform as consistently as does our coincident index for the total economy. However, both the leading and coincident indexes for the service sector are preliminary. Further work is being undertaken to improve their performance and also to identify more lagging indicators for the service sector. Nevertheless, it is believed that the results presented in this chapter help to clarify the role of the service industries in Australia's economic fluctuations.

An earlier version of this paper was presented at the Western Economic Association International's 62nd Annual Conference, Vancouver, B.C. July 7–11, 1987. I am most grateful to Dr. Geoffrey Moore for his very valuable advice and comments during the planning of this paper. I also wish to thank Mr. Michael Bednarek, Ms. Bee Fung, and Ms. Fiorenza Moppi for very helpful statistical assistance during the preparation of this paper. Of course, the usual caveat applies.

20.1   Definition of the service industries

There are problems in defining the service industries, which cover a wide and diverse range of economic activities. The Australian Standard Industrial Classification (1969) assists in providing the "industry divisions" shown in Table 20.1.

In this chapter the service industries are defined to include electricity, gas, and water; wholesale and retail trade; finance, property, and business services; transport and storage; communication; community services; and recreation, personal, and other services (see Table 20.1, part B).

The service sector in Australia has sometimes been defined to include construction and public administration and defense (see Tucker, 1977, p. 24). In a recent study (Economic Planning Advisory Council, 1987), the service sector is defined to include public administration and defense and items 2 to 7 in part B of Table 20.1. For our purposes of cyclical analysis there are merits in viewing construction as a goods-producing industry and excluding public administration and defense. We thereby provide a measure of the service industries that is largely in the private sector by excluding public administration and defense. Semi-government and statutory authorities are included. These involve varying proportions of public utilities, transport, communication, and community services that cannot be separately identified in the data available. However, the level of activity in the semi-government and statutory authorities and changes in their activity would be largely subject to cyclical influences in much the same way as in the private service industries.

20.2   The growing importance and role of Australia's service industries

The growth of the service industries in the private sector relative to the growth of the goods-producing industries is clearly revealed in Tables 20.1 and 20.2. Table 20.1 shows that over the last forty years, while Australia's total number of employed persons has just over doubled from 3.2 million in 1947 to 6.9 million in 1986, the total proportion of employed persons in the service industries has increased from a little over one-third to nearly two-thirds. Table 20.1 also shows that the two areas of the goods-producing industries that have lost significantly in their share of employed persons are manufacturing (with a decline from more than one-quarter to about one-sixth) and agriculture (with a fall from nearly one-sixth to 6 percent).

Table 20.2 presents a similar interesting picture in regard to the

Table 20.1. Employed persons. Percentage of total by industry division and total number, thousand, selected years, 1947 to 1986

	Percentage of total				
	1947 (June)	1961 (June)	1971 (June)	1976 (Aug.)	1986 (Aug.)
A. Goods-producing industries					
1. Nonfarm					
Mining	1.8	1.3	1.5	1.4	1.4
Manufacturing	27.6	26.9	24.4	21.7	16.4
Construction	8.4	9.0	8.2	8.4	7.1
Total	37.8	37.2	34.2	31.5	24.9
2. Agriculture, forestry, fishing and hunting	15.8	11.1	7.7	6.5	6.0
Total: goods-producing	53.6	48.1	41.8	38.0	30.9
B. Service industries					
1. Electricity, gas and water	1.1	2.2	1.8	1.7	2.0
2. Wholesale and retail trade	16.2	14.7	16.3	19.6	20.1
3. Finance, property, business services		5.2	7.2	7.7	10.2
4. Transport and storage	10.1	11.2	10.6	5.4	5.7
5. Communication				2.1	2.2
6. Community services	7.5	13.7	15.9	14.4	17.7
7. Recreation, personal, and other services				6.3	6.6
Total: Service industries	34.9	47.0	51.8	57.3	64.4
C. Public administration and defense	11.5	4.7	6.4	4.7	4.7
D. Total employed persons (millions)	3.196	4.225	5.240	5.899	6.886

Sources: 1947, 1961, and 1971 are census data in Boehm (1979), pp. 75 and 76; 1976 is computed from data in Australian Bureau of Statistics (1987a), p. 168; and 1986 is from Australian Bureau of Statistics (1986a), p. 26.

Table 20.2. Gross domestic product at factor cost: Percentage of total by industry of origin and total product, Australia, selected years, 1948–9, to 1985–6

	Percentage of total for year ended 30 June:			
	1949	1963	1976	1986
A. Goods-producing industries				
1. Nonfarm				
Mining	2.5	1.7	3.9	5.0
Manufacturing	26.2	26.8	20.8	17.2
Construction	6.0	7.7	9.6	7.6
Total: Nonfarm	34.7	36.2	34.3	29.8
2. Agriculture, forestry, fishing and hunting	21.3	12.6	5.4	4.3
Total: Goods-producing	56.0	48.8	39.7	34.1
B. Service industries				
1. Electricity, gas and water	1.9	3.5	3.0	3.8
2. Wholesale and retail trade	15.3	16.9	15.2	13.2
3. Transport, storage and communication	7.3	7.8	8.5	8.6

	1948–9	1962–3	1975–6	1985–6
4. Finance, property and business services	⎫ 13.9	7.3	8.8	9.3
5. Community services	⎬	⎫ 9.4	11.7	13.1
6. Recreation, personal and other services	⎭	⎭	3.8	3.8
Total: Service industries	38.4	44.9	51.1	52.0
C. Public administration and *defense*	3.7	3.4	5.4	4.7
D. *Ownership of dwellings*	4.0	5.0	6.3	11.6
E. *Less imputed bank service charges*	−2.1	−2.1	−2.5	−2.4
GDP at factor cost ($ million)	4,031	14,515	68,245	209,773

Sources: 1948–9 and 1962–3 from Boehm (1979), pp. 10–11; 1975–6 and 1985–6 computed from data in Australian Bureau of Statistics (1986b), pp. 13–15.

Note: The data for 1948–9 are not fully comparable with those for later years, especially in **B** (items 3 to 6), C, and E. This results from the adoption (in 1971) of a standard classification for economic censuses relating to the years from 1962–3.

377

shares of gross domestic product (GDP). The table reveals that the goods-producing industries now account for only a little more than one-third of Australia's output compared with more than half in the early post–World War II years. Again, the major relative declines occurred in agriculture and manufacturing. The major contributors to the relative growth in the share in total output of the service industries are finance, property, and business services; community services; and recreation, personal, and other services.

Statisticians have encountered considerable difficulties in measuring the nominal and real output in the service industries. However, the general picture conveyed by Table 20.2 is consistent with the qualitative observations that we may make about the level and the changing course and nature of aggregate economic activity and its main components.

Tables 20.1 and 20.2 clearly demonstrate that the service industries in Australia have come to play an increasingly dominant role in economic growth and social welfare. This is similar to the experiences of the service industries in other relatively developed industrialized countries, where manufacturing, construction, and agriculture have also been declining in relative importance. No credence is given to the debate inspired by Adam Smith just over two hundred years ago that the goods-producing industries manifest productive labor while the service industries involve unproductive labor.[1] Unproductive labor was believed to apply especially to community services and to recreation, personal, and other services, two areas where, as noted above, there has been substantial growth since World War II in terms of both labor employed and output.

However, Tables 20.1 and 20.2 do not provide a complete picture of Australia's employment and growth experiences. In a more complete analysis of the achievements in economic growth and of the desired and required changes in social welfare, account would need to be given to the fundamental requirement of the improvements in productivity that have been achieved in the goods-producing industries as well as in the service industries. In fact, Australia's four goods-producing industries, as classified in Tables 20.1 and 20.2, have been making major contributions to Australia's economic growth and development, with agriculture, mining, and manufacturing achieving above average trend rates of growth in productivity (GDP at constant prices per person employed) since at least 1949–50 (see Boehm, 1979, pp. 172–3; Australian Bureau of Statistics, 1986b, pp. 7 and 14).

To summarize, economic growth involving capital deepening as well

[1] For a more detailed discussion of this debate, see Tucker (1977), pp. 13–16.

as capital widening (as the Australian economy has grown from a population of 7.5 million in 1947 to just over 16 million today) has ensured significant improvements in labor productivity. In the process real living standards have risen considerably, with the increases in employment and output in the service industries helping to raise the quality of life as well as being the main avenue providing new jobs. This theme and its implications for the business cycle are discussed further in section 20.5.

20.3   General review of the indicators included in our economic indicator analysis of the total Australian economy

A major emphasis of economic indicator analysis in Australia has been on the goods-producing industries, particularly manufacturing and construction. This is true also for the United States and other industrial countries (see, for instance, Moore, 1987, as well as Layton and Moore, 1989). One reason for the emphasis on manufacturing and construction is that these industries are highly sensitive to cyclical fluctuations in demand and have experienced big economic fluctuations. These fluctuations have, in turn, largely determined the timing and severity of economic fluctuations in the rest of the economy.

The general emphasis of economic indicator analysis on the goods-producing activity appeared justifiable when this activity dominated the total economic activity of the market. Thus the monthly factory production index (which in Australia includes durable and nondurable manufactured products and power) has been used as a proxy for Australia's current economic performance and to identify the peaks and troughs of the business cycle (see, for instance, Barry and Guille, 1976, pp. 140–1). But, as we have seen above, the relative importance of factory production has been declining for some time while the cyclically more stable service industries have been growing. These trends have been occurring in other industrial countries as well (see Zarnowitz and Boschan, 1975b, p. 186; Moore, 1987).

A consequence of the historical emphasis of economic indicator analyses on the goods-producing industries is that the service industries appear to be relatively underrepresented compared with manufacturing and construction. The underrepresentation may also have increased as the service industries have progressively grown in relative importance.

Underrepresentation of the service sector in economic indicator analysis for Australia may apply especially in respect to the leading index for the total economy (see Table 20.3). Two of Australia's nine leaders relate directly to manufacturing, namely, factory overtime and the change in the price index of materials used in manufacturing, all groups;

Table 20.3. *List of indicators, total economy and service sector, Australia*

Total economy[a]	Service sector[b]	Unit	M or Q[c]	Starting dates
Leading	*Leading*			
Factory overtime (Q)	Financial liquidity, net higher/ lower, cumulated[d]	Index	Q	1969
Net demand for new telephone services (M)	Value of building approved, total commerce, in 1979–80 prices[e]	$	M	1963
Value of private non-residential building approved in 1979–80 prices (M)	Terms of trade, services[f]	Index	Q	1970
Change in price index of materials used in manufacturing, all groups, 6 months smoothed (M)	Average weekly hours worked, total services[g]	Hours	Q	1977
Australian Stock Exchange share price index, all ordinaries (M)	Australian Stock Exchange share price index, retail[h]	Index	M	1960
Gross operating surplus of trading enterprises: companies, in 1979–80 prices (Q)				
Ratio of implicit price deflator to unit-labor cost (Q)				
Overdraft limits outstanding in 1979–80 prices (M)				
Roughly coincident	*Roughly coincident*			
Household income in 1979–80 prices (Q)	Retail sales, all items (excl. motor vehicles, etc.) in 1979– 80 prices[i]	$	M	1951
Gross nonfarm product in 1979–80 prices (Q)	Employed persons, total services[g]	No.	Q	1977
Quantity of factory production (M)				

	Unit		Year
Retail sales, all items (excl. motor vehicles etc.) in 1979–80 prices (M)			
Total employed civilian labor force (M)			
Unemployment rate, inverted (M)			
Private final consumption expenditure, total services in 1979–80 prices[j]	$	Q	1960
Availability of suitable labor, net scarce/abundant[a]	Index	Q	1970
Lagging			
Stocks in relation to sales, net higher/lower, cumulated[a]	Index	Q	1969
Unemployment rate, 13 weeks and over, inverted (M)			
New capital expenditure, private, in 1979–80 prices (Q)			
Cumulated net change in stocks of raw materials, past period (Q)			
Installment credit for retail sales, balances outstanding in 1980–1 prices (M)[k]			
Labor cost per unit of output (Q)			
Commercial bills rate, bank accepted, 90-day (M)			

[a]From Boehm and Moore (1984) and Boehm (1987). The leading and coincident indexes are reported monthly in *International Economic Scoreboard* (Conference Board, New York), and, along with the lagging, in *Report on Westpac-Melbourne Institute Indexes of Economic Activity* [Institute of Applied Economic and Social Research (IAESR), University of Melbourne]. All series are seasonally adjusted except: change in price index of materials used in manufacturing; Australian share price index, all ordinaries; unemployment rate, thirteen weeks and over; and cumulated net change in stocks of raw materials, past period.

[b]All series are seasonally adjusted except: Australian share price index, retail; availability of suitable labor, net scarce/abundant; and stocks in relation to sales, net higher/lower, cumulated. The Australian Chamber of Commerce and National Australia Bank (1987) prefaces the questions on financial liquidity, availability of labor, and stocks in relation to sales (and other questions in the *Survey*) with the statement: "Excluding normal seasonal changes, what changes has your company experienced in the last three months . . . ?" Nevertheless, the response to financial liquidity displays a seasonal pattern, being generally lower in the June quarter (perhaps because of taxation payments) and higher in the September quarter and more so the December.

[c]Monthly or quarterly.

(cont. on next page)

[d]Australian Chamber of Commerce and National Australia Bank (1987). The *Survey* defines financial liquidity as "cash, bank accommodation, and short term/liquid financial asset position in relation to sales, turnover or gross earnings."

[e]Australian Bureau of Statistics (1987c). Total commerce was obtained by adding the value of approvals for hotels, hostels, etc.; shops; offices; and other business premises.

[f]Australian Bureau of Statistics (1986c, 1987d).

[g]Australian Bureau of Statistics (1987a, 1987b). Total services includes the seven subgroups shown in Table 20.1, part B. Average weekly hours worked, total services, was computed by weighting the hours worked by each subgroup by its proportion of employed persons in total services.

[h]Stock Exchange of Melbourne (1980) and Stock Exchange (1987).

[i]Australian Bureau of Statistics (1987e).

[j]Australian Bureau of Statistics (1987f, 1987g). Private final consumption expenditure, total services, was obtained by adding the expenditure on the following items: health; gas, electricity, and fuel; fares; postal and telegraph services; entertainment and recreation; financial services; and other goods and services.

[k]The publication of this series was discontinued by the Australian Statistician in January 1985. A replacement is under review from the new series on commercial and industrial finance being published by the Australian Bureau of Statistics.

and two series directly concern construction activity, namely, real value of private non-residential building approved (which also includes the service industries) and total new residential building approved. Business activity in the service sector enters the leading index as least to some extent along with the goods-producing industries in the remaining five leaders, that is, net demand for new telephone services (which is used as a proxy for new business and household formation); the Australian share price index, all ordinaries; real gross operating surplus of trading enterprises: companies; ratio of implicit price deflator to unit labor cost; and real overdraft limits outstanding.

Table 20.3 further shows that the service sector provides one of the six indicators included in our roughly coincident index of the total Australian economy. This is real retail sales, which is also appropriate to include in the coincident index for the service industries (as shown in Table 20.3). Business activity in the service sector directly contributes, along with the rest of the economy, to four of the coincident indicators of the total economy, namely, real household income; real gross non-farm product; total civilian employment; and unemployment rate, inverted. Manufacturing production is represented by the quantity of factory production, though this series also includes the production of gas and electricity, as mentioned above.

In our lagging index of the total economy, the cumulated net change in stocks of raw materials, past period, relates to the manufacturing sector. Real new capital expenditure, private, includes private services. Three of the laggers relate to the total economy including services, namely, unemployment rate, thirteen weeks and over, inverted; labor cost per unit of output; and commercial bills rate, bank accepted, ninety-day. We had a lagger relating closely to the service sector in real installment credit for retail sales, balances outstanding; but in January 1985, the Australian Bureau of Statistics discontinued publication of the series that we were using. Though more detailed monthly statistics on credit and finance in Australia began to be published from the beginning of 1985, there are no overlapping data with the previous series to permit (as yet, on the data available) a linking of a new series with the one we previously had found a reasonably reliable lagger, especially at peaks (see Boehm and Moore, 1984, p. 48).

20.4   The identification of service industry indicators

A key objective of this chapter is to see if additional indicators can be found that reflect and allow adequately for the business cycle experiences of the service sector. In selecting service industry indicators, we exploit, as noted earlier, the techniques and criteria that have a proven success in monitoring aggregate economic activity (see Boehm, 1987). Since important aspects of the service industries experience milder absolute fluctuations in some measures of their levels of activity, for instance, in employment (as discussed in section 20.5), it is appropriate to test the cyclical properties of service industry indicators by examining the fluctuations in their rates of growth. Growth cycle analysis, as developed initially at the NBER (National Bureau of Economic Research, New York; see Mintz, 1970, 1974; Moore, 1983; Klein and Moore, 1985) and now at the CIBCR (Center for International Business Cycle Research, Columbia University, New York), is well suited to do this. Likewise, in testing and selecting service industry indicators as leading, roughly coincident, and lagging indicators, it is appropriate to use as a comparable reference cycle the growth cycle chronology already established for the Australian economy (Boehm and Moore, 1984; Boehm, 1987).

Thus, one hypothesis to consider is whether our present indicator analysis for the total Australian economy could be further improved and could provide more reliable results for monitoring general business activity and short-term forecasting if additional or alternative indicators that specifically relate to the service industries are included.

In the search for Australian service industry indicators from among the available data in official and private sources, we have so far identified five series for more serious consideration as leaders (see Tables 20.3 and 20.4), three new series as coincident (in addition to retail sales already included, as noted above) (Tables 20.3 and 20.5), and one lagger (Tables 20.3 and 20.6). A number of other series (as briefly mentioned below) have been tested. Some have been rejected through not satisfying the criteria used to select economic indicators.[2]

Three of the service industry indicators (in Table 20.3), one leading, one roughly coincident, and one lagging, are from The Australian Chamber of Commerce and National Australia Bank *Quarterly Business Survey*. This *Survey* "seeks . . . views on a number of issues related to the tertiary business sector." The *Survey* covers construction (which

---

[2] The criteria, in brief, are that an indicator: (1) be a significant economic variable; (2) be statistically adequate; (3) not be subject to significant revisions; (4) reveals a consistent relationship over time with business (both classical and growth) cycle peaks and troughs; (5) associated with (4), conforms to the general cyclical movements between peaks and troughs; (6) not be dominated by irregular, erratic and noncyclical influences; and (7) be promptly, frequently, and regularly available. For more detailed discussions of these criteria, see Zarnowitz and Boschan (1975a, 1975b); U.S. Department of Commerce (1984), p. 70, n. 1; and Boehm (1987), pp. 8–10.

is included in goods-producing industries in Table 20.1) and four of the service industries subgroups in Table 20.1, part B, namely, wholesale and retail trade; finance, property, and business services; transport and storage; and recreation, personal, and other services. In terms of employment in August 1986, approximately 86 percent of the *Survey* relates to the service sector as we have defined it in this chapter, while in terms of output, it would be just over 80 percent (with allowance that communication is not covered by the *Survey* but is included with transport and storage in Table 20.2).

The series from the *Survey* included for further consideration as a leading service industry indicator is financial liquidity, the coincident indicator is availability of suitable labor and the lagging indicator is stocks in relation to sales. The logic of taking the cumulated net higher/lower experiences regarding liquidity and stocks is to place both series on a level basis comparable with the roughly coincident indicators which we use to obtain the business cycle–both classical and growth-chronologies. On the other hand, the net scarce/abundant labor situation is interpreted as being comparable to a level. As the level of business activity rises, it may be expected that the net scarce/abundant index of the availability of suitable labor rises, and vice versa.

The Australian Chamber of Commerce and National Australia Bank *Survey* also contains questions regarding changes in trading (i.e., sales, turnover, or gross earnings); number of employees; overtime; costs (of labor, purchases, and overhead in relation to sales, turnover, or gross earnings); profits in relation to sales, turnover, or gross earnings; forward orders from customers; and anticipated capital expenditure. However, on the preliminary tests conducted in the background work for this chapter, none of these appears to justify inclusion as an indicator. They have so far been rejected on grounds of one or more of the criteria already mentioned briefly, but it is planned to examine each series further.

The economic rationale for including the five service sector indicators as potential leaders (Tables 20.3 and 20.4) is that they are measures, reflections, or assessments of commitments that will affect the state of business activity in the months ahead. For instance, an improvement in financial liquidity and an increase in approvals to build foreshadow increases in the future pace and level of business activity. An anticipated general increase in economic activity in which retail trade is likely to share will also be reflected in rising share prices for retail businesses as equity values are expected to improve. One of the first business responses to an expansion of demand, or an anticipated expansion, will be to increase the number of hours worked.

Table 20.4. *Leading service industry indicators: leads (−) and lags (+) in months of turns in leading index and its components at growth cycle turns, Australia*

Growth cycle chronology[a]		Service industry indicators[b]											
		Leading index (from 1963)		Financial liquidity[c] (from 1969)		Building approved[d] (from 1963)		Terms of trade[e] (from 1970)		Weekly hours[f] (from 1977)		Share price[g] (from 1960)	
P	T	P	T	P	T	P	T	P	T	P	T	P	T
	9/61		−9										−9
4/65	1/68	−13	−14			−3	+2					−14	−14
5/70	3/72		−9	−8	−3	−2	−9		−1			−16	−12

386

								Extra cycles			
2/74	−6	−10	−5	−1	−11	−4	−3	−2			−14	−10
10/75	0	−7	−2	+17	−8	−4	−3	+28			0	−8
8/76	−2	−5	−15	+1	+9	+1	+2	0	−4	−3	−2	−5
10/77	−5	−9	−6	0	−3	−4	−3	0			−8	−10
6/81	−6	−9	−8	+4	−3	−3	−1	+6	−4	−3	−9	−10
5/83	5	3	6	9	8	4	3	15			8	3
Median	−6	−9	−6	0	−3	−4	−3	0			−8	−10
Mean	−6	−9	−8	+4	−3	−3	−1	+6	−4	−3	−9	−10
SD[h]	5	3	6	9	8	4	3	15			8	3
	2/79	5/80			9/67	9/66			5/79	5/80	2/79	5/80

[a] From Boehm and Moore (1984), pp. 38–44 and Boehm (1987), pp. 21 and 43.
[b] IAESR computed from sources noted in Table 20.3.
[c] Financial liquidity, net higher/lower, cumulated (seasonally adjusted).
[d] Real value of building approved, total commerce (seasonally adjusted).
[e] Terms of trade, services (seasonally adjusted).
[f] Average weekly hours worked, services (seasonally adjusted).
[g] Share price index, retail.
[h] Standard deviation.

388   Ernst A. Boehm

An improvement in Australia's merchandise terms of trade generally means a rise in real incomes and an expansion of general economic activity, and vice versa. The official estimate of Australia's merchandise terms of trade appears a reliable leading indicator and may be included in the revision presently being made of our leading indicators of the total economy. It seemed appropriate to review Australia's services terms of trade as a leader. Exports of services currently account for about 15 percent of Australia's exports of goods and services, while imports of services compose 22 percent of Australia's imports of goods and services. Australia has experienced a deficit on direct trade in services for decades. However, service exports are expected to grow strongly. A recent forecast by the Melbourne Institute (see McDonald and Dixon, 1987, p. 7 and Table 8) shows that service exports are likely to contribute about 40 percent of the increase in export earnings over the next year. Areas that may contribute to this expansion include educational and financial services to the close and big Southeast Asian markets. The deficit in tourism is also being reduced as Australia has been attracting increasing numbers of visitors through improvements in air travel and accommodation (see Economic Planning and Advisory Council, 1987). On our first review of terms of trade for services, longer median and mean leads were obtained than shown in Table 20.4, and on a preliminary basis it seemed reasonable to include this series in the composite index. However, on recent revised data used to obtain the results in Table 20.4, this series appears not to meet our criteria adequately and should probably be excluded.

The median and mean leads and lags reported in Table 20.4 for building approvals and average hours worked justify the inclusion of both series (though the period for hours worked from 1977 is relatively short). Building approvals for "total commerce" form part of the total economy indicator of the value of private non-residential building approved. The best performing service industry leader in terms of the leads and lags of corresponding peaks and troughs at growth cycle turns is share price index, retail. Financial liquidity of the tertiary sector has also performed well in anticipating peaks but less successfully in respect to troughs (although attention still needs to be given to the question of whether there are any special reasons for the long lag of seventeen months following the growth cycle trough in October 1977). Furthermore, financial liquidity and also terms of trade, services, produced no "extra cycles" as did the other three leading service indicators.

The leads and lags of three of the coincident service industry indicators, namely, employed persons, consumption expenditure, and availability of labor, do not rouse any immediate enthusiasm. Employed persons and consumption expenditure are already included in the roughly coincident indicators for the total economy in the series total employed civilian labor force and real gross nonfarm product, respectively. However, Table 20.5 shows that the standard deviations of the mean lags at the peaks and troughs of the availability of suitable labor are lower than those for retail sales. The latter series is also included as a roughly coincident indicator for the total economy as noted earlier. The availability of labor and the employed persons series appear worth continuing to monitor in respect to the service industries, especially to review their performance as they become longer time series.

Table 20.6 reveals that, in our search for service industry indicators, we have identified a reliable lagger in the level of the series stocks in relation to sales. It appears that this indicator would be worth including in our lagging index for the total Australian economy, thereby providing fuller representation of the state of business activity in the service industries as well as improving the quality of the lagging index and hence the usefulness of the lagging index, inverted, in short-term economic forecasting (see Boehm and Moore, 1987). The level of stocks typically continues to rise after a peak in the business cycle is reached because demand is falling while orders for stocks are still being met. When demand recovers, stocks usually continue to decline before new orders are placed and satisfied.

Table 20.7 provides a comparison of our leading and coincident indexes for both the total economy and the service industries. The comparison is in terms of the leads and lags of the peaks and troughs of the indexes in relation to Australia's growth cycle chronology. Three interesting and important findings for this chapter are highlighted by Table 20.7. First, the service industries leading index appears to compare quite favorably with that for the total economy. Both indexes provide leads foreshadowing by about six months the peaks and troughs in Australia's growth cycle. This finding is supported by both the median and mean leads of the leading indexes, though the only "extra cycle" reported in Table 20.7 is for the service industries leading index. Apart from the extra cycle, which was also revealed by two of the five individual indicators for the service industries at about the same time, as noted earlier, the leading index for the service industries performs better than the results of the individual series may have led one to expect (see Table 20.4). It appears that, in the construction of the composite index (for which the methodology developed at the U.S. Department of Commerce (1977, 1984) and CIBCR (1986) is used), some of the "noise" in the individual series is removed. Boehm and Martin (1987, p. 29) show, "as Auerbach (1982) also found . . . that not all leading indicators at

Table 20.5. *Coincident service industry indicators: leads (−) and lags (+) in months of turns in coincident index and its components at growth cycle turns, Australia*

Growth cycle chronology[a]		Service industry indicators[b]									
		Coincident index (from 1961)		Retail sales[c] (from 1960)		Employed persons[d] (from 1977)		Consumption expenditure[e] (from 1960)		Availability of labor[f] (from 1970)	
P	T	P	T	P	T	P	T	P	T	P	T
8/60	9/61		+2	−3	−4				+5		
4/65	1/68	−18	+8	−12	+16			−17	−17		
5/70	3/72	−4	−2	+11	−2			−6	+2		−1
2/74	10/75	0	−11	−1	−11			0	−14	0	−2

						Median	Mean	SD^g
8/76	-8	+2	0	+1			-4	-6	8
10/77	+2	0					0	0	6
6/81	+2			-8			-2	-2	8
5/83	0	+1	+2	+9			-3	-1	9
Extra cycles									
12/78	-8	+2	+2				+2	+2	9
10/79	-6	0	-3	-1			0	0	1
8/78	+9	+2	+2				0	-2	10
5/79	+1	0	0	0			+1	-3	10
5/79	0	+11	+1	-2			+2	+3	3
2/81	+4	0	+1	-3			+2	+1	6

^{a}As for note a in Table 20.4
^{b}As for note b in Table 20.4
^{c}Real retail sales (seasonally adjusted).
^{d}Employed persons, services (seasonally adjusted).
^{e}Real private final consumption expenditure, services (seasonally adjusted).
^{f}Availability of suitable labor, net scarce/abundant.
^{g}Standard deviation.

391

Table 20.6. *Comparison of leads (−) and lags (+) in months of turns in total economy lagging index and in level of stocks for service industries at growth cycle turns, Australia*

Growth cycle chronology[a]		Lagging index, total economy[b]		Stocks in relation to sales[c]	
P	T	P	T	P	T
	1/68		+2		+17
5/70		+9		+7	
	3/72		+11		+3
2/74		+6		+10	
	10/75		+4		+11
8/76		+3		+16	
	10/77		+19		+20
6/81		+7		+6	
	5/83		+4		+4
Median		+6	+4	+8	+11
Mean		+6	+8	+10	+11
SD[d]		2	7	4	8

[a]As for note *a* in Table 20.4.
[b]IAESR computed from indicators noted in Table 20.3.
[c]Net higher/lower (cumulated). IAESR computed form data in Australian Chamber of Commerce and National Australia Bank (1987).
[d]Standard deviation.

times help significantly in predicting cyclical variables. However, as Auerbach also notes, 'simple exclusion from the index of those series which do not individually help . . . worsens the performance of the . . . indicator in out-of-sample predictions' (pp. 594–95)" (see also Martin, 1986).

A second notable finding of Table 20.7 is that the coincident index for the total economy performs better and more consistently than does that for the service industries. This seems consistent with the conclusions above on the relatively poor and mixed performances of the four individual service industry indicators chosen for review in this paper. However, it appears that the performance of the coincident index for the service industries improved from about 1970 when a third series became available, and there was further improvement from 1977 with four series.

A third finding of Table 20.7 concerns a comparison of the months

Table 20.7. Comparison of leads (−) and lags (+) in months of turns in total economy and service industry leading and coincident composite indexes at growth cycle turns, Australia

Growth cycle chronology[a] (from 1961)		Total economy				Service industries			
		Leading index[b] (from 1961)		Coincident index[b] (from 1961)		Leading index[c] (from 1963)		Coincident index[d] (from 1961)	
P	T	P	T	P	T	P	T	P	T
	9/61		−2		0				+2
4/65	1/68	−10	−23	0	+4	−9	−14	−18	+8
5/70	3/72	−5	−1	+8	0	−13	−9	−4	−2
2/74	10/75	−6	−10	0	−7	−6	−10	0	−11
8/76	10/77	0	+5	0	0	0	−7	−8	+2
6/81	5/83	−16	−9	0	0	−2	−5	+2	0

Table 20.7. (cont.)

Growth cycle chronology[a] (from 1961)		Total economy				Service industries			
		Leading index[b] (from 1961)		Coincident index[b] (from 1961)		Leading index[c] (from 1963)		Coincident index[d] (from 1961)	
P	T	P	T	P	T	P	T	P	T
From 1961									
Median		−6	−6	0	0	−6	−9	−4	+1
Mean		−7	−7	+2	0	−6	−9	−6	0
SD[e]		6	10	4	4	5	3	8	6
From 1970									
Median		−6	−5	0	0	−4	−8	−2	−1
Mean		−7	−4	+2	−2	−5	−8	−2	−3
SD[e]		7	7	4	4	6	2	4	6
				Extra cycles 2/79		5/80			

[a]Sources as for note a in Table 20.4
[b]IAESR computed from indicators noted in Table 20.3.
[c]Table 20.4.
[d]Table 20.5.
[e]Standard deviation.

by which the leading index for the total economy leads at peaks and troughs compared with the leads of the service industry leading index. It has been observed on several occasions earlier in this chapter that the service industries have generally experienced greater stability than the goods-producing industries. This view is supported by the analysis in the next section; and it also appears to be supported by the service industry leading index, on average, peaking a month or two later than the leading index for the total economy and troughing about two to three months earlier. This means that the contraction phase foreshadowed by the leading index of the service industries has, on average, been shorter than that foreshadowed by the total economy leading index. Moreover, the longer leads at troughs given by the leading index for the service industries could be very helpful in providing earlier forecasts of recoveries than given by the leading index for the total economy. A test we plan to undertake is whether a leading index representing more fully the goods-producing industries would peak earlier and trough later than the leads (in respect to growth cycle turns) revealed by the service industry leading index. This experience of the service industry leading index peaking later and troughing earlier than the total economy index is not supported by the less robust coincident index for the service industries.

20.5 Employment experience of the service industries during growth cycles

Tables 20.8 and 20.9 furnish clear evidence of the greater stability in the service industries as far as the number and proportion of employed persons are concerned. The months shown in Table 20.8 are times of labor force surveys coinciding with or closest to successive growth cycle turns. They begin with a peak in August 1976, a trough in October 1977, and so on, as shown in Table 20.9, which presents a picture of the approximate total changes and percentage changes between the growth cycle turns.

Table 20.8 and 20.9 reveal the secular as well as the cyclical changes that have been occurring since 1977. Mining has been experiencing rising employment throughout as have the service industries, whereas manufacturing employment has declined throughout. Nevertheless, the rate of change has generally fluctuated in all industrial divisions, with the service industries experiencing slower but still positive growth in the recession periods while manufacturing has declined more steeply. Mining has also experienced continued expansion in employment throughout and, in fact, grew faster in the recession from June 1981 to May 1983 than it has since. At the same time the service industries gained

Table 20.8. *Number of employed persons by industry division (seasonally adjusted) at selected dates, Australia, 1976 to 1987 (thousand)*

	August 1976	November 1977	May 1981	May 1983	February 1987
A. Goods-producing industries					
1. Nonfarm					
Mining	80.7	82.4	91.3	97.5	103.4
Manufacturing	1287.2	1257.6	1252.6	1139.8	1128.3
Construction	497.4	480.8	485.6	411.0	503.7
Total: Nonfarm	1865.3	1820.8	1829.5	1648.3	1735.4
2. Agriculture, forestry, fishing, and hunting	382.1	398.3	426.7	419.5	424.9
Total: Goods-producing	2247.4	2219.1	2256.2	2067.8	2160.3
B. Service industries	3390.4	3495.9	3849.3	3886.6	4522.6
C. Public administration and defense	277.6	277.0	287.0	290.2	337.3
D. Total employed persons	5915.4	5992.0	6392.5	6244.6	7020.2

Note and sources: The number of employed persons is computed from data in Australian Bureau of Statistics (1987a, 1987b) for labor force surveys conducted in February, May, August, and November. The dates selected are those coinciding with or closest to the successive growth cycle turns, as shown in the next table.

Table 20.9. *Total change (in thousands) and percentage change in number of employed persons by industry division (seasonally adjusted) between growth cycle turns, Australia, 1976 to 1987*

	Peak to trough: Aug. 1976–Oct. 1977		Trough to peak: Oct. 1977–June 1981		Peak to trough: June 1981–May 1983		Trough to present: May 1983–Feb. 1987	
	000	%	000	%	000	%	000	%
A. Goods-producing industries								
1. Nonfarm								
Mining	+1.7	+2.1	+8.9	+10.8	+6.2	+6.8	+5.9	+6.1
Manufacturing	−29.6	−2.3	−5.0	−0.4	−112.8	−9.0	−11.5	−1.0
Construction	−16.6	−3.3	+4.8	+1.0	−74.6	−15.4	+92.7	+22.6
Total: Nonfarm	−44.5	−2.4	+8.7	+0.5	−181.2	−9.9	+87.1	+5.3
2. Agriculture, forestry, fishing and hunting	+16.2	+4.2	+28.4	+7.1	−7.2	−1.7	+5.4	+1.3
Total: Goods-producing	−28.3	−1.3	+37.1	+1.7	−188.4	−8.4	+92.5	+4.5
B. Service industries	+105.5	+3.1	+353.4	+10.1	+37.3	+1.0	+636.0	+16.4
C. Public administration and defense	−0.6	−0.2	+10.0	+3.6	+3.2	+1.1	+47.1	+16.2
D. Total employed persons	+76.6	+1.3	+400.5	+6.7	−147.9	−2.3	+775.6	+12.4

Source: Computed from data in Table 20.8.

only 1 percent in the most recent identified recession from June 1981 to May 1983. But in the current strong business cycle upswing, the service industries have been expanding strongly while manufacturing has continued to decline, although more slowly.

Another interesting point is that during the first growth recession period shown in Table 20.9, between August 1976 and October 1977, total employment continued to expand by nearly 77,000. This was a result of the growth of employment in the service industries of 105,500. However, in the next recession from June 1981 to May 1983, total employment fell by 148,000, with employment in the service industries growing by only 37,300. These experiences are consistent with the former recession being only a growth slowdown in Australia's aggregate economic activity (and not a classical recession, when the economy also declines absolutely). By contrast, the most recent identified recession was both a classical and growth recession (see Boehm and Moore, 1984; Boehm, 1987).

A further point revealed by Table 20.9 is that construction has contributed with manufacturing to the greater fluctuations in employment experienced during recession periods while public administration and defense have assisted the service industries in providing greater stability in employment experience.

In summary, with the service industries now providing nearly two-thirds of Australia's jobs, as noted in Table 20.1, it may be expected that in future classical and growth recessions, or in future when only growth slowdowns occur, total employment will probably be more stable. The recessions are likely to mean slower growth in the service industries. On the other hand, the goods-producing industries, notably manufacturing and construction, are likely to experience fluctuations both absolutely and relatively. But these fluctuations are likely to have a smaller impact on total economic activity than when the goods-producing industries played a more dominant role in the economy.

20.6   Major problems experienced in selecting Australia's service industry indicators

One of the main difficulties encountered in this study–as is evident in several places earlier in the chapter–is that data on at least a quarterly but preferably a monthly basis for key economic variables (to permit a comprehensive study of the economic fluctuations in the service industries in comparison with the goods-producing industries) are very limited as far as the service industries are concerned. Short-term data on services are either not available or, where they are available, do not begin until quite recently. No detailed data on output are available for the service industries on less than an annual basis. Data for the labor market, such as employed persons and hours of work, in the service industries became available on a quarterly basis for cyclical analysis only from 1977.

Caution needs to be exercised in assessing the suitability for economic indicator analysis of series available for only a relatively short period. This is because their performance as a leading, roughly coincident, or lagging indicator may vary from one cycle to another. Though there are family likenesses from one business cycle to another, hence justifying on economic grounds indicator analyses monitoring key variables that are known to behave generally in a consistent way, nevertheless each business cycle is an individual. Individuality is revealed in the way in which a particular indicator may be affected by a given stimulus and hence may perform in the indicator analysis.

In due course, given the continued publication of the indicators already identified for this chapter (from among the official and private material presently available), and the prospect of additional series on at least a quarterly basis becoming available, we should be increasingly better placed to provide a more diversified range of indicators to monitor fluctuations in particular sectors of the economy, including the service industries. As Moore (1983, p. 346) observed: "Every new recession or economic slowdown provides some additional evidence against which the indicators can be assessed."

20.7   Conclusion

The growing importance of the service industries means that Australia's business cycle experiences are no longer fundamentally dependent upon the fluctuations in the goods-producing sector. The growth of the service industries has provided an increasing dimension of greater stability in the growing economy. This may mean that future classical recessions are likely to be less severe and that the fluctuations may be more in the nature of growth slowdowns.

The evidence from economic indicator analyses of the total economy for major industrial countries reveals that the performances of the composite indexes of leading, roughly coincident, and lagging indicators have been significantly strengthened by including a diverse range of economic activity. The composite indexes are thus better able to reflect the different sources or nature of the changes in business activity. In the process the influence of "noise" occurring at varying times in individual series is minimized or overcome.[3]

[3] For a more detailed consideration of the "strength of composite indexes from diversification," see Boehm (1987), pp. 6 and 17–21.

This chapter has identified several indicators for the service industries that will be worth continuing to monitor and considering for inclusion in the economic indicator reports on the total economy prepared monthly by the Center for International Business Cycle Research in New York *(International Economic Indicators)* and by Westpac-Melbourne Institute in Melbourne *(Indexes of Economic Activity)*. The inclusion of more indicators relating specifically to the service industries will improve the diversification already achieved in Australia's leading, roughly coincident, and lagging composite indexes.

REFERENCES

Auerbach, A. J. (1982), "The Index of Leading Indicators: 'Measurement Without Theory,' Thirty-Five Years Later," *Review of Economics and Statistics, 64* (4, November), 589–95.

Australian Bureau of Statistics (1986a), *The Labour Force Australia,* August (Cat. 6203.0).

(1986b), *Australian National Accounts Gross Product by Industry, 1984–85* (Cat. 5211.0).

(1986c), *Balance of Payments, Australia–Historical Series on Microfiche* (1 July 1959 onwards), December (Cat. 5337.0).

(1987a), *The Labour Force Australia: Historical Summary 1966 to 1984* (Cat. 6204.0).

(1987b), *The Labour Force Australia,* February (Cat. 6203.0).

(1987c), *Building Approvals Australia,* February (Cat. 8731.0).

(1987d), *Balance of Payments Australia March Quarter* (Cat. 5302.0).

(1987e), *Retail Sales of Goods (Excluding Motor Vehicles, Parts, Petrol, etc), Australia,* March (Cat. 8501.0).

(1987f), *Historical Series of Estimates of National Income and Expenditure, Australia, September Quarter 1959 to June Quarter 1980 (Supplement to December Quarter 1986 issue of 5206.0)* (Cat. 5207.0).

(1987g), *Quarterly Estimates of National Income and Expenditure Australia March Quarter* (Cat. 5206.0).

Australian Chamber of Commerce and National Australia Bank (1987). *Quarterly Business Survey,* March and earlier issues.

Barry P. F., and C. W. Guille (1976), "The Australian Business Cycle and International Cyclical Linkages, 1959–1974," *Economic Record, 42* (138, June), 137–65.

Boehm, E. A. (1979), *Twentieth Century Economic Development in Australia,* 2nd ed., Longman Cheshire.

(1987), "New Economic Indicators for Australia: A Further Report," Institute of Applied Economic and Social Research Working Paper No. 4, April.

Boehm, E. A., and V. L. Martin (1987), "Testing Predictability Properties Between the Australian Leading and Coincident Indicators, 1962–85, and A Comparison with Previous Work," Research Paper No. 167, Department of Economics, University of Melbourne, January.

Boehm, E. A., and G. H. Moore (1984), "New Economic Indicators for Australia, 1949–84," *Australian Economic Review,* 4th Quarter, pp. 34–56.

(1987), "The Contribution of Leading and Lagging Indicators to Short-Term Economic Forecasting: An International Review," paper presented to the Seventh International Symposium on Forecasting, Boston, May.

Center for International Business Cycle Research (1986), *International Economic Indicators*, December, Appendix.

Economic Planning Advisory Council (1987), *International Trade in Services*, Council Paper No. 28, Pirie Printers Sales, Fyshwick, ACT, May.

Klein, P. A., and G. H. Moore (1985), *Monitoring Growth Cycles in Market-Oriented Countries: Developing and Using International Economic Indicators*, NBER Studies in Business Cycles No. 26. Cambridge, Mass.: Ballinger Publishing Company.

Layton, A. P., and Moore, G. H. (1989), "Leading Indicators for the Service Sector," *Journal of Business and Economic Statistics*, 7 (3, July), 379–86.

McDonald, D., and P. B. Dixon (1987), "Economic Developments in Australia: 1986–87 and 1987–88," *Australian Economic Review*, 2nd Quarter, 3–23.

Martin, V. L. (1986), "Cross-Spectral Estimates of the Average Lead Time Between Australia's Leading and Coincident Indicators: 1962(1) to 1985(8)," Research Paper No. 164, Department of Economics, University of Melbourne, December.

Mintz, I. (1970), *Dating Postwar Business Cycles: Methods and Their Application to Western Germany, 1950–67*, NBER Occasional Paper 107.

Mintz, I. (1974), "Dating United States Growth Cycles," in NBER, *Explorations in Economic Research*, 1 (1), Summer.

Moore, G. H. (1983), *Business Cycles Inflation and Forecasting*, 2nd ed., NBER Studies in Business Cycles No. 24. Cambridge, Mass.: Ballinger Publishing Company.

(1987), "The Service Industries and the Business Cycle," *Business Economics*, 22 (2, April), 12–17.

Stock Exchange of Melbourne (1980), *Chart Book of the Melbourne Share Price Index*, 16th ed., July.

Stock Exchange (1987), *Fact Sheet*, May and earlier issues.

Tucker, K. A., ed. (1977), *The Economics of the Australian Services Sector*. London: Croom Helm.

U.S. Department of Commerce (1977), *Handbook of Cyclical Indicators: A Supplement to Business Conditions Digest*, Bureau of Economic Analysis, Washington, D.C.

(1984), *Handbook of Cyclical Indicators: A Supplement to the Business Conditions Digest*, Bureau of Economic Analysis, Washington, D.C.

Zarnowitz, V., and C. Boschan (1975a), "Cyclical Indicators: An Evaluation and New Leading Indexes," in U.S. Department of Commerce, *Business Conditions Digest*, May; reprinted in U.S. Department of Commerce (1977, pp. 170–84).

(1975b), "New Composite Indexes of Coincident and Lagging Indicators", in U.S. Department of Commerce, *Business Conditions Digest*, November; reprinted in U.S. Department of Commerce (1977, pp. 185–98).

CHAPTER 21

Purchasing management survey data: Their value as leading indicators

Philip A. Klein and Geoffrey H. Moore

In the ongoing effort to utilize and improve the forecasting properties of leading indicators, analysts on both sides of the Atlantic and Pacific are increasingly combining quantitative indicators of the sort pioneered by Arthur F. Burns and Wesley C. Mitchell with qualitative survey data. We have in the past considered the forecasting usefulness of a number of surveys, including the surveys conducted by the European Economic Community, the Confederation of British Industry in the United Kingdom, Dun and Bradstreet, Inc., and the Michigan Survey Research Center in the United States. In a paper we presented at the September 1985 meeting of CIRET in Vienna, we explored some of the forecasting properties of the price surveys conducted by the National Association of Purchasing Management (NAPM) in the United States (Moore and Klein, 1985). One of the unique features of this survey is that it reports buying prices rather than selling prices, and we examined some of the relationships between this survey and measures of price fluctuations.

The preliminary work with the NAPM data proved so promising that we here concentrate on this source and develop the analysis not only of prices but also of other leading indicators, namely, new orders, inventory change, and vendor performance. In each case we shall compare the turning points in the NAPM series with the U.S. business cycle chronology as well as with comparable quantitative series. Correlation analyses will also be used. In this way we can evaluate the overall usefulness for forecasting of a data set that we believe has been underutilized thus far.

We are indebted to Chantal Dubrin for statistical assistance on this study, and to Theodore Torda and Michael Niemira for supplying much of the data. The National Association of Purchasing Management provided financial support for the work but is not responsible for the conclusions.

403

The NAPM has been collecting survey data monthly from about 250 companies since the late 1940s. The survey includes questions about new orders, vendor deliveries, inventories, buying prices, production, and employment. Since production and employment are not generally considered leading indicators, we omit them here. In comparing the surveys with quantitative data we shall also consider the promptness with which figures for a given month become available. Often in previous studies we have found that qualitative surveys do not lead quantitative series with which they can be compared, particularly when care is taken to treat the survey results in the correct way to make a true comparison. When the quantitative series refers to levels of activity, for example, this requires cumulating the results of monthly surveys when the latter represent changes in levels (e.g., the percentage of respondents reporting increases). Survey data of this type inherently lead levels of activity because they are a type of diffusion index and reflect changes in the activity rather than levels. Cumulation makes the comparisons equivalent, and makes the survey series considerably smoother than in their original form, but it also produces later turning points than those in the original survey series. As a result, we often find that the cumulated survey series does not lead its quantitative equivalent. However, survey data are often available anywhere from two weeks to two months earlier than the quantitative series. The result is that many survey series can be very useful in forecasting even when the turns in the survey series do not lead the turns in the quantitative equivalent.

Our correlation analyses will help to answer the important question, How well do the swings in the survey series match the size of the swings in the quantitative series? Since the surveys do not ask explicitly for the size of the change, we simply correlate the reported percent rising (including half the percent reporting no change) with the quantitative series. But this requires choosing some appropriate techniques for examining the two series. There are various ways to smooth volatile series, usually at the price of reducing or eliminating the lead in the turning points. We have experimented with a variety of ways to smooth series here. Additionally, some of the quantitative series we examine are in the form of diffusion indexes, such as the percentage of industries experiencing an increase in new orders. Thus, a diffusion index of a quantitative series is comparable to the form in which the survey data are reported.

In pursuing this study we have benefited from the earlier work of Theodore Torda at the U.S. Department of Commerce. In 1980 he developed a composite index from five of the NAPM series, including new orders, production, employment, inventories, and vendor performance. He has also made comparisons of the survey data with quantitative data, in a report published in 1985 (Torda, 1985).

Our study yields the following findings:

1. The buying price survey lags the smoothed rate of change in the *Journal of Commerce* industrial materials price index by about three months, on average, but leads the rate of change in the consumer price index by about eight months. It can therefore be used to forecast year-to-year changes in the consumer price index (CPI). The buying price survey also is a leading indicator of business cycles.

2. The new orders survey, when cumulated to reflect the level of new orders, tends to lag the actual volume of new orders by a few months. However, its movements are much smoother than new orders volume, so its cyclical turns are easier to recognize. These have led or coincided with nearly every business cycle turn. Moreover, the new orders survey data are available more promptly than the volume figures, and are not subject to revision. The survey series (not cumulated) also compares favorably with a diffusion index of new orders compiled from volume figures reported by industry.

3. The NAPM inventory survey matches the swings in inventory change closely and hence is a leading indicator of business cycles. Here the prompt availability of the survey data is of great importance since quantitative data on inventories are reported a month or so later than most other indicators.

4. The vendor performance survey figures from NAPM conform closely since 1976 with those available for prior years from the Purchasing Management Association of Chicago. They also correspond with the ratio of sales to inventories and lead the business cycle in similar fashion.

5. When the four NAPM survey series are combined into a composite leading index we find that it matches every business cycle turn since 1948. The average lead is three months. The new index usually reaches its peaks and troughs a couple of months later than the leading index compiled by the U.S. Department of Commerce. But the NAPM index is available more promptly and is not subject to revision, since all four of its components are released in final form about a week after the end of the month reported. Hence the index is a potentially useful instrument for forecasting business cycle developments.

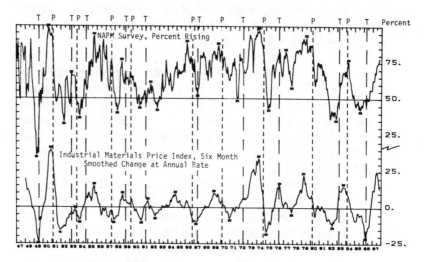

Figure 21.1. NAPM survey of buying prices versus industrial materials price index. Vertical lines are peaks (P) and troughs (T) in CPI inflation rate (see Figure 21.2).

21.1   The NAPM survey of buying prices

In our earlier study (Moore and Klein, 1985), we compared the behavior of the Purchasing Management survey of buying prices with the behavior of the *Journal of Commerce*'s index of industrial materials prices.[1] When the rate of change in the price index is measured by what we call a six-month smoothed rate (based on the ratio of the current month's index to the average index for the preceding twelve months, expressed at annual rate), the cycles in the qualitative and quantitative series track one another closely (Figure 21.1). All of the turning points can be matched, and we find that the survey results tend to lag by a few months at both peaks and troughs (Table 21.1, column 5). Since the price index is available daily, the survey data have no advantage with respect to timeliness.

In terms of the ability of the survey series to forecast the rate of inflation in consumer prices, the comparisons in Figure 21.2 and Table 21.1 are illuminating. Industrial materials prices themselves are a leading indicator of inflation, and so a comparison with changes in the con-

---

[1] The price index used was the 15 commodity index published by the *Journal of Commerce*. Since September 2, 1986, this has been replaced by a new eighteen-commodity index, also published in the *Journal*. The new index was designed by the Center for International Business Cycle Research and is used in this chapter.

Table 21.1. *Cyclical timing of consumer prices, industrial materials prices, and the NAPM survey of buying prices*

Rate of change, consumer price index (1)		Rate of change, industrial materials price index (2)		NAPM survey of buying prices, percent rising[a] (3)		Lead (−) or lag (+), in months, NAPM survey vs:			
						Consumer price index (4)		Industrial materials price index (5)	
Trough	Peak	T	P	T	P	T	P	T	P
7/49	2/51	6/49	11/50	4/49	8/50	−3	−6	−2	−3
3/53	10/53	11/51	8/53	5/52	3/53	−10	−7	+6	−5
10/54	8/57	2/54	9/55	2/54	9/55	−8	−23	0	0
3/59	10/59	11/57	11/58	4/58	10/58	−11	−12	+5	−1
6/61	—	12/60	9/61	10/60	1/62	−8	—	−2	+4
—	10/66	7/62	11/64	10/62	3/66	—	−7	+3	+16
5/67	2/70	3/67	3/69	5/67	9/69	0	−5	+2	+6
6/72	9/74	12/70	3/74	10/71	3/74	−8	−6	+10	0

Table 21.1. (cont.)

| | | | | | | Lead (−) or lag (+), in months, NAPM survey vs: | | | |
| Rate of change, consumer price index (1) | | Rate of change, industrial materials price index (2) | | NAPM survey of buying prices, percent rising[a] (3) | | Consumer price index (4) | | Industrial materials price index (5) | |
Trough	Peak	T	P	T	P	T	P	T	P
6/76	—	1/75	7/76	4/75	3/77	−14	—	+3	+8
—	3/80	11/77	3/79	11/77	7/79	—	−8	0	+4
3/86		6/82	3/79	11/82	4/84	−4	+2	+5	+7
4/86	2/84	3/86	9/83	8/85		−8		−7	
Mean						−7		+2	
At T and P							−8		+3
Median						−8		+2	
At T and P							−7		+3
Percent leads						90	89	25	27
At T and P							89		26

[a] Including half the percent reporting no change.

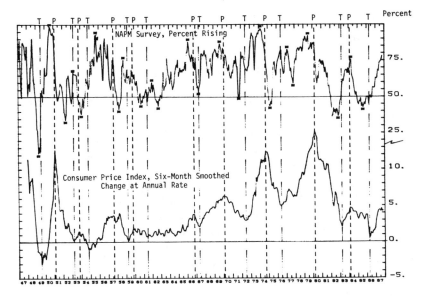

Figure 21.2. NAPM survey of buying prices versus consumer price index. Vertical lines are peaks (P) and troughs (T) in CPI inflation rate.

sumer price index represents an appropriate test of the ability of the NAPM series to forecast inflation rate change. Table 21.1 shows (column 4) that the average lead is about eight months at turns in the inflation rate cycle. Moreover, there are only two exceptions to the leading relationship: a coincident turn at the 1967 trough and a two-month lag at the 1984 peak.

The degree to which the NAPM surveys track actual changes in consumer prices can also be assessed by correlation analysis, using the six-month smoothed growth rates of the price index. For this purpose we have run cross correlograms with varying lags searching for the highest R^2 between the survey series and the growth rate in prices. We find that the maximum R^2 is .37, with the NAPM survey leading the CPI rate by six months. This is based on the monthly data for the survey and the six-month smoothed rate of change in the CPI. If we then use the December survey to forecast next year's inflation rate, which represents roughly a six-month lead, and allow for a simple time trend, R^2 is .60, with a mean absolute error over the thirty-eight years from 1948 to 1985 of 1.6 percentage points. We conclude that the NAPM price survey gives some useful clues to future inflation rates.

21.2   The NAPM survey of new orders

The new orders survey in its original form must be compared to the rate of change in new orders, or to a diffusion index of new orders. If one wishes to assess the ability of the survey results to forecast the *level* of new orders, the survey results must be cumulated. We examine the NAPM survey both ways. Initially, we compare the cumulated NAPM new orders survey with manufacturers' new orders for consumer goods and materials in 1982 dollars (Figure 21.3). It is clear that the cumulated survey series is far smoother than the actual new orders series, a common characteristic of survey results.

With regard to timing at business cycle turning points (Table 21.2), both the cumulated survey series and actual new orders exhibit a tendency to lead, especially at cycle peaks. At troughs the leads are either short or nonexistent. When the survey and the actual series are compared directly (column 6 of Table 21.2), the survey lags actual new orders at both peaks and troughs by a few months. The correlogram of the two series shows a maximum correlation ($R^2 = .93$) with the survey lagging by three months.

Although the lag is a disadvantage, there are three offsetting considerations. First, the cumulated survey data are much smoother than the actual new orders, so that cyclical turns are easier to recognize. Second, the survey data are available more promptly–about two or three weeks before the advance release of manufacturers' new orders. Third, the survey data are not revised, whereas the early data on new orders are subject to revision. Users of the indicators must weigh these factors in their evaluations.

It is also useful to compare the NAPM survey, without cumulating it, with a diffusion index of manufacturers' new orders that is compiled by the Department of Commerce. This index records the percentage of industries, among thirty-four that produce durable goods such as steel or automobiles, that report an increase in new orders over the past month or over the previous nine months. The comparison illustrates well one of the advantages of the survey method. The one-month span durable goods index is in fact more directly comparable with what the survey series measures (both show the change from the month before). However, the comparison in Figure 21.4 shows that the great volatility in the one-month span index virtually obscures any relationship that might exist between the movements in the two series. The nine-month span index is far less erratic and displays cyclical movements of much greater amplitude, closely resembling those in the survey data. The lead/lag comparison in Table 21.3 shows that both the nine-month span

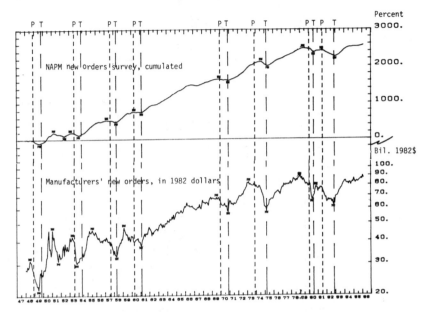

Figure 21.3. NAPM survey of new orders versus manufacturers' new orders. Vertical lines are business cycle troughs (T) and peaks (P). NAPM percent rising is cumulated monthly starting from zero in December 1947.

index and NAPM survey are highly conforming and equally consistent leaders. The direct comparison of the timing of the survey series with the nine-month span index (column 6 in Table 21.3) shows that the NAPM series usually leads at peaks, but the two are virtually coincident at troughs. The correlogram analysis indicates a maximum R^2 (.57) with the survey series leading by three months. On balance this would suggest that there is considerable forecasting advantage to utilizing the NAPM survey, particularly at peaks. This advantage is increased by factoring in the earlier availability of the survey data, as well as its freedom from revision.

21.3   The NAPM survey of inventories

A third kind of NAPM survey question that can be examined involves the behavior of inventories. Since the survey asks whether inventories are rising or falling, the percent rising reflects inventory change. We compare it with the change in manufacturing and trade inventories on hand and on order in constant dollars. A smoothed version of this monthly series is used in the Department of Commerce leading index,

Table 21.2. Cyclical timing of manufacturers' new orders and the NAPM survey of new orders, cumulated

Business cycle (1)		Mfrs. new orders (2)		NAPM survey, new orders, cumulated (3)		Lead (−) or lag (+) in months					
						Mfrs. new orders vs. bus. cycles (4)		NAPM survey, cumul. vs. bus. cycles (5)		NAPM survey, cumul. vs. mfrs. new orders (6)	
Trough	Peak	T	P	T	P	T	P	T	P	T	P
	11/48		6/48		—		−5		NA		NA
10/49		6/49		7/49		−4		−3		+1	
	—		1/51		3/51		—		—		+2
—		9/51		6/52		—		—		+9	
	7/53		4/53		2/53		−3		−5		−2
5/54		10/53		1/54		−7		−4		+3	
	8/57		7/55		3/57		−25		−5		+20

	Ref. trough	Ref. peak	NAPM low	NAPM high	Lead/lag at T	Lead/lag at P	Lead/lag at T	Lead/lag at P	Lead/lag at T	Lead/lag at P
4/58	4/60	4/58	2/59	0	−14	0	0	0	+14	
2/61	12/69	1/61	7/69	−1	−5	0	0	+1	+4	
11/70	11/73	11/70	3/73	0	−8	0	−1	0	+17	
3/75	1/80	3/75	12/78	0	−13	+2	+9	+2	+5	
7/80	7/81	5/80	10/80	−2	−9	0	−8	+2	+8	
11/82		10/82		−1		+1		+2		
Mean				−2	−10	0	−2	+2	+8	
At T and P				−6		−1		+5		
Median				−1	−8	0	−1	+2	+6	
At T and P				−4		0		+2		
Percent leads				62	100	25	71	0	12	
At T and P				81		47		6		

Note: The percent rising from the NAPM survey is cumulated monthly from zero in December 1947. NA, not available.

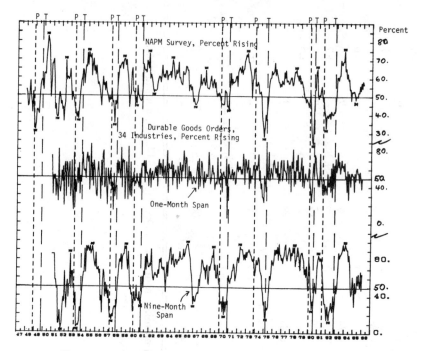

Figure 21.4. NAPM survey of new orders versus diffusion index of durable goods orders. Vertical lines are peaks (P) and troughs (T) of business cycles.

and we shall use it here for comparison with the NAPM survey since the unsmoothed series is highly erratic. The smoothing is done by a weighted four-month moving average placed in the terminal month. Both the smoothed inventory change and the survey series are quite volatile and show a number of extra cycles (Figure 21.5). Table 21.4 compares the timing of the two series with business cycles and with each other. The inventory change series has somewhat longer leads than the survey series at peaks, while the two are virtually the same vis-à-vis the business cycle at troughs. However, when the two series are compared directly, including the extra cycles that do not match the business cycle, the survey leads the actual change more often than not at peaks, while they are roughly coincident at troughs. In terms of cyclical behavior, therefore, the two series are very similar. This is supported by the correlogram analysis, which yields a maximum R^2 of .48 when the two series are coincident.

Although there is little to choose between the two series on grounds

Table 21.3. Cyclical timing of new orders diffusion indexes

| Business cycle (1) | | Mfrs. new orders, 34 industries, 9 mo. span (2) | | NAPM survey, new orders (3) | | Lead (−) or lag (+), in months | | | | | |
| | | | | | | Mfrs. new rders vs. bus. cycle (4) | | NAPM survey vs. bus. cycle (5) | | NAPM survey vs. mfrs. new orders (6) | |
Trough	Peak	T	P	T	P	T	P	T	P	T	P
10/49	—	NA	NA	1/49	6/50	NA	NA	−9	—	NA	NA
—	7/53	1/52	2/53	7/51	7/52	—	−5	—	−12	−6	−7
5/54	8/57	10/53	8/55	12/53	2/55	−7	−24	−5	−30	+2	−6
4/58	4/60	10/57	6/59	1/58	2/59	−6	−10	−3	−14	+3	−4
2/61	—	1/61	—	7/60	12/61	−1	—	−7	—	−6	—
—	—	—	5/66	6/62	7/64	—	—	—	—	—	−22
—	12/69	12/66	4/69	2/67	4/68	—	−8	—	−20	+2	−12

Table 21.3. (cont.)

| Business cycle (1) | | Mfrs. new orders, 34 industries, 9 mo. span (2) | | NAPM survey, new orders (3) | | Lead (−) or lag (+), in months | | | | | |
| | | | | | | Mfrs. new orders vs. bus. cycle (4) | | NAPM survey vs. bus. cycle (5) | | NAPM survey vs. mfrs. new orders (6) | |
Trough	Peak	T	P	T	P	T	P	T	P	T	P
11/70	11/73	6/70	4/72	11/70	1/73	−5	−19	0	−10	+5	+9
3/75	1/80	3/75	6/78	12/74	7/78	0	−19	−3	−18	−3	+1
7/80	7/81	5/80	2/81	6/80	11/80	−2	−5	−1	−8	+1	−3
11/82	—	4/82	2/84	11/81	12/83	−7	—	−12	—	−5	−2
Mean						−4	−13	−5	−16	+1	−5
At T and P							−8		−10		−3
Median						−5	−10	−10	−14	+1	−3
At T and P							−6		−9		−3
Percent leads						86	100	88	100	40	77
At T and P							93		93		61

NA = not available.

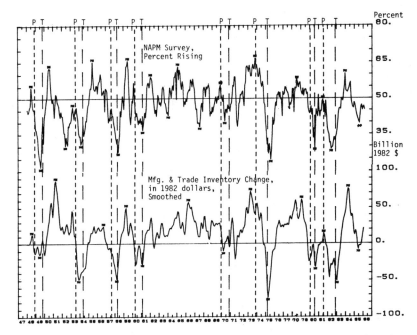

Figure 21.5. NAPM survey of inventories versus change in manufacturing and trade inventories. Vertical lines are business cycle peaks (P) and troughs (T).

of behavior, the NAPM series has a significant advantage in that it becomes available about five weeks before the inventory change figure for the same month. This publication advantage is especially important in that it puts the inventory change variable on a par with other leading indicators that are promptly available, such as new orders or housing starts or any of the other indicators used in the Department of Commerce leading index.

21.4   The NAPM survey of vendor performance

One of the more useful leading indicators is vendor performance, which is the percentage of companies reporting slower deliveries. When this increases it is a sign of expanding economic activity, with order backlogs piling up or sales outrunning inventories. We have utilized the NAPM survey reports of vendor performance for the period since 1976, linking them to a series available from the Purchasing Management Association of Chicago for earlier years. Here we relate this survey to the reciprocal

Table 21.4. Cyclical timing of inventory change and the NAPM survey of inventories

| Business cycle (1) | | Inventory change, smoothed[a] (2) | | NAPM survey inventories (3) | | Leads (−) and lags (+), in months | | | | | |
| | | | | | | Inventory change vs. bus. cycle (4) | | NAPM survey vs. bus. cycle (5) | | NAPM survey vs. inventory change (6) | |
Trough	Peak	T	P	T	P	T	P	T	P	T	P
10/49	11/48	6/49	7/48	7/49	6/48	−4	−4	−3	−5	+1	−1
—	—	—	4/51	5/52	7/50	—	—	—	—	—	−9
—	7/53	11/53	—	2/54	3/53	−6	−27[b]	−3	−4	+3	—
5/54	8/57	3/58	9/56	5/58	6/55	−1	−11	+1	−26	+2	−15
4/58	4/60	2/61	4/59	2/61	6/59	0	−12	0	−10	0	+2
2/61	—	—	—	—	1/62	—	—	—	—	—	—

Business cycle peak (P)		Specific-cycle peak		Lead (−) or lag (+), months	
—	—	—	—	—	−14
—	12/69	—	11/69	−1	−44ᶜ
11/70	11/73	3/70 / 5/70	10/73	−1	−7
3/75	1/80	4/75 / 7/75	7/78	−18	−12
7/80	7/81	8/80 / 7/80	6/81	−1	0
11/82	—	1/83 / 5/82	—	—	—

Note: the dates/leads shown include specific-cycle turns compared with reference peaks (12/69, 11/73, 1/80, 7/81) and troughs (11/70, 3/75, 7/80, 11/82); additional reference columns 1/64, 7/67, 2/65, 12/83, 4/84 also appear.

Summary statistics (months, and percent):

Mean	−2	−8	−15	−2	0	
At T and P		−8, −5			−2	
Median	0	−5	−12	−2	+2	−4
At T and P		−3			−1	
Percent leads	50	69	88	50	25	78
At T and P	75		100		53	

ᵃMonthly change in manufacturing and trade inventories on hand and on order in 1982 dollars, smoothed by weighted four-month moving average (BCD Series 36).
ᵇ4/51 peak compared with 7/53 peak.
ᶜ4/66 peak compared with 12/69 peak.

420   **Philip A. Klein and Geoffrey H. Moore**

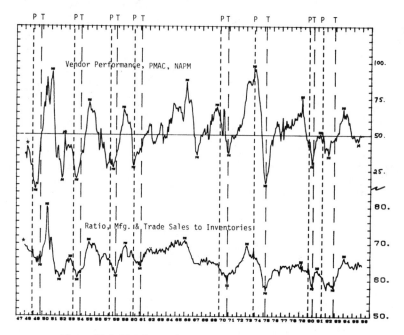

Figure 21.6. Vendor performance versus the ratio of sales to inventories. Vertical lines are business cycle peaks (P) and troughs (T).

of the ratio of manufacturing and trade inventories in 1982 dollars to sales in 1982 dollars. The reciprocal, therefore, is the ratio of sales to inventories, and can be expected to be positively related to vendor performance. When a vendor's sales to inventory ratio is high, his deliveries may slow down since he will be depending more on new production to fill orders.

Vendor performance and the sales/inventory ratio are shown in Figure 21.6, and their leads and lags are recorded in Table 21.5. The chart suggests that the two series are reasonably closely related. Table 21.5 shows that the survey series has longer leads on average at business cycle troughs, while the sales/inventory ratio has longer leads at peaks. This is confirmed in column 6 of Table 21.5, which shows that vendor performance leads the ratio at troughs but lags at peaks. The correlogram analysis, which of course does not distinguish troughs from peaks, yields a maximum correlation when the series are viewed as coincident, but the R^2 is only .27.

In short, both series contribute information about the business cycle, and both are leading indicators, although the sales/inventory ratio is usually treated as a lagging indicator in its reciprocal form. A further

Table 21.5. Cyclical timing of sales/inventory ratio and vendor performance survey

Business cycle (1)		Sales/ inventory ratio[a] (2)		Vendor performance[b] (3)		Sales/inv. ratio vs. bus. cycle (4)		Vendor perf. vs. bus. cycle (5)		Vendor perf. vs. sales inv. ratio (6)	
Trough	Peak	T	P	T	P	T	P	T	P	T	P
10/49	11/48	10/49	1/48	3/49	4/48	0	−10	−7	−7	−7	+3
—	—	12/51	7/50	3/52	2/51	—	—	—	—	+3	+7
5/54	7/53	12/53	3/53	11/53	7/52	−5	−4	−6	−12	−1	−8
4/58	8/57	4/58	4/55	12/57	4/55	0	−28	−4	−28	−4	0
2/61	4/60	1/61	5/59	3/60	2/59	−1	−11	−11	−14	−10	−3
—	—	—	1/66	5/67	3/66	—	—	—	—	—	+2
11/70	12/69	11/70	—	12/70	8/69	0	−47[c]	+1	−4	+1	—
—	11/73	—	2/73	—	11/73	—	−9	—	0	—	+9

Table 21.5. (cont.)

Business cycle (1)		Sales/ inventory ratio[a] (2)		Vendor performance[b] (3)		Leads (−) and lags (+), in months					
						Sales/inv. ratio vs. bus. cycle (4)		Vendor perf. vs. bus. cycle (5)		Vendor perf. vs. sales inv. ratio (6)	
Trough	Peak	T	P	T	P	T	P	T	P	T	P
3/75	1/80	3/75	3/79	2/75	4/79	0	−10	−1	−9	−1	+1
7/80	7/81	6/80	1/81	5/80	4/81	−1	−6	−2	−3	−1	+3
11/82	—	10/82	1/84	3/82	11/83	−1	—	−8	—	−7	−2
Mean						−1	−16	−5	−10	−3	+1
At T and P						−8		−7		−1	
Median						0	−10	−5	−8	−1	+2
At T and P						−4		−6		−1	
Percent leads						50	100	88	88	78	30
At T and P						75		88		53	

[a] Ratio, manufacturing and trade sales to inventories in 1982 dollars (reciprocal of BCD series 77).

[b] Percent reporting slower deliveries, Purchasing Management Association of Chicago through 1975, National Association of Purchasing Managers from 1976. Data are seasonally adjusted.

[c] 1/66 peak compared to 12/69 peak.

point to be noted is that the vendor performance survey is available on a timely basis whereas the sales/inventory ratio is subject to the same publication lag as noted above for inventory change.

21.5 A composite leading index of NAPM surveys

When we bring together the results of our analysis of the four components of the NAPM survey, we find that three of them clearly display a leading relationship to business cycles and one (cumulated new orders) could best be described as roughly coincident. Even this series, however, leads at more turns than it lags (see Table 21.6). These results suggest that it might be useful to combine the four components into a composite index, using the same procedure employed by the Department of Commerce in constructing its leading index for *Business Conditions Digest.*

The results of this exercise are shown in Figure 21.7, where the new NAPM index is compared with the BCD index. The NAPM index shows clear cyclical movements, closely matching those in the BCD index. At three of the eight business cycle troughs, it leads, while it is virtually coincident with the other five. At peaks, it leads at every turn but one (see column 6 in Table 21.6). On average it leads the business cycle by two or three months. This is a shorter lead than that achieved by the BCD leading index, where the leads average about six months. Hence the NAPM index lags the BCD index by a couple of months at nearly every turn. The correlation between the two indexes is dominated by the long-run trend in both indexes, but is at a maximum with the NAPM index lagging by two to six months. For each of these lags $R^2 =$ .982. The lag can be pinned down more closely by taking six-month smoothed growth rates of both indexes (Figure 21.8). Then the maximum correlation occurs with the NAPM growth rate lagging the BCD growth rate by two months, and $R^2 = .80$. In practice the lag in timing would be partly offset by the prompter availability of the NAPM index, by about three weeks. Moreover, the index is not subject to revision, since each component is available in final form when first released. We conclude that the new NAPM leading index is a promising tool for monitoring the ebb and flow of the business cycle.[2]

---

[2] There are several differences between the leading index developed here and the one constructed by Torda and published currently by the NAPM. We do not include production or employment because these are basically coincident variables and the survey data for them show leads only because they represent rates of change. Also, for the same reason, we use the new orders survey data in cumulated form. Finally, we use the composite index method for combining the components, rather than averaging the survey figures directly.

Table 21.6. Timing at business cycle turns: NAPM surveys and BCD leading index

Business cycle (1)		NAPM buying prices (2)		NAPM new orders, cumulated (3)		NAPM inventories (4)		PMAC + NAPM vendor performance (5)		NAPM leading index (6)		BCD leading index (7)	
Trough	Peak	T	P	T	P	T	P	T	P	T	P	T	P
	11/48		—		—		−5		−7		−5		−10
10/49	7/53	−6	−4	−3	−5	−3	−4	−7	−12	−4	−4	−4	−4
5/54	8/57	−3	−23	−4	−5	−3	−26	−6	−28	−3	−7	−6	−23
4/58	4/60	0	−18	0	0	+1	−10	−4	−14	0	−10	−2	−11
2/61	12/69	−4	−3	0	−1	0	−1	−11	−4	−7	−2	−2	−8
11/70	11/73	+11	+4	0	+9	−6	−1	+1	0	+1	+2	−1	−8

Leads (−) and lags (+), in months, at business cycle turns

3/75	+1	+2	+4	−1	+1	−1
1/80	−6	−8	−18	−9	−9	−10
7/80	—	0	0	−2	0	−2
7/81	—	−1	−1	−3	−2	−3
11/82	0	+1		−8	0	−8
At troughs and peaks						
Mean	−4	−1	−5	−7	−3	−6
Median	−3	0	−3	−6	−2	−5
Percent leads	62	47	73	88	62	100
Extra cycles						
Troughs	5/52, 10/62, 5/67, 11/77, 8/85	6/52	5/52, 1/64, 7/67, 7/85	3/52, 5/67, 4/85	5/52, 5/67, 7/85	8/51, 12/66
Peaks	8/50, 1/62, 3/66, 3/77, 4/84	2/53	7/50, 1/62, 2/65, 12/83	2/51, 3/66, 11/83	1/51, 8/66, 4/84	8/50, 3/66

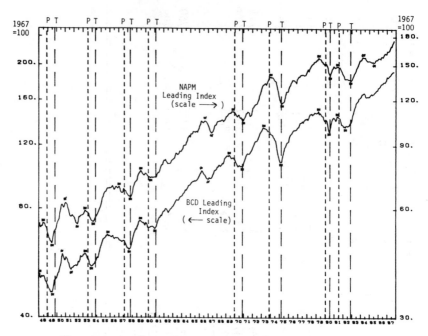

Figure 21.7. NAPM leading index versus BCD leading index. Vertical lines are business cycle peaks (P) and troughs (T).

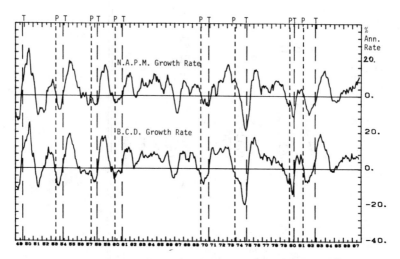

Figure 21.8. NAPM leading index growth rate versus BCD leading index growth rate. Vertical lines are business cycle peaks (P) and troughs (T). Growth rates are six-month smoothed rates.

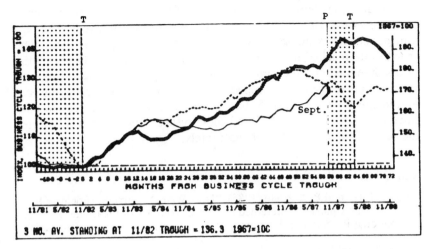

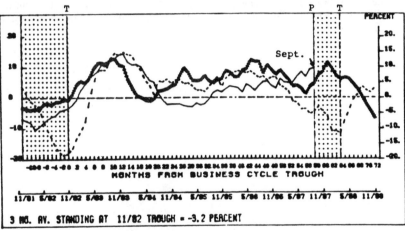

Figure 21.9. Recession-recovery patterns for the NAPM index. Solid line = 1982-7 expansion; heavy line = 1961-9 expansion; dashed line = 1975-80 expansion. Top: NAPM leading index. Bottom: NAPM leading index, growth rate.

Figure 21.9 illustrates one way of using the NAPM leading index for this purpose. The top panel compares the course taken by the index during the current recovery, which began in November 1982, with its pattern during two previous long-lasting recoveries. The index did not lead the 1982 upturn in the economy but reached bottom in exactly the same month (November) after having leveled off during the preceding nine months. In this respect it resembled its behavior in the 1961 recovery.

428   Philip A. Klein and Geoffrey H. Moore

After that the current upswing was much like the two earlier recoveries until the summer of 1984, when it slumped for about a year. The bottom panel makes the same comparison in terms of growth rates. The growth rate reached its sharpest rate of decline nine months before the recession ended and then moved into a rapid growth phase in line with the previous recoveries. It dipped into negative territory during the economic slowdown of 1984–5, but has been on an upward growth path since the summer of 1985. In all these respects the index has reflected the state of the economy quite accurately.

REFERENCES

Moore, G. H., and P. A. Klein (1985), "How Well Do Surveys Anticipate Inflation Rate Changes?" presented at 17th Conference of the Center for International Research on Economic Tendency Surveys, Vienna, Austria, September 11.
Torda, T. S. (1985), "Purchasing Management Index Provides Early Clue on Turning Points," *Business America,* U.S. Department of Commerce, June 24, 1985.

CHAPTER 22

An agenda for inventories input to the leading composite index

Feliks Tamm

A broadly based agreement exists among students of economic conditions that inventories play an important role in the periodic economic fluctuations from boom to bust and back again to boom. That finding by economists should not be praised as an extraordinary piece of brain work, however, because every manufacturer and trader, plus various functionaries, such as business managers and purchasing agents, and even sales clerks, can independently come to the same conclusion by observing the production, sales, and inventory records. In fact, the inventory data are collected with the help of those production and sales agents. The economists may have differences of opinion about how to best use and evaluate the inventory data so collected. This chapter, in effect, is concerned with the use of various inventory data for evaluation of current and future economic conditions.

22.1 Inventory data as a business cycle indicator

The application of inventory data may create misunderstanding when one does not carefully distinguish between flow and stock concepts relating to inventories. The flows and stocks have different timing sequences. To begin with, the flows are equivalent to changes and lead the cyclical timing in the stocks or aggregates (also referred to as levels). The accumulation of inventory stock has normally slowed down by the time the economic activity reaches a peak because the inventory flow (called inventory investment or buildup) has reached its peak some time prior to the cyclical peak and has been slowing down from that time point on.

The views expressed in this chapter are those of the author and do not necessarily reflect those of the U.S. Department of Commerce.

Obviously, the stocks start declining when the inventory buildup turns negative.

In regard to the Department of Commerce data on inventories, used in the leading index, there is another important timing sequence of flows and stocks relating to the orders and unfilled orders to complete the second part of the series definition—inventories on hand and on order. The change in unfilled orders (the excess of new orders over shipments) leads new orders. Since the cyclical timing of new orders occurs earlier than that in shipments, the change in unfilled orders (or buildup of inventories on order) also leads – by long intervals – shipments and aggregate (stocks of) unfilled orders.

Often individual analysts have questioned why an increase in inventories was a good business cycle omen. They erroneously think in terms of inventory stocks rather than inventory buildup. The increasing rate of inventory buildup (i.e., change in inventory stocks) signifies the public's trust in the current economic strength. All participants concerned expect the expansion to continue, and those offering goods for sale are willing to replenish their inventory stocks to maintain increased current and future sales and thus realize greater profits. At some point, the rate of inventory buildup begins to decline. This is because the sellers have developed a notion about deteriorating future sale and profit opportunities. An analogous scenario of economic revival could be easily developed with reversed basic movements and with an inverted expectational pattern.

To summarize, the timing sequences discussed above tell us that, as a rule, the stocks of inventories on hand and on order are a lagging indicator; that is, they lag the turning points in the aggregate economic activity.[1] In fact, a lead–lag relationship can be observed in most, if not all, economic time-series, where the stock-flow family relationship exists, and in summary indicators, such as the diffusion indexes. This interesting relationship renders the lagging indicators very useful analytical tools, as noted below.

The lagging series represent variables that influence the development and implementation of production plans in anticipation of future profits. For example, declines in inventories and interest rates during a business contraction lead to an improved outlook for profitability, new

---

[1] A broad concept lacking precise statistical representation. It can be determined only by approximation in empirical research. A combination of data on employment, production, income, and trade is often considered a fair representation. According to Wesley C. Mitchell and Arthur F. Burns a meaningful entity for measuring aggregate economic activity would be GNP restricted "to the portion of the national product that passes through the 'market'" (Burns and Mitchell, 1946).

orders, and production. Plans and commitments for future growth in economic activity (leading indicators) lead to growth in employment, production, earnings, and consumption (coincident indicators) until certain associated processes reflecting elements of rising costs and falling profits (lagging indicators) develop into effective constraints that discourage planning for new commitments and, eventually, production. The timing of these processes established an "order of sequence" for the cyclical indicators in which the lagging composite index leads the leading composite index, bearing a message relevant for the subsequent business cycle phase. The peaks in the lagging index signal that the imbalances that constrain future production and investment are about to decrease; the outlook for an upturn in the business cycle is now improving – a favorable message that a new economic expansion is not far away. Similarly, the trough in the lagging composite index would indicate that the imbalances and stresses are about to increase. The record shows that increases in these imbalances have continued, on average, twenty-six months before an absolute decline is recorded—a period long enough for corrective measures, possibly neutralization of depressive forces, or even reversal of the course of events.

The relationship of the laggers to the two other categories of indicators is where the development of a theoretical structure of the cyclical indicators approach should begin. It is the focal area for both behavioral and causal relationships. Causal conditions, relations, and dispositions are largely present between individual indicators or certain "families" of indicators. These relationships could be more closely defined and formalized, perhaps on the basis of elaborated theories, if adequate resources were employed.

22.2   Inventory data in the Department of Commerce leading composite index

Data for inventories both on hand and on order are compiled from data collected each month by the Bureau of the Census in shipments, inventories, and orders surveys and in surveys of merchant wholesalers and retail trade. Probability samples and modern data-processing technologies are used. The compiled dollar values are adjusted for seasonality and trading days, and are converted into the constant dollars.

It is apparent that those inventory data meet fully the customary functional quality requirements to justify the conceptual suggestion that the inventory data be included in the leading composite index. But apart from the conceptual appeal, the change in inventory stocks is subject to certain inherent features, and it displays behavioral characteristics that make it a difficult time-series for practical applications. One problem is that the change in inventories on hand and on order has two weak characteristics, which, like twin sisters, demand equal and simultaneous attention – inadequate smoothness and a lack of prompt availability."

Data on inventory buildup are typically computed by taking the first differences in the inventory levels. The differences in terms of dollars can be analytically related to other economic aggregates expressed in terms of monetary units, such as sales and GNP data, to produce meaningful comparisons.[2] Monthly changes, whether differences or percentage changes, are subject to irregular fluctuations to an extraordinary degree. The irregular movements are residuals after seasonal adjustment procedures have identified and removed the systematic patterns, such as the seasonal and trading day variations, and have also taken into account a smooth underlying data curve called the trend-cycle curve. As the irregular fluctuations do not follow any systematic pattern but display characteristics of a random series, they can only be moderated by using a smoothing formula that, in effect, fully or partially cancels out the high extremities against the low ones.

Traditionally, moving averages (MA) have been used for smoothing away irregular fluctuations. The Bureau of Economic Analysis (BEA) is presently using a four-term MA, with weight pattern of 1, 2, 2, 1, for smoothing inventory data and certain other composite index components. A more advanced technique for smoothing is an approach developed by Statistics Canada – the minimum phase-shift filtering involving "autoregressive moving average (ARMA) filters" – and BEA has been experimenting with that methodology. (For more detail, see Appendix A.)

Moving averages and other smoothing formulas have a serious drawback – a loss of data at the ends of data arrays with a corresponding shift of timing. For example, a four-term MA loses three data positions because four data values are needed to calculate one MA value. If the MA is placed at the center of the four-month smoothing interval, as it preferably should be, the array would lose one and one-half months of data at both ends. In other words, the series would lose currency, but the cyclical timing or the "lead" is not affected. On the other hand, if the MA is placed at the end of the interval, all data positions at the cur-

---

[2] Percent changes would be the preferable form of data when historical comparisons are made. They provide, as a rule, a meaningful comparison of economic forces over time. Therefore, percent changes are preferable input data in the summary measures, such as composite indexes, over the differences, especially where such measures are computed for a long time period.

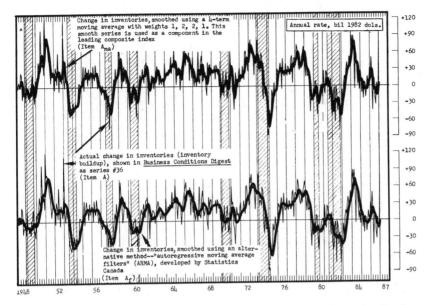

Figure 22.1. Change in manufacturers' and trade inventories on hand and on order. Inventory buildup series 36 in BCD. Item letters are shortcuts to identify series for Table 21.1. *Source:* Bureau of Economic Analysis, Statistical Indicators Division, April 20, 1987.

rent end of the interval would be filled. (The far end of the data array would lose values for three months, which is not a serious loss for analytical purposes.) But the cyclical timing is altered – shifted forward by one and one-half months. Thus placing MA values at the end of intervals reduces the lead time of data. In either case, a price is being paid for smoothing in the form of creating a distortion in the original data constellation.

Figure 22.1 provides some basis for comparing the effectiveness of the two smoothing formulas mentioned above. The results produced by the BEA's four-term weighted MA and those calculated by the ARMA filters of Statistics Canada are placed in juxtaposition. The latter appears to be decisively superior to the former, and serious thought is entertained at BEA for adopting the ARMA filtering methodology as a standard smoothing formula. From here on the ARMA filters are used for smoothing data in this chapter. Table 22.1 shows analytical figures for judging the smoothness and various other characteristics of the two smoothed series discussed above as well as for other data series shown

Table 22.1. *MCD and related measures of variability*

Line title	Period covered	C̄I	Ī	C̄	Ī/C̄	MCD	Ī/C̄ for MDC-span	Average duration of run (ADR)			
								CI	I	C	MCD
Item A	2/48–2/87	18.98	18.12	3.83	4.74	6	...	1.67	1.58	7.43	2.97
Item Ama	5/48–2/87	6.05	2.77	4.53	0.61	1	0.61	3.50	2.22	6.55	3.50
Item Af	2/48–1/87	4.06	1.30	3.59	0.36	1	0.36	4.53	1.89	7.92	4.62
Item B	1/48–3/87	2.88	2.46	1.25	1.96	3	0.78	2.35	1.64	8.55	4.42
Item Bf	1/48–3/87	2.81	0.46	2.65	0.17	1	0.17	7.83	2.06	9.79	7.83
Item C	1/48–3/87	19.53	17.34	6.72	2.58	3	0.99	1.98	1.58	6.81	3.55
Item D	1/48–3/87	18.58	16.15	7.60	2.13	3	0.83	1.97	1.63	7.34	3.97
Item E	1/48–3/87	8.73	8.38	1.95	4.29	5	0.88	1.72	1.54	6.71	3.05
Item F	1/48–3/87	5.82	5.07	2.40	2.11	3	0.83	2.03	1.64	8.70	3.90
Item Ff	1/48–3/87	6.20	1.09	5.80	0.19	1	0.19	8.10	2.18	10.00	8.10
Item G	1/48–3/87	3.24	2.96	1.08	2.74	4	0.77	2.04	1.54	8.10	4.21
Item Gf	1/48–3/87	5.50	1.16	5.10	0.23	1	0.23	6.91	1.90	9.40	6.91
Item H	1/47–3/87	1.86	0.81	1.59	0.51	1	0.51	3.65	1.54	13.39	3.65
Item I	1/45–3/87	1.01	0.57	0.77	0.75	1	0.75	3.75	1.69	11.00	3.75
Item J	1/58–3/87	1.70	0.50	1.61	0.31	1	0.31	5.38	1.56	19.44	5.38
Item K	1/45–3/87	0.35	0.16	0.30	0.53	1	0.53	5.06	1.54	16.87	5.06
Item L	12/47–3/87	0.51	0.11	0.48	0.23	1	0.23	8.26	1.73	14.27	8.26
Item M	12/47–3/87	2.05	0.52	1.98	0.26	1	0.26	8.56	1.73	14.27	8.56
Item N	1/53–2/87	1.06	0.36	0.97	0.38	1	0.38	5.38	1.59	14.10	5.38
Item O	2/48–1/87	15.65	15.55	1.78	8.72	6	...	1.48	1.49	9.94	2.60
Item Of	2/48–1/87	2.67	1.04	2.27	0.46	1	0.46	3.99	1.69	7.66	4.06
Item P	2/48–10/86	9.98	9.08	2.87	3.16	4	0.94	1.81	1.61	6.36	3.57
Item Pf	2/48–10/86	2.79	0.74	2.50	0.30	1	0.30	5.59	1.94	7.86	5.59

Note: The following are brief definitions of MCD and related measures of variability; more complete explanations appear in *Electronic Computers and Business Indicators*, by Julius Shiskin, issued as Occasional Paper 57 by the National Bureau of Economic Research, 1957 (reprinted from *Journal of Business*, October 1957). $\overline{CI}$ is the average month-to-month percentage change, without regard to sign, in the seasonally adjusted series (i.e., the series after adjustment for measurable seasonal, trading-day, and holiday variations). $\overline{C}$ is the same for the cyclical component, a smooth, flexible moving average of the seasonally adjusted series. $\overline{I}$ is the same for the irregular component, obtained by dividing the cyclical component into the seasonally adjusted series. MCD (months for cyclical dominance) provides an estimate of the appropriate time span over which to observe cyclical movements in a monthly series. It is small for smooth series and large for irregular series. In deriving MCD, percentage changes are computed separately for the irregular component and the cyclical component over one-month spans (Jan.–Feb., Feb.–Mar., etc.) two-month spans (Jan.–Mar., Feb.–Apr., etc.), up to twelve-month spans. Averages, without regard to sign, are then computed for the changes over each span. MCD is the shortest span in months for which the average percentage change (without regard to sign) in the cyclical component is larger than the average percentage change (without regard to sign) in the irregular component, and remains so. Thus, it indicates the point at which fluctuations in the seasonally adjusted series become dominated by cyclical rather than irregular movements. All series with an MCD greater than 5 are shown as 6. $\overline{I}/\overline{C}$ is a measure of relative smoothness (small values) or irregularity (large values) of the seasonally adjusted series. It is shown for one month spans and for spans of the period of MCD. When MCD is 6, no $\overline{I}/\overline{C}$ ratio is shown for the MCD period. Average Duration of Run (ADR) is another measure of smoothness and is equal to the average number of consecutive monthly changes in the same direction in any series of observations. When there is no change between two months, a change in the same direction as the preceding change is assumed. The ADR is shown for the seasonally adjusted series CI, irregular component I, cyclical component C, and the MCD curve. The MCD curve is an unweighted moving average (with the number of terms equal to MCD) of the seasonally adjusted series. A comparison of these ADR measures with the expected ADR of a random series gives an indication of whether the changes approximate those of a random series. Over one-month intervals, the expected ADR of a random series is 1.5, and the actual ADR falls between 1.36 and 1.75 about 95 percent of the time. Over one-month intervals in a moving average (MCD) of a random series, the expected ADR is 2. For example, in a series with ADR measures of 1.56 for CI, 1.45 for I, 8.71 for C, and 3.15 for MCD, the 1.56 for CI indicates that one-month changes in the seasonally adjusted series reverse sign, on average, about as often as expected in a random series. The 1.45 for I and 8.71 for C suggest that the seasonally adjusted series has been separated into an essentially random component and a cyclical (nonrandom) component. This 3.15 for MCD indicates that the MCD moving average of the seasonally adjusted data reverses direction, on average, about every three months. Thus, for this series, month-to-month changes in the MCD moving average usually reflect underlying short-term trend movements while month-to-month chages in the seasonally adjusted series usually do not.

on graphic presentations. See also the Table 22.1 explanatory note describing those measures. Please note that lines of information are identified by shorthand line titles that also appear in the figures.

A second, but perhaps a more serious shortcoming of inventory data is caused by certain definitional features and the time schedule of data collection. Since inventories are taken at the end of an accounting period (e.g., a month), their availability to statistics users is always behind that of promptly available statistics,[3] some of which are often estimated on the basis of returns covering but a segment of the first part of the period. (Strictly speaking, the delay in the preliminary release of inventories is not quite one-half month if compared with new orders.) For that reason, the initially published leading and lagging composite index estimates do not include the contribution of inventory data.

The composite indexes are a target for an increasing volume of criticism because of subsequent revision of the initially published data. A great share of the revision is due to that predicament. Revisisons caused by the missing values may result in troublesome revision situations. This is especially true now because the public view of the composite indexes has changed drastically. The leading index is no longer looked upon as a mere statistic, but rather as a forecasting device of some consequence. Such forecasting devices have to meet more rigid criteria than ordinary statistics. Yet those criteria, as set by different individuals, may vary widely. Nevertheless, this criticism must be taken seriously.[4]

One possibility for increasing the reliability of the inventory statistics' contribution to the leading and lagging composite indexes would be to delay the publication of the indexes by three to five days during which period the inventory data compilers in the Census Bureau would be in a position to provide a rough preliminary estimate. This idea, however, is not appealing to those who desire a rapid release of the leading composite index.

For many series, preliminary data, based on incomplete reporting, are speedily released with an understanding that a short time later a revised figure will be released that is superior to the preliminary figure. Inventories have a one-month publication lag and, therefore, are not included in the current month estimate of the leading index. Next month the index estimate is revised by including the inventory value.

---

[3] A promptly available statistic is a figure referring to the given month, but published in the following month; such a statistic is said to have no monthly publication lag. A statistic referring to the given month but published next to the following month – actually two months later – displays a one-month publication lag.

[4] Not all analysts are concerned about revisions of data. Corrected or revised figure may be preferable to a faulty figure that will never be corrected.

Depending on the index computation method, if the contribution of an inventory figure is greater than the average contribution of the series that were included last month, the inclusion of the missing inventory figure causes un upward revision of the index. Conversely, if the contribution is less than the average contribution of the series that were included last month, the inclusion of the missing inventory figure causes an upward revison of the index. Conversely, if the contribution is less than the average, the last month's figure of the index is revised down. This index problem is sometimes referred to as *prompt availability (or currency) of data versus revision due to publication lag.*

Inventory data are involved in another index problem, referred to as *currency versus smoothness.* Since inventory buildup data (or change in inventory stocks) are subject to erratic fluctuations (or statistical noise), they are smoothed using a four-term moving average with weights 1, 2, 2, 1. Normally, the moving average values are centered within the moving average span, resulting in a loss of currency. See also Appendix A for further discussion.

22.3   Diffusion index from the NAPM survey on purchased materials survey on purchased materials inventories – some data problems

It has been suggested that data from other sources be substituted for the Census data to overcome the publication lag. A candidate for substitution is a diffusion index extracted from a monthly opinion survey conducted by the National Association of Purchasing Management (NAPM). The survey is based on a sample of 250 business firms selected from a population of approximately 25,000 member firms, reportedly stratified among twenty-one major manufacturing industries and diversified geographically by states according to value added. The diffusion index measures for each month the percentage of respondents experiencing higher inventories of purchased materials in the given month, as compared to the preceding month. Data are usually released to the public on the first Monday after the end of the month and thus would be technically available to fill the information gap on inventories. As to whether, and how well, the NAPM data are qualified to substitute for the Census data, which are based on actual monetary values obtained from a scientifically designed sample of business firms, will have to be examined.

It should be a sobering observation that compilation and refinement of inventory data are difficult tasks, but considering the importance of the subject matter, the effort appears worthwhile. The U.S. Census Bureau's role in collecting and refining the basic data and aggregates and specific categories, shown in *BCD,* are summarized in Appendix B. Census data are recorded as monthly inventory levels in terms of dollars, and changes (or inventory buildup) are computed from those levels. The NAPM data are based merely on reports about the direction of change. Hence they are a measure of change in which the magnitude of change is not recorded and remains an unknown factor. It is reasonable to assume that a change in any activity derived directly from substantive data is far superior to a similar statement lacking such proof. To accept a statistic not based on substantive data represents an act of good faith on part of the analyst.

Some good faith is needed in statistical work, in fact, in any work, but it should be kept within proper limits. Objective statistical data are preferable to subjective data because the former are not affected by personal feelings or prejudices of the reporting agent, but the latter (subjective) rely on one's own opinions, attitudes, moods, and biases, and possibly on systematic policy considerations. Data taken from written records and reported in terms of quantities, monetary units, normally in writing, are thought to be objective data. On the other hand, information passed from the reporter to the collecting agent as broad relationships is usually thought to be subjective data. No doubt, the Census data are objective while data from the NAPM survey must be considered subjective. Hence, Census Bureau data are to be preferred to NAPM data, other things being equal. Subjective data can be useful, especially if they are subjected to accuracy controls and stand the test of time.

The NAPM questionnaire (elements of which are given in Appendix C) does not seek information on the magnitude of change. It solicits three responses: are inventories "higher" or "lower" than a month ago or the "same" as a month ago. The NAPM interprets the "same" response as an accurate judgment of the inventory situation, although it is possible that the response is motivated by a lack of information on which to base the judgment. For example, the "same" response could mean "I don't know"; "I don't have time to find out"; "under given circumstances, it is impossible to say (and/or find out) what the situation is"; and the like.

What is extraordinary is the huge "same" response. For the period 1966 through March 1987 the "same" response was 53 percent, on average, with 26 percent of respondents reporting "lower" and 21 percent "higher" inventories. Figures 22.2 and 22.3 view the distribution of monthly responses. To neutralize the large "same" response, the NAPM divides it equally between the two discriminate response groups, thus establishing that, on average, 52.5 percent reported lower and 47.5 per-

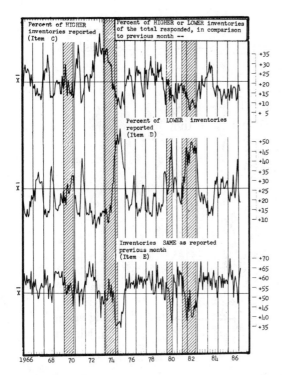

Figure 22.2. Data from inventories survey by the National Association of Purchasing Management (NAPM). *Source:* Bureau of Economic Analysis, Statistical Indicators Division, April 20, 1987.

cent higher inventories. This "adjustment" procedure is objectionable under the given circumstances.

The NAPM method of handling the "same" response is similar to the methodology used by BEA in computing diffusion indexes, but there is an important difference. BEA compares the level of two numbers, and if they are identical or differ by less than 0.25 percentage point (in the case of the symmetrical percent formula), zero-change (numbers are the same) is recorded. Aside from the fact that such a "tie" occurs seldom, two actual recorded values are compared. That is a good justification for breaking the tie into halves of equal sizes and transferring one half to the "yes" position and the other half to "no" position. In the case of an opinion survey with more than 50 percent of the sample staying neutral, it would be appropriate to allocate the neutral response proportionally to "yes" and "no" responses.

Figure 22.4 compares cyclical performance of the presently used cen-

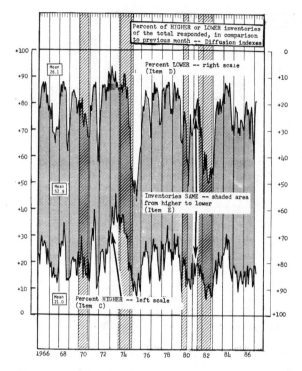

Figure 22.3. Data from inventories survey by the National Association of Purchasing Management (NAPM). Comparison of principle data categories – diffusion. *Source:* Bureau of Economic Analysis, Statistical Indicators Division, April 20, 1987.

sus data and the NAPM purchased materials and supplies diffusion index. To analyze these data and the adjustment procedure, let us use data for an important benchmark, the specific peak of July 1978 in the NAPM inventory diffusion index. In that month 33 percent of respondents judged their inventories to be "higher" than a month ago, 13 percent said that they were "lower," and 54 percent reported that inventories were the "same" as a month ago. The response rate for higher inventories exceeded that for lower by twenty percentage points (33 percent − 13 percent = 20 percent). Taking into account that reportedly 80 percent of a sample of 250, on average, have been responding to the questionnaire each month, we find that only 40 individuals from a population of 25,000, or 0.16 percent, thought that inventories were higher than a month ago. Application of a similar procedure to the adjusted

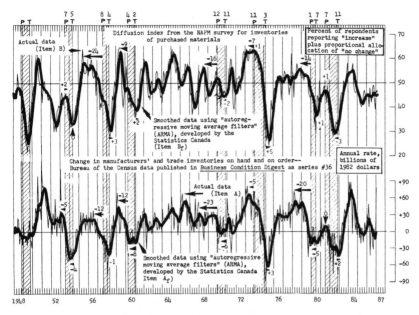

Figure 22.4. Change in inventories. Actual smoothed data. National Association of Purchasing Management (NAPM) and Bureau of the Census. Numbers 1–12 stand for business cycle peak or trough months. Item letters are shortcuts to identify series for Table 21.1. See footnote 18. *Source:* Bureau of Economic Analysis, Statistical Indicators Division, April 20, 1987.

data yields an equal number and the same low percentage of "higher" responses.

Let us now convert the 60 percent response for "higher" inventories in the NAPM adjusted data into would-be actual responses. It appears that 120 individuals out of a total population of 25,000, or 0.48 percent, reported higher inventories as compared with 66 individuals, or 0.27 percent, when the original data were used. We can conclude that by the "adjustment" NAPM has accomplished a rare data enhancement feat: it has made the survey results more respectable by eliminating an overwhelming "same" response and has increased the apparent substantive response absolutely and relatively against the total population. The elimination of the troublesome "same" response by allocating it as equal shares to "higher" and "lower" responses is hard to justify. The process flattens the resulting series around the cyclical turning points. It also would misrepresent normal human behavior and oversimplify sound statisitical procedure.

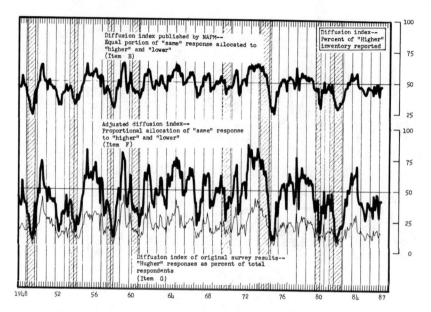

Figure 22.5A. Inventories of purchased materials (diffusion indexes) from NAPM survey. Three alternative forms of actual data. *Source:* Bureau of Economic Analysis, Statistical Indicators Division, April 29, 1987.

It is unlikely that a large proportion of respondents, presumably homogeneous with respect to intimate knowledge of the state of the inventory in question, would form a pattern of response vastly different from that of the segment which was prepared to give a definite answer to the question asked. Therefore, it would be more appropriate to allocate the "same" response in proportion to the sizes of the "higher" and "lower" responses. In fact, the proportional allocation enhances the "respectability" of the survey and its results, as it increases the share of the "higher" responses corresponding to a business cycle peak and the "lower" responses corresponding to a business cycle trough, and in an orderly fashion retains the proportions within the sample and the population. For example, the approximate size of the group expected to report higher inventories would be 143, or 71.7 percent of all respondents, and of that reporting lower inventories 57, or 28.7 percent of all respondents. The ratio of "higher" reporters over "lower" reporters would be 2.5, which is approximately equal to the ratio based on actual results.

Figure 22.5A provides a comparison of the three versions of the NAPM diffusion indexes of purchased materials inventories depicting

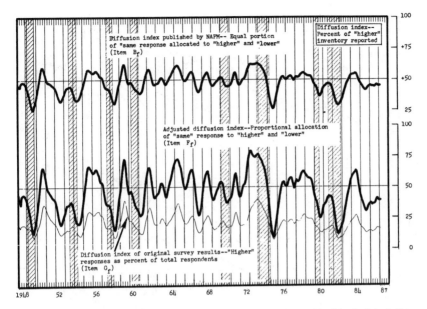

Figure 22.5B. Inventories of purchased materials (diffusion indexes) from NAPM survey. Three alternative forms of data in Figure 22.5A smoothed using Statistics Canada ARMA technique. See Figure 22.5A for series definitions. *Source:* Bureau of Economic Analysis Statistical Indicators Division, April 29, 1987.

the unsmoothed data. Figure 22.5B shows the same three versions using data smoothed by ARMA filters.

22.4   Diffusion index as a measure of stocks and flows

The diffusion index summarizes the direction-of-change in any number of selected time-series. Since the diffusion index is a measure of change, it represents flows. The flows in a diffusion index can be cumulated, similar to flows in a single time-series, in order to obtain a series of "stocks," generally referred to as a cumulative diffusion index. In their cumulative form the diffusion indexes tend to emulate the underlying cyclical and secular behavior of their aggregate parent series. In fact, this characteristic makes the diffusion index a powerful analytical tool.

The calculation of a cumulated diffusion index is straightforward. First the central value of fifty is subtracted from a *common diffusion index* and the residuals for each month (called the *net diffusion index*) are cumulated on a selected convenient base. It follows that if the mean of the common diffusion index is above the fifty level, the cumulated

444   **Feliks Tamm**

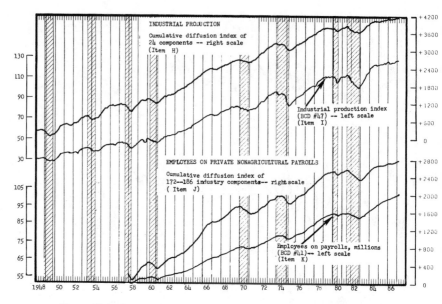

Figure 22.6. Cumulative diffusion indexes and their aggregate parent data for selected series. *Source:*. Bureau of Economic Analysis, Statistical Indicators Division, April 20, 1987.

diffusion index will have a rising trend. On the other hand, if the mean is less than fifty, that newly created level series will have a falling trend. The swings in the cumulated diffusion index so generated tend to correspond to those in the aggregate parent. Figure 22.6 illustrates the close correspondence between two pairs of cumulative diffusion indexes and the corresponding parent series that are shown in *BCD*.[5]

Following up the logic presented in the preceding paragraphs, we could submit any diffusion index to tests by comparing its cumulated form to its aggregate parent series. Figure 22.7 shows the NAPM published diffusion index (equal portion of "same" response added to the "higher" and the "lower" responses) and the proportionally adjusted common diffusion index, in the cumulated form, along with the closest parent compiled by the Bureau of the Census, which is shown in *BCD* as series 78 – Manufacturers' inventories, materials, and supplies. As can be seen, the NAPM cumulated diffusion indexes appear to be poor

---

[5] The industrial production index (series 47) has a broader coverage than the diffusion index of twenty-four industrial production components. Strictly speaking, it is not an aggregate parent to the cumulated diffusion index. Yet the relationship between the two stands out quite prominently.

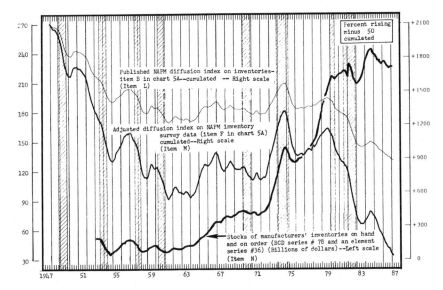

Figure 22.7. Testing the cumulative NAPM diffusion index against a "parent" aggregate. See Figure 22.5A for series definitions. *Source:* Bureau of Economic Analysis, Statistical Indicators Division, April 29, 1987.

relatives to the Census aggregate. The two NAPM cumulated diffusion indexes and the Census parent have little in common.[6]

Although there are no precedents as to whether and when to reject a diffusion index because of poor family resemblance between the cumulated diffusion index and its aggregate parent, the underlying logic strongly suggests that such a test ought to be considered for inclusion in the tool box of indicators analysis and construction of summary measures.

22.5 Why the NAPM inventories diffusion index is not an appropriate replacement for census data

It has been suggested that the present inventory component in the leading index be replaced with the NAPM inventories diffusion index (see Chapter 21). The promoters of such change bring out what appear to be

[6] The comparison is imperfect because the Census Bureau series includes an inflationary trend that may be, at least partly, absent from the NAPM data. But even so, Census and NAPM data seem to have behaved quite differently in 1950s and early 1960s when inflation was not an important factor.

the only strong features of these data—a relatively early compilation of the data and the finality of the initially released numbers. Yet, there are a number of characteristics that fall short of fully satisfactory inventory investment data.

Limited coverage: The NAPM inventories diffusion index measures manufacturers' purchased materials and supplies and thus covers only a very narrow slice in the change in inventories (series 36), included in the leading index. The latter consists of manufacturers' inventories (including finished goods, goods in process, and purchased materials and supplies), wholesale and retail inventories, and unfilled orders for eight durable-goods and four nondurable-goods industry components. Thus the NAPM inventory series would not fully qualify as a substitute for the presently used inventory component in the leading index.

Statistical inadequacy: The sample of 250 out of a total population of 25,000 is rather small (about 1 percent), and the average monthly response rate is 80 percent. A discussion with those at one time responsible for the survey implementation revealed that the sample had not been selected on a probability basis; rather, the members questioned were handpicked, giving preference to larger outfits. That method of sample design was said to have an advantage over probability sampling because, by virtue of their positions, the reporting officials would allegedly have a better insight into the production/trade policies of the establishment. Further, the finality of the initially released data is not necessarily a strong feature, contrary to some allegations. A correction of errors of all types may be considered a strong feature instead, especially from the point of view of longer-range dispositions. All in all, inadequate statistical procedures appear a serious shortcoming of the NAPM inventory data.

Subjective evaluation vs. a written record Subjectively created data definitely inferior to a written data record passed on to the statistics-collecting staff as mentioned earlier. The intimate knowledge of production/trade policies, said earlier to be favorable condition, may in reality be a serious drawback–the policy consideration may be misleading and actually distort the true inventory picture. The latter is the main concern here and not a forecasting of the future inventory situation.

An unfavorable evaluation by the NAPM: It should be noted that an unfavorable testimonial is given by the NAPM officials themselves on their inventories diffusion index. In constructing a composite diffusion index that is being considered by some forecasters and media as a major business indicator, the NAPM seems to hold the inventories diffusion index in low esteem, as it is given a low weight of 10 out of a total of 100. The other four component diffusion indexes from the same survey are given greatly higher weights: 30 for new orders and 20 each for production, employment and vendor performance.

Although the idea of constructing composite diffusion indexes is basically good, what is needed is a carefully designed, conceptually sound measure. If conceptually different cyclical elements, such as leaders and coinciders, are combined into the same summary measure, it loses its analytical purpose. Figuratively speaking, it becomes a hybrid misfit who has absorbed "genes" from two or more "thoroughbred species" but may neither "swim" nor "race." There is no point in generating crystal balls to serve as conversation pieces when you can build a worthwhile measuring instrument on the basis of tested relationships and past knowledge.

Internal inconsistencies in some of the survey results: A careful study of all diffusion indexes resulting from the NAPM survey reveals a behavioral pattern in the new orders and production indexes that seems to be atypical of cyclical indicators. A comparison of the "high" level responses in new orders to those in production shows that all major turning points, most minor turns, and even the erratic wiggles appear to occur in the same time points in the two series. The same is true for "low" levels and "same" responses. The two cumulated diffusion indexes show remarkable uniformity in cyclical timing. In several instances the turns in the production index slightly lead those in new orders – a condition that runs against the grain of business cycle analysis.

It is true that a common diffusion index leads its parent and also the cumulated deviations from the central value the same way the first differences lead their aggregate levels, and that all follows from a definition. However, one should examine carefully the prospective data conditions to discover irregularities and inconsistencies. For example, if two input series come from a single source as a package with their processes closely connected, such as new orders and production, the two must be thoroughly tested before being accepted as two independent data series and assigned a prominent place in a summary measure. In fact, they may have to be treated as two equivalents and only one be selected.

Mathematical means, especially in today's computer age, are often used to justify the employment of various statistical data, especially to select them for important summary measures. Correlation coefficients and other regression measures are often produced under circumstances where the data do not lend themselves to a stable analysis. Even worse, if and when the meaningless coefficients are thrown around as a proof of the solidity of a measure, one is fooling the "modern" analyst who is awestruck by such techniques. If an arrangement is lacking conceptual structure and justification by sound economic logic, it should not be presented as a sound economic device for evaluating economic conditions; although it may be worth recognition as a great intellectual achievement.

Supplemental role for NAPM data: The foregoing discussion may wrongly convey an impression that the NAPM survey results on inventories are entirely useless. The inventory data from the NAPM survey were found unqualified as a substitute for the Census data.[7] Therefore, it would be venturesome to replace the inventory component in the leading index by the NAPM diffusion index of a limited scope. In spite of some characteristics that would not fully measure up, there are several ways NAPM inventory data could be used as a part of the inventory investment input in the leading index, as noted below.

22.6   Conclusions and recommendations

The presently used inventory component in the leading index should be disassembled into its basic components and reorganized into more appropriate groupings for inclusion in the index. The inventories-on-order portion (unfilled orders) must be separated and included as an independent entity, which it really is, to take advantage of its prompt availability (no publication lag!). As an element of the presently used inventory series, it selectively excludes approximately two-thirds of the available unfilled orders data. Now, all industry components of unfilled orders will have to be reviewed and the qualified elements included. The

---

[7] Another important conceptual reason for the position taken here is the circumstance that if NAPM inventories on purchased materials and supplies were selected as the sole representative of inventories in the leading index, with a weight of 1.00, the index would include two components from the same NAPM survey. Moreover, both are subjective series, using a common questionnaire for a relatively small and otherwise statistically inadequate sample. Hence, possibilities for close correlation between the series are infinite. To recommend inclusion of both series in the leading index would equal proposing significantly lowering the customary structural quality of the composite index system. It should be noted that it has been decided to drop the presently used vendor performance component (series 32) from the leading index and to replace it by the vendor performance data – a diffusion index – collected by the NAPM. That issue was discussed in the Albany conference.

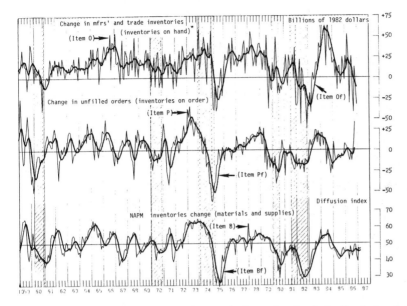

Figure 22.8. Investment in inventories input data for the leading index. Actual and smooth data. The data for changes in manufacturers' trade inventories include materials and supplies. ARMA filters used for smoothing. *Source:* Bureau of Economic Analysis, Statistical Indicators Division, April 20, 1987.

materials and supplies element will have to be taken out of the present inventories-on-hand segment. The NAPM inventories of material and supplies is to be substituted for this element. The remaining elements of the inventories on hand portion are organized into two subcomponents—manufacturers' inventories (composed of finished goods and goods in process) and trade inventories (including wholesale trade and retail trade). Each of the four basic subcomponents should be assigned 0.25 weight in the index. The inventory input may take different forms as discussed above. Figure 22.8 shows these components except that manufacturers' and trade inventories are combined.

Scenario A: Each of the four subcomponents enters the leading index as a separate entity with a weight of 0.25. The three Census components, traditionally presented as changes in deflated monetary units (manufacturers' and trade inventories and unfilled orders), are to be converted into percent changes to eliminate the growth bias that would be significant over the forty-year period of index coverage. The NAPM purchased materials and supplies data are to be included as a diffusion index. There is a solid logic behind this method. Each of the four represents a different aspect of inventory investment and each comes from a different source. From the point of view of analysis, it would be advantageous to know the contribution of each of the subcomponents, each of which has a somewhat different lead structure.

Two of the components are promptly available, but two have a one-month reporting lag. That situation opens up at least three possibilities of index treatment.

Scenario A-1: A preliminary estimate for the current month is calculated and released as usual. Two inventory components are included and only two are missing, thus reducing the weight of the unavailable inventory components from 1.00 to 0.50. Research may establish that the other series with publication lags – change in business and consumer credit outstanding (series 111) – can be treated a similar way. A revised index may be issued ten to fifteen days later, when information is available for the missing elements. This would be best of the two worlds – no delay in the initial release, but the magnitude of revision is reduced, followed only a short time later by a release containing complete data.

Scenario A-2: A modified A-1 scenario is used, but the regular monthly index release is delayed by ten days or whatever time is needed to come up with a relatively stable figure for the current month – revision-proofing the initially released figure but foolishly sacrificing currency!

Scenario A-3: Fundamentally, scenario A-1 is used, but a radical (up to this point considered radical if not sacrilegious) modification is suggested. Shift the latest manufacturers' and trade inventories figure forward by one month (theoretically only one-half month), just into the currently empty time cell. A violation of statistical rules? Yes! But, violations of rules seem to have enough precedents. For example, when smoothing formulas are applied, the smoothed data are often assigned to the end of the interaction period instead of placing them at the center of the period, to mention one. Moreover, many private practitioners of the art of forecasting are combining the latest data available, regardless of their precise timing, into summary indicators.

One should note that inventories are taken on the last day of the month, and therefore they actually lag the center of the following month by one-half month. When a new monthly business period begins, information on inventories is carried from the end of last month to the beginning of the current month as a going concern. Inventories might as well be included in the current statistical measures because the last month's inventories are the latest measures of that kind available to a business-

Table 22.2. *Specific peak and trough dates for selected cyclical indicators in relation to (NBER reference) business cycle peak and trough dates (employed as components of the composite indexes)*

A. Specific peak dates

Leading indicators series	Specific peak dates corresponding to business contractions beginning in (NBER reference peaks)							
	July 1981	Jan. 1980	Nov. 1973	Dec. 1969	Apr. 1960	Aug. 1957	July 1953	Nov. 1948
1. Average workweek, production workers, mfg.	1/81 (−6)	3/79 (−10)	4/73 (−7)	10/68 (−14)	5/59 (−11)	11/55 (−21)	4/53 (−3)	12/47 (−11)
5. Initial claims, unemployment insurance (inverted)	7/81 (0)	9/78 (−16)	2/73 (−9)	1/69 (−11)	4/59 (−12)	9/55 (−23)	9/52 (−10)	1/47 (−22)
8. New orders, consumer goods, 1972 dollars	5/81 (−2)	1/79 (−12)	3/73 (−8)	11/68 (−13)	2/59 (−14)	7/55 (−25)	4/53 (−3)	6/48 (−5)
32. Vendor performance, slower deliveries	4/81 (−3)	3/79 (−10)	5/73 (−6)	6/69 (−6)	10/59 (−6)	10/55 (−22)	7/52 (−12)	10/48 (−1)
12. Index of net business formation	12/80 (−7)	10/78 (−15)	10/72 (−13)	4/69 (−8)	3/59 (−13)	6/55 (−26)	1/53 (−6)	*1/48 (−10)
20. Contracts and orders, 1972 dollars	12/80 (−7)	3/79 (−10)	11/73 (0)	4/69 (−8)	3/59 (−13)	11/56 (−9)	2/53 (5)	*4/48 (−7)
29. New building permits, private housing	9/80 (−10)	6/78 (−19)	12/72 (−11)	2/69 (−10)	11/58 (−17)	2/55 (−30)	11/52 (−8)	10/47 (−13)
36. Change in inventories on hand and on order, 1972 dollars (smoothed)[a]	7/81 (0)	5/78 (−20)	4/75 (−7)	12/68 (−12)	4/59 (−12)	9/56 (−11)	2/53 (−5)	*7/48 (−4)
99. Change in sensitive prices (smoothed)[a]	9/80 (−10)	4/79 (−9)	4/73 (−7)	2/69 (−10)	10/58 (−18)	9/55 (−23)	NSC	*7/48 (−4)
19. Index of stock prices, 500 common stocks	11/80 (−8)	NSC	1/73 (−10)	12/68 (−12)	7/59 (−9)	7/56 (−13)	1/53 (−6)	6/48 (−5)
106. Money supply (M2), 1972 dollars	NSC	2/78 (−23)	1/73 (−10)	2/69 (−10)	NSC	4/56 (−16)	NSC	*1/47 (−22)
111. Change in credit outstanding	5/81 (−2)	1/79 (−12)	2/73 (−9)	1/69 (−11)	6/59 (−10)	6/55 (−26)	10/52 (−9)	*11/47 (−12)
Average timing[b]	−5.0	−14.2	−8.1	−10.4	−12.3	−20.4	−6.7	−9.5
Standard deviation[c]	3.6	4.5	3.1	2.2	3.2	6.4	2.8	6.9

Table 22.2. (cont.)

B. Specific trough dates

Leading indicators series	Specific trough dates corresponding to business expansions beginning in (NBER reference troughs)							
	Nov. 1982	July 1980	Mar. 1975	Nov. 1970	Feb. 1961	Apr. 1958	May 1954	Oct. 1949
1. Average workweek, production workers, mfg.	9/82 (−2)	7/80 (0)	3/75 (0)	9/70 (−2)	12/60 (−2)	4/58 (0)	4/54 (−1)	4/49 (−6)
5. Initial claims, unemployment insurance (inverted)	9/82 (−2)	5/80 (−2)	3/75 (0)	10/70 (−1)	2/61 (0)	4/58 (0)	9/54 (+4)	10/49 (0)
8. New orders, consumer goods, 1972 dollars	10/82 (−1)	6/80 (−1)	2/75 (−1)	10/70 (−1)	1/61 (−1)	4/58 (0)	10/53 (−7)	6/49 (−4)
32. Vendor performance, slower deliveries	5/82 (−6)	6/80 (−1)	2/75 (−1)	12/70 (+1)	3/60 (−11)	12/57 (−4)	12/53 (−5)	3/49 (−7)
12. Index of net business formation	9/82 (−2)	6/80 (−1)	2/75 (−1)	8/70 (−3)	1/61 (−1)	4/58 (0)	3/54 (−2)	7/49 (−3)
20. Contracts and orders, 1972 dollars	7/82 (−4)	5/80 (−2)	12/75 (+9)	10/70 (−1)	3/61 (+1)	3/58 (−1)	3/54 (−2)	7/49 (−3)
29. New building permits, private housing	10/81 (−13)	4/80 (−3)	3/75 (0)	1/70 (−10)	12/60 (−2)	2/58 (−2)	9/53 (−8)	4.49 (−6)
36. Change in inventories on hand and on order, 1972 dollars (smoothed)[a]	NA	8/80 (+1)	4/75 (+1)	1/71 (+2)	12/60 (−2)	3/58 (−1)	9/53 (−8)	1/49 (−9)
99. Change in sensitive prices (smoothed)[a]	12/81 (−11)	6/80 (−1)	4/75 (+1)	3/70 (−8)	2/61 (0)	3/58 (−1)	11/53 (−6)	6/49 (−4)
19. Index of stock prices, 500 common stocks	7/82 (−4)	NSC	12/74 (−3)	6/70 (−5)	8/60 (−6)	11/57 (−5)	NSC	5/49 (−5)
106. Money supply (M2), 1972 dollars	NSC	5/80 (−2)	1/75 (−2)	4/70 (−7)	10/60 (−4)	1/58 (−3)	NSC	8/48 (−14)
111. Change in credit outstanding	12/82 (+1)	5/80 (−2)	3/75 (0)	10/70 (−1)	4/61 (+2)	2/58 (−2)	12/53 (−5)	7/49 (−3)
Average timing[b]	−4.4	−1.3	+0.1	−3.0	−2.2	−1.8	−4.0	−5.4
Standard deviation[c]	4.2	1.1	2.9	3.6	3.5	1.7	3.6	3.4

Note: Specific peak and trough dates mark the cyclical turning points in individual series, whereas reference peak and trough dates indicate the cyclical turning points in business activity as a whole. This table shows the specific peaks and troughs corresponding to post–World War II business cycles for the major cyclical indicators. Numbers in parentheses indicate the leads (−) or lags (+) of the specific dates in relation to the reference dates. The determination of the specific peaks and troughs is not an entirely objective matter, and honest disagreement may exist among individual analysts. Therefore, the dates above should not be considered absolute. See Burns and Mitchell (1946) for further information on the selection of specific peaks and troughs. NA (not available) indicates that the data necessary to determine a turning point are not available. NSC, (no specific cycle) indicates that no specific turning point corresponding to the indicated reference data is discernable. An asterisk preceding a date indicates that this is not necessarily the peak but is the high point in the available data.

[a] This is a weighted four-term moving average (with weights 1, 2, 2, 1) placed on the terminal month of the span.

[b] The average timing is based on all available indicators, including those not performing as expected.

[c] Standard deviation about the average timing.

man or a manager and thus are relevant current information indeed. Furthermore, any respondent to an opinion survey on inventories makes an evaluation based on the available "latest past" data, simply because "latest current" data are not available. The talk about the accurate current readings on inventories by manager is basically a "sales talk."

The view taken here would effectively eliminate both the data currency problem and the problem of revision because of missing data. An important condition attached to this solution is that a leading indicator so treated would retain enough lead time to make the operation worthwhile. Tables 22.2A and B represent lead times for the leading index components during eight post–World War II business cycles. There is enough evidence that change in inventories on hand and on order had enough lead time at the specific peaks, so that a one-month loss would not be detrimental. The lead time at troughs is normally short, and the inventory data were no exception to that condition. Forecasting of the upper turning point, however, is more crucial to the economic community than of the lower turning point.

Scenario B: Leave out inventory data and by implication also change in business and consumer credit outstanding. A few suggestions have been made along these lines. The suggestion is usually supported by an argument that neither change in inventories nor change in credit series is good for the leading index. The erratic fluctuation spoils the otherwise well-behaving measure of business cycle developments. The answer to such a suggestion is, of course, that without inventory investment and credit expansion contributions the leading index may stop being well-behaving.

Timing cyclical movements in the inventory buildup data, which actually represents change in the stocks of inventories, is a thankless undertaking. Because it is an erratically fluctuating series, the operation is likely to reflect individual biases of the people involved as the existing operational rules provide inadequate guidance. Figure 22.4 amply illustrates an imperfect outcome. Smooth data are used to improve chances for picking the true cyclical turns, relevant to the analysis. The smooth data should be placed at the center of the span of smoothing interaction, but in Figure 22.4 smooth data are plotted at the terminal end of the span.

The modest smoothing action here is aimed to smooth away the random fluctuations (statistical noise). A host of fluctuations of somewhat longer duration, reminiscent of extra short cyclical movements that may be explained on economic or institutional grounds, is left behind or generated. Some segments of the choppy line, traced by the data, appear hopelessly inadequate as a business cycle series. In other segments, the data approximate high and low grounds for somewhat longer periods, forming plateaus intercepted by minor fluctuations. Such high and low grounds normally correspond to business cycle peaks and troughs, but the turns are usually difficult to pinpoint and as a rule are arbitrarily placed. The following examples will demonstrate the difficulty and a lack of consensus. For the NAPM data (top line of Figure 22.4) a specific peak is placed here at the end-month of 1973, but traditionally it would be placed at the end of 1972 (the later point is slightly higher but the earlier point also seems significant as the point at which data reached the "peak zone" and stayed longer than a year before dropping). In the Census data a specific peak is placed at September 1956 (the terminal point of the peaking zone). Perhaps July 1955 should be recognized as the peak (the beginning of the peaking zone).

A point worth making here is that in a difficult data situation, such as described above, an analyst inclined to be overly zealous concerning "rules" might disqualify a series that would actually be an asset to a composite index. If blended into a great many other components, its choppiness is offset by other data, and its broad but well-formed plateaus, reaching beyond the expected turning points, may be helpful to form proper turns in the composite index or the subindexes, especially if and when the series is conceptually an important one, such as the inventory investment series. The thrust of the matter is that timing determination is important, but choppy data, such as inventory investment and credit expansion, ought to be pursued with pragmatism. By no means should these series be removed from the index because they are difficult to handle. The conceptual need to include these data should overrule convenience.

It is high time to turn the composite indexes into a sophisticated analytical system, utilizing the almost unlimited opportunities the accumulated knowledge in cyclical indicators offers. For example, the number of components included in the leading index can be more than doubled as even new economic process groups could be added. The index ought to become a "superindicator" consisting of subindexes that would, in effect, represent all relevant processes or their meaningful groups. It would become a systematic presentation of relevant data—a comprehensive general indicator. Process indexes are to be constructed using all components included in the comprehensive index. The process indexes will replace the present haphazardly compiled group indexes, which appear to have been ignored by forecasters and members of the public interested in economic affairs. The reconstituted index system, if

properly maintained, overhauled promptly when a need arises, and fully
explained to the public by competent officials, would become a central
feature for evaluating current economic conditions.

Appendix A: Treatment of irregular fluctuations

Seasonally adjusted data, as a rule, are free of systematic variations,
other than the long-range trend and cyclical movements, but they still
contain irregular fluctuations, or statistical noise, which are a mixture
of various unsystematic fluctuations. Some of those are extreme movements, brought about by extraordinary events, such as strong excep-
tional economic developments (e.g., strikes), reactions to unexpected
powerful political events, unseasonable weather, major errors of measurement, and the like. Often an extreme movement in a given month
may give rise to a rebound next month, creating a seesaw game that
serves no rational purpose but complicates data interpretation. Many of
the extreme movements in data can be identified and a basis for direct
individual modification of extremes may be found. When individual
modifications are not feasible, a degree of extremeness can be designated
in each instance by a straightforward scheme, such as that used in the
X-11 seasonal adjustment program.

A plan could be set up for testing the irregular movements using the
standard deviations of the series. The scheme would amount to a systematic assessment of the level of the disturbance caused by the extreme
movement. The modification of the extremes would depend on the size
of each individual movement and the size of the standard deviation. For
example, an extreme movement measuring two to three standard deviations would be replaced by 80 percent of the original value; those
extreme values falling between three and four standard deviations would
be replaced by 60 percent of the original value, and so on. The algebraic
signs of the movements are not arbitrarily changed. The nature of data
and other relevant considerations should be taken into account while
designing the scale and designating the extent of modification for a given
series.

The bulk of residuals are irregular movements reminiscent of random
series, and will have to be treated as such. (See notes to Table 22.1 for a
test of approximate randomness.) Appropriate smoothing formulas will
have to be employed for offsetting typical irregular fluctuations.

Irregular fluctuations or statistical noise obscures the underlying
cyclical movements and secular trend. Thus, statistical noise interferes
with the reliability in the analytical readings of data. Another aspect of
data relevant to evaluation of the current economic developments is the

promptness of availability, or timeliness, of data. There is a tradeoff between reliability and timeliness, and the objective is to minimize the loss of timeliness and maximize the degree of reliability. Moving averages are widely used to offset irregular movements and thus to increase reliability, but a gain in reliability is achieved only by giving up some timeliness, that is, lead-time.

Statistics Canada, under leadership of Darryl Rhoades, has devised a technique that "minimizes the timeliness sacrificed to achieve a given degree of reliability" by using "autoregressive moving average (ARMA) filters." The filters are produced with the help of spectral analysis techniques that are employed to derive certain least-squares functions. The procedures employed "result in a sequence of filters each of which increases reliability by a different amount, and each of which minimizes the timeliness lost in exchange for a given increase in reliability." The designers of the filters draw a conclusion (Rhoades, 1980) as follows:

> We have shown that, besides collecting additional information, one can improve the reliability of a given set of time series measurements by processing it appropriately. We have indicated that such attempts to improve reliability are practiced commonly but not efficiently. A technique for designing efficient ARMA filters was sketched and the results presented when three such filters were applied to the U.S. Commerce Department's leading indicators. It is our belief that similar results will be obtained when the filters are applied to a broader range of series relevant to current economic analysis in general. We further believe that current analysis based on a broad range of filtered economic indicators will enable clearer interpretation of the current situation and will help in detecting earlier and more certainly, changes in the current cyclical phase.

The staff of BEA's Statistical Indicators Division has been experimenting for some time with different moving averages, some with complex smoothing patterns, but none of those have matched the effects and capabilities of the ARMA filtering technique invented by Dr. Rhoades and his colleagues at Statistics Canada. It is high time that more attention is given to this ingenious methodology.

Appendix B: Description of series on manufacturing and trade inventories and sales

Source: U.S. Department of Commerce, Bureau of the Census and Bureau of Economic Analysis (Data contained in these series are seasonally adjusted; sales and shipments are adjusted also for holiday and working day differences.)

These series measure the inventories or sales of manufacturing, merchant wholesalers, and retail establishments. Inventories and sales of agriculture, forestry, and fishing; mining; construction; nonmerchant wholesalers (sales branches of manufacturing companies, agents, brokers, and commission merchants); transportation, communication, electric, gas, and sanitary services; finance, insurance, and real estate; and services are excluded. The series are compiled from data collected each month by the Bureau of the Census in the shipments, inventories, and orders survey and in the merchant wholesalers and retail trade surveys. They are adjusted to benchmarks from the 5-year censuses of manufactures, wholesale trade, and retail trade and to interim annual surveys.

The monthly series on manufacturers' inventories and sales have been compiled by the Census Bureau since 1957; prior to that year, the survey was conducted by the Bureau of Economic Analysis (BEA). Merchant wholesalers' inventories and sales and retail sales have been collected and published by the Census Bureau since 1954 and 1951, respectively. Retail inventories have been collected and published by the Census Bureau since January 1979. For prior years, these series were published by BEA from sample data collected by the Census Bureau.

Manufacturers' inventories are book values of stocks-on-hand at the end of the month, and include materials and supplies, work in process, and finished goods. Inventories associated with nonmanufacturing activities of manufacturing companies are excluded. Inventories are valued according to the valuation method used by each company, and the aggregates are a mixture of LIFO (last-in-first-out) and non-LIFO values. Annual information is obtained on the portions of inventories valued by the various accounting methods.

Merchant wholesalers' and retail inventories are also book values of merchandise-on-hand at the end of the month. Goods held on consignment by wholesalers and retailers are excluded.

Manufacturers' sales are the value of their shipments for domestic use of export. Shipments are measured by receipts, billings, or the value of products shipped (less discounts, returns, and allowances) and generally exclude freight charges and excise taxes. Shipments from one division to another within the same company in the United States and shipments by domestic firms to foreign subsidiaries are included, but shipments by foreign subsidiaries are excluded. For some aircraft and all shipbuilding, the "value of shipments" is the value of the work done during the period covered, rather than the value of the products physically shipped.

Merchant wholesalers' sales include sales of merchandise and receipts from repairs or other services (after deducting discounts, returns, and allowances) and sales of merchandise for others on a commission basis. Sales taxes and Federal excise taxes are excluded.

Retail sales include total receipts from customers after deductions of refunds and allowances for merchandise returned. Receipts from rental or leasing of merchandise returned. Receipts from rental or leasing of merchandise and from repairs and other services to customers are included also. Since 1967, finance charges, and sales and excise taxes collected from customers and paid to tax agencies by the retailer are excluded.

Manufacturers' inventories and sales of defense products are based on separate reports covering only the defense work of large defense contractors in the ordnance and accessories; communication equipment; aircraft, missiles, and parts; and shipbuilding and tank industries. These defense products cover only work for the U.S. Department of Defense and orders from foreign governments for military goods contracted through the Defense Department.

Series 36. Change in manufacturing and trade inventories on hand and on order in 1972 dollars

Series 36 measures the month-to-month amount of change, in constant (1972) dollars, in manufacturing and trade inventories and manufacturers' unfilled orders (excluding unfilled orders for capital goods and defense products). The components of each series are deflated separately and then combined into a total from which monthly changes are computed.

The constant-dollar manufacturing and trade inventories component is series 70, described above. Manufacturers' unfilled orders measure the end-of-month constant-dollar value of orders that have been received but have not yet passed through the sale accounts. (See the *New and Unfilled Orders* section in this *Handbook.*) The unfilled orders data are deflated separately at the 2-digit Standard Industrial Classification (SIC) industry level, using appropriate Producer Price Indexes beginning with 1953 for the eight durable-goods industries and beginning with 1958 for the four nondurable-goods industries. Prior to these dates, the aggregate durable and nondurable levels were each deflated using fixed-weighted averages (1958 weights) of Producer Price Indexes as deflators.

The series is shown in *BCD* as the month-to-month amounts of change and as 4-term moving averages of the monthly changes (weighted 1,2,2,1) and placed on the terminal month of the span.

In *BCD*, series 36 appears under the economic process "inventories and inventory investment."

(See *Handbook of Cyclical Indicators* for more complete information.)

Appendix C: Segments of the NAPM questionnaire

Report for NAPM business survey committee

Note: Check marks and comments should reflect conditions in your own business. But, whenever possible, please include additional remarks on prevailing local conditions. Refer to explanation sheet for further details.

1. GENERAL BUSINESS CONDITIONS:

Production
(Check)

Remarks (Explain fully):

- Better than month ago
- Same as month ago
- Worse than month ago

New Orders
(Check)

- Better than month ago
- Same as month ago
- Worse than month ago

3. PURCHASED MATERIALS INVENTORIES:

(Check)

Remarks (Explain reason for change from previous month):

- Higher than month ago
- Same as month ago
- Lower than month ago

6. VENDOR DELIVERIES:
(Check)

- Faster than month ago
- Same as month ago
- Slower than month ago

7. ITEMS IN SHORT SUPPLY: (Explain reason for shortage.)

8. GENERAL REMARKS: (Give frank opinion on general business condition and any conditions, local or national, which affect purchasing policies.)

Use reverse side or attach separate sheet if additional space is necessary

REFERENCES

Burns, A. F., and W. C. Mitchell (1946), *Measuring Business Cycles.* New York: National Bureau of Economic Research.
Rhoades, D. (1980), "Converting Timeliness into Reliability in Economic Time Series or Minimum Phase Shift Filtering of Economic Time Series," *Canadian Statistical Review,* February.

Index